Pasta Improvvisata

How to Improvise in Classic Italian Style

Erica De Mane

Pasta Drawings by Laura Hartman Maestro

S C R I B N E R

Scribner
1230 Avenue of the Americas
New York, NY 10020

Designed by Barbara M. Bachman
Pasta drawings by Laura Hartman Maestro
Set in ITC Officina and Rage Italic

Manufactured in the United States of America
10 9 8 7 6 5 4 3 2 1

Library of Congress Cataloging-in-Publication Data
De Mane, Erica.
        Pasta Improvvisata : how to improvise in classic Italian style / Erica De Mane.
            p.   cm.
        1. Cookery (Pasta)   2. Cookery, Italian.   I. Title.
    TX809.M17D429   1999
    641.8'22—dc21   99-21363
                                                           CIP

    ISBN 0-684-82972-X

Dedicated to my parents,

Maureen and Richard De Mane,

with love, and with gratitude

for raising me in a

modern Italian-American style.

Contents

Pasta Drawings

I loved my family's southern Italian American cooking when I was a child, and even back then, before I was aware of where it all came from, I was proud to invite my friends over for a dinner of lasagne layered with ricotta and my mother's long-simmered meat sauce.

My family also ate out a lot, almost exclusively at Italian restaurants, and I always ordered pasta. That was where I first learned that the world of pasta went beyond the tomato, garlic, and dried oregano triumvirate of my home and into the creamy Alfredo sauces that in the 1960s and '70s became the hallmark of high-class Italian restaurant cooking (the dish was always made tableside by a tuxedoed waiter using elaborate arm movements). I noticed the attention and care that were paid to the preparation of food, not only in these restaurants but in my own family. And my dedication to the art of cooking took hold.

As a teenager, I began by experimenting. My first great discovery was *aglio e olio* (garlic and oil sauce), which was something my family never cooked because my father was not a fan of the straight taste of olive oil. As I entered adulthood, I'd make an *aglio e olio* sauce toward dawn for friends after a night of disco-hopping. It wasn't long before I varied the garlic-and-olive-oil base by adding anchovies, prosciutto, hot pepper, fresh parsley, and basil from my father's garden. Cooking was starting to become a life focus for me, a way of expressing myself.

Pasta sauces lend themselves beautifully to the kind of improvisation I was doing. Even in Italy, where town feuds are fought over the correct ingredients for a true Bolognese sauce, each cook makes the classic sauces a little differently. While traveling through the provinces of Campania and Puglia in the south of Italy on the way to my grandmother's birthplace a few years back, I stopped at many small trattorias and was served at least a dozen different versions of the ubiquitous (in that region) baked ziti with tomato sauce: one had mozzarella; one was seasoned with oregano; one included Pecorino and sausage; another had tiny meatballs. Each restaurant called the dish the specialty of the region, but no two made it the same way. I realized that this was what good cooking was all about—placing your personal stamp on the food you love best.

This is a book about the innumerable possibilities for combining Italian flavors. My recipes show you the many approaches you can take with the ingredients you are working with. I give examples to help you discover what herbs and vegetables go well together, how different cooking techniques vary the taste of the same ingredients, and how to substitute with seasonal produce or simply to use up something in the refrigerator.

I also experiment with each key ingredient to show you how much freedom you really have. For me the most interesting part of any cookbook is the options the author provides. After most recipes, I've added a section called "Ideas," where I offer Italian regional variations and then suggest different directions in which you can take the dish. For example, a pasta sauce with tomato, shallots, and a touch of cream can easily be made piquant by omitting the shallots and cream and replacing them with garlic and green olives.

The wonderful thing about starting your culinary improvisation with pasta is that an extremely diverse range of ingredients can make their way into a pasta sauce and still retain Italian style. Looking through old Italian cookbooks, I've come across sauces containing beets, dried apricots, cabbage, squid ink, sweetbreads, walnuts, even chocolate!

My love is for pasta in true Italian style, and I favor using ingredients most Italians would approve of, so you won't find cilantro or miso paste here. Not that you can't make a great pasta dish using them; I just want to preserve the flavors and the feeling of real Italian cooking. My aim is to teach you how to use recipes creatively but within the framework of the Italian flavor palate. My recipes can be taken as starting points, with many enticing variations suggested.

As I show, Italian pasta sauces fall into two general categories: long-cooked and short-cooked. You can make a classic southern Italian sauce of calamari and tomato that is long-simmered, with a stewed, mellow character, or you can use the same ingredients, quick-sauté the squid just until it turns opaque and tender, add chopped fresh tomatoes and herbs, and have it ready to eat in four minutes. The sauce will be bright and the squid tender. Same ingredients, two different tastes.

Your memory will gradually become a resource you instinctively rely on to make such choices and improvise in the kitchen. The more you cook, the more olfactory memory you will acquire as well, enabling you to imagine beforehand what will result from a certain combination of ingredients or cooking techniques. Of course, there will always be surprises. I've been eating at a small Italian restaurant in my neighborhood since it opened four years ago. I frequently order the same dish, which is listed as farfalle with squid and saffron, a combination or variation of which I often make at home. The restaurant's version tastes different, deeper. For ages, each time I ordered it, I tried to figure out what was special about it. The sauce is yellow from saffron. It contains white wine, probably a fish stock, and butter instead of the olive oil I invariably reach for when I cook squid. But there was something else in the sauce. One night I figured it out. The cook added rosemary with the saffron. An unusual combination. I would have thought a strong herb like rosemary would overpower the delicate saffron. But it didn't. It blended into a delicious, rich taste. And the rosemary must have been added to the stock and strained out so no little green flecks appeared. That combination might never have occurred to me, but now I use it as a flavoring for seafood dishes—it works particularly well with shellfish. Even if you've cooked for many years, you'll always make discoveries, and those discoveries will stay with you. So don't be intimidated by lack of experience. It will make cooking all the more exciting.

I have always felt that the best cooks are those who have a naturally inquisitive palate. I've always had one. I remember as a child accepting a sandwich filled with bacon and cocktail olives from a kid down the street. I didn't realize it was meant as a joke, and she laughed hysterically when I tasted it, but I actually thought it had potential. Constant tasting is extremely important for any cook. If you follow a recipe without tasting as you go along, you're not really cooking; you're just following orders. By tasting, you learn how each addition to a dish changes it. Tasting while you cook is also a big part of the fun of cooking. You absorb a knowledge of what different foods are and what happens to them when they're cooked. Before adding the tomatoes, taste the chopped leek you've just sautéed in olive oil as a base for your sauce. Maybe you'll decide you don't need the tomatoes, and dine on a dish of fettuccine with leeks.

In the recipes in this book, I give general amounts for all seasoning ingredients such as fresh herbs or capers, so you'll have some leeway. My hope is that I'll encourage you to think about what you are doing and participate more fully in the process. I do give fairly specific amounts for main ingredients, such as one large eggplant, two pounds of tomatoes, or half a pound of shrimp. This is to ensure that the quantity will come out to the desired serving size (all the recipes in this book are designed for four main-course pasta servings or six first-course servings, or for sauce for one pound of dried pasta).

It's also important to study a recipe for guidance before you begin. Get a sense of what the cooking style and principles are. Will you be sautéing or baking or grilling? Or simmering something in liquid? When you really start to become confident, try not bringing the book into the kitchen with you when you cook. You've got your ingredients, you know roughly the quantities you want to use, you understand the basic cooking method. Maybe you won't need to look at the recipe again. Maybe you'll want to take a look at it after you've finished, to see if what you did was what the recipe told you or if you went off and did something easier, better, or more suited to your own style. That is real liberation!

The last thing you should worry about is making mistakes. Very few dishes are literally inedible, and unusual is almost always better than boring. In most cases what you consider a mistake your guests or family will find delicious. Don't tell them you screwed up the recipe; you'll just make them feel wrong to enjoy it.

It takes a while to train your nose to sniff out flavor. Marcella Hazan, the great cooking teacher and author, once wrote that she could smell the salt in food. I thought this was amazing and tried to do it myself. I couldn't. I still can't, although I can now tell whether or not pasta water has already been salted by smelling it. But I cannot smell a tomato sauce and make this same determination. Maybe someday.

I'm still learning. Cooking, after all, is a continuous process of discovery. Out of discovery will emerge your personal style and the real joy that comes from pleasing your family and friends with your creations. Don't be afraid to grab a little freedom in your kitchen. You'll pick up techniques and learn while you cook. And there's nothing more inspiring than the flavors of Italy to serve as your well-seasoned guide.

Pasta and Vegetables

Vegetables are the heart of Italian pasta cooking and always make up the majority of recipes in any pasta cookbook. They are the food Italians (and many Americans) live on. I eat pasta with a vegetable sauce at least three times a week, sometimes as a first course, more often as a main dish, maybe with a chunk of salami or cheese alongside, the way they do in southern Italian households. The combinations and varied seasonings you can create with vegetables for pasta sauces are all but endless.

For me, the charm of a good vegetable sauce lies in its clear, well-defined flavors. After years of throwing every herb available, plus garlic and onions, into every sauce I made, I learned discretion. Now I'll choose one herb for a zucchini sauce and maybe leave out the garlic if I'm using leeks. Anything superfluous is left out. I adhere to this idea especially when cooking with vegetables, because I don't want to overwhelm fresh produce with too many adornments. This doesn't mean every vegetable sauce has to be bone simple, but it needs to be well-thought-out and carefully constructed. For example, a pasta primavera might contain five different vegetables, but each one should be added to the sauce with respect for its cooking time so you don't wind up with a half-raw, half-mushy vegetable mess. If you think about this when choosing ingredients for your vegetable sauces, you'll be one step closer to creating dishes with beauty and integrity.

Since the subject is so broad, I've divided the pasta-and-vegetable chapter into sections, each one containing ways to begin with the basic recipes and build from them. The tomato sauce chapter, for example, lists many approaches to cooking a tomato sauce, in addition to examples of how to embellish each sauce to create more complex dishes. And under each dish I offer several variations to stimulate your own creativity. Tomato sauces serve as platforms for more intricate pasta sauces. If you dissect a puttanesca or an amatriciana sauce, you will discover a simple tomato base to which tasty ingredients have been added. I do the same in the garlic section. There is also a section on traditional vegetables used to dress pasta and ways for you to produce unique dishes. Next you'll see some inspirational ways to use seasonal produce. Our own supermarket vegetables such as leeks, squash, parsnips, snap peas, and cabbage make surprisingly good pasta sauces and stuffings for lasagne and ravioli.

Making Tomato Sauce

Tomatoes can be the basis for a sauce, or they can be the sauce itself. After you've mastered a few basic tomato sauces, you'll discover how many other pasta sauces start with such a simple foundation. For example, adding anchovies, olives, and capers to a tomato base gives you an instant puttanesca. Spice up a plain tomato sauce with fresh or dried hot chiles, and you've got an arrabbiata sauce. Brown a little pancetta along with the chile and you've made a classic amatriciana sauce from the Abruzzo. Letting a handful of clams open in the tomato sauce creates a classic red clam sauce. You can also perk up yesterday's plain tomato sauce by adding sautéed mushrooms or artichokes or by simmering shrimp or scallops in the sauce while you gently reheat it. Afterthoughts are easily incorporated into tomato sauces, which are accepting of your whims.

Sometimes it's not apparent when you look through a cookbook that a group of recipes actually share the same foundation, but it can be especially true of pasta sauces. It's a matter of adding or omitting an ingredient or two to create a different taste and the illusion of something unknown and mysterious.

Matching Pasta with Sauce

Despite the fact that pasta has become quite whimsical in the hands of many American and even Italian chefs, several traditional thoughts governing what sauce goes with what pasta still make sense to me. I wouldn't prepare a cream sauce with dried spaghetti any sooner than I would make an *aglio e olio* (garlic and oil sauce) with fresh egg tagliatelle. But some of my thinking has changed. In my travels to southern Italy, I've noticed a restaurant trend toward serving fresh egg tagliatelle with white or red clam sauce. This is a dish that I've always had with dried spaghetti or other long, thin dried pasta such as bucatini or capellini. But this new dish seems fresh to me, and less austere than the original spaghetti version.

Try to use an artistic eye when matching sauces with pasta shapes. Ingredients can be cut in different ways to accommodate different pasta shapes. I love cutting celery, carrots, and onions in small cubes, sautéing them in olive oil, and tossing the mix with tubetti—which is basically the same shape. Small cubes of zucchini look pretty nestled in the hollowed rounds of orecchiette. Thin strips of sautéed bell pepper wrap nicely around penne or fusilli. The recipes that follow reflect my current thoughts on pairing sauce with pasta. Some are based on strict tradition, and others bend the rules a bit.

On Measuring

When I worked in the test kitchen of a major food magazine, I discovered firsthand just how subjective taste really is. I would prepare recipes and then the editors would all taste the dishes and write their reactions on a chart. I noticed that their comments on saltiness always varied greatly. "Too salty," and, of the same dish, "needs salt" or "way too bland" or "horrendously oversalted." This perplexed me. People's taste for salt obviously varies greatly. Many cookbooks and magazines include salt quantities in their recipes. This, I think, is a bad idea. Personal salt tolerance aside, it is extremely hard to judge without tasting the intrinsic and varying saltiness of many ingredients—ham, for instance, or cheeses—how much salty flavor these foods will add to a dish.

And speaking of salt as it pertains to pasta, it actually is *crucial* that you salt your pasta water. You cannot make up for lack of it by salting the sauce—the dressed pasta will always taste flat. This is the same as the need to salt meat or fish during a preliminary sautéing, even though ingredients may be added later or the dish is to be simmered, as in a stew. Without that early salting, the dish will remain somewhat bland and never be what it could be. You need that initial infusion to round it out.

Saltiness, like many other aspects of flavor, is a matter of personal taste. Constant tasting is vital to good cooking. There is really no way to season food without following the cooking process with your tongue and nose. Sauces reduce, and many qualities, especially saltiness, intensify with long cooking and evaporation. The flavors of fresh herbs, however, tend to diminish after long cooking.

How much of an ingredient you add to a dish will depend on the freshness and quality of that ingredient. Fresh garlic has a much milder flavor than older dried garlic, and the longer it stews, the milder its flavor becomes. Olives vary greatly in saltiness and pungency, so it is a good idea to taste any olives—or capers or prosciutto or anchovies or Pecorino cheese—or anything—before adding them to a dish, just to get an idea of what you are working with. Then you can decide how much of the ingredient you want or whether you want it at all.

A problem I've had with many cookbook and food magazine recipes is that the amounts of certain ingredients called for are so small that they could never contribute to the recipe. Three basil leaves in a tomato sauce meant to feed six? What is the point? You go out and buy a big bunch of basil, only to use three leaves? Three grindings of black pepper? One scraping of nutmeg? Taste to see what the written recipe produces, and if you want more basil, add it. You'd be amazed to know the quantities of seasonings that go into good restaurant cooking. I almost inevitably add a bit more of whatever is called for, partly because my taste tends to favor the robust but also because I find that people who follow recipes religiously tend to make rather bland meals.

As a general rule, try not to measure when you cook, unless you are baking. Learn to trust your eye and palate. When deciding how much tomato to add to a pasta sauce, look at the amount of pasta and judge how much sauce will cover it. Some cooks get used to placing small amounts of ingredients, such as chopped garlic, pepper, or herbs, in the palm of their hand before adding them to a dish. This provides a frame of reference and separates the ingredient from the others scattered over the kitchen counter. Try to think not in terms of adding a tea-spoon or a cup but of how weak or strong a taste you want a certain ingredient to have in re-lationship to the whole. How oniony do you want your sauce to be? Should it be spicy? Do you want to taste the wine or just use it as a subtle component to bring the dish together? Do you want a full-out tomato sauce or just pieces of tomato for accent? Are you making a meat sauce, or will you just sauté a little pancetta to give richness to the vegetables? Usually when I cook I have an idea of the end result I want, and I start by thinking about how I'm going to get there.

Some Basic Information for Cooking Pasta

The most important point when cooking pasta is to make sure your cooking water returns quickly to a boil after you drop in the pasta. Pasta left cooking in slow-simmering water will become mushy and have a tendency to clump. For a pound of pasta, choose a large pot (6 to 8 quarts). Fill it slightly more than three-quarters full with cold water (my cold tap water tastes better than the hot water, which picks up more residue from the pipes, so I prefer to use it, and in general this is a good practice). Bring the water to a boil, then add the salt. Pasta water is always salted after it comes to a boil to avoid its taking on a slight metallic taste. I find this less of a problem now that I use sea salt, but it is a good rule to follow. I use at least 2 tablespoons salt; otherwise I find the pasta tastes flat no matter how well seasoned my sauce is. Taste the water after you salt it. It should taste salty. If it doesn't, your pasta won't have much flavor either. After salting, let the water return to a rolling boil. Then add the pasta all at once. Stir it briefly with a wooden spoon to keep it from sticking together. Make sure the heat is on high. The water should return to a rapid boil after a few seconds. You can cover the pot to bring the water back to a boil quickly, but be sure to remove the cover as soon as the water boils or the pasta will steam and become mushy. Stir the pasta gently with a wooden spoon once or twice during cooking to prevent sticking. Some cooks add a drizzle of oil to the pasta water. In my experience this doesn't prevent the pasta from sticking together, but does discourage the sauce from clinging to the pasta, so I would avoid doing it.

Fresh pasta, if really moist, can cook in less than a minute. When properly cooked, it will be tender but still slightly firm to the bite, never soft or mushy. Taste-test a piece the minute you see it start to float to the top of the water. Fresh filled pastas can be difficult to judge. They need to cook long enough to heat the filling, but you don't want to overcook the delicate pasta casing. When you taste-test one, check to see if the edges where they are sealed are still a little firm and need a few more seconds to cook to become tender. Dried pasta cooking times vary, depending on the shape and the hardness of the product. Thick rigatoni, for instance, will take longer to cook than thin spaghettini. Start taste-testing the pasta a few minutes before it has reached the recommended cooking time on the package. It should be cooked al dente, chewy to the bite, but with no hardness in the center. When cooked, the color will have lightened somewhat and the pasta will look a bit swollen. If the pasta is still somewhat rigid and inflexible, it needs more cooking.

The minute the pasta is perfectly cooked, drain it in a colander. Don't shake all the water off. Pasta should remain a bit moist. Toss it with sauce immediately so it doesn't stick together. (Don't rinse it with cold water before saucing it. This cools off the pasta and washes away the surface starch that helps the sauce adhere. I rinse pasta only when I'm making a pasta salad.) Some very delicate fresh pastas such as ravioli or lasagne should be lifted from the cooking water with a large, flat strainer because the relatively violent act of pouring the pasta with its water into a colander can sometimes tear the pasta.

A pound of pasta will expand quite a bit when cooked, so if you plan to return it to the saucepan for a brief cooking with the sauce, make sure the pan is large. I always use a 13-inch skillet for this purpose.

All the recipes in this book are for one pound of dried pasta, unless fresh is specified. Only dried pasta is cooked al dente. Fresh egg pasta, even raw, is quite soft; cooking should take it from doughy to firm but tender, so all the recipes call for cooking it until tender.

One pound of pasta serves four as a main course or six as a first course.

General Quantities to Keep in Mind When Shopping for Pasta Sauce Ingredients

*I*f you want to create a pasta sauce from your imagination but are not sure how much of a certain ingredient to buy, here are some tips that may help you along. All the ingredient amounts are designed for 1 pound of pasta, which makes 4 main-course or 6 first-course servings.

Olive Oil

For a sauce that will be almost all olive oil, such as an *aglio e olio* (garlic and oil sauce), figure on at least ⅓ cup of oil. You'll need enough to coat all the pasta. Otherwise, a few tablespoons are usually enough for sautéing vegetables, fish, or meat. And keep in mind that if the dish seems dry after tossing the pasta with the finished sauce, a drizzle of fresh olive oil can loosen the sauce and help it cling to the pasta. It will also provide a flavor boost, especially if you use a first-rate oil.

Tomatoes

One 35-ounce can of Italian plum tomatoes with their juice will give you plenty of sauce to coat the pasta lightly. If you drain the tomatoes and are not adding any other ingredients, you may want to use one large can and one small (approximately 15-ounce) one, depending on how tomatoey you want the sauce to be. If you're going to thin the sauce with broth or wine or stretch it with a lot of onion and celery, one drained can may suffice. Two pounds of plum tomatoes (about 15) will make enough sauce for a pound of pasta. Four or five round summer tomatoes (about 2½ to 3 pounds), seeded and chopped, are enough for an uncooked tomato sauce.

Vegetables

One large onion, 3 shallots, 2 or 3 leeks, or 6 scallions are enough for a flavor base (your soffritto). But if you want a heavily laced onion sauce, you'll have to use about twice as much. Greens cook down considerably, especially arugula and spinach. Sturdier greens like kale and chard add more bulk to a sauce. In general, 1½ pounds of raw greens is about right for an all-greens sauce. One pound of mushrooms is about enough for an all-mushroom ragù or olive oil–based sauce. If you add another vegetable or mix it with meat, use about ½ pound of mushrooms. Use 1 pound of large eggplant for an all-eggplant sauce, or 1 pound of zucchini for an all-zucchini sauce. If you're making a sauce with zucchini and another vegetable, 2 medium zucchini should be about right. For an all-pepper sauce, use 5 bell peppers, or 2 if you're mixing them with another ingredient.

Fish

One to 1½ pounds of fish fillets should be enough when mixed with other ingredients such as tomatoes, wine, or broth. If you're adding a vegetable to the sauce, you can even use a little less fish. Two pounds of mussels or clams will give you a generous shellfish sauce. One to 1½ pounds of shrimp or scallops should be about right. If you're adding a lot of other ingredients, you can get away with a little less.

Meat

For a ragù, 1½ pounds of chopped meat or stew meat will give you an ample sauce. One pound of sausage is enough for a pasta sauce that will include tomatoes or a small amount of vegetables. If the sausage is very rich, use less. If you want to add something bulky, like broccoli rabe, you can get away with ½ pound of sausage, since it becomes more of an accent. About 1 pound of chicken livers or sweetbreads or veal scallops is enough for a nicely flavored sauce with small pieces of chopped meat.

Cheese

Use approximately 1 cup of grated cheese for an Alfredo-type sauce that will be predominantly cheese and cream. For a tomato or vegetable sauce, ½ cup is about right, added at the last minute for body and flavor. One cup of ricotta will coat 1 pound of pasta. One cup of cream will serve for cream sauce. To add richness to a tomato or meat sauce, you'll want just a few tablespoons to about ½ cup.

Pasta Lunga (Long Pasta)

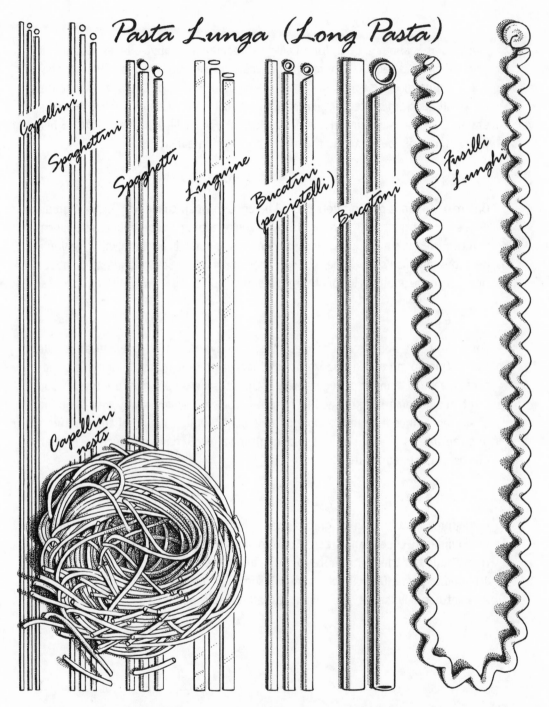

Capellini

Spaghettini

Spaghetti

Linguine

Bucatini (perciatelli)

Bucatoni

Fusilli Lunghi

Capellini nests

For spicy or pungent sauces like puttanesca or arrabbiata. Also a good choice for *aglio e olio* (garlic and oil sauce) or olive oil–based tomato and other Mediterranean vegetable sauces made with small pieces of zucchini or artichoke. Long pasta is classic with red or white clam sauces, sardines, or mussels.

Sauce of Plum Tomatoes, Shallots, and Butter

A Sweet Sauté of Plum Tomatoes

The best fresh plum (also called Roma) tomatoes are available in the summer, but I often see acceptable-looking ones during the fall and early winter, and if they're dark red, soft, and smell like tomatoes, I buy them. Sometimes they're quite good; sometimes they're mealy and tasteless, so taste one before you cook with it. This is a quick sauce that blends excellently with fresh egg pasta. Note the use of shallots and butter instead of the usual onion and olive oil. This produces a sweeter, more delicate sauce.

[Makes enough sauce for 1 pound of pasta]

2 to 3 tablespoons unsalted butter	Salt
4 shallots, thinly sliced	Freshly ground black pepper
15 ripe plum tomatoes (2 to 2½ pounds), peeled, seeded, and chopped into small dice	

- In a large skillet, melt the butter over medium heat. Add the shallots and sauté until soft, 3 to 4 minutes. Add the tomatoes, turn up the heat a bit, and cook until they soften and give off juice, another 5 to 6 minutes. Cover the pan while cooking the tomatoes if you want more liquid in your sauce. The sauce will taste sweet, like a slightly heightened ripe tomato, and be bright red. Add salt and pepper and a little extra butter if desired. I like this sauce a little chunky, but if you want a smoother texture, pulse it briefly in a food processor.

Ideas

If you like the taste of green tomatoes, substitute them here. The sauce will be tart but lively. Choose ones with tiny flecks of red on the skin. Very firm green tomatoes are a bit too sour.

Tagliatelle with Plum Tomatoes, Pine Nuts, and Chanterelles

This sauce is absurdly easy to make but comes off as special. It is an elegant elaboration on the Sauce of Plum Tomatoes, Shallots, and Butter. The addition of a few ingredients produces a subtle sauce that harmonizes with the butter and shallot theme.

[Makes 4 main-course or 6 first-course servings]

2 to 3 tablespoons unsalted butter

About 2 dozen chanterelle mushrooms, cleaned with a damp rag if dirty and cut in half lengthwise or quartered if very large

A generous handful of pine nuts

Salt

Freshly ground black pepper

A splash of brandy

1 recipe Sauce of Plum Tomatoes, Shallots, and Butter (page 21)

A few gratings of nutmeg

5 or 6 sage leaves, cut in thin strips*

1 pound Plain Egg Pasta (page 364), cut for tagliatelle

½ cup mascarpone cheese

- In a large skillet, melt the butter over medium heat. When the butter is hot and just bubbling, add the chanterelles and pine nuts and sauté until the mushrooms start to soften and the nuts turn golden, about 4 minutes. Salt and pepper lightly.
- Pour the brandy into the pan, stir to loosen all the browned cooking juices, and let the liquid boil to almost nothing (this way you capture every bit of mushroom flavor from the pan). Add the plum tomato sauce, nutmeg, and sage and simmer over low heat for about 4 minutes to incorporate the flavors and to make sure the mushrooms are tender (chanterelles can be hard to digest if they're not cooked through).
- Cook the tagliatelle until tender and drain. Place them in a large serving bowl.
- Stir the mascarpone into the sauce; the sauce should be warm enough so the cheese melts easily. If you make the sauce ahead of time and it needs to be reheated, gently simmer for a few seconds over very low heat (mascarpone can separate if cooked too long over high heat). The sauce will be dark pink. Taste for salt and pepper. Pour the sauce over the pasta and toss well.

---

* To keep delicate herbs and greens from bruising when cutting them into strips (which can occur with a repeated chopping motion), simply roll 3 or 4 leaves widthwise into a loose round and slice into very thin strips. It helps to have a very sharp knife so you can get nice clean strokes. The leaves will unroll into thin strips that fall gracefully into a sauce or can be scattered on top for garnish.

Note: Mushrooms can also be added while sautéing the shallots for the plum tomato sauce. They cook along with the tomatoes. This is the way I cook white mushrooms or sturdy portobellos, but when adding chanterelles, I like to preserve their delicate flavor and not let them simmer in a tomato sauce.

Freshly grated cheese, such as Parmigiano-Reggiano or Asiago, is not generally served with mushroom-sauced pasta in Italy. I don't always hold to this thinking, but with mushrooms like chanterelles, where you need to be careful not to overwhelm their exquisite perfume, it makes sense.

Ideas

Mushroom and tomato sauces are made throughout Italy and sometimes referred to as *boscaiola,* which means "woodsman style." You can make them with fresh or dried mushrooms. This one, with chanterelles and mascarpone, is a subtle sauce, but a heartier version can be made with porcini or portobellos and a bit of garlic.

Two other interesting mushroom and tomato sauces are made with white cultivated mushrooms and a little anchovy or with hedgehog mushrooms and capers.

Add a few chopped sprigs of gentle fresh herbs like parsley or chervil at the end of cooking—either one will impart sprightly flavor to the sauce without overpowering it. Fresh tarragon, an herb not used much in Italian cooking, goes particularly well with mushrooms and is another good herb choice. If you use one of these herbs, leave out the sage.

Crème fraîche in place of the mascarpone will add a note of acidity to your sauce. Heavy cream will add richness but has a slightly blander flavor.

Sautéing Vegetables for Flavor

*I*t's always a good idea to sauté any vegetable that will become part of your pasta sauce. Plain boiled vegetables have little flavor. Sautéing not only toasts the outside of the vegetable, releasing its natural sugars, but also brings out its juices, adding to the depth of any sauce. The difference between a pasta primavera you are served in Italy and the sort you are often served here is a quick sautéing of blanched or raw vegetables before the cream or other liquid is added. There are two ways to incorporate vegetables (or any other ingredients, for that matter) into a sauce. The first is to add them at the beginning, when you want the vegetables to simmer and impart rich flavor (you'd make a tomato-based eggplant sauce this way). The other is to add them at the end. You'd do this either because you don't want delicate vegetables (fresh peas or chanterelle mushrooms, for instance) to cook too long and lose their charm and freshness, or because the addition was an afterthought (the way you might incorporate leftovers or odds and ends from your refrigerator). In either case, the sautéing step is crucial for obtaining maximum flavor.

Sauté some chopped onion in a little olive oil and taste it. Then sauté some in unsalted butter. Note the different flavor each fat imparts to the onion, remembering that the fat and onion you choose will provide the backbone of the finished sauce.

Onion of some sort shows up in so many sauce recipes that you can easily mistake it for a neutral presence. Taste its sweetness (or slight sourness) before adding other ingredients. Next add the tomatoes and note how the onion mingles with their acidity. Do the same when adding shallots, leeks, scallions, Vidalia onions, or red onions, as they are subtly yet considerably different in their effects on a sauce.

Note: For quick-cooked (15 minutes or under) tomato sauces with a bold taste, use a large sauté pan instead of a saucepan. Its big surface encourages evaporation and cooks the sauce quickly while preserving its bright red color. Longer-simmered sauces can cook more slowly, allowing seasonings and the sweetness of the tomatoes to open up and create a more complex flavor.

Tomato and Orange Sauce with Farfalle

Orange and tomato is a surprisingly successful combination. The oil from the orange zest blends with the butter to form a perfumed cooking fat, creating a third dimension. This sauce makes a good base for seafood additions (see Ideas). Serve it without cheese.

[Makes 4 main-course or 6 first-course servings]

1 recipe Sauce of Plum Tomatoes, Shallots, and Butter (page 21)	**1 pound farfalle**
Zest of 2 oranges	**A handful of basil leaves, cut in thin strips**
Juice of 1 orange	

- Make the plum tomato sauce, adding the orange zest and juice with the tomatoes. Proceed as in the original recipe.
- Cook the farfalle until al dente, drain, and transfer to a serving bowl. Pour on the sauce, add the basil, and toss well.

Ideas

Many interesting flavors can be added to a basic tomato sauce while still keeping it simple. Orange is one. A splash of Marsala wine adds amazing depth and creates an ideal base for additions such as sausage or mushrooms.

Mint leaves make an interesting substitute for the basil. Or use half mint and half basil. Thyme is another option, but will give you a slightly sharper result.

Toss the pasta with about ½ cup ricotta before adding the tomato and orange sauce. I sometimes add a tiny drop of orange flower water to the ricotta to accentuate the sweetness of the ricotta even further.

Shrimp or scallops can be added to this sauce and poached until just tender, about 2 minutes, depending on the size of the shellfish. Or add precooked crab or lobster meat. Rings of sliced raw squid are also wonderful here; let them simmer at least 30 minutes in the sauce to become tender. And if you want this dish to taste even more like bouillabaisse, add a splash of Pernod or other anise-flavored liqueur when you add the fish.

This sauce can also become a base for puttanesca: add a handful of capers, some pitted black olives, a pinch of cayenne, a few chopped anchovy fillets, and, if you like, a can of tuna packed in olive oil and drained to your cooked tomato sauce and let this all simmer over low heat 2 to 3 minutes to blend the flavors.

Cherry Tomato Sauce with Garlic and Olive Oil

A Tomato Sauce Cooked on Very High Heat

I love cooking this sauce because I get to watch the tomatoes burst open in the pan—and when they do, the sauce is done. A mild acidity is characteristic of most cherry tomatoes and is part of their appeal. Yellow or orange cherry tomatoes provide unexpected color but tend to taste even sharper than the red. Taste one before cooking it and add a pinch of sugar, if necessary, to the sauce.

[Makes enough sauce for 1 pound of pasta]

2 to 3 tablespoons olive oil

2 pint baskets cherry tomatoes (about
   3 dozen), stemmed

2 or 3 garlic cloves, thinly sliced

Salt

A small piece of fresh red chile,
   seeded and finely chopped

- In a skillet large enough to hold all the tomatoes in a single layer, heat the olive oil over high heat until very hot and just starting to smoke. Add the tomatoes. You should hear the sizzle when the liquid in the tomatoes hits the hot oil. Shake the pan a bit, letting the tomatoes brown slightly on all sides. After a few minutes they will start to burst.
- Add the garlic, salt, and red chile and continue cooking over high heat until most of the tomatoes have opened and let off juice, another 2 to 3 minutes. The tomatoes will have burst but still be in large chunks. The sauce shouldn't be cooked down to the point where the skins start falling off the tomatoes.

Ideas

A very thinly sliced red onion is an intelligent substitute for the garlic because its sharpness complements the gentle acidity of this sauce. This sauce is wonderful with Black Pepper Pasta (page 368), cut for tagliatelle.

Spaghetti with Cherry Tomatoes, Capers, Anchovies, Marjoram, and Lemon Zest (A Puttanesca Sauce)

A robust mix of pungent and salty ingredients in a tomato base, puttanesca features capers, black olives, anchovies, fresh or dried oregano, and plenty of garlic. Sometimes hot red peppers and a splash of red wine vinegar are added, but it is not a fixed recipe. The only constant is that it should have a sharp taste. There are many ways to achieve this. Here is one.

[Makes 4 main-course or 6 first-course servings]

1 recipe Cherry Tomato Sauce with Garlic and Olive Oil (page 26)

5 or 6 anchovy fillets, chopped

A handful of black olives, pitted and cut in half (I use oil-cured Moroccan olives)

A handful of capers, preferably salt-packed, soaked and rinsed

Zest of 1 lemon

A few marjoram sprigs, leaves chopped

1 pound spaghetti

- Heat the cherry tomato sauce over medium-low heat. Add the chopped anchovies, stirring them into the sauce to dissolve (some brands are saltier and fishier than others, so it's best to taste one first and decide how many to add). Add the olives, capers, lemon zest, and marjoram and simmer a minute to blend the flavors.
- Cook the spaghetti until al dente, drain, and place in a large serving bowl. Toss with the sauce and serve.

Ideas

My mother always added canned, drained olive oil–packed Italian tuna to puttanesca, which made a substantial main course. If you'd like to try this, add the tuna at the end and just let it heat through. Canned tuna is best in a sauce when not allowed to cook.

I've chosen marjoram for this version, but experiment with other strong herbs; mint goes well with all sorts of olives.

Experiment with different olives. Using oil-cured black olives will warm up your dish; green olives will create a sharper sauce.

Simmered Tomato Sauce

A 30-Minute Sauce with an Old-Fashioned Taste

Hardly anyone these days cooks dark brown tomato sauces that sit on the stove all day developing a heavy crust around the rim of the pot. I think that style of cooking evolved out of a misinterpretation of southern Italian ragùs—robust tomato and meat sauces that do need long cooking to tenderize coarse cuts of meat. Twenty to 30 minutes of simmering is sufficient to produce a rich tomato sauce with some complexity of flavor. Long cooking is, in fact, appropriate only for meat sauces in which proteins need to be broken down.

[Makes enough sauce for 1 pound of pasta]

2 to 3 tablespoons olive oil

About 2 tablespoons unsalted butter

1 large sweet onion, such as Vidalia or
  Walla Walla, cut in small dice

2 small carrots, cut in small dice

2 tender inner celery stalks, cut in
  small dice, plus leaves, chopped

A few garlic cloves, crushed with the
  back of a knife

A small wineglass of dry white wine

One 35-ounce can Italian plum tomatoes with their juice, chopped

A few thyme sprigs, leaves chopped

A large handful of flat-leaf parsley
  leaves, coarsely chopped

A large handful of basil leaves,
  coarsely chopped

Salt

Freshly ground black pepper

- Heat about 2 tablespoons each of the olive oil and butter in a large skillet over medium heat. Add the onion, carrots, celery, and celery leaves and sauté until soft and just starting to brown slightly, about 10 minutes. Add the garlic and sauté a minute longer, just to bring out the flavor, not to brown it. Add the wine and let it bubble a minute or so to cook out the alcohol. Crush the tomatoes with your hands (or use a food processor) and add them with their juice to the pot. Add half of the fresh herbs and season lightly with salt and pepper.
- Cook, uncovered, at a lively simmer over medium heat, stirring occasionally, until the sauce loses its watery appearance and has thickened, 15 to 20 minutes. Check the seasoning and add the remaining fresh herbs. The sauce will have a mild sweetness and be bright red.

Ideas

This is another basic tomato sauce that is ideal with spaghetti or other string pasta. But its full-bodied taste also makes it perfect for lasagne, cannelloni, or ravioli.

You can use fresh plum tomatoes when they are ripe and juicy (peeled, seeded, and chopped).

This sauce can be made richer by adding a splash of heavy cream immediately before serving.

Vary the flavor base by adding leeks, fennel, shallots, or scallions instead of, or in addition to, the onion.

By browning about ½ pound of crumbled skinless veal or pork sausage along with the onion, celery, and carrot, you create the taste of a simmered meat sauce in about 30 minutes.

If you add a cup or more of homemade chicken stock to the finished sauce and then stir in ½ cup of cooked small pasta such as orzo or acini di pepe right before serving, you will have an elegant soup. Top with a sprinkle of freshly grated Grana Padano cheese and a drizzle of extra-virgin olive oil.

Garganelli with Simmered Tomato-Fig Sauce

While eating a dish of chicken stuffed with figs in tomato sauce at an eclectic Italian restaurant, I was amazed at how well figs and tomatoes go together. So I came up with this sauce, which has an indefinable sweetness balanced by the acid of the tomatoes. It is a rich, warming dish of pasta, good for a cold night and especially inviting for vegetarians, who need a little variety in their lives. Freshly grated Parmigiano-Reggiano cheese goes very well with it.

[Makes 4 main-course or 6 first-course servings]

5 or 6 dried figs (softer, lighter figs such as Calimyrna work best)

Ingredients for 1 recipe Simmered Tomato Sauce (page 28)

1 pound garganelli (Plain Egg Pasta, page 364, cut for tagliatelle, is a good alternative)

About ½ cup heavy cream

Freshly grated Parmigiano-Reggiano cheese

- Chop the figs into small pieces. Make the tomato sauce, letting the figs soak for 30 minutes in the white wine. Add a little warm water if necessary just to cover the figs. Add the figs with their soaking liquid to the sauce when the wine is added to the recipe. Proceed with the recipe.
- When the sauce has cooked, taste for balance. You might need extra salt to offset the sweetness imparted by the figs.
- Cook the garganelli until al dente and drain. Stir the cream into the sauce at the end of cooking. The sauce will be bright orange and the figs will have dissolved into the sauce. Toss with the hot pasta, adding a handful of grated Parmigiano-Reggiano. Serve extra cheese at the table if desired.

Note: I like the texture the fig seeds add, but if you want a more refined sauce, pass it through a food mill before serving.

Ideas

Try sour cream instead of fresh; it will add a bit of tartness that complements the sweet figs.

Thyme goes wonderfully with figs; you can add the leaves from a few sprigs along with the other herbs or in their place.

Prosciutto with figs is a classic Italian antipasto. Try adding a few slices of chopped prosciutto to this sauce (add them just before tossing with the pasta so the prosciutto doesn't cook too much in the sauce).

MAKING A SOFFRITTO

This simmered tomato sauce and many other simmered sauces in this book begin with a gentle sautéing of onions, carrots, celery, and often other aromatic vegetables such as fennel or garlic. Occasionally finely chopped fresh herbs such as parsley, sage, or rosemary are included. This sauce base is known in Italian as a soffritto. A carefully made soffritto can help to ensure a flavorful, rich base for many sauces. A soffritto can be sautéed in olive oil, butter, or a mix of both. Sometimes pancetta or salt pork is added for additional flavor. The gentle browning of these vegetables in oil creates a light caramelization and sweetness that serve as a solid underpinning for any ingredients that will later be added. It's what gives Italian cooking its depth of flavor.

Quick-cooked sauces can benefit from a soffritto too, but usually a simpler one, possibly consisting only of sautéed leeks, shallots, and perhaps a bit of garlic. I like experimenting with different members of the onion family when making a soffritto. Your choice of leeks or scallions over a yellow Spanish onion, for instance, can make a huge difference in the taste of the finished sauce. Try sautéing some chopped onion in a little olive oil and taste it. Then try the same with leeks or shallots. In each case note the sweet or sharp undertones each vegetable releases into the oil. Then sauté the same vegetables in butter. Note the different flavor each fat imparts, remembering the fat and onion you choose will provide the backbone for the finished sauce.

Quick Sauté of Drained Canned Tomatoes (A Marinara Sauce)

A Quick Winter Sauce for Canned Tomatoes

When I want the taste of summer tomatoes in winter, I come close by draining high-quality canned plum tomatoes and quickly sautéing them over very high heat. This produces a taste similar to that of a fresh Neapolitan pizza sauce and serves as a vibrant base for many variations. This is a marinara sauce, which in its classic form is a base of sautéed garlic in olive oil with chopped tomatoes added.

[Makes enough sauce for 1 pound of pasta]

One 35-ounce can Italian plum tomatoes, plus one 15-ounce can Italian plum tomatoes, crushed a bit with your fingers and well drained

2 to 3 tablespoons olive oil

3 or 4 garlic cloves, peeled and minced

Salt

Freshly ground black pepper

A few large sprigs each of fresh oregano and marjoram, stemmed, leaves left whole (see Note)

- Chop the tomatoes roughly and drain them very well in a colander (they should sit at least 15 minutes so that most of the liquid will drain out).
- In a large skillet, heat enough olive oil over high heat to very generously cover the bottom of the pan. When the pan is very hot, add the garlic and drained tomatoes at the same time, shaking the pan to sear them evenly. This should take 2 to 3 minutes. The sauce will be fairly thick and bright red. Season with salt, pepper, and the oregano and marjoram.

Note: In southern Italy this marinara sauce would be made with dried oregano, which is preferred to fresh in many Mediterranean countries. Fresh oregano can sometimes be harsh, but it does have a wonderful biting flavor. I've found that mixing fresh oregano with fresh marjoram, which has a similar taste but is mild and flowery, tames the oregano and adds a Mediterranean perfume to this sauce.

Orecchiette with Drained Canned Tomatoes Flavored with Soppressata and Pine Nuts

I make this sauce in 5 minutes when I have a chunk of soppressata or other salami in the refrigerator. The oil from the sausage flavors the sauce, giving it pungency. It's best with a sturdy dried pasta and a sharp-tasting grating cheese.

[Makes 4 main-course or 6 first-course servings]

Ingredients for 1 recipe Quick Sauté of
    Drained Canned Tomatoes (page 32)
2-inch or bigger chunk of soppressata,
    pepperoni, salami, or other dried
    sausage, skinned and cut in
    small dice
A generous handful of pine nuts,
    lightly toasted

1 pound orecchiette (fusilli, penne,
    and rigatoni are other good
    pasta choices)
Freshly grated Pecorino Toscano or
    Romano cheese

- Heat the oil for the tomato sauce and add the soppressata, browning it quickly. Then proceed with the tomato sauce recipe, cutting down on the amount of olive oil if you wish. (Depending on the sausage you choose, you may have a fair amount of fat in your pan.) Add the pine nuts just as the sauce finishes cooking.
- Cook the orecchiette until al dente, drain, and add to the pan. Toss well to coat the pasta. Pass bowls of the freshly grated cheese at the table.

Ideas

This sauce provides an opportunity to use up leftover prosciutto ends or even previously cooked fresh sausage, such as sweet Italian, in place of the dried. Shredded pieces of roasted duck are wonderful here in place of, or in addition to, the soppressata. Add it in the last minutes of cooking, just to warm through.

Make a vegetarian version by sautéing red and yellow bell pepper strips or adding grilled eggplant or zucchini cut into strips in place of the sausage.

Uncooked Tomato Sauce

Perfect Summer Tomatoes

When you find fragrant summer tomatoes, this is the sauce to make. This was one of the sauces my mother added to her repertoire in the early 1970s, using my father's backyard tomatoes (I think she found it in a magazine; it was not a family standard). It was a revelation to me that pasta could taste so fresh. Try this marvelous sauce over hot pasta or in a cold pasta salad—it can become the starting point for a seemingly infinite number of variations using cooked or uncooked ingredients. But save it for your very best seasonal tomatoes.

[Makes enough sauce for 1 pound of pasta]

5 ripe summer tomatoes (about 3 pounds), seeded and cut in medium dice

5 scallions, cut in very thin rounds, including some tender green

1 or 2 garlic cloves, very finely minced

A large handful of basil leaves, lightly chopped (see Note)

A few tablespoons of extra-virgin olive oil

A tiny splash of balsamic vinegar

Salt

Freshly ground black pepper

- Drain the chopped tomatoes in a colander for 20 minutes to remove excess water. Place all the ingredients in a large bowl and let sit for at least 30 minutes so they can develop flavor. The amount of olive oil you add to this sauce is entirely a matter of taste. I like quite a bit, about ⅓ cup. Aside from providing a luscious taste, it helps the sauce adhere to the pasta.

  A note about summer tomatoes: I find an amazing variety of heirloom tomatoes at my farmers' market during the summer—some with deep ridges, some in gorgeous burnished tones of mauve, dark pink, or ochre yellow. The old forgotten varieties that farmers are now growing again from heirloom seeds are especially suited for uncooked sauces. Some of these tomatoes have an exciting acidity you don't find in common commercial tomatoes. They can also be extremely juicy, so make sure you drain them after chopping and before mixing with oil and other ingredients.

A note about olive oil for this sauce: Since this is a raw sauce and the oil remains uncooked, it is best made with a high-quality extra-virgin olive oil, whose flavor will really shine.

A note about peeling tomatoes: To give any tomato sauce a polished, elegant finish, you might want to remove the skins. This is very easy to do. Just drop the tomatoes into a large pot of boiling water for a minute or two. Lift them out with a large strainer and put them in a large bowl of ice water right away to stop the cooking. The skins should slip off easily. The only problem is that this cooks the tomato a bit and some cooks object to the compromise. You can also remove the skin with a sharp paring knife. (I haven't had luck with standard vegetable peelers. They tend to just rip at the skin instead of shaving it off in a neat slice. The longer, swivel-bladed type of peeler works well if it is sharp.) I usually leave the skin on ripe summer tomatoes because it's thin and sweet, and if the tomatoes aren't going to be cooked, the skin is not a problem because it stays intact and doesn't float around loose in the sauce.

Remove tomato skins whenever you want a more refined, smooth sauce. Make any of these tomato-sauce recipes with either peeled or unpeeled tomatoes. Even concassé (chopped raw tomatoes in small dice) can be left unpeeled, if you desire.

A note about chopping herbs for uncooked sauces: Herbs should be chopped as little as possible to preserve their flavorful oils and prevent them from turning into a mush. This is especially important if they're to be left uncooked, as in this sauce or when tossed into a cooked sauce at the last minute. Use a sharp knife and give them a few quick strokes. Large pieces of herbs are perfectly suited to the slightly casual quality of most pasta sauces.

Ideas

Aside from showing off beautiful tomatoes, this sauce can also showcase fresh summer herbs. I like a mix of fresh tarragon and chervil in place of the basil. Parsley, an herb many people take for granted, really stands out here.

This is also a good time to take advantage of sweet garden onions and fresh garlic, since you can add them raw.

A summer version of puttanesca, popular in Naples, starts with uncooked tomatoes, to which classic puttanesca flavorings are added—usually anchovies, capers, olives, and garlic. See A Puttanesca Sauce, page 27.

After dressing the pasta with this sauce, top each bowl with sautéed or grilled shrimp or baby squid. The juices from the seafood trickle down into the pasta, mixing with the uncooked tomatoes and enriching the sauce with sweet sea flavor. See Grilled Paprika Shrimp on Spaghetti with Summer Tomato Sauce, page 186.

Whimsical Shapes

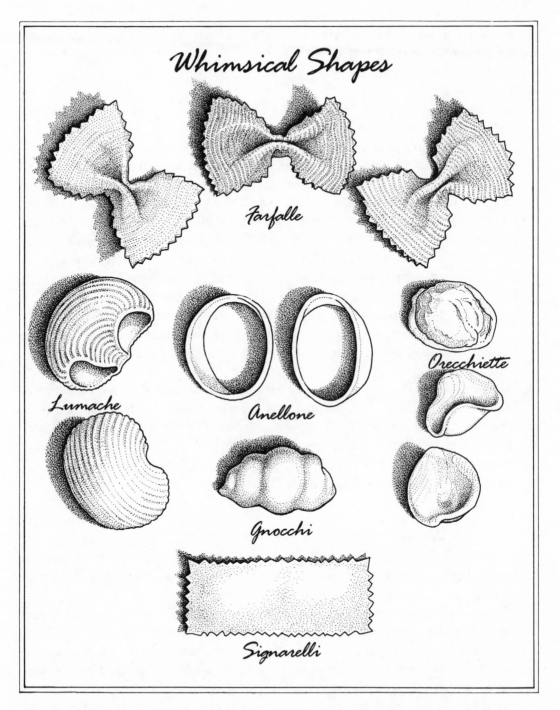

Farfalle

Lumache

Anellone

Orecchiette

Gnocchi

Signarelli

Choose sauces with pieces that can lodge inside these lovely shapes. These shapes work well with both robust and delicate sauces. Farfalle suggest a subtle sauce, one with peas and prosciutto, or a tomato sauce with a touch of cream. Sturdy orecchiette can stand up to a spicy lamb or sausage sauce or one with broccoli rabe, garlic, and a shot of hot chile.

Uncooked Tomato Sauce with Arugula, Avocado, and Croutons Tossed with Lumachine

Avocado, a very non-Italian ingredient now used by cooks in Italy, adds creaminess and body to any uncooked pasta sauce. Its suave blandness responds nicely to little bursts of flavor, like capers, for instance, which I've added here as well. Croutons give crunch and make the dish taste a bit like *panzanella*, the Tuscan bread salad.

[Makes 4 main-course or 6 first-course servings]

A dozen or so ½-inch stale Italian
    bread cubes
A bit of olive oil
Salt
Freshly ground black pepper
1 bunch arugula, washed, stemmed,
    and dried
A handful of capers (salt-packed if
    possible), soaked and rinsed
    (see page 343)

A small fresh red chile, finely minced
    (include seeds if you like a very
    spicy sauce)
1 ripe Hass avocado, peeled and
    cut in small cubes
1 recipe Uncooked Tomato Sauce
    (page 34)
1 pound lumachine (penne and ziti
    are other good choices)

- Toss the croutons with olive oil and season with salt and pepper. Sauté in a large skillet over medium-high heat a few minutes to brown lightly.
- Add the croutons, arugula, capers, chile, and avocado to the uncooked tomato sauce. Taste for seasonings.
- Cook the lumachine until al dente, drain, and toss with the sauce.

Oven-Roasted Tomato Sauce

Oven-Roasting to Concentrate Flavor

Roasting tomatoes in high heat produces a concentrated flavor similar to that of sun-dried tomatoes, but in this recipe they're cooked quickly, so they stay moist inside. This effortless sauce takes well to bold additions like hot chiles and black olives and to sturdy dried pastas like penne, ziti, and rigatoni.

[Makes enough sauce for 1 pound of pasta]

About 15 plum tomatoes (2 to 2½ pounds), coarsely chopped

Salt

Freshly ground black pepper

A few tablespoons olive oil

2 or 3 garlic cloves, thinly sliced

A small handful of flat-leaf parsley leaves, coarsely chopped

A small handful of fresh basil leaves, coarsely chopped

- Preheat the oven to 500°F.
- Place the chopped tomatoes on a baking sheet. They shouldn't be too crowded, so if you think it is necessary, use 2 baking sheets. Sprinkle the tomatoes with salt and pepper and drizzle liberally with olive oil. Mix the tomatoes with your hands until they are well coated with oil. Distribute them evenly in one layer on the baking sheet. Roast about 10 minutes, stirring the tomatoes once or twice so they cook evenly. Sprinkle the garlic and the herbs on top of the tomatoes and mix briefly. Roast another 5 to 10 minutes. The tomatoes should be slightly browned around the edges of the pan but still moist. Transfer the tomatoes to a bowl, and while still hot, break them up a bit with a fork, saving all the juices.

Ideas

You can also make this sauce with well-drained canned plum tomatoes, coarsely chopped. A 35-ounce can is enough for a pound of pasta.

This is an intensely tomatoey sauce. When seasoning it, think in terms of assertive herbs, such as mint, basil, or oregano, whose bouquets won't be lost in the sauce.

I like to use this sauce as the base for a red clam sauce. Make sure the clams are free of sand, scrape the roasted tomato sauce into a large pot, and add a splash of white wine and the clams. Cook over lively heat until the clams open, usually about 5 minutes. Pour over hot cooked linguine or bucatini and toss.

Ziti with Oven-Roasted Tomato Sauce, Prosciutto, Black Olives, and Chile Pepper

The addition of strong, contrasting flavors (sweet, spicy, and piquant) illustrates how easily you can add uncooked ingredients to the oven-roasted tomato sauce at the last minute to change its character. This is where a well-stocked Italian pantry comes in handy.

[Makes 4 main-course or 6 first-course servings]

Ingredients for 1 recipe Oven-Roasted
    Tomato Sauce (page 38)
3 or 4 thin slices prosciutto, trimmed of
    some fat, cut in small pieces
A large handful of black olives, pitted
    and cut in half (I use Gaeta here)

1 fresh red or green chile, seeded and
    very finely minced (taste a bit of the
    flesh to see how hot it is; you may
    want to add only a tiny amount)
1 pound ziti

- Make the tomato sauce and, while it is still warm, mix in the prosciutto, olives, and chile.
- Cook the ziti until al dente, drain, and toss with the sauce.

Ideas

This sauce also makes a terrific pasta salad. Simply let the sauce cool and toss it with penne that has been cooked al dente, rinsed under cold water, and drained thoroughly.

Add a cup of cooked chickpeas (ceci) or white beans plus a ladle of their cooking liquid to this sauce, and you'll have an intensely flavored, though unorthodox, *pasta e fagioli* (pasta and beans).

Substitute a handful of chopped sun-dried tomatoes for the olives for a complex and pungent two-tomato sauce.

Oven-Dried Tomatoes

A Basic Recipe

You can create a respectable homemade version of sun-dried tomatoes by cooking halved plum tomatoes in a very low oven for a very long time. The result may not be as intense as the real thing, but it's still very useful for adding to sauces and salads or using as a sauce on its own.

[Makes about 2 cups dried tomatoes]

15 ripe plum tomatoes (about 2 pounds)   **Freshly ground black pepper**
About 5 garlic cloves, finely slivered   **Olive oil**
Salt

- Preheat the oven to 200°F.
- Cut the plum tomatoes in half lengthwise and place them cut side up on an oiled baking sheet. Insert thin slivers of garlic in each tomato, salt and pepper the tomatoes liberally, and drizzle with the olive oil. Roast until they are dried and shriveled looking, 2 hours or more. (These tomatoes will never look as dry and shriveled as commercially made sun-dried. They will always retain a bit of moisture, but their flavor will be concentrated and intense.)
- The tomatoes will keep, refrigerated, at least 5 days.

A note about using your hands as kitchen utensils: You'd be surprised how often restaurant chefs use their hands to mix food, especially when making large quantities. There's no better way to sense what's going on in the pot. When mixing chopped tomatoes with oil, salt, and herbs, you can actually feel when the oil has distributed itself evenly through the tomatoes. This is especially important with salt, and if you use coarse salt, you can feel the grains mix in with the other ingredients. When mixing cooked ingredients with your hands, you can press on them to see if they have cooked long enough or have overcooked—if the meat has firmed up, if the vegetables have softened. The most efficient way to take stewed meat off the bone is with your fingers; you waste nothing because you can feel where the meat ends and the bone begins. And the best way to separate eggs is through your fingers; the fastest way to crush canned tomatoes is with your fist.

Tubi (The Maccheroni Group)

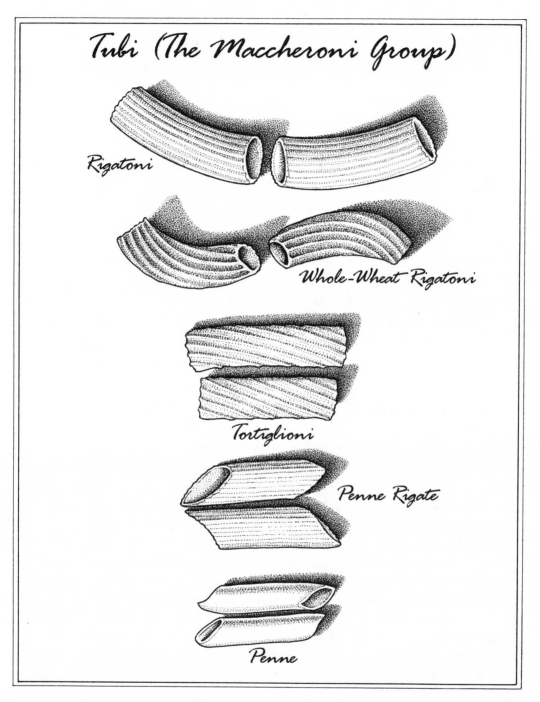

Rigatoni

Whole-Wheat Rigatoni

Tortiglioni

Penne Rigate

Penne

These pasta shapes are the best choice for chunky sausage or vegetable sauces where pieces can nestle in the holes. They are wonderful with a thick tomato or wild mushroom sauce and great for baking.

Tubetti Salad with Oven-Dried Tomatoes, White Beans, Sage, and Celery

This is a version of the classic Tuscan white bean salad to which I've added pasta. The beans are creamy, the celery is uncooked, and the pasta is al dente, resulting in a marvelously textured dish that doesn't compromise the Italian concept of pasta salad.

[Makes 4 main-course or 6 first-course servings]

1 cup dried cannellini beans, soaked overnight and drained

1 large red onion, peeled and cut in small dice (save the ends and skin to cook with the beans)

4 tender inner celery stalks, plus leaves, cut into small dice (save celery ends and 1 outer stalk to cook with the beans)

About 6 sage leaves, chopped

Red pepper flakes

Salt

Olive oil

1 recipe Oven-Dried Tomatoes (page 40), thinly sliced

Freshly ground black pepper

1 pound tubetti (or penne or farfalle)

- In a large pot, place the beans, onion ends and skin, celery ends and outer stalk, about half of the sage, and a pinch of red pepper flakes. Cover with cold water and bring to a boil. Turn the heat to low, cover the pot, and simmer until the beans are tender but not falling apart, at least 1 hour, depending on the beans. Salt the beans about halfway through the cooking so they don't become tough.
- Drain the beans, removing and discarding all the flavoring vegetables, and place them in a large serving bowl. While still warm, toss liberally with olive oil. Add the oven-dried tomatoes, chopped onion, the diced celery and leaves, and a few chopped fresh sage leaves. Season with salt and pepper.
- Cook the tubetti until al dente, place in a colander, and run cold water over them to stop the cooking. Drain thoroughly and add to the beans. Toss well, adding extra olive oil if needed to help coat the pasta. Taste for seasoning, adding more red pepper flakes if you like.

Ideas

Italians usually season bean salads very simply. Sage and good olive oil are often it. But that doesn't mean you can't play around. Adding pasta turns this classic into a full meal. And a little meat or fish makes it into a substantial main course.

Add about ¼ pound smoked trout, flaked with your fingers, or smoked salmon, chopped, or a few chopped anchovies. Chopped soppressata or another type of salami is nice in this too. If you add fish or meat, think about changing the herb. Basil is good with salmon; dill or parsley goes well with smoked trout or fresh shrimp. Choose rosemary or marjoram with soppressata.

Steam a pound of mussels open in a little white wine, shell them, and add to the beans along with the cooking liquid if you like. Steamed shrimp are also delicious.

Tomato Concassé

Adding Bursts of Fresh Tomato Flavor

Tomato concassé (peeled, seeded, and diced fresh tomatoes) is served mostly as a restaurant garnish, but can be an exciting way for home cooks to add a fresh tomato taste to pasta dishes. Sprinkle it on a finished dish of pasta, toss it into a pasta salad, or add a handful of it to a sauce during the last minutes of cooking to add color and a burst of fresh tomato.

[Makes 1½ cups]

3 large round tomatoes (about 1½ pounds)

- Place the tomatoes in boiling water for several minutes (see Note below). The skins should split slightly. Lift them out of the water with a large slotted spoon and run them under water to cool. The skins should slip off easily. Cut the tomatoes in half and remove the seeds. Cut into small dice.

Note: Blanching the tomatoes will cook them slightly. If you want really raw tomatoes, remove the skins with a sharp knife or swivel-bladed vegetable peeler.

Fusilli with Cream, Grappa, and Tomato Concassé

Grappa is a brandylike drink distilled from the skins and seeds of grapes after winemaking. In addition to being a fiery eye-opener, it's also very good to cook with, imparting a taste somewhat like that of French marc or brandy. Lemon thyme is excellent in cream-based pasta sauces because its subtle acidity cuts the richness. This is the kind of simple pasta dish I love to make for a first course and can usually pull together from ingredients on hand.

The sauce contains a fair amount of cream, which adds a sweet richness that is best balanced by a slightly acid or sharp flavor; the tomato concassé adds this needed touch.

[Makes 4 main-course or 6 first-course servings]

1 pound fusilli	Salt
3 tablespoons unsalted butter	A pinch of red pepper flakes
4 shallots, finely minced	1 recipe Tomato Concassé (page 43)
3 garlic cloves, thinly sliced	A handful of basil leaves, cut in
A generous splash of grappa (or marc	thin strips
or brandy)	A few small sprigs of thyme, leaves
½ cup (or up to 1 cup) heavy cream	chopped (use lemon thyme if
1 or 2 fresh bay leaves	you can get it)

- Start cooking the fusilli.
- Melt 2 tablespoons of the butter in a large skillet over medium heat. Add the shallots and sauté until soft. Add the garlic and sauté until very lightly golden, about 1 minute. Add the grappa and cook until it has almost boiled away. Add the cream and bay leaves (I've suggested ½ cup cream; add more if you want a richer sauce) and season with salt and red pepper flakes. Let this simmer a few minutes over low heat. Add the tomato concassé and heat through. Do not cook the sauce more than a few minutes or the tomatoes will soften too much. The diced tomato needs to remain firm. Taste for seasoning.
- When cooked al dente, drain the fusilli and add them to the pan. Add the basil and thyme and toss well over low heat 1 minute. At this time you can decide if you'd like to add a bit more butter for enrichment. Check for seasoning. Serve right away.

Ideas

This is a variation on *penne alla vodka,* which is made with tomatoes, vodka, cream, and a bit of hot red pepper. Grappa lends a less pungent taste to the finished sauce. You can try other types of brandy or fortified wines. Cognac or dry Marsala is especially good in this sauce.

This nice clean sauce can be embellished in many subtle ways. Try sautéing a handful of sliced wild mushrooms or artichoke hearts along with the shallots. Fresh peas can be added when you add the cream and simmered until tender.

Shrimp or scallops can be added along with the cream and allowed to gently poach for a few minutes, until tender.

I've used basil here, but sage is another herb that blends well with cream-based sauces. If you use sage, add a grating of fresh nutmeg as well.

Also try this sauce with Herb Pasta flavored with basil or parsley (page 368), cut for tagliatelle.

Cooking with Garlic and Olive Oil

Spaghetti with garlic and olive oil is a dish many college students learn to cook out of financial desperation or late-night hunger. Yet it is one of the best pasta dishes you can eat. My mother never made this at home—I think she thought it was too ordinary—but I would order it at restaurants every chance I got. Sometimes it was sublime; sometimes it was terrible. When I started cooking it for myself, I immediately realized its potential as a platform for improvisation.

Once you learn how to make a garlic and oil sauce *(aglio e olio),* you can add to it in any number of ways to create any of your own customized olive oil–based pasta sauces. Clams, parsley, and a splash of white wine added to an oil and garlic base produce an authentic white clam sauce within minutes. Zucchini or asparagus sautéed in oil and garlic give you two seasonal vegetable sauces just as quickly. A classic marinara sauce is nothing more than an *aglio e olio* with tomatoes added.

The only tricky aspect of cooking with garlic is that it burns quickly, more quickly than onions. It will darken immediately upon contact with hot oil. Often recipes are to blame, instructing the cook to heat the oil, add chopped onion and garlic, and sauté until soft. The garlic will burn by the time the onions are soft. What you should do is cook the onions first and then add the garlic.

When I sauté garlic for an *aglio e olio* sauce, I like to start with unheated oil and cook the garlic in it at a low temperature. This way I have some control. There's nothing that sticks in your taste memory more than burned garlic. A still-vivid memory from my childhood involves badly burned garlic and rancid oil tossed with mushy spaghetti, served to me at several restaurants in New York's Little Italy. It wasn't until I started making this sauce myself that I realized I could have control over the garlic in the pan. It should be cooked gently and lightly, anywhere between barely warmed through to just turning golden. If you've let it go a little too far, you can always stop it from browning further by adding a splash of wine or water to the pan.

Young garlic is sweeter than older garlic. Summer is when you can find the best young garlic in the market, and it makes improvisational cooking a pleasure. That's when it's wonderful used raw, tossed with pasta, good olive oil, and fresh herbs. Try a pasta sauce of young garlic sautéed with sliced sautéed artichoke hearts and a little fresh mint. And use it raw in pasta salads.

Here are some basic ways to create pasta sauce with a garlic and olive oil base, plus many ideas on how to custom-make your own garlic-based pasta sauces.

Preserved Garlic

Oil-Braised Garlic Cloves

When I have a jar of these tender braised garlic cloves in my refrigerator, I know I can make a successful pasta sauce at a moment's notice. You can also use them to boost a sauce that didn't turn out as flavorful as you'd hoped, adding them even after the pasta has been tossed and brought to the table. I like a sauce of nothing but cooked penne tossed with preserved garlic cloves, oil, and a little salt and coarsely ground black pepper.

This slow-braising method produces garlic with a sweet, refined garlic taste, so if you like garlic, don't be afraid to use a lot of it. The cloves look beautiful whole, but you can mash them up if you like.

[Makes 4 heads of garlic]

4 heads of garlic, cloves peeled
Extra-virgin olive oil (not your most
prized oil, but one with a strong
olive taste) to cover the garlic

- Place the garlic cloves and olive oil in a large skillet fitted with a cover (the cloves should be in one layer). Cook over very, very low heat, covered, for about 20 minutes, or until the cloves are soft but not mushy. Check the garlic a few times during the cooking to make sure it isn't coloring too much (be careful when lifting the lid; condensation on the underside might hit the hot oil and make it spatter). The cloves should be golden, have a sweet taste, and still retain their firmness when cooked through. You can use the preserve and its cooking oil immediately or keep it for up to 1 week. Allow the cloves to cool. If all the cloves are not covered by the oil, add more oil and store, refrigerated, in a tightly covered glass jar.

Ideas

If you object to the large amount of olive oil used in this method of cooking (although very little actually remains in the garlic cloves), you can blanch whole garlic cloves in simmering water to soften their flavor. They won't have the same deep, olive oil–infused sweetness, but their texture will be similar for adding to sauces either whole or pureed. Simply place peeled cloves in a pan, cover with water, and simmer over low heat until soft and tender, about 10 minutes. Try to use them within a day or two of making, as they don't last as long as oil-covered garlic.

The garlic–infused cooking oil can be used to sauté vegetables. A tablespoon or so can be added to your pasta sauce, but remember it will have a powerful garlic flavor.

Gemelli with Haricots Verts, Potatoes, and Preserved Garlic

This is actually a pasta dish adapted from a string bean salad I often make in the summer. I've used French haricots verts here because I like the way the thin beans mingle with the thin gemelli pasta, but feel free to substitute fresh American string beans. If you do use the thicker American beans, choose a sturdier pasta like penne or ziti.

[Makes 4 main-course or 6 first-course servings]

2 medium baking potatoes, peeled and cut in small cubes

A large handful of haricots verts (about ¼ pound), stem ends trimmed

1 pound gemelli (or penne or fusilli)

A few tablespoons olive oil

2 slices slab bacon, thinly sliced and cut in small chunks

About 2 dozen preserved garlic cloves (about 3 heads, see page 46)

Salt

Freshly ground black pepper

A splash of balsamic vinegar

About ½ cup homemade Chicken Broth (page 374) or low-salt canned

A large handful of basil leaves, coarsely chopped

A handful of whole blanched almonds, lightly toasted

Freshly grated Pecorino Toscano cheese

- Set up a large pot of salted water to cook the pasta. Bring to a boil, drop in the potatoes, and cook until just tender, 4 or 5 minutes. Lift them out with a large strainer and drain well. Now add the haricots verts to the water and blanch for a minute or two, until tender but still firm. Remove with the strainer and run under cold water to preserve their color; drain well.
- Start cooking the gemelli.
- In a large skillet, heat enough olive oil to generously cover the bottom of the pan (you can use some of the garlic cooking oil, but remember it will give the finished dish a strong garlic taste, not the gentle one you'll get using the cloves alone). Add the bacon and sauté until it just starts to crisp. Add the potatoes and sauté over medium heat until very lightly browned, 3 or 4 minutes. Add the beans and preserved garlic cloves, season with salt and pepper, and sauté a minute, just to blend the ingredients. Add the balsamic vinegar and let it boil away. Add the chicken broth and simmer for a minute or two. You should still have some liquid left in the skillet. Taste for seasoning.

- When the gemelli are al dente, drain them and add to the pan. Add the basil and almonds. Toss well. Add a drizzle of fresh olive oil for enrichment if you like. Pass the grated Pecorino Toscano around at the table.

Ideas

I also make this dish substituting mushrooms for the potatoes. Simply slice them and add after you've browned the bacon. If you can find wild mushrooms such as morels, they'll add a good strong flavor, but some of the more interesting cultivated mushrooms, like shiitakes and portobellos, add another dimension to the sauce without overwhelming the delicate string beans.

Haricots verts are thin, elegant string beans, but substitute fresh green or yellow wax beans in season. Also watch for the purple variety; they look beautiful against pasta.

I like the smoked flavor of American bacon in this dish, but for a more authentic Italian accent, use pancetta.

Asparagus makes an exciting substitution for the string beans.

If you want to take this recipe in another direction, use blanched green chard or broccoli rabe instead of string beans to give the dish an earthy character.

Roasted Garlic

Roasting Whole Heads of Garlic

- Choose young, firm heads of garlic that have not yet begun to sprout. Drizzle them with a little olive oil, wrap in aluminum foil, and close tightly. Place them on a baking sheet in a 350°F oven for about 30 minutes, or until they are soft. When cool enough to handle, slice the bottoms (the wider root ends) off the bulbs. You will now be able to squeeze the roasted garlic cloves from their skins into a bowl (they will be rather sticky). The resulting soft garlic paste can be added directly to a finished sauce or added during cooking.

Green Tagliatelle with Red Pepper and Roasted Garlic Purée

Roasted garlic purée is very versatile. It can be added to tomato sauces or cream- or ricotta-based sauces. You can stir it into a clam sauce or a meat ragù. Here I've mixed it with red bell peppers for a smooth, mellow sauce. I've chosen green tagliatelle because it contrasts beautifully with the red sauce, but a fresh herb pasta—one made with basil or marjoram, for instance—will also enhance the sauce.

[Makes 4 main-course or 6 first-course servings]

About 1 tablespoon unsalted butter

A few tablespoons olive oil

4 large, ripe red bell peppers, charred over a flame until black, peeled, seeded, and roughly chopped (for more ideas on cooking bell peppers, see page 77)

2 or 3 thyme sprigs

Salt

Cayenne pepper

4 or 5 heads of Roasted Garlic (page 49), cloves squeezed into a bowl

1 pound Green Pasta (page 367), cut for tagliatelle

A handful of flat-leaf parsley leaves, coarsely chopped

A few tarragon sprigs, leaves chopped

- In a large skillet, heat the butter and 1 tablespoon of the olive oil over medium-low heat. Add the roasted peppers and thyme sprigs (butter lends a sweet taste to red peppers, which can sometimes be bitter). Season with salt and a pinch of cayenne and cook until very soft, about 10 minutes. Remove the thyme sprigs and puree the peppers in a food processor until smooth. Add the roasted garlic and blend until very smooth. If the sauce seems stiff, add a bit of olive oil (you can also add cream or pasta cooking water to thin it out).
- Cook the tagliatelle until tender. Drain, leaving a bit of water clinging to the pasta, and transfer it to a large bowl. Toss it well with the sauce, adding the parsley and tarragon. I like this dish without cheese, but a freshly grated sweet, mellow cheese like Parmigiano-Reggiano tastes very good on it.

Ideas

Roasted garlic works well here because it mellows the acidity in the peppers. The garlic purée by itself makes a very simple but highly flavored sauce. If it is too thick, loosen it with some chicken broth or heavy cream. Also try adding leaves from a few sprigs of a fresh herb; marjoram, thyme, and savory are good choices.

Toss the hot tagliatelle with about a cup of ricotta or a small log of soft goat cheese before adding the red pepper and garlic purée.

A dollop of basil pesto mixed into pepper purée in place of the roasted garlic creates a bright, summery sauce.

To add texture and bursts of flavor, add a handful of capers or pitted black olives to the dish while tossing the pasta. You'll break up the texture of the smooth sauce with bits of color and vibrant taste.

Change the sauce completely by substituting tomato sauce for the red peppers. That makes, in fact, a fabulous sauce that's very good eaten cold.

Try experimenting with different vegetable purées. Broccoli purée with roasted garlic is wonderful. If you have a food processor, you can easily turn a pound of cooked vegetables into a smooth sauce for pasta. Other good possibilities include cauliflower, zucchini, asparagus, and eggplant.

Also see Ziti with Roasted Garlic and Butternut Squash (page 120).

Tubi (The Maccheroni Group)

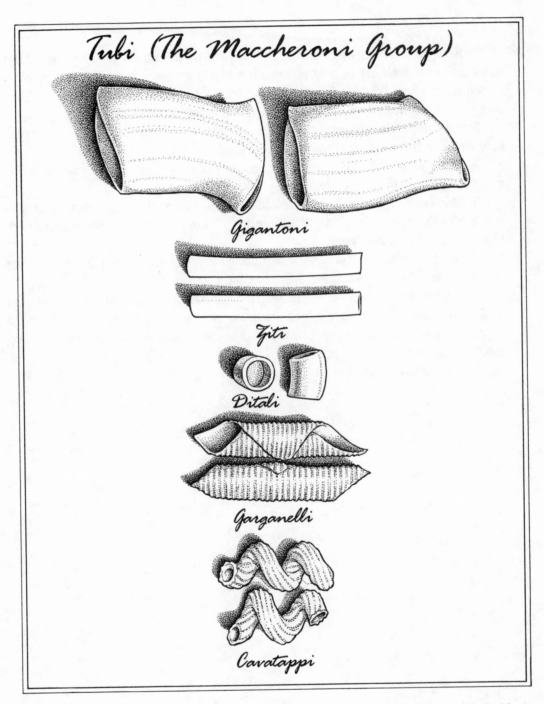

Gigantoni

Ziti

Ditali

Garganelli

Cavatappi

Here are additional tube shapes that take chunky sausage or vegetable sauces and also work well with rustic ragùs.

A Talk About Wasting Food

*F*ear of wasting food, even more than fear of failure, prevents many home cooks from being creative in the kitchen. Food is precious and costs money, and some of us live on tight budgets. But creativity, that unique human gift, is precious too. We cook to make other people happy. We create to satisfy ourselves.

What better way to learn how to become a creative cook than by learning how to improvise with pasta, an inexpensive, easily available food? Dried pasta can sit on your kitchen shelf for months and still be fine. And only serious over-cooking can make it inedible (and then some people, including all kids, still love it). Maybe save the homemade saffron tagliatelle with lobster sauce for a time when you're feeling especially confident, but don't think twice about opening up a box of ziti and messing around with a few zucchini and a leftover chunk of salami.

Picky eaters are by nature wasteful. It makes me sad to hear someone say, "I don't eat that." My sister has become a very picky eater lately. She loves anchovies but hates them mixed in with anything. She loves fish but loathes it when cooked with pasta. These are perplexing idiosyncrasies that make me nuts if I think about them too long. Unless you're dealing with a food allergy, as a good cook you should try everything. Once you open your mind and palate to more tastes, you'll find it easier to use up what's in your refrigerator and cupboard. Adventurous taste buds lead to creativity. "I eat chicken, but I only like it fried." Why? You like tomatoes? Yes. You like garlic and onions? Yes. So what about sautéing chicken with tomatoes, garlic, and onions and tossing it with pasta? "I don't eat that" is not a valid response for the cook who wants to become creative. The more you taste, the less you'll waste. You'll influence those around you (kids, for instance) to try unusual food. The kitchen will have few barriers for you, only possibilities.

People who love to cook tend to be somewhat nurturing, and nurturing people want everyone to be happy. So have fun in the kitchen and don't worry much about wasting food. Painters waste paper and canvas; writers waste time. The more you experiment in the kitchen, the better you'll become at imagining how to use leftovers and stray ingredients. The short-term solution is to make your family or friends eat everything you cook. Your goal is to learn to cook well by improvising.

Spaghetti with Sautéed Aglio e Olio (Garlic and Oil)

Aglio e Olio (Garlic and Oil) Two Ways

[Makes 4 main-course or 6 first-course servings]

1 pound spaghetti (or other string pasta)	Salt
⅓ to ½ cup high-quality (but not prized) extra-virgin olive oil	Freshly ground black pepper
4 or 5 young garlic cloves, finely sliced	A small handful of chopped flat-leaf parsley

- Start cooking the spaghetti.
- Place the olive oil and garlic in a skillet. (The amounts I've suggested seem about right to sauce 1 pound of dried pasta. You can use more or less to taste.) Turn the flame on low and sauté the garlic slowly (adding garlic to hot oil can cause it to burn; this way you have control), stirring it around, until it just starts to turn golden. Remove the pan from the heat to stop the cooking.
- When the spaghetti are al dente, drain them well and add them to the pan. Return the pan to the stove and add salt and pepper. Over low heat, toss the pasta to coat with the oil and sauté lightly. Transfer to a warmed serving bowl, add the parsley, and serve very hot.

Spaghetti with Sautéed Aglio e Olio (Garlic and Oil), Black Olives, Anchovies, Orange Zest, and Bread Crumbs

Here the flavors of a French tapenade (olive paste) translate into a sauce for spaghetti. Tapenade usually consists of chopped olives combined with small amounts of flavoring agents such as garlic, capers, cognac, and sometimes orange zest. I've increased the proportion of flavoring ingredients so they stand out.

This sauce should just coat each strand of spaghetti with flavor, with none to spare at the bottom of the bowl. This is an example of how you can take a garlic and oil base and add a few simple ingredients to it to create an entirely new dish.

Ingredients for 1 recipe Spaghetti with Sautéed *Aglio e Olio* (page 54)

About 10 anchovy fillets (salt-packed are preferable, but oil-packed are a fine alternative), chopped

About ½ cup black olives, pitted and chopped (I use Niçoise olives)

A handful of salt-packed capers, soaked, rinsed, and chopped (see page 343)

Grated zest of 2 oranges

A thyme sprig, leaves chopped

A splash of cognac or brandy

A large handful of flat-leaf parsley leaves, chopped

Freshly ground black pepper

Additional extra-virgin olive oil, if needed

About ½ cup bread crumbs, toasted (page 340)

- Start cooking the spaghetti.
- Make the sautéed *aglio e olio*. When it is done, keep the heat on low and add the anchovies, olives, capers, orange zest, and thyme. Sauté about 1 minute, just to blend the flavors. Add the cognac and let it boil away completely.
- By this time the spaghetti should be al dente. If it needs a little more time, the sauce won't suffer from sitting in the pan off heat for several minutes. Drain the spaghetti well and add it to the skillet. Add the parsley and a few grindings of black pepper. Toss over low heat 1 minute, just to coat the pasta, adding more olive oil, if needed, to coat it well. Serve hot, topped with a sprinkling of toasted bread crumbs. (You probably won't need salt in this sauce, but taste to make sure.)

A note about chopping ingredients for this sauce: Chop all the ingredients by hand separately so each one remains distinct. If you throw everything into a food processor (which you can do when making an actual tapenade), you'll wind up with a homogenous paste rather than with little recognizable pieces scattered throughout the spaghetti. I think this is important for presentation and flavor.

Ideas

Before you cook the garlic, sauté a handful of finely diced celery until softened. This makes an extremely fragrant sauce with some depth of flavor.

Previously grilled or sautéed tuna or swordfish added to this sauce turns a simple dish into an elegant main course.

A chopped, seeded fresh tomato tossed into the pan at the last minute and not allowed to soften gives a summery finish. If it's ripe, you can add it off the heat.

Almonds go well with orange flavor; add a handful of lightly toasted sliced almonds at the last minute.

Uncooked Aglio e Olio (Garlic and Oil)

Use green spring garlic here for especially good results. An immature garlic bulb with a scallionlike stem, it is very mild and sweet. If it's not in season, use fresh garlic that has not begun to sprout. In May I look for purple-streaked bulbs with thin, sticky skins. They are usually sweeter than the white, papery bulbs.

[Makes ⅓ to ½ cup]

⅓ to ½ cup high-quality extra-virgin olive oil

2 or 3 garlic cloves, finely minced

Salt

Freshly ground black pepper

- Pour the olive oil into a bowl and add the garlic. Season with salt and pepper. Let the sauce sit about 15 minutes to develop flavor. Since garlic loses its freshness very quickly after it has been cut, this sauce is best eaten within an hour after it has been made.

Ideas

Toss with 1 pound hot spaghetti, or for a cold pasta salad, toss with penne cooked al dente, rinsed under cold water, and drained. Use a little less sauce, to taste.

A WORD ABOUT PASTA SALADS

Italians do eat pasta salads, especially in the warm south, and they treat them with as much respect as they treat hot pasta dishes. Don't turn a pasta salad into a second-class citizen by throwing in frozen peas, vinegary jarred artichoke hearts, or a confusion of mismatched ingredients. Delicate stuffed pasta such as tortellini belongs in a broth or a light sauce, not in a cold salad. Stay with sturdy dried pasta. Cook it with plenty of salt in the water (you'll be running cold water over the pasta, so a lot of the salt will be washed away).

Look for ingredients that are seasonal, that harmonize on the tongue, and that make sense together visually. Think about how you want the dish to look. Do you want long, graceful strips of color? Short, confettilike dots? Choose the pasta accordingly. Make the dish simple, picking two or three flavorful main ingredients. Use good olive oil and fresh herbs. Think about some of the things you like in an antipasto course and how they might be included in an interesting pasta salad.

Tubetti with Uncooked Aglio e Olio (Garlic and Oil), Parsley, and Celery Leaves

I used to throw away the leaves from celery stalks until I started working in restaurants and got yelled at for wasting money. So I began using them in soups and stocks when I wanted a strong celery flavor. But I also found that their flavor is released when they're chopped and combined with hot pasta. Try adding a handful of celery leaves to a dish of pasta with beans, or sauté some along with onions and other aromatic vegetables as part of a soffritto.

[Makes 4 main-course or 6 first-course servings]

Leaves from 2 bunches of celery	**Freshly ground black pepper**
A large handful of flat-leaf parsley leaves	**Salt**
1 recipe Uncooked *Aglio e Olio*	**1 pound tubetti**
(page 56)	

- Chop the celery and parsley leaves gently and add to the *aglio e olio*. Season with a generous amount of black pepper and a little salt.
- Cook the tubetti until al dente, drain, toss with the sauce. Serve hot.

Ideas

Let the dressed pasta come to room temperature and serve as a pasta salad. It's a light but flavorful first course to serve before grilled fish or shrimp.

Add chopped fennel tops with the celery leaves. If you like lovage, you can add a little here. It has a strong celery taste.

This is also a good opportunity to use any edible flowers that might be in season. Chive blossoms or julienned zucchini flowers add flavor as well as color.

Instead of using garlic and olive oil as a sauce base, try sautéing 4 or 5 shallots in olive oil and then adding the herbs.

Celery is a wonderful base for seafood. Try topping each bowl of pasta with grilled shrimp or squid.

Classic Italian Vegetable Sauces: How to Make Them Your Own

After pasta with tomato sauce in all its myriad interpretations, certain vegetables come to mind when considering classic Italian pasta cooking. I immediately think of eggplant, then zucchini, red bell peppers, broccoli, and cauliflower. These bold and beautiful vegetables are the staples of cooking in southern Italy, where vegetables are in the forefront of pasta cooking. There exist many time-honored classic combinations, such as *pasta alla norma* with eggplant, garlic, and tomatoes; penne with broccoli, garlic, and hot red pepper flakes; and pasta with zucchini slices browned in olive oil. But there's no reason to stop with the classic combinations. Eggplant doesn't have to be cooked with tomatoes.

Pasta with Eggplant and Zucchini: Playing with Different Flavorings

Many people avoid cooking eggplant because they think it has to be greasy. Zucchini some people find boring. I suppose the latter may have an element of truth, but if you choose firm, young vegetables, they are a fragrant delight to cook with. One crucial thing to remember is that both vegetables taste best when cooked through. Crunchy eggplant can be bitter; hard zucchini has little flavor. Italians do have a tendency to overcook their vegetables, but there is some logic to it. Tender eggplant and zucchini make sense in a pasta sauce because they break down into a rough purée coating and cling to each piece of pasta, adding great flavor to the finished dish. And the flavor of both vegetables is greatly improved by browning. I usually start my sauté on high heat to brown the surface and then lower the heat a bit so the vegetable pieces can cook until tender. This method also permits you to use less oil when sautéing eggplant, because the lower heat gives the eggplant time to release liquid, which facilitates cooking.

One wonderful aspect of cooking with eggplant is the chance to look at it. I've always found this vegetable fascinating. Its color can range from bright white to a deep, blackish purple, and the shininess of its skin reminds me of thickly lacquered wood. I usually leave the skin on for cooking because it provides color and texture, but you can remove it if you prefer a smoother sauce. There is no bitterness in eggplant skin; most of the bitterness comes from the seeds.

Many home cooks and professional chefs salt and drain eggplant to remove the bitterness. My mother did this, and I used to do it. But does it really get rid of the bitterness? I think it does not. What it does is rid the vegetable of excess water, which makes browning easier (excess water in any food will cause steaming instead of sautéing). If you really want to avoid bitterness, choose youngish eggplants, which have tight, shiny skins and a firm texture with no soft spots.

Even though eggplant has a unique flavor (which is wonderfully enhanced by being cooked in olive oil), in a pasta sauce it can be made piquant or mellow depending on what you add to it. Adding vinegar, capers, and olives produces a vibrant sauce much like Sicilian caponata, the eggplant condiment. Adding ricotta and roasted tomatoes makes eggplant taste rich and mellow. Eggplant also blends surprisingly well with meat and fish to form more complex pasta dishes.

You can treat zucchini, a milder-tasting vegetable, in different ways as well. Zucchini seasoned with mint or fresh oregano and garlic produces a robust pasta dish. Starting with a base of sautéed shallots and butter produces a refined and elegant zucchini sauce to toss with fresh egg pasta, such as tagliatelle or fettuccine.

Zucchini, like so many other things in life, is best young. I always look for small ones because of their tender skin; big zucchini tend to be thick-skinned and full of seeds. Zucchini blossoms first appear in the market in late spring, and you can still find them into the middle of the summer. You can cut zucchini blossoms in thin strips and add them to any zucchini dish. Or stuff and fry them to use as a delicious garnish on pasta. For more information on cooking with zucchini blossoms, see Spaghetti with Asparagus, Zucchini Blossoms, and Eggs (page 88).

On the following pages, I've provided eggplant and zucchini pasta recipes that employ Italian seasoning and flavor combinations. They are a little less familiar but still produce Italian-tasting results.

Orecchiette with Roasted Eggplant, Walnuts, Ricotta, and Cinnamon

I love any pasta dish in which hot pasta is tossed with ricotta and then an additional sauce is ladled on or mixed in. The taste is rich and creamy without the burden of heavy cream. Walnuts and eggplant are an old-fashioned Italian combination not used much anymore, but the pairing is luscious, especially when the walnuts are roasted. Cooks tend to reach for pine nuts when making Italian dishes. Try walnuts instead.

[Makes 4 main-course or 6 first-course servings]

1 large, firm eggplant (about 2 pounds), cut in small cubes (I like to leave the skin on)

1 large onion, cut in small dice

A large pinch of ground cinnamon

Salt

Freshly ground black pepper

Olive oil for roasting

A large handful of walnuts, roughly chopped

1 cup ricotta cheese

A handful of flat-leaf parsley leaves, coarsely chopped

Freshly grated mild Pecorino cheese

1 pound orecchiette

- Preheat the oven to 425°F.
- Place the eggplant and onion on a large baking sheet. Sprinkle with the cinnamon and season with salt and pepper. Drizzle liberally with olive oil and bake, stirring around occasionally until browned and fork tender, about 30 minutes. About 5 minutes before the eggplant is cooked, scatter the chopped walnuts on top and let them roast along with the vegetables.
- In a large serving bowl, blend together the ricotta, parsley, a generous handful of the grated cheese, and salt and pepper to taste.
- Cook the orecchiette until al dente and drain, saving about 1 cup of the pasta water.
- Add the pasta to the serving bowl and mix well with the ricotta, adding enough pasta water to loosen the sauce. Add the eggplant and walnut mix and toss well. Serve hot, and pass extra grated cheese at the table.

Ideas

Eggplant dishes in Sicily, such as caponata, sometimes contain a pinch of cocoa powder, which counters the vegetable's natural bitterness. You might try this instead of, or in addition to, the cinnamon.

Try experimenting with different varieties of eggplant: round lavender eggplants; long, skinny white ones; tiny round black ones. They all have slightly different tastes.

Mixing a handful of crumbled ricotta salata instead of Pecorino in with the fresh ricotta produces a pleasantly pungent sauce.

DRIED HERBS

I like to use fresh herbs when I cook, and I've become spoiled because I can now buy them year-round, either from the local farmers' market in summer or from the supermarket the rest of the year, where they carry greenhouse-grown herbs. If you use dried herbs, use them sparingly, as they can be quite potent. Add them toward the beginning of cooking so they have time to open up in the sauce. Certain dried herbs (oregano, basil, and sage in particular) can taste musty. Dried rosemary I find bitter and lacking in the essential oil that gives this wonderful herb its charm. I know many cooks are fans of dried oregano, but I'm not one of them. Maybe it has bad memory associations for me, but I think it overpowers everything it comes in contact with. When I don't have any fresh herbs, I make pasta sauces that taste good without them or add a splash of vinegar or wine to wake up the sauce. (See also "Herb Overkill," page 101.)

Rigatoni with Eggplant, Italian Frying Peppers, and Shaved Provolone

The long, green Italian "frying" peppers of my childhood seem to have been ignored lately in favor of bell peppers. Slightly sharp-tasting, these light green peppers are used to make the classic southern Italian sausage and peppers. Here I've replaced the sausage with eggplant for a vegetarian version of that dish. You can bake the eggplant, but if you want a smoky taste, grill it instead. Directions for both follow.

[Makes 4 main-course or 6 first-course servings]

Olive oil

3 small eggplants (about 2 pounds), cut into rounds, leaving the skin on (if you use 1 large eggplant, cut the rounds in half before tossing with the pasta)

Salt

Freshly ground black pepper

5 green frying peppers, seeded and cut into strips

1 large onion, thinly sliced

A few savory sprigs, chopped, plus a few whole sprigs for garnish

A splash of dry white wine

1 pound rigatoni

A small chunk of provolone cheese, thinly shaved with a vegetable peeler

- Preheat the oven to 400°F.
- Sprinkle olive oil on 2 baking sheets. Place the eggplant slices on the pans in one layer. Season with salt and pepper and drizzle more olive oil on top. Bake, turning once, until lightly browned and tender, 20 to 25 minutes.
- Meanwhile, in a large skillet over medium-low heat, slowly sauté the peppers, onion, and savory in several tablespoons of olive oil until tender and fragrant, about 15 minutes (green frying peppers are a bit sturdier than bell peppers and take longer to become tender). Season with salt and pepper. Add the wine and let it boil away. Transfer to a large serving bowl.
- Cook the rigatoni until al dente and drain, leaving some water clinging to the pasta. Place in a serving bowl and add the eggplant slices and a generous amount of thinly shaved provolone. Toss gently, keeping the eggplant as intact as possible. Garnish with savory sprigs.

A note on grilling eggplant: Grilling is one of the easiest ways to cook eggplant. Simply slice it thin, leaving the skin on. Brush the slices with olive oil and sprinkle with a little salt and pepper. Cook on an outdoor grill or a preheated stovetop grill plate, turning once, until both sides have grill marks and the slices are fork tender.

Ideas

One of the loveliest summertime dishes is grilled eggplant slices tossed with hot ziti or penne, a drizzle of extra-virgin olive oil, and a generous handful of chopped summer herbs, such as basil, mint, and parsley. A handful of capers or a splash of balsamic vinegar will add a vibrant note.

This sauce combines three strong flavors: eggplant, green pepper, and sharp provolone cheese. For a subtler approach to this theme (and a more traditional one), try roasted red pepper strips and ricotta mixed with the eggplant. Or sautéed yellow peppers, mild Japanese eggplant, and Parmigiano-Reggiano cheese.

Sicilian pepato, a tangy Pecorino cheese with black peppercorns, is a good substitute for the provolone. Because of the peppercorns, it is easier to grate than to slice.

If you sauté a few sliced zucchini with the peppers, you'll create a taste like that of ratatouille; ground lamb makes it like moussaka.

For a different look and flavor, instead of mixing the eggplant into the sauce, drape the slices on top of the pasta before serving; top with the sliced provolone. This keeps the flavors clear and separate, changing the character of the finished dish.

Zucchini, Roasted Tomatoes, Tarragon, and Mozzarella with Ditali

This dish combines many southern Italian flavors in a modern way. I've chosen a short, round pasta and cut the zucchini the same size so both look pretty and uniform in the bowl. The oven-dried cherry tomatoes give this mild sauce a bit of punch.

[Makes 4 main-course or 6 first-course servings]

2 dozen ripe cherry tomatoes, stemmed and cut in half

Salt

Freshly ground black pepper

Olive oil

A few tablespoons unsalted butter

5 small zucchini (about 1 pound), cut in small cubes

About 10 scallions, cut in thin rounds, with some green

1 pound ditali

A few large tarragon sprigs, leaves chopped

Freshly grated Grana Padano cheese

½ pound fresh mozzarella cheese, cut in small cubes

- Preheat the oven to 500°F.
- Place the cut cherry tomatoes on a baking sheet. Season with salt and pepper and drizzle with a good amount of olive oil. Bake until brown around the edges, about 15 minutes. (What you are making here is essentially Oven-Roasted Tomato Sauce, page 38, using cherry tomatoes instead of plum.)
- In a large skillet, heat about a tablespoon each of the butter and olive oil (or use all olive oil if you prefer) over medium heat. Add the zucchini and scallions, season with salt and pepper, and sauté until the zucchini is brown and tender, about 8 minutes.
- Cook the ditali until al dente, drain, and transfer to a large serving bowl. Add the zucchini and scallions, tomatoes, tarragon, a handful of Grana Padano, and the mozzarella. Season with more salt and pepper. Toss well. Serve immediately.

Ideas

Thyme and black olives are another good combination for zucchini. Add them with or without the tomatoes and mozzarella.

Instead of the roasted tomatoes, try punctuating this dish with sautéed mushrooms (they can be sautéed along with the zucchini).

Roasted Zucchini, Fennel, and Gruyère Tossed with Penne

My mother's sauce of sliced zucchini and onion sautéed in olive oil was sweet and unexpectedly flavorful because the vegetables were caramelized lightly at the edges. The roasting method in this recipe produces a similar result.

[Makes 4 main-course or 6 first-course servings]

6 or 7 small zucchini or a few larger ones (about 1½ pounds), cut in 1-inch sticks	Salt
	Freshly ground black pepper
	Olive oil
2 medium fennel bulbs, cored and thinly sliced (save some of the feathery tops, if you have any, for garnish)	A large handful of pine nuts
	1 pound penne
	Extra-virgin olive oil
1 large onion, thinly sliced	Freshly grated Gruyère cheese
A small handful of fennel seeds	(about ½ cup)

- Preheat the oven to 425°F.
- Place the zucchini, fennel, and onion in one layer on a large baking sheet (use two sheets if it seems crowded). Sprinkle with the fennel seeds. Salt and pepper generously and drizzle with the olive oil. Mix well with your hands and roast until the vegetables are soft and golden, about 30 minutes. Sprinkle the pine nuts on top of the vegetables during the last 5 minutes of cooking to toast lightly.
- Cook the penne until al dente and drain, leaving some water clinging to the pasta. Transfer to a serving bowl. Toss with the vegetables, adding a drizzle of extra-virgin olive oil to help coat the pasta and for a little flavor boost. Taste for seasoning. Garnish with fennel tops and top with grated Gruyère. Serve immediately.

Ideas

Fresh thyme and basil are wonderful with zucchini, especially when the zucchini is cooked with unsalted butter.

I like the combination of scallions and garlic very much in this dish (add the garlic along with the pine nuts in the last 5 minutes of roasting so it doesn't burn).

Drained chopped canned tomatoes (one 15-ounce can) added in the last 5 minutes of cooking impart a subtle acidity and change the character of this sauce dramatically.

A touch of cream can work well here.

Grated Zucchini Soup with Saffron and Acini

Here's an altogether different way to combine pasta and zucchini. Grated zucchini has a different flavor from sliced zucchini because the amount of water released by grating makes browning almost impossible. The resulting taste after sautéing is fresher, less caramelized. The great French chef Roger Vergé, in his book *Vegetables in the French Style,* states that sliced tomatoes taste different from tomatoes cut in wedges. I've never noticed that, but it's an example of the individual taste perceptions that make each chef's point of view unique.

[Makes 4 main-course or 6 first-course servings]

About 2 thin slices pancetta, finely chopped

A few tablespoons olive oil

5 or 6 small zucchini or a few larger ones (about 1 pound), grated with a food processor or mandoline

1 or 2 garlic cloves, minced

Salt

Freshly ground black pepper

1½ quarts (more or less) homemade Chicken Broth (page 374)

A pinch of cayenne pepper

A pinch of ground nutmeg

A generous pinch of saffron threads, ground to a powder with a mortar and pestle (see page 352)

½ cup acini, cooked until al dente and tossed with a little olive oil

2 eggs, lightly whisked

Freshly grated Parmigiano-Reggiano or Grana Padano cheese (you need a mellow cheese for this)

Grated zest of 1 lemon

A handful of flat-leaf parsley leaves, chopped

A few zucchini blossoms, if available, cleaned and thinly sliced (see page 89)

- In a large soup pot, sauté the pancetta over medium-low heat with a tablespoon of the olive oil until crisp. Add the zucchini and garlic, season with salt and black pepper, and sauté over medium-high heat until just starting to soften. Add the chicken broth and bring to a boil. Turn off the heat. Add the cayenne, nutmeg, saffron, and cooked acini. Taste and add more salt if needed.
- Place the eggs, cheese, lemon zest, parsley, and zucchini blossoms (if using) in a small bowl and mix. Add a large ladle of hot soup and mix well. Gradually pour this mixture into the pot with the rest of the soup and stir to blend. The soup will thicken slightly. Check the seasonings. Serve immediately. Because this soup contains tempered eggs, it will curdle if reboiled.

Ideas

Once you cook enough pasta dishes, you will realize that many of them can be turned into good soups simply by adding broth. I do this with pasta and bean dishes all the time. If you have leftover sauced pasta, try adding broth and correcting the seasoning. Dishes made with short, stubby pasta such as tubetti, ditali, or little shells work best transformed into soup. Fresh egg pasta becomes mushy with a second cooking. It's easy to brighten up this type of soup with a handful of chopped fresh herbs; a few chopped quick-cooking greens such as spinach, arugula, or green chard; or a squeeze of lemon juice.

A little cumin—not a spice used much in Italian cooking—is good sautéed with the zucchini (you can use a few whole cumin seeds or a pinch of ground). A pinch of ground cloves or allspice will also blend well with the saffron and can be added with, or instead of, the nutmeg.

If you have a handful of flavorful mushrooms, such as chanterelles or shiitakes, chop them fine and sauté them with the zucchini to add a whole new dimension.

Use veal broth or, in classic Italian style, a mix of veal and chicken broth instead of all chicken (see page 373 for ideas on how to make broths).

How Much Oil and What Kind?

*I*t's difficult to recommend a specific quantity of oil when making a pasta sauce. So much depends on personal preference and what type of sauce a cook wants to create. I've noticed that food magazines in Italy hardly ever give quantities for olive oil. It's just listed as an ingredient. This is no doubt partly because most Italian cooks have grown up cooking with olive oil and are familiar with how it interacts with different ingredients. But it is also, I believe, a reflection of Italy's generous and more informal approach to cooking and eating.

An *aglio e olio* (garlic and oil) sauce should coat each strand of pasta thoroughly, but ideally you shouldn't end up with a pool of oil in your bowl when you've finished eating. In general, when adding olive oil, butter, or some other oil to a pan for sautéing vegetables, you should use at least enough to cover the bottom of the pan, but if you want a richer sauce, add more. Just remember, you can always add more oil at any time during cooking or even when tossing the pasta with the finished sauce.

I almost always use olive oil rather than other vegetable oils when cooking pasta. It blends beautifully with all Mediterranean vegetables, brings out the best in garlic and tomato, and is a fragrant platform to carry the essence of fresh herbs. You can buy extremely mild olive oil when you want subtle flavor, and since this type of oil is inexpensive, it is good for frying ingredients like eggplant or zucchini that will become part of your dish. I almost always use a medium-bodied, relatively inexpensive extra-virgin olive oil for sautéing. I use high-quality extra-virgin oil when I want a strong, clean olive taste, as in an *aglio e olio* (garlic and oil), or when the sauce will be uncooked. A drizzle of extra-virgin olive oil added when tossing the pasta is a wonderful flavor boost. Butter can serve the same purpose, especially in a cream sauce or a meat ragù. I often mix olive oil with butter when sautéing winter vegetables like cabbage or squash. The combination is also a sweet base for a sauce with a soffritto of onion or shallots. (See "Improviser's Pantry," page 346, for more on choosing olive oils.)

Pork fat from pancetta, prosciutto ends, salt pork, or lard can add rich meat flavor to vegetable-, meat-, and some fish-based sauces. A little goes a long way, and you can mix it with olive oil for sautéing a soffritto.

I've had some luck with grapeseed oil, which blends well with bitter greens, but canola oil, I find, adds a musty taste reminiscent of badly prepared health food. Sunflower-seed oil is used a lot in Italy, and its flavor is unobtrusive; corn oil I find especially greasy and peculiar tasting when mixed with any type of pasta sauce. Nothing beats fruity olive oil for bringing out the best flavor in just about any pasta dish incorporating warm-weather vegetables or any fish-based pasta sauce.

The Spicy and Mellow Sides of Broccoli, Cauliflower, and Broccoli Rabe

Broccoli and cauliflower have never been the shining stars of American cooking. But in the hands of Italian cooks these vegetables come alive.

The way to bring out the best flavor in all these vegetables is with a quick blanching in abundant rapidly boiling salted water, followed by a quick sauté over high heat in fragrant olive oil, which will lightly caramelize the surface and remove any gassy taste. Broccoli, cauliflower, and the rich, beguilingly bitter broccoli rabe take very well to strong seasonings, which tend not to disguise but to enhance their natural flavors. I look for inspiration to the noble cooking of Sicily, where a pasta sauce of humble cauliflower and onion is raised to exotic heights with the addition of pine nuts, raisins, fennel seeds, and saffron.

Broccoli florets sautéed with hot red pepper flakes, garlic, and anchovies make a memorable pasta sauce. Broccoli rabe tossed with orecchiette and little bits of browned sausage is a dish I frequently crave. A pasta sauce based on any of these wonderful vegetables can be sweetened with roasted garlic or perked up with a handful of capers. When looking for cheeses to include in these sauces, try a bold Pecorino or ricotta salata instead of a more sophisticated Grana like Parmigiano-Reggiano.

Herbs can be a little tricky, because these vegetables are so strongly flavored there's a chance many delicate herbs might get lost in the mix. To me, a scattering of parsley leaves on a broccoli and pasta dish is completely pointless, but thyme, marjoram, oregano, savory, or a tiny bit of rosemary will work if you keep in mind the other ingredients in your sauce. Cauliflower blends well with all the above herbs and will not overpower gentle herbs like parsley or chervil. The main point to remember when dreaming up pasta dishes using these vegetables is that you are creating a first or main course, not a side dish that will play a supporting role. So make sure they are well seasoned with fruity olive oil and bold counterpoints to make a satisfying, complete dish.

Broccoli, broccoli rabe, and cauliflower are interchangeable in the following recipes.

Cavatelli with Broccoli Rabe, Mortadella, Pistachios, and Tomatoes

This sauce is a variation on the classic broccoli rabe and Italian pork sausage combination of Puglia. I've replaced the sausage with mortadella, a mild, creamy-textured sausage from Bologna. Mortadella is often studded with pistachio nuts, which add wonderful flavor to this pasta sauce. I add extra pistachios to the sauce as well.

[Makes 4 main-course or 6 first-course servings]

1 large bunch broccoli rabe (about 1 pound), washed and thick stems removed

1 pound cavatelli

A few tablespoons olive oil

1 large red onion, cut in small dice

¼ pound (or a little more) chunk of mortadella, cut in small cubes

2 or 3 garlic cloves, thinly sliced

Salt

Freshly ground black pepper

3 large, ripe tomatoes (about 1½ pounds), peeled, seeded, and cut in medium dice

A handful of shelled unsalted pistachios

- Set up a large pot of salted water to cook the pasta. Bring to a boil and drop in the broccoli rabe. Blanch quickly, about 2 minutes, and scoop it out with a large strainer. Run it under cold water to stop the cooking. Drain well, pressing on the broccoli rabe to extract excess water. Chop roughly.
- Start cooking the cavatelli.
- In a large skillet, heat about 3 tablespoons of olive oil over medium heat. Add the onion and mortadella and sauté until the sausage starts to brown lightly (the sausage is precooked, so it needs only light sautéing to release flavor). Add the garlic and cook 1 minute. Add the blanched broccoli rabe, season with salt and pepper, and sauté until well coated with oil. Add the tomatoes and pistachios and heat through, 1 or 2 minutes. The tomatoes should cook very briefly and retain their shape and bright red color.
- When the cavatelli are al dente, drain them and add them to the skillet. Sauté briefly, adding more olive oil if needed to coat the pasta. Check the seasoning.

Note: I blanch broccoli rabe in the boiling pasta water before sautéing it, then rinse it under cold water to preserve its green color. But the old Italian way is to sauté slightly wet, raw broccoli rabe in a covered pan with olive oil until soft. This way it steam-sautés, producing gray, mushy broccoli rabe with pronounced bitterness, which was admired by older southern Italians.

Ideas

Cacciatorini or capocollo, two dried sausages, are excellent choices here in place of the mortadella and can be cooked exactly the same way.

Broccoli rabe also makes a great sauce on its own. Try it sautéed with nothing but a little garlic, fresh hot red chile, and olive oil. Other common additions to broccoli rabe sauce are anchovies, capers, raisins, pine nuts or pistachios, and black olives.

To make a classic broccoli rabe and Italian pork sausage sauce, remove the casings from 3 sweet Italian sausages and crumble the meat. Add it to the sauce with the onion and brown over medium-high heat. Make this with or without the tomatoes. If you leave them out, add a bit more olive oil to help coat the pasta.

Tagliatelle with Broccoli Rabe and Mascarpone

I always thought of broccoli rabe as a strong and alluringly bitter vegetable that could be accented only by equally strong ingredients such as sausage, anchovies, garlic, hot pepper, or olives. That was the only way I had ever seen it prepared. But then at an Italian restaurant I was served a dish of broccoli rabe with mascarpone and saw its slight bitterness in a new light. All of which shows how your cooking style can be turned around when you stay open to new ideas. Here is my version.

[Makes 4 main-course or 6 first-course servings]

1 large bunch broccoli rabe (about 1 pound), washed, stemmed and chopped into small pieces

About 3 tablespoons unsalted butter

4 medium shallots, finely chopped

A few gratings of nutmeg

Salt

Freshly ground black pepper

A splash of dry white wine

1 pound Plain Egg Pasta (page 364), cut for tagliatelle

About 1 cup mascarpone cheese

About ½ cup freshly grated Grana Padano cheese

- Set up a large pot of salted water to cook the pasta. Bring to a boil and drop in the broccoli rabe. Blanch for 3 to 4 minutes and scoop it out with a large strainer. Run it under cold water to preserve its green color. Drain well, pressing on the broccoli rabe to extract excess water. Keep the water boiling while you proceed with the sauce. (The few little bits of greens left in the water from blanching the broccoli rabe will not color the pasta, but if you like, you can remove them with a fine strainer.)
- In a large skillet, melt the butter over medium heat. Add the shallots and sauté until soft. Add the broccoli rabe and nutmeg, season with salt and pepper, and sauté a few minutes. Add the wine and let it boil away completely. The broccoli rabe should be a little on the soft side.
- Drop the tagliatelle into the boiling water.
- Add the mascarpone to the skillet and let it melt over very low heat. Turn off the heat. Drain the pasta well and add it to the skillet. Add the Grana Padano and mix well. Taste for seasoning. Transfer to a serving bowl. Serve very hot.

Ideas

Mascarpone really sets the tone of this dish and dictates any additions you can make. I wouldn't reach for olives or hot pepper here, but a handful of toasted pine nuts or chopped almonds will further accentuate the mellow flavors of this sauce. A small amount of chopped pancetta sautéed along with the shallots will add a rich supporting taste.

In spring, use scallions or sweet white onions instead of shallots.

Italian sausage removed from its casing and browned along with the shallots is also a good addition. The delicacy of the dish will be lost, but you'll gain robustness and a main-dish pasta.

This is another master sauce in which the broccoli rabe can be replaced by lightly blanched and sliced spring asparagus, chopped spinach (no need to blanch; just add it, slightly wet, to the pan after sautéing the shallots and it will cook in a minute), any type of wild mushroom (added with the shallots), or chopped roasted red pepper strips.

Baked Penne with Feta, Black Olives, Broccoli, and Thyme

This is a dish of strong, contrasting flavors that shows another way to construct a pasta dish. Instead of layering a few soft flavors with bits of bold additions, such as a handful of capers or olives, experiment with all the bold flavors that complement each other in an exciting way.

[Makes 4 main-course or 6 first-course servings]

1 medium bunch broccoli (about 1½ pounds), cut in small florets, plus some of the tender stalk, peeled and thinly sliced

1 pound penne

Olive oil

1 large onion, cut in medium dice

3 or 4 garlic cloves, thinly sliced

Salt

Freshly ground black pepper

½ pound feta cheese (see Note), crumbled

3 or 4 thyme sprigs, leaves chopped

A small rosemary sprig, leaves chopped

A large handful of pitted black olives (such as Gaeta), cut in half

A handful of oil-packed sun-dried tomatoes, thinly sliced

About ½ cup bread crumbs, toasted (page 340)

- Set up a large pot of salted water to cook the pasta. Bring to a boil and add the broccoli. Blanch for 1 or 2 minutes and remove with a large strainer. Drain well and set aside.
- Preheat the oven to 425°F.
- Drop the penne into the pot of boiling water.
- Meanwhile, in a large skillet, heat about 3 tablespoons olive oil over medium heat. Add the onion and sauté until soft. Add the garlic and sauté a minute longer, just until the garlic gives off aroma. Add the blanched broccoli, season with salt and pepper, and sauté a minute or two to bring out the flavor.
- When the pasta is al dente, drain it well and place in a 13 x 9 x 2-inch baking dish or equivalent (wide and shallow is better than small and deep because you need more surface to develop a crisp top). Add the broccoli mixture, feta, thyme, rosemary, olives, sun-dried tomatoes, and a bit more black pepper (it shouldn't need more salt because of the saltiness of the feta). Give the mixture a good toss, adding a drizzle of olive oil to help coat the pasta. Top with the bread crumbs and another drizzle of olive oil and bake, uncovered, until crisp on top and bubbling, about 20 minutes.

A note about feta cheese: Feta is a strong sheep's milk cheese from Greece, and Greek cooks use it in pasta sauces all the time. I tried this dish with a French feta I found at my cheese shop and the flavor was a little less sharp and sweeter than the Greek variety, but the texture was the same. If you can find French feta, use it in this dish.

Ideas

If you prefer a milder baked dish, use about 1 cup of ricotta instead of the feta. Ricotta salata blends exceptionally well with broccoli and greens such as escarole and green chard and it can also be used in place of the feta, but it doesn't melt as well and the baked dish won't be quite as creamy.

There is a famous Greek dish called *garídes mikrolímano* that is made with shrimp baked with feta and tomatoes and sometimes black olives and oregano. It is absolutely delicious. While I was testing this pasta, I realized it contained many of the same ingredients, so I made it again, substituting a pound of peeled medium shrimp for the broccoli, and came up with a hit. Add the shrimp when you add the garlic and sauté only about 1 minute (remember, the shrimp will cook again in the oven). You can substitute oregano for the thyme if you like.

Cauliflower, Saffron, Basil, and Preserved Garlic Sauce with Ziti

Many cauliflower sauces in Italian cooking contain tomato. I prefer them without. This recipe produces a lovely pale-colored sauce with plenty of flavor.

[Makes 4 main-course or 6 first-course servings]

1 medium cauliflower (about 2 pounds), cut into very small florets

Olive oil

Cloves from 2 heads of Preserved Garlic (page 46)

3 or 4 anchovy fillets, chopped

A generous splash of dry white wine

A large pinch of saffron threads, ground to a powder with a mortar and pestle (see page 352)

½ cup homemade Chicken Broth (page 374) or low-salt canned, warmed

Salt

Freshly ground black pepper

1 pound ziti

A large handful of blanched almonds, lightly toasted and coarsely chopped

A large handful of basil leaves, coarsely chopped

- Set up a large pot of salted water to cook the pasta. Bring to a boil and add the cauliflower. Cook the florets until they smell like cauliflower, about 4 minutes. Scoop them out with a strainer and set aside.

- In a large skillet, heat about 2 tablespoons olive oil over medium heat (or use the oil from the preserved garlic for a very garlicky sauce). Add the cauliflower and sauté quickly, just to bring out the flavor. Add the preserved garlic and anchovies and sauté 1 minute to blend the flavors. Add the wine and let it bubble until boiled away. Stir the saffron into the warm chicken broth and add it to the pan. Season with salt and pepper and let the sauce simmer while the pasta is cooking (the sauce will thicken a bit because of all the softened garlic).

- Cook the ziti until al dente, drain, and place them in the skillet. Over low heat, sauté with the sauce for a minute or two, just to coat the pasta well, adding a drizzle of fresh olive oil for added richness. Check the seasoning. Add the almonds and basil and toss briefly. Transfer to a large serving bowl and serve very hot.

Ideas

Saffron and cauliflower are often used together in Sicilian cooking. For a classic Sicilian pasta sauce, sauté cauliflower with pine nuts, raisins, saffron, onions, and 3 or 4 chopped anchovies; toss with cooked bucatini. The traditional topping for this pasta is toasted bread crumbs (see page 340), but if you want to serve grated cheese instead, try Pecorino Sardo or Pecorino Toscano.

To make a good cauliflower soup, put this sauce (without the almonds or basil) in the food processor along with enough chicken broth to thin it out, and puree until smooth. Add ½ cup cooked small pasta such as orzo. Add the basil when serving.

If you don't want to bother making the preserved garlic, add instead 3 or 4 fresh garlic cloves, thinly sliced, to the pan when you're heating the olive oil and sauté to a very light golden tan. Then add the blanched cauliflower and proceed with the recipe. This sauce will not have the sweetness provided by the preserved garlic.

Seasoning Bell Peppers for Pasta

In southern Italy the mellow and versatile condiment peperonata is made from roasted sweet peppers sautéed with other flavorings, usually tomatoes, garlic, basil, and onion. It shows up as a hot or cold antipasto or as a simple lunch dish to be eaten with bread. You'll find jars of it in Italian grocery shops, but the bottled version always tastes a little sour. It is easy to make, and you'll be amazed at how sweet and fragrant a homemade version tastes.

Peperonata is one of the mother sauces of southern Italian cooking and is almost as versatile as tomato sauce. It can be left chunky and seasoned with strong tastes like capers, olives, and anchovies and tossed with stubby dried pastas such as rigatoni and ziti. Or you can puree it and add a little fresh cream and a scattering of a soft herb like basil or chervil. You can blend it into a tomato sauce. If you use all yellow or orange peppers, you'll have a dish of pasta that looks like sunshine.

About the Color of Bell Peppers

The green bell peppers in supermarkets are usually immature red bell peppers. Yellow and orange bell pepper varieties start out green as well. I find deep red bell peppers the sweetest. The yellow and orange varieties can be sweet but sometimes lack flavor. I sniff mature peppers to check for the faint sweet-pepper aroma they have when they're truly ripe and flavorful. You can use green bell peppers in a peperonata sauce, but they are sharp and crunchy and occasionally bitter, so don't use more than one. I sometimes use one or two that are halfway between red and green. These impart a pleasant sharpness but no bitterness to a peperonata.

Peperonata Sauce

Peperonata doesn't have to contain tomatoes, onions, or anything other than sliced roasted peppers and olive oil. My basic recipe is the way it's classically prepared for a pasta sauce.

[Makes enough for 1 pound of pasta]

5 or 6 bell peppers (red, yellow,
    or orange)
Olive oil
1 onion, thinly sliced
3 or 4 garlic cloves, lightly crushed
3 ripe plum tomatoes, peeled, seeded,
    and chopped

A handful of basil leaves, chopped
A handful of flat-leaf parsley leaves,
    chopped
Salt
Freshly ground black pepper

- Roast the peppers over a gas flame until charred on all sides. Place in a paper bag to steam. When cool enough to handle, remove the charred skins, wiping off excess black spots. Seed the peppers and cut into thin strips. (You can, if you like, run the charred peppers under cool water to remove the little bits of black skin that stick to them, but this also removes some of the flavorful oils and juices from the peppers. A few little blackened bits are actually characteristic of this sauce.)
- In a large skillet, heat about 3 tablespoons olive oil over medium heat. Add the onion and sauté until soft, about 4 minutes. Add the roasted peppers and sauté a minute to blend the flavors. Add the garlic and cook about 1 minute longer, just to release its aroma. Add the tomatoes, basil, and parsley; season with salt and pepper; and simmer over low heat for 10 minutes, just until all the ingredients begin to thicken and the flavors come together. You can cover the pan if you like a sauce to have a little more liquid. Check the seasonings. The peppers should have a touch of sweetness but also a pleasant acidity.

Ideas

You can also finish cooking the peperonata in a preheated 400°F oven. Mix the roasted pepper slices with the other ingredients, toss well, and roast for about 20 minutes.

Add capers, olives, hot pepper, or anchovies for a more pungent sauce.

Play around with different herbs. Mint, oregano, thyme, and marjoram can all stand up to the strong taste of peppers. Summer savory is also wonderful with peppers. And for a fresher herb flavor, add them at the end of cooking.

A deep-tasting sauce can be made by chopping and sautéing a strip of bacon until crisp and then adding the onions and the rest of the ingredients for peperonata. Toss this sauce with spaghetti or bucatini. Pancetta would be a more traditional Italian choice, but I love the way the smokiness of regular bacon blends with the sweetness of roasted peppers. A small amount (½ cup or less) of heavy cream will enrich the sauce and mingle with the pepper juices for a mellow sauce; add it at the end.

You don't need to roast the peppers. If you don't mind their skins, simply seed and slice the peppers and sauté them along with the onions until soft. The final result will be a little less sweet.

Dried Egg Pasta

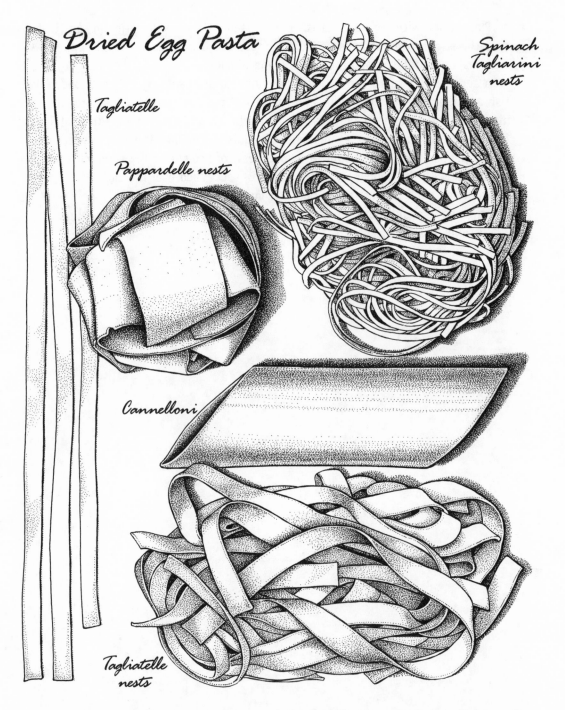

Tagliatelle

Spinach Tagliarini nests

Pappardelle nests

Cannelloni

Tagliatelle nests

A good alternative to fresh when you can't make your own or find high-quality, store-made egg pasta. I've been finding these in all sorts of novel flavors, including jalapeño pepper and cilantro. I usually stick with plain, spinach, or one with an Italian herb flavor.

Creating Liquid for a Sauce

*P*asta should not drown in its sauce. A fine coating is generally appropriate and in keeping with Italian style. I've seen many recipes in Italian cookbooks that tell you to toss a cooked vegetable with the hot pasta and then add a tablespoon of olive oil or butter. The resulting sauce is not only flavorless but almost nonexistent. There are several ways to create more liquid for a pasta sauce:

- Leave a bit of the hot cooking water clinging to the pasta. Don't shake the colander too much but instead quickly transfer the pasta to a serving bowl. Add the prepared sauce and toss. The water blends easily, even with oils, becoming almost an emulsion.
- Add extra olive oil or unsalted butter.
- Add meat or fish stock or canned broth.
- Add hot pasta cooking water. Rich, concentrated sauces like basil pesto often need diluting, not only to achieve a looser consistency but to diffuse the flavor. Adding hot water to pesto opens it up, releasing its fragrance. Pasta cooking water is also good for loosening up ricotta- or cheese-thickened cream sauces. Many cooks add a little pasta cooking water to a pasta dressed with *aglio e olio* (garlic and oil sauce), but I find that this prevents some of the sauce from clinging to the pasta and, as a result, dilutes the taste. I prefer simply to add a bit more extra-virgin olive oil when tossing.
- Toss the pasta well, eliminating the need for an overly liquid sauce. As long as each piece of pasta is well coated, the taste will come through.
- Puree part of the sauce, removing some bulk while leaving some chunkiness.
- Toss the cooked pasta briefly in the pan with the sauce over low heat, coating it well and infusing it with flavor. This will give you a lot of taste with a little sauce. I'm more inclined to do this with dried pasta such as orecchiette or penne than with fresh egg pasta, which doesn't take as well to additional cooking. If you want to toss fresh egg tagliatelle in the saucepan, do it quickly (a few seconds) over very, very gentle heat and serve right away.
- Dried pasta can take a little more handling, and it is sometimes beneficial to lightly sauté cooked dried pasta with its sauce, especially if it's an olive oil–based one. This can deepen the flavor. But even with dried pasta, don't let it cook too long in the pan. A minute should be the maximum.

Ziti with Peperonata, Almonds, and Green Olives

Almonds and green olives are a combination I find absolutely delicious and often serve together as appetizers. For this recipe, I use whole almonds, but if you prefer, use sliced ones. They may be a little easier to eat. Picholine are a good choice here because of their slight sweetness, but a sharper Sicilian green olive would also work well.

[Makes 4 main-course or 6 first-course servings]

Ingredients for 1 recipe Peperonata Sauce (page 78)

A generous handful of blanched almonds, lightly toasted

About ½ cup pitted green olives, cut in half

A splash of balsamic vinegar

Salt

Freshly ground black pepper

A pinch of cayenne pepper

1 pound ziti

- Prepare the peperonata sauce and add all the remaining ingredients except the ziti. Heat gently over medium-low heat in a large skillet for 2 or 3 minutes to warm through and blend the flavors. Check the seasoning.
- Cook the ziti until al dente, drain, and add to the pan. Toss well and check the seasoning. Serve hot. This dish also tastes wonderful at room temperature.

Ideas

Equal amounts of capers and pistachios substitute well for the almonds and green olives. Black olives and pine nuts give the dish a sweet, less acerbic flavor.

Add 3 or 4 whole anchovy fillets with the garlic and let them dissolve into the sauce. For more pronounced flavor, finely chop them and add them at the last minute. Try to use the salt-packed variety (see page 338.) They have a better flavor and are my choice for using uncooked or lightly cooked.

Poach shrimp, scallops, or small cubes of salmon right in the sauce (add them in the last few minutes and simmer over low heat until just tender). Or even better, sauté the fish in a separate pan with a little olive oil over high heat. Season with salt and pepper.

When just cooked through, deglaze the pan with a tiny splash of balsamic vinegar and add to your peperonata.

For a delicious but very non-Italian dish, drape small slices of grilled skirt or hanger steak over a peperonata-dressed pasta.

Farfalle with Ricotta, Mint, and Sweet Pepper Purée

Fresh ricotta with a little mint is used to dress spaghetti in Sicily and is a classic combination in Lazio. Here I've used it as a base and added a peperonata sauce to create layers of flavor. I've pureed the peperonata to give it a more refined character.

[Makes 4 main-course or 6 first-course servings]

1 recipe Peperonata Sauce (page 78)	**A handful of mint leaves,**
1 pound farfalle	**cut in thin strips**
¾ cup ricotta cheese	**Salt**
½ cup grated caciocavallo cheese	**Freshly ground black pepper**

- Puree the peperonata sauce in a food processor until very smooth. If the sauce is very thick, add a tablespoon or two of hot water or chicken broth to loosen it slightly. Check the seasoning.
- Start cooking the farfalle.
- In a large warmed serving bowl, combine the ricotta, caciocavallo, and mint. Season with salt and pepper and mix gently. When the farfalle are al dente, drain them, leaving some water clinging to the pasta, and add them to the bowl. Toss well. Add the peperonata purée and toss again.

Ideas

For a sauce with similar ingredients but a completely different character, toss the hot pasta with fresh goat cheese, ladle it onto the peperonata, left unpureed, and toss well.

If you don't like mint, substitute parsley or basil.

For a beautiful, though slightly sharper, yellow sauce, omit the tomato and use all yellow peppers in the peperonata.

WHEN NOT TO ADD GRATED CHEESE TO PASTA— A LOOK AT TRADITIONAL ITALIAN THINKING ON THE SUBJECT

*M*any Americans believe that a heavy shower of grated Parmigiano-Reggiano or other Italian grating cheese is suitable for all pasta dishes except those containing fish. But there are other times when grated cheese is considered inappropriate. Here is a short list of the traditional don'ts. Remember that all these cheese/no-cheese traditions came about by a general consensus about taste. Let taste be your guide when it comes to abiding by or breaking these rules.

- *Aglio e olio* (garlic and oil sauce) is traditionally a no-cheese sauce. It is more likely to be finished with a scattering of chopped parsley and a grating of coarsely ground black pepper. Pasta with olive oil and chopped fresh herbs (with or without garlic) is also usually served without grated cheese.
- Many olive oil–based vegetable sauces, such as those with zucchini, broccoli, potatoes, or sweet peppers, are served without grated cheese, but there is no hard rule about them, and the style varies from region to region. Marinara Sauce (page 32), which traditionally consists of olive oil, garlic, and lightly cooked tomatoes, is never served with cheese.
- Generally speaking, pasta dishes containing hot red pepper, such as an arrabbiata sauce, are not served with cheese. *Penne alla vodka,* which contains a bit of red pepper, is served without cheese. But the classic amatriciana pasta sauce from the Abruzzo region, which contains pancetta and red pepper, is traditionally topped with grated Pecorino Romano cheese; this is one of the exceptions to the rule. Almost all tomato-based sauces that are seasoned with hot red pepper are classically served without cheese.
- Puttanesca sauces, with their strong flavors of olives, capers, anchovies, garlic, and sometimes hot pepper, are traditionally served without grated cheese.
- Mushroom sauces, especially those in an olive oil base, are thought to be best without the addition of grated cheese. The same is true for most pasta sauces containing truffles. There are regional exceptions.
- No cheese on pasta sauces containing fish. Toasted bread crumbs are often used as a substitution because they add an appealing crunchy texture. There are a few exceptions to this rule. Cheese is occasionally added on the rare occasions the sauce contains milk or cream. Sicily has several traditional pasta recipes pairing tuna or swordfish sauces with local caciocavallo cheese. In various parts of Italy, classic stuffed pasta dishes combine

fish with cheese and are sometimes finished with a grating of cheese as well.

- Pasta with rabbit or hare sauces are usually served without cheese.
- Many long-simmered meat sauces are traditionally accompanied by a grating cheese of that region, but some meat sauces, especially those that include mushrooms, hot pepper, or olives, are served without cheese. Some complex mixed-meat sauces and some Neapolitan meat sauces containing large pieces of stewed meat are served without grated cheese as well. Pork sausage sauce is usually served with grated cheese.

Pasta with Spring and Summer Vegetables: Warm-Weather Cooking

Often in spring I'll walk to the farmers' market just to lift my spirits. The colors and smells of spring produce start to alter my attitude about cooking, pulling me away from slow-cooked meals with many subtle flavors toward a more straightforward approach to cooking.

Thinking seasonally sharpens your improvisational skills. Choosing the freshest just-picked ingredients gives you such a tremendous head start on flavor. It's unfortunate so much is now available year-round in our markets. If you are open to seasonal cooking, you can go to the market armed with a recipe for fettuccine with prosciutto and fresh peas, discover you have just missed the season for fresh peas, and grab the just-fresh local asparagus to adapt your recipe to.

You can't go far wrong playing with spring or summer produce. Try planning a meal around your favorite color or around one herb. I occasionally make pasta primavera or a summer minestrone using all light green vegetables, such as young fennel, zucchini, asparagus, fava beans, baby artichokes, and celery. These dishes have a harmony that pleases me greatly. I can never quite believe the color of real summer tomatoes or those thin, bright orange summer squash that taste so good flash-sautéed with a handful of bright green parsley leaves. In fact, a surefire way to come up with something good is by chopping any fresh vegetable in small chunks and sautéing it quickly in a hot pan with some fragrant extra-virgin olive oil and a bit of salt (maybe sea salt). If you have an herb, chop it lightly and add it at the end of cooking. Toss the result with hot pasta.

Thinking seasonally will clear your mind, because many of the big decisions are already made for you; you cook what jumps out at you in the market. The best way to simplify and ultimately improve your warm-weather cooking is by shopping at your local farmers' market.

I've arranged the following recipes roughly in the order in which the vegetables appear in the market. For more ideas on warm-weather pasta, see "Classic Italian Vegetable Sauces" (pages 58–83), for recipes with tomatoes, eggplant, zucchini, and bell peppers—all summer produce.

Saffron Tagliatelle with Asparagus, Orange Zest, and Ramps

Two Asparagus Pastas

In the spring I make asparagus with orange vinaigrette, and I like this combination so much I've applied it to a pasta sauce. Orange zest also goes surprisingly well with Parmigiano-Reggiano or Grana Padano cheese. Ramps are wild leeks that are sold at farmers' markets on the East Coast in early spring. Scallions make a fine but more assertive substitute.

[Makes 4 main-course or 6 first-course servings]

2 pounds asparagus, tough ends trimmed, peeled if thick-skinned, and cut in small pieces on the diagonal

About 3 tablespoons unsalted butter

About 15 ramps, cleaned and trimmed but left whole

Zest of 1 large orange

Salt

Freshly ground black pepper

Juice of 1 large orange

⅓ cup homemade Chicken Broth (page 374) or low-salt canned

½ cup heavy cream

A handful of basil leaves, chopped

A few savory sprigs, chopped

1 pound Saffron Pasta (page 368), cut for tagliatelle

Freshly grated Grana Padano or Parmigiano-Reggiano cheese

- Set up a large pot of salted water to cook the pasta. Bring it to a boil and add the asparagus pieces. Boil until just tender, about 2 minutes. Lift the asparagus from the pot with a large strainer and run under cold water to stop the cooking and to preserve the bright green color. Drain.
- In a large skillet, melt the butter over medium heat. Add the ramps and sauté until just starting to soften, about 3 minutes. Add the asparagus and orange zest, season with salt and pepper, and sauté 1 minute to blend the flavors. Add the orange juice and chicken broth and let the sauce simmer over medium heat for 2 or 3 minutes to blend the flavors. Add the cream, basil, and savory. Check the seasoning and simmer over low heat a few minutes longer.
- Cook the tagliatelle until tender, drain well, and add to the pan. Sauté briefly over very low heat, just to coat the pasta, adding a small handful of grated cheese. Transfer to a large serving bowl. Pass additional cheese at the table.

Ideas

Asparagus alone make an exquisite pasta sauce, simply blanched then sautéed in a little butter. But many vegetables complement asparagus. I find the combination of asparagus and morel mushrooms, another spring vegetable, unbelievably good. Slice a handful of morels and add them at the same time as the ramps; sauté both until just starting to soften and then proceed with the recipe. Other good seasonal choices are fresh fava beans, baby artichokes, spring lettuces, or snap peas.

A few thin slices of chopped prosciutto are always wonderful with asparagus. Add them when you add the savory and leave out the orange.

For a light main-dish pasta, add a pound of shelled small shrimp to the sauce while the broth is simmering. Cook only until tender, 2 to 3 minutes. Omit the grated cheese.

Spaghetti with Asparagus, Zucchini Blossoms, and Eggs

Zucchini blossoms and asparagus start appearing at my green market at about the same time—usually the beginning of May—so I decided to combine their flavors. This dish is made in the style of pasta alla carbonara, with raw eggs tossed in hot pasta to cook the sauce into a thick creaminess.

[Makes 4 main-course or 6 first-course servings]

1 bunch thin asparagus (about 15), ends trimmed, cut in small pieces on the diagonal

A dozen zucchini blossoms (see Note)

2 large eggs, at room temperature

About ½ cup freshly grated Pecorino Toscano cheese

Salt

About 3 tablespoons unsalted butter

5 thin slices pancetta, cut in small dice

1 medium onion, cut in small dice

A splash of dry white wine

1 pound spaghetti

Freshly ground black pepper

- Set up a large pot of salted water to cook the pasta. Bring to a boil and add the asparagus. Blanch for about 2 minutes. Lift the asparagus from the pot with a large strainer and run them under cold water briefly to stop the cooking and to preserve their bright green color. Drain.
- Wash the zucchini blossoms gently in a bowl of cool water. Remove the stamens and check the insides for bugs or dirt. Dry them with paper towels.
- In a large warmed serving bowl, mix the eggs with the grated cheese. Add a little salt.
- In a large skillet, heat the butter over medium heat. Add the pancetta and sauté until crisp. Add the onion and cook until tender, 3 or 4 minutes. Add the asparagus, season lightly with salt, and sauté a minute or two to bring out the flavor. Add the zucchini blossoms and sauté about 1 minute longer. Add the wine and, with a wooden spoon, loosen any bits of onion and pancetta on the bottom of the pan. Let the alcohol cook away.
- Cook the spaghetti in the same water in which you blanched the asparagus. When the pasta is al dente, drain, leaving some water clinging to the strands, and add to the serving bowl with the egg mixture. Add the asparagus sauce and a generous amount of black pepper. Toss very well. Serve immediately.

A note about zucchini blossoms: The best pizza I've ever eaten was topped with zucchini blossoms, mozzarella, and anchovies. I was served this in Rome in early spring when zucchini blossoms turn up stuffed, sautéed, in risotto and pasta, soups, and even on pizzas. I find these gorgeous dark yellow blossoms at my farmers' market and occasionally in grocery stores starting in early May and through the middle of the summer. The blossoms are best when first picked and just starting to open or newly fully opened. After a day or two they start to close their petals and shrivel. You can prolong their freshness about a day by sticking their stems in a glass of water and refrigerating them.

The blossoms should be gently washed in a bowl of cool water to remove dirt and any little bugs that might be trapped inside. Remove the stamen of each flower and let the flowers dry on paper towels. They are now ready to use whole or sliced in pasta sauces. Add them to a recipe in the last few minutes of cooking so they remain fresh tasting.

Ideas

You can make this sauce without the asparagus if you would like to highlight a bunch of beautiful zucchini blossoms you found at the market. Or leave out the asparagus and the zucchini blossoms and you'll create a classic carbonara sauce.

If you'd like to add a fresh herb, think delicate flavor so as not to mask the spring perfume of these two vegetables. A few coarsely chopped basil or parsley leaves tossed in at the last minute would add spark to the sauce without overwhelming the vegetables.

Cavatelli with Morels, Montasio Cheese, and Arugula

Using Spring Mushrooms

When I worked as a line cook at the restaurant Le Madri, in New York City, one of my jobs was to fill morel mushrooms with Parmigiano-flavored mashed potatoes. These were grilled to order and served on arugula. I loved this dish so much I adapted it for pasta. I've chosen Montasio, a cow's milk cheese from Friuli (near Venice); it is mild and mellow, softening the slight bitterness of the arugula.

[Makes 4 main-course or 6 first-course servings]

6 new potatoes, cut in quarters
   (I use creamer potatoes)

1 pound cavatelli

Olive oil

1 large spring onion, thinly sliced

Salt

Freshly ground black pepper

½ pound morels, cleaned, trimmed,
   and cut in thick slices

3 garlic cloves, thinly sliced

A splash of dry sherry

About ½ cup low-salt canned chicken
   broth

2 bunches arugula, washed, stemmed,
   and dried

Freshly grated Montasio cheese

- Set up a large pot of salted water to cook the pasta. Bring to a boil and add the potatoes. Blanch for 2 or 3 minutes. The potatoes should stay a bit firm because they will cook further in the sauce. Scoop the potatoes from the water with a large strainer and drain.
- Bring the water back to a boil and start cooking the cavatelli.
- In a large skillet, heat about 3 tablespoons olive oil over medium heat. Add the onion and sauté until soft. Add the potatoes, season with salt and pepper, and sauté until the potatoes brown lightly, about 3 minutes. Add the morels and garlic and sauté until the mushrooms begin to soften and the garlic gives off its aroma, about 2 minutes. Add the sherry and let it bubble 1 minute to evaporate the alcohol. Add the chicken broth and simmer gently for a minute or two, just until the mushroom pieces are tender. Taste for seasoning.

- When the cavatelli are al dente, drain them well and add them to the skillet. Sauté over low heat for a minute to blend the ingredients, adding a generous drizzle of olive oil to help the sauce coat the pasta. Taste for seasoning. Add the arugula and a handful of grated Montasio. Remove from the heat and mix well (the arugula will immediately start to wilt from the heat of the pasta and will not require further cooking). Transfer to a large serving bowl. Pass extra Montasio at the table if you desire.

Note: Dry Marsala, dry vermouth, and dry sherry are good flavorings for mushrooms, removing their slight soil taste and bringing out their desirable musky undertones.

Ideas

I make variations on this dish with different mushrooms and different greens: chanterelles with spinach, oyster mushrooms with escarole, portobellos with chard. Montasio cheese is just a suggestion; Grana Padano or a mild Pecorino are good substitutes.

Cooked dandelion greens are enticingly bitter, a little more so than cooked arugula, and I like the way they blend with mushrooms. If you use dandelion greens instead of arugula, chop them and add with the mushrooms to allow this slightly tougher green to soften. If you don't like bitterness, substitute spinach or a mild lettuce.

If you can find green spring garlic, use it in place of the mature garlic for a slightly sweeter taste.

Spring Mushroom and Sorrel Soup with Ditali

Many Italian vegetable soups contain some sort of pasta. Minestrone almost always does, but so can a quick-cooked, cleaner-tasting soup like this one. In the spring I like a mix of spinach and sorrel, which I think works well because the sweet spinach tempers the sourness of the sorrel.

[Makes 4 main-course or 6 first-course servings]

About 7 cups homemade Mixed-Meat Broth (page 375) or Vegetable Broth (page 377)

About 2 tablespoons olive oil

A small piece of fresh salt pork or prosciutto end, cut in small cubes

2 or 3 small carrots, cut in small dice

6 or 7 scallions, cut in thin rounds, including some tender green

1 pound mixed spring mushrooms (morels, chanterelles, and a handful of cultivated ones such as portobello and cremini), stemmed and cut in small dice (save all the stems and trimmings; see Note)

5 or 6 small waxy potatoes (I use fingerlings), cut in small cubes

A few stalks green garlic, trimmed and finely chopped

Salt

Freshly ground black pepper

A large handful of fresh sorrel leaves, washed, stemmed, and cut in thin strips

A large bunch of spinach, washed, stemmed, and cut in thin strips

A thyme sprig

A bay leaf

About 1 cup ditali, cooked until al dente, drained, and tossed with a little olive oil

Freshly grated Grana Padano cheese

- Heat the broth in a large saucepan.
- In a heavy-bottomed soup pot, heat the olive oil over low heat. Add the salt pork or prosciutto end and sauté until all the fat is rendered and the pieces are crisp and lightly browned. Add the carrots and scallions and sauté 1 minute to bring out the flavors. Add the mushrooms, potatoes, green garlic, salt, and pepper and sauté just until the

mushrooms start to soften and you smell the sweetness of the garlic. Add the sorrel, spinach, thyme sprig, and bay leaf and sauté briefly.

- Add the hot broth and bring to a boil. Lower the heat to medium and simmer for about 10 minutes, bringing together all the flavors. The potatoes and carrots should be tender, with no hardness to them. Add the cooked ditali and let them heat through. Taste for seasoning. Serve hot or at room temperature, with Grana Padano sprinkled on top of each bowl.

- To preserve the freshness of this light soup, I suggest not reheating it but serving any leftover at room temperature.

A note about the broth for this soup: If you are making broth specifically for this soup, add all the mushroom trimmings and stems to the pot along with the other vegetables. If you already have broth or are using canned broth, simmer the stems in the broth for about 30 minutes and then strain.

Ideas

Sorrel is a delicate leafy green with a subtle sourness. It is perfect in soup because it just about melts into the broth, leaving a jolt of flavor that has the effect of a squirt of lemon juice. It goes extremely well with most varieties of mushrooms.

Chopped, seeded tomato can be added and simmered briefly in the broth for a taste more like minestrone.

Green Penne with Baby Artichokes, Fava Beans, and Anchovy Cream

Here is an early spring version of pasta primavera. I hesitate to give recipes involving fava beans, because they take so long to peel. But they're so delicious I can't resist. You can substitute fresh spring peas or use just artichokes.

[Makes 4 main-course or 6 first-course servings]

1 to 1½ dozen (depending on size) baby
    artichokes (see Note)
Juice of 1 lemon
About 3 tablespoons olive oil
Freshly ground black pepper
2 or 3 garlic cloves, finely minced
½ pound or more fava beans, shucked
    and peeled (see Note)

About 10 anchovy fillets, chopped
3 ripe tomatoes (about 1½ pounds),
    peeled, seeded, and diced (see
    Tomato Concassé, page 43)
Zest of 1 lemon
About 1 cup heavy cream
1 pound green penne

- Trim and quarter the artichokes, placing them in a bowl of cold water with the lemon juice. Drain the artichokes and dry them with paper towels.
- In a large skillet, heat the olive oil. Add the artichokes and season generously with pepper (hold back on adding salt; remember, you will be adding a large amount of anchovies to this dish). Sauté until just starting to color. Add the garlic and sauté only 1 minute. Add a splash of water, cover the pan, and simmer until the artichokes are tender but still firm, about 5 minutes.
- Uncover the pan and add the fava beans, anchovies, tomatoes, lemon zest, and cream. Simmer until the anchovies are dissolved and the fava beans are tender, about 5 minutes. Taste for seasoning.
- Cook the penne until al dente, drain, and add to the pan. Toss over medium heat until well coated.

A note about baby artichokes: These tiny artichokes usually don't have chokes, so all you need to do is peel off the tough outer leaves and trim the remaining leaf tips and stems. If you buy slightly more developed small artichokes, simply slice them in quarters and remove any just-forming fuzzy choke.

A note on peeling fresh fava beans: The fava beans we find in our markets are usually a bit more mature than the very young beans found in Italy in the spring. Our slightly older beans have usually developed a tough inner peel that can be bitter and needs to be removed. Remove the beans from their pods. Blanch the beans in the boiling salted pasta cooking water for about a minute. Lift the beans from the water with a large strainer spoon and run under cold water. The tough peel should now slip off easily.

Ideas

If you think of this as a pasta primavera, you'll see that many seasonal vegetables can be substituted. Asparagus and young fennel is a good combination. Try artichokes with peas or string beans.

Anchovy cream makes an interesting sauce for a variety of green vegetables. So does Parmigiano cream (see page 138).

Pasta is good simply tossed with anchovy cream, leaving out the other ingredients. Try anchovy cream with fresh egg tagliatelle.

Pasta Primavera in Shades of Green

Born-Again Pasta Primavera

I've been so disappointed by uninspired pasta primavera made with boiled out-of-season vegetables that I've stopped ordering it in restaurants. I make it at home with interesting mixtures of farmers' market vegetables that I sauté separately and then season with sweet onions, sometimes spring garlic, and fresh herbs. When making primavera, choose a mix of all delicate vegetables (lettuce, peas, asparagus, fava beans) or a mix of meatier ones (artichokes, bell peppers, eggplant). Cut the vegetables up small so they cook quickly and have a uniform appearance. In this version I've chosen all green vegetables, not only because of the taste but because of the way they look together. When choosing vegetables for a primavera sauce, take your cue from the market. Most vegetables that ripen at the same time will make sense in your composition.

I think of this primavera not so much as a delicate sauce but as a spring vegetable stew, so I've chosen sturdy ziti as the pasta. But try fresh egg tagliatelle to see how it lightens the character of the dish.

[Makes 4 main-course or 6 first-course servings]

1 cup freshly shucked peas

2 small bunches asparagus, tough ends trimmed, cut in small pieces

Olive oil

6 spring scallions, cut in thin rounds, with some of the green

2 inner celery stalks, plus leaves, cut in small dice

1 small fennel bulb, trimmed and cut in small dice

Salt

Freshly ground black pepper

3 small zucchini, cut in small dice

A generous splash of semidry, fruity white wine (a non-oaky Chardonnay is perfect here)

1 pound ziti

Extra-virgin olive oil

2 or 3 thin slices prosciutto, chopped

A small handful of basil leaves, chopped

A handful of chives (use garlic chives if possible), finely chopped

- Set up a large pot of salted water to cook the pasta. Bring to a boil and add the peas and asparagus. Blanch until tender but still firm, about 3 minutes. Lift the peas and the asparagus from the water with a large strainer, run under cold water, and drain.
- In a large skillet, heat about 3 tablespoons of olive oil over medium heat. Add the scallions, celery, and fennel. Season with salt and pepper and sauté until fork tender but still firm. Add the zucchini and sauté until just starting to soften, about 4 minutes. Add the asparagus and peas and sauté until tender and fragrant. Add the wine and let it boil down to almost nothing. Add a splash of water, cover the pan, and let the vegetables cook a few minutes to become tender. Taste and add more salt and pepper if needed.
- Cook the ziti in the same water you used to boil the vegetables. When they are al dente, drain them and add to the skillet. Toss well, adding a drizzle of extra-virgin olive oil for a fresh flavor boost. Add the prosciutto, basil, and garlic chives and toss briefly. Transfer to a serving bowl.

Ideas

In the spring, Sicilians make *frittella,* a stew of young peas, fava beans, and artichokes seasoned with a little white wine vinegar; it makes a lovely pasta sauce. If you would like to make it, follow the general directions for the above recipe, first sautéing spring onion in olive oil, then sliced artichokes, allowing them to sauté together a few minutes. Then add the peas and fava beans and a tiny splash of good white wine vinegar. Add a little water, cover the pan, and simmer until the vegetables are tender, about 5 minutes. Season with basil, tarragon, or parsley if you like.

Many vegetable stews are perfect tossed with pasta. The great Provençal summer stew, ratatouille, is great tossed with rigatoni, topped with crumbled fresh goat cheese, and thrown into a medium-hot oven to heat through and melt the cheese.

Summer Couscous with Chanterelles, Yellow Squash, and Basil

A Summer Couscous

Chanterelles start showing up in the market around midsummer. They're wonderful simply sautéed in butter and tossed with penne, but try them with couscous. This is a good vegetarian main course and works well as a side dish with grilled chicken.

Couscous is a small grainlike pasta usually made from semolina. In Sicily it is used much the same way as it is in Morocco—as a base for stews (in Sicily fish stew is the norm). Here I've taken a modern approach and mixed it with sautéed seasonal vegetables for a fluffy, light dish. You can easily use this sauce with traditional pasta such as tagliatelle or even penne.

[Makes 4 main-course or 6 first-course servings]

1 to 2 cups homemade Chicken Broth (page 374) or Vegetable Broth (page 377), flavored with any chanterelle trimmings you have

1 cup couscous (not quick-cooking)

Salt

Freshly ground black pepper

A pinch of sugar

A few gratings of nutmeg

Unsalted butter

Olive oil

1 large onion, cut in medium dice

½ pound chanterelles, cleaned, stems lightly trimmed, and cut in half lengthwise if large (otherwise, leave whole)

4 or 5 small yellow summer squash, cut in medium dice

A large handful of basil leaves, cut in thin strips, plus a few left whole for garnish, if desired

A handful of fresh chervil, long stems trimmed

Freshly grated Parmigiano-Reggiano cheese

- In a small saucepan, heat the chicken or vegetable broth to boiling.
- Place the couscous in a large serving bowl. Season it with salt and pepper, the sugar, and the nutmeg. Dot the top with 2 or 3 tablespoons of butter. Pour about 1 cup hot broth over the couscous and stir. Cover the pan with aluminum foil and let stand for about 10 minutes.

- Meanwhile, heat about 2 tablespoons each of butter and olive oil in a large skillet. Add the onion, chanterelles, and squash, season well with salt and pepper, and sauté over medium-high heat until the vegetables are tender and fragrant, about 5 minutes. Add a splash of broth and mix with a spoon to loosen any caramelized solids on the bottom of the pan, which will add flavor to the dish. Simmer a minute or two to blend the flavors.
- Fluff the couscous with a fork. If the grains are not tender enough, add a little more hot chicken broth, let it stand a minute, and fluff again.
- Add the basil strips, chervil, a handful of the grated cheese, and the mushroom-squash mixture to the couscous. Toss. Transfer to a large serving platter and top with a sprinkling of Parmigiano-Reggiano and a few whole basil leaves if you like. Serve warm.

Ideas

This is a good way to present any combination of spring or summer vegetables. Experiment with different mushroom and vegetable combinations. Porcini go well with spinach and other greens. Try portobello with tomatoes or roasted peppers. Morels can be accented with peas or asparagus. Zucchini works well with white button mushrooms, garlic, and a grated mild Pecorino. You can use the above recipe as a general guideline, keeping in mind that for the couscous to remain fluffy and light, the vegetables should be cooked until tender but not mushy and they should be rather dry.

A drizzle of truffle oil mixed into the vegetables just before serving creates a richer flavor.

Vegetable stock can replace the chicken broth for a completely vegetarian dish.

Toss the vegetable mixture with a sturdy dried pasta such as penne or farfalle.

Another good way to use chanterelles for a pasta sauce: Sauté the mushrooms in onion, thyme, and olive oil. Toss cooked pasta with fresh mild goat cheese until well coated. Top with the mushrooms and toss again.

Spaghetti with Sautéed Summer Herbs

Recipes for Summer Herbs

Lightly sautéing whole herb leaves in olive oil toasts the outside but keeps all the oils inside, so the big taste comes when you start eating and all the trapped herb oils explode on your tongue. This sauce tastes best without cheese.

[Makes 4 main-course or 6 first-course servings]

1 pound spaghetti

About 1 cup assorted whole herb leaves,
   washed, stemmed, and dried
   I suggest:
   About 2 dozen whole basil leaves
   About 10 sprigs flat-leaf parsley
      leaves
   About 6 or 7 spearmint leaves

About a dozen marjoram leaves

About 5 sprigs of tarragon leaves

5 or 6 young garlic cloves, very thinly
   sliced

Extra-virgin olive oil

Salt

Freshly ground black pepper

- Start cooking the spaghetti.
- Place the herbs, garlic, and about ⅓ cup olive oil in a large skillet. Turn the heat to low and sauté gently until the garlic is soft and the herbs are fragrant, 5 to 6 minutes.
- Drain the spaghetti well and add to the pan. Season with salt and a generous amount of pepper. Sauté a few minutes over medium heat to coat the pasta with the herbs and oil. You can add a drizzle of fresh oil just before serving for a flavor boost.

Ideas

My herb suggestions result in a mild sauce, but for an even subtler blend, try a mix of basil, parsley, chervil, and fennel tops. Scallions might replace the garlic in this case. Or choose a mix of bold herbs with heavy oils, such as rosemary, summer savory, thyme, sage, and oregano. Half a cup of these stronger herbs will be enough to flavor a pound of pasta.

Using butter instead of olive oil makes the finished dish much richer. Butter and cream are richer still.

Sauté rosemary leaves alone with a generous amount of extra-virgin olive oil. Toss with tagliatelle and serve before a plate of pan-fried lamb chops. I sometimes add the grated zest of a lemon or an orange to this rosemary-scented pasta.

HERB OVERKILL

*I*t became popular sometime in the 1980s for restaurant chefs to scatter fresh herbs over every dish that came out of the kitchen. I love herbs, but they need to be used with care. Fresh herbs add much to many pasta sauces, but you don't have to put them in every sauce. Sometimes a tomato sauce just needs to be a tomato sauce. If you have a very fresh seasonal vegetable such as asparagus, you might not want to include any herb because it's more important to show off the fresh taste of asparagus.

There are good pasta dishes, however, that use a mix of several herbs (see Spaghetti with Sautéed Summer Herbs, page 100). In these sauces the herbs usually dominate and sometimes constitute the entire sauce, and during the summer, when fresh herbs abound, there is nothing more intoxicating than a mouthful of soft perfumes caressing your palate. But the purity of flavor achieved from using one herb to flavor a pasta dish, as in basil pesto, is something I highly respect. In general, when adding herbs to a meat-, vegetable-, or fish-based sauce, it's best to decide on one flavor that goes well with your other ingredients. A mix of five fresh herbs mixed into a clam sauce is confusing to the taste buds and results in a generalized "herb" flavor that does not enhance the herbs or the clams. So try not to be nonchalant about using them. Think about the flavor a certain herb will impart and how it will blend with the other flavors in your dish, and then decide if that's what you want to taste in your pasta dish.

Spaghetti Nest with Genoese Pesto and Goat Cheese-Stuffed Tomatoes

Goat cheese and basil pair beautifully, and I'm always experimenting with different ways to put them together. Here I've placed cheese-filled baked summer tomatoes on top of a pesto-dressed pasta. The tomatoes look like little eggs sitting in their nests. When the tomato juices mix with the basil, garlic, and goat cheese, you get all the taste of high summer in one bite. The success of this dish depends greatly on superb basil from your farmers' market (or your garden) and plump, juicy tomatoes that have never seen the inside of a refrigerator.

[Makes 4 main-course or 6 first-course servings]

For the pesto:

About ½ cup pine nuts, plus a handful, lightly toasted, for garnish

1 or 2 young garlic cloves, peeled

About 2 loosely packed cups basil leaves, washed and well dried

About ¼ cup freshly grated mild Pecorino cheese (Toscano is good here)

About ¼ cup freshly grated Grana Padano cheese

About ½ cup olive oil (I like a green Tuscan oil for pesto, but a lighter oil from Liguria is more traditional)

Salt

Freshly ground black pepper

For the tomatoes:

One 11-ounce log unaged goat cheese

About ¼ cup heavy cream

Freshly ground black pepper

Salt

4 to 6 small round tomatoes (1 per serving: 4 for main course or 6 for first course)

Olive oil

1 pound spaghetti

- In a food processor, place the pine nuts and garlic and chop roughly. Add the basil leaves and process a few seconds, until they can start to break down. Add the cheeses and blend everything until you have a rough, dry paste. Now add enough olive oil (about ½ cup) to achieve a rich, smooth paste. Season with salt and pepper and process a second to blend. I like pesto not too finely ground, but instead with a bit of texture. I think this gives it a brighter flavor.

- Preheat the oven to 425°F.
- To prepare the tomatoes, mix the goat cheese with enough cream to make it soft and spreadable. Season with pepper and if needed, salt. Cut the top off the tomatoes and scoop out the insides. Salt lightly and place, cut side down, on paper towels to drain for 20 minutes.
- Spread a little pesto on the inside of each tomato and fill to the top with goat cheese. Place the tomatoes in a lightly oiled baking dish. Drizzle a little olive oil over each one and bake until the tomatoes start to shrivel and the cheese is lightly browned, about 20 minutes. (Don't cook them any longer or at a lower temperature. You want them to cook quickly to retain their shape and juiciness.)
- Cook the spaghetti until al dente, reserving about 1 cup of the pasta cooking water. Drain, leaving a bit of water clinging to the pasta, and transfer to a large serving bowl. Toss with the pesto, adding a bit of pasta water if necessary to loosen the pesto further. Divide the pasta among individual bowls and place a tomato in the middle of each serving. Top with a sprinkling of toasted pine nuts. Serve hot. The tomatoes are best served hot, but they can also be served warm on top of the hot pasta. The main point is that the goat cheese should be warm enough to be runny so it can blend easily with the pesto and tomato juices.

Ideas

Italians love to stuff vegetables, and many of the classic stuffed-vegetable dishes, I've found, are wonderful placed on top of a dish of pasta, creating multilayered tastes. Stuffed zucchini or stuffed zucchini flowers are delicious over pasta in tomato sauce. Classic mushrooms stuffed with garlic and bread crumbs look and taste great on top of a dish of pasta with mushroom sauce or over spaghetti dressed with a parsley-flecked *aglio e olio* (garlic and oil sauce).

When choosing vegetables to stuff and serve over pasta, think small—mushrooms, small tomatoes, small onions, and zucchini blossoms are good choices. Large vegetables like bell peppers, globe artichokes, and large tomatoes will overwhelm the pasta and are best served as a separate course.

PESTO

*G*enoese-style pesto is a great love of mine. Strangely, it is never as good in a restaurant as it is when you make it yourself. I'm not sure why. Maybe it's fresher, or possibly it just tastes better because you make it the way you like it. Restaurants are always messing it up by adding cream or too much garlic or acrid garlic or poor-quality cheese.

Everyone has his or her own way of making it perfect. I like mine with plenty of pine nuts and very little garlic. There are no common measurements for pesto, just common ingredients: basil, pine nuts, garlic, Pecorino or Grana cheese (or a mix of both), olive oil, and salt. Some people add a bit of butter; some mix in walnuts with the pine nuts. I like a bit of black pepper, which is not a traditional ingredient. In Genoa, pesto is made with the local Pecorino. The measurements in this recipe are to my taste; you don't have to match them, just use them as a starting point.

My only suggestion, outside of letting your taste be your guide, is to buy the best ingredients you can. Even though basil is available year-round now, I make pesto only in the summer, when I can buy beautifully perfumed basil from my farmers' market. And toward the end of August, when the basil stalks become woody and the leaves take on a strong, harsh flavor, I stop making it and wait until next year. In a good pesto, you're looking for a perfect balance, yet every ingredient can be tasted true and clear. Purchase fresh pine nuts, and make sure your olive oil is really fresh and delicious. If your cheese has a slight refrigerator taste, this will be apparent in your pesto. Since pesto is a raw sauce, there is nowhere for inferior ingredients to hide. Another important thing to keep in mind is to make sure your basil leaves are very dry before putting them in the food processor. Water in your pesto will darken it to an olive green instead of the vibrant bright green it should be.

One final comment: You hear a lot of talk about how much better pesto tastes when it's made the old-fashioned way—with a mortar and pestle. I'm not really interested in spending time doing this when I have a food processor, especially when I'm serving a dozen people. I've made small batches of pesto with my mortar and pestle and they've come out fine, but in my opinion, if you use a food processor and do not overpuree the ingredients, you will have a beautifully textured, vibrant pesto in no time.

Tomato Tagliatelle with Basil Butter and Almonds

This is really a variation on Genoese basil pesto, using butter instead of olive oil and almonds in place of pine nuts. The taste is lush, making for a rich and fragrant first course. Tomato-flavored tagliatelle adds another summer flavor to this dish. It can be bought at many Italian specialty shops. Most versions are flavored with tomato paste. I make mine with pureed sun-dried tomatoes.

[Makes 4 main-course or 6 first-course servings]

1 cup whole blanched almonds, plus a handful, lightly toasted, for garnish

2 young garlic cloves, peeled

½ cup (1 stick) unsalted butter, softened

About 1 cup basil leaves

Zest of 1 lemon

Freshly grated Parmigiano-Reggiano cheese

Salt

Freshly ground black pepper

1 pound Tomato Pasta (page 369), cut for tagliatelle

- In a food processor, grind the cup of blanched almonds with the garlic until you have a fine paste. Add the softened butter and process until blended. Add the basil leaves, lemon zest, a large handful of grated Parmigiano, salt, and pepper and process until the basil is chopped and just blended into the paste. Taste for seasoning. This pesto has a sweeter, more delicate flavor than traditional basil pesto made with olive oil. Either use right away or store, refrigerated, in a tightly covered bowl until ready to use (it will retain its flavor for about 2 days).
- Cook the tomato tagliatelle until tender. Drain, leaving some water clinging to the pasta, and place in a warm serving bowl. Add the basil butter in small pieces and toss until it melts and coats the pasta. Add as much basil butter as you like; you might not want to use all of it. Garnish with a handful of whole or sliced toasted almonds. Serve very hot.

Ideas

The basil butter can become parsley butter or mixed-herb butter. You can replace the almonds with walnuts, pistachios, pine nuts, or even olives or capers.

Basil butter is also good melted over a fish fillet or a steak. If well wrapped, it can be frozen for about a month.

Anchovy butter goes wonderfully with spaghetti. In a food processor, blend a stick of softened butter with 9 or 10 anchovy fillets and toss with hot spaghetti or linguine.

Late-Summer Minestrone with Tomato, Fennel, and Broken Spaghetti— Served with Aioli

Many pasta sauces make good soups if you thin them with broth or even water. Conversely, ingredients that make good Italian soups can also make excellent pasta sauces. It's true for this soup, which contains summer tomatoes, fennel, potatoes, saffron, garlic, thyme, and spaghetti—just leave out the broth. Many tomato-based sauces and also many meat sauces can be thinned to produce wonderful soups if the texture and cut of the ingredients lend themselves to it. This is another way to think about altering pasta sauces to serve different purposes.

Minestrone is traditionally a rather thick soup with very soft, long-cooked vegetables. I like mine thinner than most Italians would eat it, but you can adjust the amount of broth to suit your taste.

Aioli, a Provençal garlic mayonnaise, goes very well with tomatoes and fennel, but you can serve the soup instead garnished with freshly grated Pecorino Toscano cheese and a drizzle of extra-virgin olive oil.

[Makes 4 main-course or 6 first-course servings]

2 medium red onions, cut in small dice

3 or 4 small summer fennel bulbs, or 1 large one, trimmed and diced (save the feathery tops and chop fine)

Olive oil

4 or 5 small waxy potatoes, such as new or fingerling, cut in small chunks

A few thyme sprigs

A few fennel seeds, ground

1 or 2 bay leaves, fresh if possible

2 or 3 garlic cloves, thinly sliced

2 small zucchini, cut in small dice

Salt

Freshly ground black pepper

4 large summer tomatoes (about 2 pounds), peeled, seeded, and cut in small dice

A pinch of saffron threads, ground to a powder with a mortar and pestle (see page 352)

A tiny splash of Pernod

About 6 cups homemade Chicken Broth (page 374)

4 ounces spaghetti, broken in small pieces, cooked until al dente, and tossed in a little olive oil

For the aioli:

3 young garlic cloves, peeled	About 1 cup light, fruity olive oil (a Ligurian oil is perfect here)
2 egg yolks, at room temperature	A squeeze of lemon juice
	Salt

- In a large soup pot, sauté the onions and fennel in about 2 tablespoons olive oil over medium heat until soft and fragrant. Add the potatoes, thyme sprigs, ground fennel, bay leaves, and garlic and sauté until the garlic and spices give off aroma, a minute or two. Add the zucchini and sauté 1 minute to release its flavor. Season with salt and pepper. Add the tomatoes, saffron, Pernod, and chicken broth (if you like your soup a bit thicker, use about 1 cup less, remembering you can always add more broth or even a little water later if the consistency is not right for you).
- Bring to a boil, then turn the heat to medium and cook, uncovered, at a lively simmer about 10 minutes to bring all the flavors together and to finish cooking the vegetables. The tomatoes should remain bright red and fresh tasting, so don't cook the soup much longer than that. Add the pasta and fennel tops. Check the seasoning. Serve hot, with a dollop of aioli in each bowl.
- To make the aioli, have all the ingredients at room temperature. Place the garlic in a food processor and grind until well chopped. Add the egg yolks and process a few seconds. With the machine running, start adding the olive oil in a thin stream. You will notice it start to catch after a few seconds, and the sauce will start to become thick and pale yellow. Continue adding the oil until it is used up. Add a squeeze of lemon juice to flavor and loosen the aioli just a bit. Season with salt.

Ideas

I tend to like minestrones that highlight only two or three vegetables instead of the more classic medley of six or more. Pick two or three that appeal to you at any given time. For instance, I like a soup of all summer squash and tomato. If you like a more elaborate minestrone, there are no rules. Just choose vegetables that are seasonal and fresh, and the soup should work itself out by natural design.

A dollop of basil pesto is delicious on this soup instead of aioli and is traditional with a minestrone.

Another interesting garnish is unaged softened goat cheese thinned with a little heavy cream. The cheese melts into the soup, adding a mild tartness that goes well with tomatoes.

Tarragon is an excellent herb to use instead of basil, blending well with both fennel and tomato.

Orecchiette with Roasted Corn, Red Peppers, and Ricotta Salata

Using American Produce in an Italian Way

I chose orecchiette for this sauce because I like the way the corn kernels get caught in the rounded hollows of the pasta. Corn's sweetness and texture, I think, go well with the wheaty taste of dried pasta. The pancetta is cut in slightly bigger pieces than we are used to in this country (I learned this style from eating pasta carbonara at restaurants in Rome), which gives the finished dish an earthy texture that stands up well to a sturdy pasta. If you don't have a grill, roast the peppers over a gas flame and roast the corn in a hot oven.

[Makes 4 main-course or 6 first-course servings]

4 red bell peppers

4 ears fresh corn

4 thin slices pancetta, cut in small cubes

2 tablespoons olive oil

10 scallions, cut in thin rounds, with some of the green

Salt

Freshly ground black pepper

1 pound orecchiette

A tiny splash of sherry vinegar

A large handful of basil leaves, chopped

About ½ cup freshly grated ricotta salata cheese

- Roast the peppers over a hot grill until well charred on all sides. Roast the corn in their husks (or husk and wrap in aluminum foil), turning several times, until tender and lightly browned (this should take about 10 minutes, depending on the heat of your grill; a medium-hot grill with low flames is best). Peel and seed the peppers and cut them in small cubes. Remove the corn kernels with a sharp knife. Set aside.
- In a large skillet, sauté the pancetta in the olive oil over medium-low heat until it gives off most of its fat and becomes crisp and golden brown. Add the scallions and sauté a minute longer. Add the corn and peppers, season with salt and pepper, and sauté until all the vegetables are soft and fragrant, 3 or 4 minutes.
- Cook the orecchiette until al dente. Drain, leaving a little water clinging to the pasta, and add to the pan. Add the sherry vinegar and toss well over low heat. Add the basil and ricotta salata. Toss well and taste for seasonings. Transfer to a serving bowl.

Ideas

I also like corn with lima beans or string beans, both of which can be blanched and then briefly sautéed in this sauce, replacing the bell peppers. Fresh corn kernels sautéed with chanterelle mushrooms, loosened with a splash of white wine and finished with a scattering of chopped parsley make a fabulous sauce for fresh egg pasta.

Corn sautéed with chopped summer tomatoes and spiked with fresh hot chiles is great tossed with green penne and topped with crumbled fresh goat cheese.

Replace the pancetta with bacon for a very American pasta dish.

Play with the herbs. I think corn goes best with basil or parsley.

Grilled or sautéed sausage cut in small pieces is a good addition; try merguez, Moroccan lamb sausage, or chorizo for a spicy touch.

Use yellow bell peppers, and you'll have a pretty pasta dish with all yellow vegetables.

If you don't want to grill the vegetables, make the entire dish in a sauté pan, sautéing the corn and peppers along with the scallions until tender. The dish will lack smoky flavor but will still satisfy if you let the vegetables brown a bit to become sweet.

GARNISHES FOR PASTA

A bowl of pasta can be a humble sight, and that's certainly what it should be at times. But when you want formality, garnishes can make a big difference.

Without going overboard you can easily find creative ways to dress up pasta. In the summer a few fried zucchini blossoms, which are not only beautiful but delicious, make a lovely garnish for a bowl of penne tossed with sautéed zucchini. Chive blossoms are both gorgeous and edible and are especially welcome on pasta salads that include chives or some type of onion. Whole fried artichoke hearts provide a suitable garnish for any pasta with an artichoke-based sauce. When you make linguine with clam sauce, place a handful of the nicest clams in their shells on top of each portion along with a scattering of whole flat-leaf parsley leaves.

Just be mindful that the garnish be related to the dish, either as a component of the recipe or as a complement to the flavors. You probably wouldn't want to sprinkle caviar over a pasta dressed with veal ragù, but you'd like it on ravioli filled with salmon or crab. Here are a few simple ways to dress up pasta, appropriate for individual servings or family-style platters or bowls.

Whole herb leaves and herb sprigs: Choose unblemished sprigs of basil, parsley, rosemary, chervil, or fennel tops, but only if they pick up a flavor in the sauce.

Thin strips of herb leaves: Cut leafy herbs or greens into thin strips by rolling a few leaves together into a thin cigarette-shaped tube and cutting crosswise. Basil, arugula, and sorrel can be cut like this and look attractive on pastas dressed with cream-based or tomato sauces.

Fried sage and parsley leaves: Whole fried herb leaves are a delicious way to highlight an herb used in a pasta sauce. For instance, garnish a sauce of butter and chopped sage with whole sage leaves. Fry the whole leaves in an inch or so of hot olive oil in a small sauté pan until crisp. Drain on paper towels. Parsley, chervil, and small basil leaves can be fried too.

Pepper and herb oils: A drizzle of glistening herb oil shines out on pasta soups. Hot-pepper-flavored oil enlivens pasta and bean dishes while putting a shiny red swirl on the pasta.

Tomato Concassé (page 43): Chopped fresh tomatoes are all you can want on top of many summer pasta dishes, especially pasta salads containing basil, vegetables, and fruity olive oil.

Diced roasted peppers: These give added flavor to tomato sauces, especially those mixed with cream or ricotta. Diced red, yellow, or orange peppers look beautiful on herb sauces and *aglio e olio* (garlic and oil sauce).

Fried capers: Capers fried in hot olive oil open up like little flowers and have a crunchy texture. Scatter them on piquant tomato, puttanesca, oil and garlic, and fish sauces.

Nuts: Whole toasted or slivered nuts work well as garnishes if they're a component of the dish. For instance, scatter pine nuts over pasta with basil pesto or lightly toasted almonds over a cauliflower pasta containing chopped almonds.

Shaved cheese: Shave Grana or semihard cheeses such as Pecorino with a vegetable peeler to make thin strips. These look lovely and melt into the sauce for added flavor. They are especially becoming on tomato sauces or on rustic pasta dishes such as penne with sausage sauce or pasta with broccoli.

Bread crumbs: Use with fish and vegetable sauces and on baked pastas.

Croutons: Homemade garlic or herb-flavored croutons are a natural on brothy fish pastas and summer tomato sauces.

Caviar: This special garnish is perfect for seafood ravioli or any other simple but elegant pasta and fish dish, such as tagliatelle dressed with lobster or scallops. A sprinkling of sevruga or osetra caviar is heaven on a dish of fresh egg pasta tossed with poached oysters and cream, but it's also superb on spaghetti dressed with olive oil and garlic or chopped summer herbs. Tagliatelle with fresh or smoked salmon looks very elegant finished with a scattering of bright pink salmon roe.

Pasta with Fall and Winter Vegetables: Cold-Weather Cooking

The vegetable color palate changes dramatically at summer's end—from the bright, dark, and clear to the burnished. Your mind-set starts to change too—away from quick and fresh cooking to slow, simmered, nurtured dishes. Maybe it takes a little more time and tinkering to compose tantalizing pasta sauces from hard-skinned squashes, nuts, leeks, and cooked greens, but the resulting flavors are deep and rewarding.

In fall and winter I am seduced by the cooking of northern Italy, in which pumpkin, braised kale, and cabbage are used to make stuffings and sauces for pasta. You can braise or roast Belgian endive or radicchio with onions and classic Italian seasonings such as anchovies, garlic, and capers to create sauces for pasta or a flavor base for layering into lasagne. Fall mushrooms are abundant and make glorious pasta sauces. Many winter vegetables may seem too starchy to pair with pasta, but pasta cooked with potatoes, lentils, or beans is standard Italian comfort food. Don't overlook simplicity just because it's winter. Try pasta sauces that are all onion, for example, or nothing but celery or baked fennel. Highlighting a seemingly mundane winter staple is a good way to discover its neglected charms and to experience, for instance, what a leek really tastes like.

Canned and sun-dried tomatoes can be cooked with shallots, dark, rich olive oil, and black olives to produce a winter version of pasta with tomato sauce—a very different sauce from its summer counterpart, but one with its own multilayered taste. You'll find that the liquid you're left with after soaking dried mushrooms is a real flavor booster. And you'll be reaching more for anchovies, pancetta, shallots, heavy cream, and reduced wine than for fresh herbs. But that's the way it should be.

I've arranged these cold-weather dishes by vegetable, trying to group recipes with similar ingredients to illustrate how they can be cooked in different ways to achieve different results.

Farfalle with a Soffritto of Fennel and Parsnips

A soffritto, used as a base for many sauces (page 31), stands alone here. Softening and browning the vegetables gives them a complex, sweet flavor.

[Makes 4 main-course or 6 first-course servings]

Olive oil

Unsalted butter

3 medium parsnips, peeled and cut in small dice

1 large onion, cut in small dice

1 large fennel bulb, trimmed, cored, and cut in small dice (save and chop the feathery tops)

4 tender inner celery stalks, cut in small dice (save and chop the leaves)

About ½ teaspoon fennel seeds

Salt

Freshly ground black pepper

1 or 2 garlic cloves, finely minced

1 pound farfalle

A large handful of flat-leaf parsley leaves, chopped

Freshly grated Grana Padano cheese

- In a large skillet, heat about 2 tablespoons each of olive oil and butter. Add the parsnips, onion, diced fennel, diced celery, and fennel seeds. Season well with salt and pepper and sauté over medium-low heat, stirring often, until the mixture is soft and just starting to brown, about 25 minutes. If it is browning too fast, turn the heat down. At the last minute, add the garlic and sauté until it just begins to give off aroma. Add a splash of warm water to the skillet to loosen the sauce slightly.
- Cook the farfalle until al dente. Drain well and add to the skillet. Over low heat, mix the pasta into the sauce. Add more olive oil or butter if needed to coat the pasta. Add the fennel tops, celery leaves, and parsley and toss well. Sprinkle with cheese and serve hot.

Ideas

Experiment with a mix of parsnips and carrots or parsnips and butternut squash. Or substitute leeks for the fennel for a great pasta sauce.

Sage, thyme, and winter savory all go well with parsnips.

A splash of sweet vermouth or Marsala, added after the vegetables are browned and cooked out, boosts the natural sweetness of this vegetable combination.

Tubetti with Celery, Potatoes, and Hot Green Pepper Sauce

My mother always made pasta and beans with a huge amount of celery. We always ate the dish with plenty of dried red pepper flakes. I really like the mix of mild, fragrant celery with something spicy, and here I've added jalapeño peppers. I cut the celery the same size as the pasta for a handsome, uniform look. You can make this without the potatoes, but I love the body and texture they add.

[Makes 4 main-course or 6 first-course servings]

2 medium baking potatoes, peeled and cut in small dice

Olive oil

Tender inner stalks from 1 large bunch of celery (save tough outer stalks for soup), cut in small dice (about 1 cup), plus the leaves, coarsely chopped

About 10 scallions, cut in thin rounds, with some of the green

2 garlic cloves, finely minced

1 jalapeño pepper, seeded and finely minced

Salt

1 pound tubetti

A handful of flat-leaf parsley leaves, coarsely chopped

- Set up a large pot of salted water to cook the pasta and bring it to a boil. Drop in the potatoes and cook until just tender, about 4 minutes. Remove with a strainer.
- In a large skillet, heat about 3 tablespoons olive oil over medium heat. Add the diced celery stalks and the scallions and sauté until tender and fragrant, about 8 minutes. Add the garlic, jalapeño, and potatoes. Season with salt and sauté a minute or two longer, just until the garlic and jalapeño release their fragrances and the potatoes are fork tender.
- Cook the tubetti until al dente, drain, and add to the sauté pan. Add the parsley and celery leaves and a generous drizzle of olive oil. Over low heat, sauté lightly, just to coat the pasta with sauce and release flavor from the herbs. Taste for seasoning. Serve very hot, without cheese.

Ideas

This is a perfect spicy base for all types of shellfish. Cook a few dozen clams or mussels in a large pot with a small wine glass of dry white wine until they open. Shuck the shellfish, strain the cooking broth, and add both to the just-cooked celery sauce.

Chop a few anchovies and add them toward the end of the cooking so they don't burn.

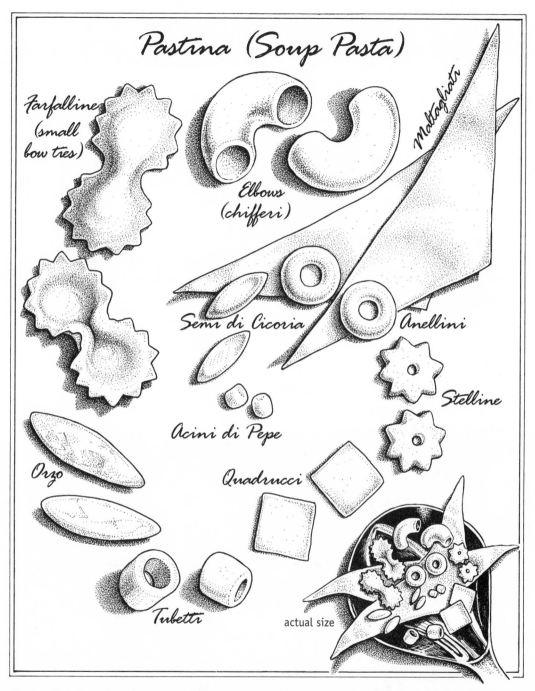

Pastina (Soup Pasta)

Farfalline (small bow ties)

Elbows (chifferi)

Mattagliati

Semi di Cicoria

Anellini

Stelline

Acini di Pepe

Orzo

Quadrucci

Tubetti

actual size

Pastina, *little pasta* in Italian, are tiny shapes (often scaled-down versions of big pasta) that make perfect additions to homemade broth. Tubetti or elbows, slightly sturdier little pasta shapes, are traditional in pasta and bean soups. Orzo and acini di pepe are excellent in a spring vegetable soup or added to an American-style chicken soup.

Baked Spinach Tagliatelle with Endive, Leeks, and Prosciutto Cotto

Endive and Radicchio Add Pleasant Bitterness to Pasta Sauces

The idea for this pasta came from a dish of baked endive wrapped in ham I cooked from a recipe in an Italian food magazine.

[Makes 4 main-course or 6 first-course servings]

4 leeks, cleaned, white part sliced in
    thin strips
Olive oil
4 large Belgian endives, cored and sliced
    lengthwise in thin strips
Salt
Freshly ground black pepper
A generous squeeze of fresh lemon juice
A few gratings of nutmeg
About ½ cup homemade Mixed-Meat
    Broth (page 375) or Chicken Broth
    (page 374)

1 cup heavy cream
¼ pound thinly sliced prosciutto cotto
    or another high-quality cooked ham,
    cut in thin strips
A handful of flat-leaf parsley leaves,
    coarsely chopped
1 pound Green Pasta (page 367), cut for
    tagliatelle
About 1 cup freshly grated Grana
    Padano cheese

- Preheat the oven to 425°F.
- In a large skillet, sauté the leeks in a few tablespoons olive oil over medium heat until soft and tender, about 5 minutes. Add the endive and sauté a minute or two, just to release the flavor. Season with salt and pepper and add the lemon juice and nutmeg. Add enough chicken broth to allow the endive to simmer gently until soft, about 5 minutes. Add the cream and let it simmer and cook down, about 5 minutes more. Add the ham and parsley and mix well. Taste for seasoning, adding a few grindings of black pepper.
- Cook the tagliatelle, leaving it slightly underdone. Drain well.
- Choose a wide, shallow baking dish (I use a 13 x 6 x 2-inch oval) that will allow the pasta to bake quickly and form a crust. Mix the tagliatelle with the endive sauce, adding a large handful (about ½ cup) of grated cheese as you toss it. Taste for seasoning. Spoon the pasta into the baking dish and top with a generous sprinkling of cheese. Bake, uncovered, until the top is browned and the sauce is bubbling, about 15 minutes. Let stand a few minutes before serving. The pasta should remain loose and creamy beneath a crisp cheese crust.

Ideas

This loose, unstructured baked pasta is a bit different in texture from the rather firm (translate overcooked) dishes I remember eating in Italian restaurants as a kid. Any tomato, cream, or ragù sauce can be transformed into a baked pasta by giving it a little body and a good crust. The easiest way to do this is by tossing it with cheese that will melt and help hold the thing together. A good crust can be made with grated cheese, bread crumbs (see page 340), or a mix of both. Cook baked pasta dishes in a 425°F oven for 15 to 20 minutes so they heat quickly and the top develops a nice crust.

AUTHENTIC ITALIAN PASTA: EVEN ITALIANS TAMPER WITH TRADITION

*I*taly has a long history of pairing certain sauces with certain pastas, and there are writers, home cooks, chefs, and historians who make it their life's work to cook and record these classic couplings, helping to keep them alive. In Emilia-Romagna cappellacci are always stuffed with sweet squash. In Genoa pesto sauce is served with trenette, a long, thick pasta, or gnocchi—and rarely anything else. It's comforting to see regional traditions upheld.

The first time I had smoked salmon with pasta, however, was not on Long Island but in Florence. The first time I had French goat cheese in ravioli was in Rome. Chefs in Italy do create new dishes and thereby influence American chefs. My approach here is to keep the ingredients and the finished dishes recognizably Italian. I do make reference to Provençal flavors, because that cooking is Italian in spirit. When you bring together olive oil, garlic, and tomatoes, you may well be reminded of something you ate in Nice or cooked from a southern French cookbook.

Looking through the cooking magazines of Italy, you will find all sorts of maverick pasta dishes—penne with zucchini blossoms and American bacon, for instance. Sometimes I get ideas for pasta dishes by paying attention to the way Italian restaurant chefs put together antipasto or first-course dishes. Appetizers tend to translate well into pasta sauces. A mussel and cannellini-bean salad I ate in a restaurant in New York made the transition to pasta easily. I made the same salad, adding white wine to loosen the sauce, and tossed it with orecchiette. Even though tradition runs strong in Italian regional cooking, everyone wants new dishes, and everyone improvises. So don't feel that you're destroying, feel that you're adding to a cuisine so rich and secure that it can't be intimidated but only flattered by tinkerers like you.

Garganelli with Roasted Radicchio, Anchovies, and Black Olives

I frequently make this dish without pasta, as a side dish or first course. With pasta, it is one of my favorites.

[Makes 4 main-course or 6 first-course servings]

Olive oil

3 medium heads round radicchio (see Note), cored and cut in thick strips

3 or 4 garlic cloves, very thinly sliced

Salt

Freshly ground black pepper

10 anchovy fillets, chopped, or 6 whole salt-packed anchovies, rinsed, filleted, and chopped

A large handful of oil-cured black olives, pitted (I use Gaeta)

½ cup homemade Chicken Broth (page 374) or low-salt canned

About ½ cup toasted bread crumbs (see page 340)

1 pound garganelli (or penne or fusilli)

A few marjoram sprigs, leaves chopped

- Choose a large skillet fitted with a lid. It should be large enough to hold the pasta and radicchio. Heat about 4 tablespoons olive oil over medium heat. Add the radicchio and garlic and season very lightly with salt and more generously with black pepper. Sauté until the radicchio starts to wilt and the garlic gives off aroma, 3 or 4 minutes. The color will start to change from a bright pink to a dark burgundy. Stir in the anchovies and olives. Add the chicken broth, cover the pan, and cook until the radicchio is soft and tender, about 5 minutes.

- In a small sauté pan, heat about 1 tablespoon olive oil. Add the toasted bread crumbs, season with salt and pepper, and sauté over medium heat until lightly toasted, about 2 minutes.

- Cook the garganelli until al dente, drain well, and add to the radicchio. Sprinkle with the marjoram and toss over low heat, adding more olive oil if needed to coat the pasta. Check the seasoning (it probably won't need extra salt because of the anchovies and the olives). Transfer to a large serving bowl and top with the toasted bread crumbs.

A note about radicchio: The common tight, round heads of radicchio found in most U.S. markets are known in Italy as radicchio di Chioggia, and this is what I use for this recipe. I've also made pasta dishes using a long-leafed variety call radicchio di Treviso, which appears in some Italian markets in the winter. While all radicchio is enjoyed for its slight bitterness, the Treviso variety has a slightly sweet edge to it, making the flavor a bit more complex and interesting, especially when cooked. If you can find this type, substitute about 5 medium bunches of it for the Chioggia variety.

Ideas

Radicchio is a member of the chicory family, which also includes endive, chicory, frisée, and escarole. All these vegetables have a gentle bitterness that is pleasantly heightened by cooking. And they're all good in pasta sauce.

Small cubes of fresh mozzarella tossed into the serving bowl and allowed to melt into the pasta are delicious.

Another excellent radicchio-based pasta sauce I sometimes make includes cooked cannellini beans. Add a cup of tender, cooked white beans to this dish, along with about ½ cup of the bean cooking water in place of the chicken broth. Omit the anchovies and olives, but keep the marjoram, which goes beautifully with white beans. Also try sautéed radicchio finished with a handful of toasted walnuts and about ½ cup crème fraîche. Sprinkle the finished dish with grated Grana Padano or a mild Pecorino.

Ziti with Roasted Garlic and Butternut Squash

A Sauce with Fall Colors

The butternut squash here cooks into a rough purée that adds body to the sweet sauce. Fresh sage and roasted garlic add depth of flavor. The result would work nicely, I think, as a first course before a Thanksgiving turkey.

[Makes 4 main-course or 6 first-course servings]

3 heads of garlic

Unsalted butter

Olive oil

1 large butternut squash (about 1½ pounds), peeled, seeded, and cut in small cubes

Salt

Freshly ground black pepper

1 bay leaf

A few gratings of nutmeg

Zest of 1 large orange

1 cup homemade Chicken Broth (page 374) or low-salt canned

About 2 heaping tablespoons crème fraîche

About 6 fresh sage leaves, cut in thin strips

About 6 large flat-leaf parsley sprigs, leaves coarsely chopped

1 pound ziti

About ½ cup freshly grated Grana Padano cheese

- Preheat the oven to 400°F.
- Wrap the garlic heads together in a large sheet of aluminum foil and squeeze the top to seal it. Roast until soft and fragrant, about ½ hour.
- Meanwhile, heat about 2 tablespoons each of butter and olive oil in a large skillet over medium heat. Add the squash, season with salt and pepper, and sauté a few minutes to lightly caramelize the surface of the cubes. Add the bay leaf, nutmeg, orange zest, and chicken broth, cover the pan, and cook until the squash is just tender but still holding its shape, about 8 minutes. At this point, most of the broth will have been absorbed, but you should have a few tablespoons left to form your sauce. Add the crème fraîche, sage, and parsley. Mix well and taste for seasoning.
- Start cooking the ziti.
- Slice off the root ends and squeeze the garlic from the roasted heads into a bowl. Mash it to form a paste, adding about a tablespoon of pasta cooking water to give it a creamy consistency.

- When the ziti are al dente, drain them and transfer them to a large serving bowl. Add the roasted garlic paste and the Grana Padano. Toss. Add the squash sauce, a bit of fresh black pepper, and a drizzle of olive oil and toss again. Check for seasoning.

Ideas

You can puree this sauce in a food processor, adding the herbs at the end so they don't become too finely chopped. A good pasta for this purée is fusilli, which will allow the thick, smooth sauce to cling to it.

Substitute about 4 medium leeks, thinly sliced, for the roasted garlic (sauté them along with the squash). For this, contemplate using Plain Egg Pasta (page 364) or Herb Pasta flavored with sage (page 368).

Rosemary is an herb often paired with winter squash and can replace the sage (use very little, a few small sprigs only).

An altogether different flavoring for winter squash or pumpkin—this one borrowed from Sicilian cooking—is fresh mint, a splash of vinegar, and hot red pepper flakes. If you would like to make this, sauté squash cubes in olive oil and garlic. Add a splash of red wine vinegar and a few red pepper flakes. Pour in enough chicken broth or water to allow the squash to simmer until tender and absorb most of the liquid. Add chopped fresh mint leaves and toss with cooked penne or ziti.

Pappardelle with Duxelles, Cognac, and Walnuts

Two Mushroom Sauces with Different Tastes

Duxelles were the first thing I learned to make in cooking school. This finely diced sauté of mushrooms also makes a delicious pasta sauce. I've added walnuts to the sauce—an idea I picked up from chef Daniel Boulud, who uses this flavor combination in several of the mushroom dishes served at his New York restaurant, Restaurant Daniel.

[Makes 4 main-course or 6 first-course servings]

Unsalted butter

Olive oil

1 pound mixed fresh mushrooms (porcini, chanterelle, oyster, hedgehog, cremini, portobello, or white button), stemmed and cut in small dice (save stems for a quick mushroom broth)

4 shallots, finely chopped (save peels for mushroom broth)

2 garlic cloves, finely minced (save skins for mushroom broth)

A handful of flat-leaf parsley leaves, chopped (save stems for mushroom broth)

About 3 small thyme sprigs, stemmed, leaves chopped (save stems for mushroom broth)

Salt

Freshly ground black pepper

½ cup walnuts, roughly chopped

A generous splash of cognac

1 pound Plain Egg Pasta (page 364), cut for pappardelle

About 1 cup freshly grated Parmigiano-Reggiano cheese

- To make the mushroom broth, heat 1 tablespoon each of butter and olive oil in a medium saucepan over medium heat. Add the mushroom stems, shallot and garlic skins, and herb stems and sauté a minute just to release their flavors. Add cold water just to cover and bring to a boil. Turn the heat to low and simmer, uncovered, for about 30 minutes. Strain. Season with salt and pepper.
- In a large skillet, heat 1 tablespoon butter and 2 tablespoons olive oil over medium heat. Add the shallots and walnuts and sauté until the shallots are tender and the

walnuts are lightly toasted and give off a good nut smell, about 4 minutes. Add the garlic and sauté until it gives off aroma, about 1 minute. Add the mushrooms, season with salt and pepper, and sauté until they just start to give off some liquid, about 5 minutes. Add the cognac and let it bubble a minute to cook out the alcohol. Add about ½ cup of the mushroom broth and simmer over low heat, uncovered, until the mushrooms are very tender and the sauce has thickened, about 5 minutes. Add the herbs. Taste for seasoning.

- Cook the pappardelle until tender and drain well. Transfer to a large serving bowl. Add a tablespoon each of olive oil and butter and a small handful of the grated Parmigiano-Reggiano. Toss. Add the duxelles and toss again. Serve the remaining grated cheese at the table.

Ideas

A finely chopped sauté of mushrooms makes a delicious filling for ravioli or cannelloni. To use as a filling, omit the mushroom broth from the recipe and add about ½ cup untoasted bread crumbs (see page 340) and 1 large egg. Mix well and let cool before filling your pasta.

I love a tablespoon or two of Gorgonzola dolce or Taleggio cheese melted into this mushroom sauce at the last minute. When the sauce is finished, turn off the heat, add the cheese, and stir until melted and well mixed.

Cutting the mushrooms in thick slices gives the sauce an entirely different, more robust character, suitable for a sturdy pasta such as ziti or rigatoni.

Fusilli Lunghi with Mushrooms, Black Olives, and Anchovies

This is a version of a fall pasta dish I enjoyed at a Jewish restaurant in Rome. The dish was deep, haunting, and delicious. I thought I detected rosemary in the sauce, so I've added some here.

[Makes 4 main-course or 6 first-course servings]

A handful of dried porcini mushrooms (about ½ cup), soaked in warm water to cover

Olive oil

3 garlic cloves, minced

About 6 anchovy fillets

About ½ pound cremini mushrooms, stemmed and thickly sliced

Freshly ground black pepper

A splash of dry white wine

One 35-ounce can plum tomatoes, drained and chopped

A generous handful of pitted black olives, cut in half (I use Niçoise)

A few small rosemary sprigs, leaves chopped

1 pound fusilli lunghi

Salt, if needed

- Lift the porcini mushrooms from their soaking liquid and slice them thin. Strain the soaking liquid through a fine-mesh strainer and save.
- In a large skillet, heat a few tablespoons of olive oil over medium heat. Add the garlic, anchovies, and cremini mushrooms and sauté just until the garlic gives off aroma and the mushrooms start to soften. Season with black pepper. Don't add any salt yet; aside from all the anchovies you've just added, you'll be adding olives soon, so it's best to judge saltiness at the end of cooking. Add the white wine and let it boil away to nothing.
- Add the tomatoes to the sauce, along with the porcini and about ½ cup of the strained soaking liquid. Cook, uncovered, over medium heat until the sauce thickens a bit, about 5 minutes. Add the black olives and rosemary. Check the seasoning.
- Cook the fusilli lunghi until al dente, drain, and add to the pan. Toss well for a minute over low heat to coat the pasta. Transfer to a large serving bowl.

Ideas

Mixing dried porcini with a mild cultivated mushroom is standard practice to produce a rich mushroom sauce when you cannot find fresh wild mushrooms at the market. If you can find fresh porcini mushrooms (imported from Italy or domestic), use them in place of this mix of fresh and dried.

With thick, chunky sauces, I sometimes like to toss the cooked pasta with olive oil and then pour the sauce on top, letting my guests mix in the sauce themselves. Naked pasta peeking out from a mass of chunky sauce can be a surprisingly lovely sight.

I actually like this sauce as much without any mushrooms at all. What results is a light tomato sauce flavored with anchovies and black olives.

If the combination of mushrooms and anchovies doesn't appeal to you, substitute 3 thin slices of chopped pancetta or a little prosciutto fat for the anchovies. Sauté it until crisp before adding the garlic. This will give your tomato base some backbone.

Onion and Marsala Sauce for Baked Ziti

An All-Onion Sauce for Pasta

This sauce, basically all onions, illustrates the Italian respect for unadulterated flavors. It is uncomplex but can be elaborated on without losing its simple charm.

[Makes 4 main-course or 6 first-course servings]

4 large sweet onions, such as Vidalia or
    Walla Walla, thinly sliced

2 or 3 whole thyme sprigs

Olive oil

Salt

Freshly ground black pepper

A generous pinch of ground nutmeg

A pinch of ground allspice

½ cup dry Marsala

½ cup Mixed-Meat Broth (page 375)

About 2 tablespoons unsalted butter

1 cup toasted bread crumbs
    (see page 340)

1 pound ziti

About 1 cup freshly grated Parmigiano-
    Reggiano cheese

- In a large skillet, sauté the onions with the thyme sprigs in about ⅓ cup olive oil over low heat (you need more than enough oil to coat the bottom of the pan, because the onions must cook a long time without burning). Season with salt and pepper and let the onions cook slowly for about 30 minutes, stirring occasionally, until soft and a light golden brown. Add the nutmeg, allspice, and Marsala to the pan and cook until the onions are almost dry. Add the meat broth and butter and let the sauce simmer for a minute or two over low heat. Remove the thyme sprigs.
- Preheat the oven to 425°F.
- Choose a large, relatively shallow baking dish (about 12 x 10 x 2 inches). Coat it lightly with olive oil and sprinkle with about 2 tablespoons of the bread crumbs, distributing them evenly to lightly coat the dish.
- Cook the ziti until al dente (leave the ziti a bit less tender than usual, remembering they will cook further in the oven). Drain and add them to the skillet with the onions. Add about ½ cup Parmigiano-Reggiano, toss well, and spoon into the casserole. Mix the remaining bread crumbs with the rest of the Parmigiano and sprinkle over the top of the ziti. Drizzle with olive oil and bake, uncovered, for about 20 minutes, or until the dish is bubbling and the top is nicely browned.

Ideas

Cooking onions in some sort of alcohol until they're tender and golden brown produces a rich and fragrant sauce. Here I've used Marsala, but sweet red vermouth will also work well. Remember to add the alcohol and let it boil away to burn off the raw alcohol taste, then add a light broth to mellow and round out the sauce.

This all-onion sauce looks and tastes wonderful if you accent it with bits of vegetable. Peas with onions is an Italian classic. Add about ¾ cup fresh peas to the pasta cooking water during the last minute of cooking the pasta. Drain them along with the cooked pasta and toss with the onions. You can also include roasted red pepper chunks or blanched asparagus tips. My favorite addition is a handful of pitted black olives tossed into the onions after they've finished cooking.

WHICH DRIED PASTA SHOULD I BUY?

*P*eople ask me this question all the time, and I always say, "Buy Italian." This might seem just snobbish, but I do find a textural difference, no matter what brand. American brands are designed to cook up softer, supposedly because Americans like their pasta soft. The technology and machinery are imported from Italy, and our wheat is superb, so there's no reason why our pasta can't be almost identical—except the big American companies choose not to make it that way. So if you want dried pasta with good texture and flavor, choose an Italian brand. Of course, even the Italian brands vary in quality. I prefer dried pasta made by the smaller southern Italian companies, which still use slow-drying, old-fashioned methods. For more on these artisanal brands of pasta, see "The Improviser's Pantry," page 350.

Tubetti Soup with Kale, Potatoes, Lemon Zest, and Rosemary

Two Pastas with Cooked Greens

My grandfather worked as a golf pro in Westchester, New York, and at some point the family lived near the course where he worked. My grandmother was a well-assimilated Italian American who nonetheless felt compelled, possibly by her peasant heritage, to collect soup greens, mostly dandelion weeds, from the golf course, gathering them up in a bulging apron. She made great pasta soups loaded with greens and studded with chunks of Italian sausage. Here is my version of one of her wonderful soups.

[Makes 4 main-course or 6 first-course servings]

A few tablespoons olive oil

1 medium red onion, cut in small dice

5 or 6 scallions, cut in thin rounds, with some of the tender green

3 shallots, minced

½ pound garlic sausage (the French *saucisson à l'ail*), skinned and cut in very small cubes

A large bunch of kale, trimmed and coarsely chopped

5 or 6 small red new potatoes, cut in small chunks

Zest of 2 lemons (see Note)

A few small rosemary sprigs, leaves chopped

Salt

Freshly ground black pepper

About 6 cups homemade Mixed-Meat Broth (page 375) or Chicken Broth (page 374)

About 1 cup tubetti, cooked until al dente and tossed with a little olive oil

Freshly grated Sicilian Pecorino cheese

- In a large soup pot, heat the olive oil over medium heat. Add the onion, scallions, shallots, and garlic sausage and cook until the sausage is lightly browned and the onion is soft. Add the kale, potatoes, lemon zest, and rosemary, season with salt and pepper, and sauté a few minutes. Add the broth and bring to a boil. Turn the heat to medium and cook at a lively simmer until the potatoes and greens are tender, about 20 minutes.
- Stir in the pasta. Check the seasoning. Serve hot or at room temperature. Top each bowl with a sprinkling of the grated Pecorino.

A note on lemon zest: Lemon zest is a chef's secret for brightening up dull sauces. A little goes a long way. The zest from one lemon is usually enough to enliven a sauce meant for 1 pound of pasta. Too much can make a sauce bitter, especially if you dig up too much of the white pith while grating. That is the most bitter part.

Ideas

A type of kale known in Tuscany as *cavolo nero* (black cabbage) is now being grown in the United States, usually by the name of black or Tuscan kale. It is long, dark, and leafy and has an earthy taste somewhere between cabbage and kale. If you find it, use it in this soup. It also makes a great pasta sauce when sautéed in olive oil with garlic and finished with a splash of white wine.

Lemon with rosemary is one of my favorite combinations, and I've used it to flavor this soup. Other good accents for kale are bacon, garlic, a touch of cream, or a splash of good vinegar.

Orecchiette with Chicory, Bacon, Walnuts, and Capers

The inspiration for this pasta dish comes from a French bistro salad. I've replaced the toasted croutons with pasta. The result is a sophisticated mix of flavors using rustic ingredients.

[Makes 4 main-course or 6 first-course servings]

2 medium heads of chicory, trimmed, washed, and roughly chopped

About 2 tablespoons olive oil

2 slices slab bacon, thinly sliced and chopped

1 large red onion, peeled and cut in small dice

3 garlic cloves, thinly sliced

About ½ cup walnuts, roughly chopped

Salt

Freshly ground black pepper

About ½ cup capers, rinsed

About ½ cup homemade Chicken Broth (page 374)

1 pound orecchiette

Freshly shaved Fiore Sardo cheese

- Set up a large pot of salted water to cook the pasta. Bring to a boil and add the chicory. Blanch for 2 minutes, then lift from the water with a large strainer. Rinse the chicory under cold water to preserve its color and drain well, squeezing it to remove excess water.
- In a large skillet, heat the olive oil over medium heat. Add the chopped bacon and cook until almost crisp (if you have too much oil in your pan at this point, drain some off, making sure to leave at least a tablespoon or so to ensure a good sauce to coat the pasta). Add the onion and sauté until soft. Stir in the garlic and walnuts and sauté 1 minute to release their flavors. Add the blanched chicory and sauté 1 minute to blend all the flavors. Season with salt and a generous amount of pepper. Add the capers and chicken broth and let the sauce simmer over low heat while the pasta is cooking.
- Cook the orecchiette until al dente, drain, and add them to the skillet. Sauté briefly to mix all the flavors and to coat the pasta well with sauce. Top with the shavings of cheese.

Ideas

Chicory can be seasoned in many ways to produce highly flavored, rustic pasta sauces. I love it blanched and then briefly sautéed in olive oil with garlic and hot pepper flakes. Or try the popular combination of pine nuts and raisins. Another direction is to add anchovies, garlic, and capers.

Whimsical Shapes

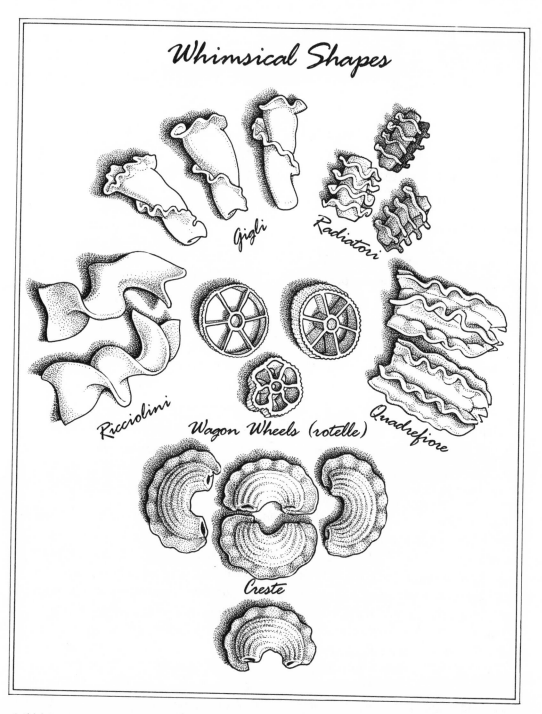

Gigli

Radiatori

Ricciolini

Wagon Wheels (rotelle)

Quadrefiore

Creste

A thick tomato sauce enriched with ricotta clings perfectly to the little openings of rotelle or radiatori. Vegetable purées made from roasted peppers or asparagus are another excellent choice. A soffritto of finely diced mixed seasonal vegetables briefly sautéed in olive oil and herbs enhances these curvy, sensuous shapes.

Cavatappi with Cabbage and Kidney Beans

Two Pasta and Bean Dishes

Having had my head for the most part in southern Italian cooking, but wanting to incorporate more northern ingredients into my repertoire, I came up with this winter dish. Braised cabbage and beans make excellent cold-weather eating.

[Makes 4 main-course or 6 first-course servings]

1 cup dried kidney beans, soaked overnight in cold water to cover if very dry (see page 339)

1 large onion, cut in medium dice (save trimmings to cook with the beans)

A few whole garlic cloves, crushed

A few thyme sprigs

Salt

Olive oil

3 thin slices of pancetta, cut in small dice (see Note)

2 or 3 garlic cloves, finely minced

2 juniper berries, crushed

2 tablespoons unsalted butter

1 small Savoy cabbage, cored and thinly sliced

Freshly ground black pepper

A tiny splash of sherry vinegar

1 pound cavatappi

Asiago cheese, shaved into thin slices with a vegetable peeler

- Place the beans in a large pot and add cold water to cover them by about 3 inches. Add the onion trimmings, a few lightly crushed whole garlic cloves, a few thyme sprigs, or whatever aromatic vegetables or herbs you might have on hand. Bring to a boil. Turn the heat to low and simmer, covered, at least an hour, probably longer, depending on the beans. Add salt about halfway through the cooking. The beans should be tender to the bite but still hold their shape. Drain the beans, reserving all the cooking liquid. Remove all the flavoring vegetables and herbs from the beans and discard.
- In a flameproof casserole or large skillet, heat about a tablespoon of olive oil over medium heat. Add the pancetta and cook until crisp, 3 or 4 minutes. Add the onion and sauté until soft. Add the minced garlic, juniper berries, butter, and the cabbage. Season lightly with salt and pepper and sauté, stirring often, until the cabbage has started to wilt, about 5 minutes. Add the sherry vinegar and let it cook out. Add enough bean cooking liquid to cover the cabbage about halfway. Simmer, uncovered, stirring occasionally, until the cab-

bage is tender and the liquid has reduced by about half, at least 20 minutes. Add the beans to the pan. Check the seasoning. Let the sauce simmer a few minutes over low heat while the pasta is cooking.

- Cook the cavatappi until al dente, drain, and place in a large warmed serving bowl. Add the cabbage sauce and toss. If the sauce seems dry, add a little more of the bean cooking liquid. Add a small handful of shaved Asiago, toss briefly, and serve.

A note on cooking pancetta: If the pancetta is very fatty, I start cooking it first and don't add oil to the pan. If it looks fairly lean, I'll add the onion or other soffritto base along with it, plus a bit of oil or butter. The reason is that pancetta needs to render its fat, which may take a while, and you don't want the other vegetables, such as onions, leeks, garlic, and celery, to burn while you're waiting for the pancetta to crisp up.

Ideas

I've experimented with various types of cabbage in combination with pasta and found I like the crinkly, thin-leaf Savoy cabbage best because its flavor doesn't overwhelm pasta. The smooth, thick-leaf green and red cabbages take longer to cook and are a bit too strongly flavored when matched with pasta.

Cabbage can be seasoned in various ways to produce robust wintry pasta sauces. Try a mix of cabbage, anchovies, garlic, and thyme tossed with penne. I also like cabbage with rosemary, tomato, and prosciutto.

For a more robust flavor, braise the cabbage in veal or beef stock.

A traditional pasta dish from the Valtellina region of nothern Italy combines cabbage with string beans and sometimes potatoes. Substitute a handful of chopped blanched string beans for the kidney beans used in this recipe. Cook them in the pasta water and add them to the cabbage at the last minute. You can also add blanched potatoes instead of the beans.

A few slices of braised cotechino sausage cut in cubes and sautéed with the cabbage are a hearty addition.

Fresh Neapolitan Pasta with Chickpeas, Celery, and Carrots

My family made pasta and beans in several different styles. Sometimes they combined tubetti and cannellini beans in a celery-scented tomato sauce and sometimes they made a similar sauce without the tomatoes. But I also remember a dish our neighbor made with chickpeas and fresh short pasta in a brothy sauce. Its lightness intrigued me. Here is my updated version.

[Makes 4 main-course or 6 first-course servings]

For the beans:

1 cup dried chickpeas *(ceci),* soaked
    overnight in cold water to cover
1 tablespoon olive oil
A few garlic cloves, smashed
A few leek trimmings
1 tough outer celery stalk
1 carrot, roughly chopped
1 bay leaf
Marjoram stems
2 cloves
A few black peppercorns
Salt

For the sauce:

About 3 tablespoons olive oil
A small chunk of prosciutto fat or fresh
    salt pork
3 medium leeks, cleaned, white part cut
    in small dice
3 tender inner celery stalks, thinly sliced,
    plus celery leaves, chopped

2 small carrots, cut in small dice
2 garlic cloves, thinly sliced
A few marjoram sprigs, leaves chopped
A splash of dry white wine
4 plum tomatoes, peeled, seeded, and
    cut in small dice
Salt
Freshly ground black pepper

For the pasta:

1 pound Plain Egg Pasta (page 364),
    cut as for tagliatelle but
    shorter, in 3- to 4-inch lengths
    (see Note)
A few flat-leaf parsley sprigs,
    eaves chopped
Olive oil
About 1 cup freshly grated Pecorino
    Toscano cheese

- Drain the beans. Place all the bean-cooking ingredients except the salt in a large pot with the beans. (You can wrap up the herbs and spices in a bouquet garni, but I enjoy picking the loose herbs out of the cooked beans). Add cold water to cover the beans by about 3 inches. Bring to a boil, cover, turn the heat to low, and simmer until the beans are tender. This can vary wildly, especially with chickpeas, which can be very dry and hard, so taste them every once in a while. Expect them to cook for at least an hour and a half. Salt the beans about halfway through the cooking. Drain the beans, saving the cooking liquid. Discard the vegetables, herbs, and spices.
- To make the sauce, heat the olive oil in a large skillet over medium heat. Add the chunk of prosciutto or salt pork, the leeks, the celery and celery leaves, and the carrots and sauté over medium heat until the vegetables are tender and fragrant, about 5 minutes. Add the garlic and marjoram and sauté a minute longer, just to release their flavors. Add the wine and let it boil away to nothing. Add the tomatoes, season with salt and pepper, and sauté about 2 minutes. Add the chickpeas and about ½ cup of the bean cooking liquid. Let the sauce simmer a few minutes while the pasta is cooking. Taste for seasoning. Remove the salt pork or prosciutto.
- Cook the pasta until tender, drain, and transfer to a large warmed serving bowl. Add the bean sauce, parsley, and a drizzle of fresh olive oil. Toss. Serve with Pecorino Toscano or another mild Pecorino at the table.

A note about the traditional pasta for this dish: In southern Italy chickpea sauce is usually served with laganelle (also called lagane in dialect). It is a short, fresh pasta made partly with semolina flour and no eggs. It is cut the same way I've recommended you cut the tagliatelle for this recipe. To make it, mix 1 cup unbleached white flour with 1 cup semolina flour, about ½ cup water, and a pinch of salt. Follow the directions for making Plain Egg Pasta (page 364).

Ideas

Another chickpea dish I remember my family making was a garlicky tomato sauce tossed with chickpeas, tubetti, and lots of red pepper flakes. A dish I sometimes make, although not a traditional one, is penne with chickpeas, pancetta, and a generous amount of caramelized onions. Another simple sauce can be made by sautéing the cooked chickpeas with garlic and fresh sage and loosening the sauce with cooking liquid.

All sorts of greens go very well with chickpea sauces. Try dropping dandelion or arugula into the boiling water along with the pasta, drain, and toss with the sauce.

For a creamier dish, puree half the chickpeas in a food processor along with about ½ cup of their cooking liquid. Add this to the skillet along with the whole chickpeas.

Vegetable Lasagne

In Italian cooking, lasagne is meant to be an elegant dish, usually made with thinly rolled egg pasta and one or two carefully chosen vegetables.

When constructing a vegetable lasagne in your head, think about one vegetable—mushroom, for instance—and then imagine seasonings you'd like with it—garlic maybe, possibly sage. Try to recall other mushroom dishes you've eaten and why you liked them. How were they seasoned? And then think about how you want to hold it together. Béchamel is traditional in the north and south; ricotta is a rich presence in many southern lasagne; other cheeses, such as fontina or Parmigiano-Reggiano, can also help give form to your dish. They are part of the classic lasagne construction. But many lighter, more modern approaches work equally well. You could make your lasagne with nothing but sautéed greens and pasta sheets. Or include a tomato sauce. Many lasagne are meant to be loose. Some are not even baked (the pasta sheets are simply boiled and then layered with a sauce). You won't go far wrong if you keep it simply but highly seasoned.

In my childhood I ate many lasagne dishes made from curly-edged dried lasagne, a contribution of Neapolitan immigrants. Every Italian American I knew used it, and the result, even though I had nothing at the time to compare it to, struck me as heavy. If you want to make a lasagne that has integrity, you need fresh egg pasta rolled very thin. This makes it a bit more difficult to handle, but the finished dish is worth it. So stretch the dough out a bit thinner than you would for making tagliatelle.

Many traditional Italian lasagne preparations can become elaborate, such as the classic lasagne for carnival from Naples. I love these dishes, bursting with meatballs, ragù, and hard-boiled eggs. But here I want to concentrate on a different type of lasagne, a simple one with purity of flavor, because this approach is just as Italian but less often cooked in this country. I've eaten lasagne layered with nothing but toasted bread crumbs and raisins or butter and poppy seeds.

Another way to come up with good ideas for a vegetable lasagne is to think of your favorite pasta sauces. I love sautéed eggplant with ricotta salata and tomato, tossed with penne. So I tried the same sauce layered in lasagne, and it made a lovely dish. I also like sautéed zucchini and onions as a lasagne filling.

I like my lasagne a little loose, so I've suggested baking it in high heat, covered for the first 15 minutes or so and then uncovered so it can brown. This way, not as much liquid evaporates and the pasta sheets stay firm and don't absorb too much sauce, becoming mushy.

These lasagne recipes are for a baking dish about 12 by 10 by 2 inches. I sometimes make lasagne in a long oval dish and let the uneven pasta ends hang over the edge. They get nicely browned, and I notice my guests like to pick them off and nibble on them when I bring the dish to the table.

A note on buying and cooking pasta sheets for lasagne:
I've found a shop in my neighborhood where I can buy lasagne sheets rolled very thin, and these work well (almost as well as homemade, in fact). If you purchase pasta sheets for lasagne, make sure to request that they be rolled extra thin.

I always boil fresh lasagne sheets before baking so that the finished pasta is light and the dish retains its moisture. Baking uncooked sheets results in a heavier, drier lasagne, because the slow cooking forces the pasta to soak up all the moisture from the filling.

Baking lasagne at a higher temperature, at least 425°F, is best because it cooks quickly, leaving the pasta firm (not mushy from long, slow cooking), the ingredients moist, and the sauce not too concentrated and thick.

Roasted Asparagus Lasagne with Fontina

Roasting Vegetables Intensifies Their Flavor in Lasagne

Asparagus roasted with butter and Parmigiano-Reggiano cheese is one of my favorite dishes. Here I've translated it into a simple lasagne with a Parmigiano cream sauce instead of the traditional béchamel. This version also includes fontina cheese, which provides even more flavor and just enough body to hold the dish together.

[Makes 4 main-course or 6 first-course servings]

About 2 pounds medium-thick asparagus, ends trimmed, stalks peeled, and cut in half

2 large Vidalia or Walla Walla onions, thinly sliced

Olive oil

Unsalted butter

Juice of 1 lemon

Zest of 1 lemon

Salt

Freshly ground black pepper

4 or 5 savory sprigs, leaves chopped

For the Parmigiano cream:

About ¾ cup freshly grated Parmigiano-Reggiano or Grana Padano cheese

1½ cups heavy cream

A few gratings of nutmeg

A handful of fresh chives, finely chopped

1 recipe Three-Egg Black Pepper Pasta (page 368) or Three-Egg Pasta (page 365), cut for lasagne

½ pound fontina cheese, thinly sliced or grated

- Preheat the oven to 450°F.
- Place the asparagus and onions on a large baking sheet. Drizzle with a few tablespoons of olive oil, dot with a few tablespoons of butter, and squeeze on the lemon juice. Scatter the lemon zest on top and season well with salt and pepper. Mix the vegetables well with your hands to make sure they're uniformly covered with all the seasonings. Bake until soft and just starting to brown, about 20 minutes. When they give off a concentrated, sweet asparagus aroma and are fork tender, they're ready. Sprinkle with the fresh savory.
- Lower the oven temperature to 425°F.
- In a small saucepan, stir the Parmigiano-Reggiano into the cream and mix well. Simmer gently over low heat until the cheese is melted and the sauce is fairly smooth (there will

always be a slight graininess to the sauce because of the texture of the cheese). Season with the nutmeg, black pepper, and a pinch of salt. Add the chives.

- Cook the lasagne sheets in a large pot of boiling salted water until tender (I usually do this in batches of 2 or 3 sheets). Drain and rinse with cold water. Lay the lasagne out in one layer on paper towels.
- Lightly coat a 12 x 10 x 2-inch baking dish with olive oil. Make a layer of pasta. Make a layer of asparagus and onion and top with a thin layer of grated or sliced fontina. Salt and pepper lightly. Add another layer of pasta and top with more asparagus, half of the Parmigiano cream, and another thin layer of fontina. Repeat until you use up the ingredients, ending with a layer of pasta. Pour the remaining Parmigiano cream on top, letting it run down the sides a bit.
- Cover the dish with aluminum foil and bake for about 20 minutes. Remove the foil and bake until the filling is bubbling and the top is golden, 15 to 20 minutes longer. Let stand about 5 minutes before cutting.

Ideas

Roasting intensifies the flavor of many vegetables. Eggplant slices, small chunks of butternut squash, sliced bell peppers, zucchini, leeks, tomatoes, or artichoke hearts can all be coated with olive oil (or a mix of oil and unsalted butter), roasted until browned and fragrant in a hot oven, and layered in a lasagne, either with just a few thin layers of grated cheese or with the Parmigiano cream and fontina used in this recipe.

Puree half the roasted asparagus, mixing it with half the Parmigiano cream. Use that in place of one roasted asparagus layer.

Lasagne with Basil-Almond Pesto and Béchamel

Pesto as a Filling for Lasagne

This is a variation on a basil pesto lasagne that is a specialty of Liguria, Italy. Thin lasagne sheets are cooked, layered with pesto and a sprinkling of Parmigiano-Reggiano cheese, and lightly baked. This makes an especially delicate and fragrant lasagne and was a revelation to me when I first tasted it. Here I've used a Sicilian pesto, which contains tomato and almonds in addition to fresh basil. I've also included a few thin layers of béchamel sauce, which gives this dish a beautiful, rather formal finish.

[Makes 4 main-course or 6 first-course servings]

For the pesto:

¾ cup blanched almonds, lightly toasted

2 garlic cloves, peeled

3 loosely packed cups basil leaves, washed and dried well

1 cup grated Parmigiano-Reggiano cheese

2 medium, ripe tomatoes (about 1 pound), peeled, seeded, and roughly chopped (if very juicy, drain for about 30 minutes)

About ½ cup olive oil

Salt

Freshly ground black pepper

For the béchamel:

3 tablespoons unsalted butter

¼ cup unbleached all-purpose flour

2 cups cold whole milk

1 bay leaf

A pinch of freshly grated nutmeg

A pinch of ground cloves

A pinch of cayenne pepper

Freshly ground black pepper

Salt

1 recipe Three-Egg Pasta (page 365), cut for lasagne

- To make the pesto, place the almonds in a food processor and grind to a chunky consistency. Add the garlic and basil and process to a very rough paste. Add the cheese (saving a small handful for the top of the lasagne) and tomatoes. Pour the olive oil in through the top tube and process until you have a thick paste. Leave the pesto with a slightly rough texture (when making pesto, I find I have more control over the finished texture if I use the pulse button). Season with salt and pepper.

- To make the béchamel, melt the butter in a large saucepan over medium heat. Add the flour and whisk until you have a smooth paste. Let it bubble and cook a few minutes to remove the raw flour taste. It should start to smell a bit sweet, like cake batter. Add the cold milk all at once and whisk to incorporate the flour. Add the bay leaf. Cook, whisking frequently, until the sauce just comes to a boil. It should be thick and smooth. Add the nutmeg, cloves, cayenne, black pepper, and salt and let the sauce simmer over low heat for about another 5 minutes, whisking often. Remove the bay leaf. Place a piece of plastic wrap over the surface to prevent a skin from forming.
- Preheat the oven to 425°F.
- Cook the lasagne sheets in batches. Remove from the water with a large strainer and run under cold water. Lay them out in a single layer on paper towels.
- Lightly coat a 12 x 10 x 2-inch baking dish with olive oil. Place a layer of lasagne sheets in the dish and spread them lightly with béchamel. Make another layer of lasagne and spread it more generously with pesto. Repeat until all the pasta is used up, ending with a layer of pasta covered with a thin layer of béchamel. Sprinkle the top with the reserved Parmigiano. Bake (see Note below), uncovered, for about 25 minutes, or until bubbling. The top should be golden brown.

Note: Since this is a thin lasagne, the cooking time is shorter than for other lasagne recipes in this section. And because it cooks quickly, it's not necessary to cover it at all during the cooking.

Ideas

Another way to make a pesto lasagne—the way it is often done in Genoa—is not to bake it at all. You simply layer hot lasagne sheets (don't run them under cold water) with pesto on a large serving platter. Top the lasagne with a sprinkling of Parmigiano-Reggiano cheese and a few toasted pine nuts and serve it right away. It's a free-form presentation, which is fresh tasting because the pesto remains uncooked.

Other types of pesto can easily be made in the food processor. A few that are excellent in this lasagne in place of the basil-almond pesto are sun-dried tomato pesto; parsley and capers (a classic Italian green sauce); and Arugula Almond Pesto (page 202).

Lasagne with Sautéed Greens, Mascarpone, and Olives

A Lasagne of Sautéed Greens—with Many Variations

The filling in this lasagne consists of different greens, a style typical of Campania, where greens are often used to fill calzone and double-crusted pizzalike tarts.

[Makes 4 main-course or 6 first-course servings]

1 medium bunch chicory, trimmed, washed, and chopped

1 medium bunch escarole, trimmed, washed, and chopped

1 medium bunch dandelion greens, trimmed, washed, and chopped

About ¼ cup olive oil

4 garlic cloves, thinly sliced

About 8 anchovy fillets

A generous splash of dry white wine

1 cup black olives, pitted and cut in half (Gaeta are a good choice)

½ cup pine nuts, lightly toasted

Freshly ground black pepper

A pinch of cayenne pepper

Salt

1 cup mascarpone cheese

About ½ cup heavy cream

1 recipe Three-Egg Pasta (page 365), cut for lasagne

About 1 cup toasted bread crumbs (see page 340)

- Set up a large pot of salted water to cook the pasta. Bring to a boil, add the greens, and blanch for 1 minute. Lift the greens from the water with a large strainer and run under cold water. Drain the greens well, squeezing out any excess water with your hands. Give the blanched greens an extra chopping to make sure there are no large pieces.
- In a large skillet, heat the olive oil over low heat. Add the garlic and anchovies and cook for 1 minute, breaking up the anchovies with your spoon. Add the greens, turn the heat to medium, and sauté well, about 4 minutes. Add the wine and let it boil away. Add the olives, pine nuts, black pepper, cayenne, and salt if needed (the anchovies may provide enough salt, but taste to make sure). Mix well.
- Preheat the oven to 425°F.
- In a small saucepan, gently heat the mascarpone with the cream over very low heat, just until it reaches a pourable consistency, less than a minute. Turn off the heat. Season with a pinch of salt and black pepper.

- Cook the lasagne sheets in batches, lifting them out with a large strainer when tender. Run under cold water, drain, and lay out in a single layer on paper towels or kitchen towels.
- Pour a thin layer of mascarpone cream on the bottom of a 12 x 10 x 2-inch baking dish and spread it out more or less evenly. Add a layer of lasagne and top with a layer of greens and a drizzle of mascarpone cream. Put down another layer of pasta sheets, top with more greens and another drizzle of mascarpone cream. End with pasta, the remaining cream, and an even sprinkling of bread crumbs.
- Cover the dish with aluminum foil and bake for 20 minutes. Uncover and bake an additional 15 minutes or so, or until bubbling and lightly browned.

Ideas

When deciding on a filling for lasagne, consider classic vegetable dishes for inspiration. A vegetable tart filled with greens, Pecorino, pine nuts, and raisins is a dish native to Liguria. It also makes an excellent lasagne filling: Replace the black olives in this recipe with about half the amount of currants or golden raisins, omit the anchovies, and mix about ½ cup grated Grana Padano or a mild Pecorino cheese into the greens.

Spinach with ricotta is a popular filling for ravioli and cannelloni. I love this layered into a lasagne along with a few thin slices of prosciutto. Top with grated Parmigiano-Reggiano cheese.

Greens and goat cheese, a dish I usually make in its salad form, is an especially good combination for lasagne. Blend a small log (about 6 ounces) of fresh goat cheese with about ½ cup milk and a handful of chopped fresh herbs (savory, thyme, basil, and parsley are good choices). Use this in place of the mascarpone cream.

Orange Lasagne with Tomato and Orange Sauce and Fennel-Flavored Ricotta

A Classic Combination of Tomato and Ricotta

This is a variation on the classic tomato and ricotta lasagne of Naples, usually made with thin spinach pasta. Because of the quickly cooked tomato sauce, this lasagne has a very fresh taste and bright color.

[Makes 4 main-course or 6 first-course servings]

4 large fennel bulbs, cored and very thinly sliced, plus the feathery tops, chopped

Olive oil

Salt

Freshly ground black pepper

2 cups fresh ricotta cheese

About 1 cup freshly grated Pecorino Toscano cheese

1 large egg

Zest of 2 oranges

A small handful of fennel seeds (about 1 teaspoon), lightly toasted and ground to a powder with a mortar and pestle

A small splash of pastis, such as Pernod

1 recipe Three-Egg Pasta (page 365), cut for lasagne

2 recipes Tomato and Orange Sauce (page 25)

A large handful of basil leaves

- Preheat the oven to 425°F.
- Place the sliced fennel on a baking sheet and toss with olive oil, salt, and pepper. Roast until tender and lightly browned, about 30 minutes.
- In a large mixing bowl, blend together the ricotta, a large handful of Pecorino Toscano (save a handful to sprinkle on top of the finished lasagne), the egg, chopped fennel tops, black pepper, orange zest, ground fennel seeds, pastis, and salt. Mix well and set aside.
- Cook the lasagne sheets in batches of 2 or 3 at a time. Run them under cold water and lay out on kitchen towels or paper towels.
- Make a thin layer of tomato-orange sauce in a 12 x 10 x 2-inch baking dish. Add a layer of lasagne sheets and top with a smooth layer of the ricotta mixture. Add a layer of fennel and a scattering of basil leaves. Continue with the same pattern until all the ingredients are used up, ending with a layer of lasagne covered with a thin layer of tomato sauce. Sprinkle the top with the remaining Pecorino Toscano.

- Cover with aluminum foil and bake for 20 minutes. Remove the foil and bake 15 to 20 minutes longer, or until the top is golden and the sauce is bubbling hot.

Ideas

Ricotta can be flavored in many ways. Here I've chosen an orange and fennel seasoning. The most traditional ricotta flavoring for lasagne is a mix of grated Parmigiano-Reggiano cheese, chopped parsley, and bit of grated nutmeg. Other Italian additions you can experiment with are a pinch of ground cinnamon, a tiny splash of orange flower water, chopped prosciutto, grated ricotta salata, freshly chopped herbs (I especially like mint, basil, or thyme), a handful of pitted green or black olives, and chopped blanched spinach.

Any of the tomato sauces on pages 21–40 can be used as a component of a lasagne, all imparting a slightly different character to your finished dish. The quick-cooked sauces will add a fresh taste, while the simmered sauces will lend a more mellow, richer quality.

PASTA—FIRST OR SECOND COURSE?

Have you ever wondered why an American restaurant-size serving of fettuccine Alfredo is so hard to finish? It's because in Italy pasta is almost always meant as a first course, and many very rich, buttery, creamy, or stuffed pastas were created with small servings in mind. In southern Italy, where life has traditionally been hard (and where dried durum pasta was born), dried pasta with a simple vegetable sauce has very often sufficed for an entire meal for a big family. There is nothing wrong with eating a lightly sauced dried pasta dish as a main course, but a big dish of tortellini bolognese is too rich and filling to be eaten in any but small servings. I prefer most stuffed pastas as a first course, except lasagne, especially when it has a meat or fish filling.

On the other hand, a big dish of pasta with tomato or a plain vegetable sauce can be filling but not quite satisfying. You may be happier serving small bowls of a simple pasta and then moving on to a main course, as is usually done in Italy. To me, pasta with any type of fish sauce or a meat ragù always constitutes a full and satisfying meal. It might not be eaten that way in Italy, but it seems right to my American soul.

Vegetable and Cheese Fillings for Pasta

The recipes in this section are not intended to represent classic Italian stuffed pastas, which tend toward strict regional definitions. Rather, they are modern interpretations of the classic forms, inspired by Italian ingredients and imagination.

I've given recipes for stuffed pasta shapes that are easy to make at home, mainly large ravioli and cannelloni. Both are less fussy than smaller stuffed pastas like tortellini, but just as rewarding in terms of flavor and presentation.

In Italy there are many regional names for what we know as ravioli. So I refer to all closed filled pastas as ravioli but have provided ideas on how to create round or triangular, big or small ones. I like making big filled ravioli that take no time, and serve two or three per person. I don't worry about making each one uniform. In Italy I've been served all sorts of free-form ravioli, some looking like big comfortable pillows. I think they're very pretty this way.

You have enormous leeway when choosing ingredients for vegetable fillings, but the most important consideration is texture, especially when making fillings for ravioli. All fillings should be cooled to room temperature or slightly chilled before you attempt to stuff ravioli. Warm fillings will make your pasta sheets soggy. The ravioli should also be well sealed so that no water seeps in during cooking. Ravioli fillings need to be quite dry. Excess water in the filling will cause the pasta casing to become limp before it's cooked. Ingredients should be finely chopped. Big pieces can jut out, making the pasta pockets hard to close or even tearing holes in very thin pasta.

I enjoy making cannelloni because the pasta is easy to cut and gives me more freedom with the texture of the fillings. Because the pasta is boiled before it's filled and then nestled securely in a baking dish, the fillings can be looser and moister, with larger pieces of ingredients if you prefer.

Sauces for filled pasta should be very simple and not too chunky. I think anything that detracts from the suaveness of the stuffed pasta should be avoided in favor of something simple, flavorful, and complementary to the filling you've chosen. Herb-flavored butters and oils, simple vegetable purées, warmed cream or light cheese sauces, vegetable or light meat broths, or simple tomato sauces work best. I also like a sauce containing one thinly sliced, sautéed vegetable, such as mushrooms, if it has some logical relationship to the filling.

Watercress, Prosciutto, and Goat Cheese Ravioli with Pine Nut Pesto

This adaptation of my watercress salad with toasted pine nuts, prosciutto, and goat cheese makes a highly flavored dish of ravioli.

[Makes 4 main-course or 6 first-course servings]

For the filling:

About 2 tablespoons olive oil

4 bunches watercress, thick stems removed, finely chopped

Salt

One 11-ounce log unaged goat cheese, such as Montrachet or Coach Farms, at room temperature

½ cup ricotta cheese, well drained

1 garlic clove, finely minced

A few thyme sprigs, leaves chopped

A few drops of grappa or cognac

3 thin slices prosciutto, finely chopped

Freshly ground black pepper

For the pasta:

1 recipe Three-Egg Pasta (page 365), cut for ravioli

For the sauce:

About 1 cup pine nuts

1 large garlic clove, peeled

½ cup freshly grated Pecorino Toscano cheese

A few flat-leaf parsley sprigs, leaves removed, plus a few sprigs left whole for garnish

Olive oil

Salt

Freshly ground black pepper

- To make the filling, heat the olive oil in a large skillet over medium heat. Add the watercress and a little salt and sauté until wilted, about 5 minutes. Drain off any excess water (squeezing the watercress dry in the palm of your hand if very watery) and let cool completely.
- In a mixing bowl, combine the goat cheese, ricotta, garlic, thyme, grappa, prosciutto, and watercress. Season with salt and pepper and mix well. Chill in the refrigerator a few minutes to firm up the filling.
- Lay out the pasta sheets on a floured surface and fill and form into ravioli (see page 370).
- To make the sauce, place the pine nuts and garlic in a food processor and grind to a rough consistency. Add the Pecorino, parsley leaves, and enough olive oil (at least ¼ cup) to smooth out the sauce. Process again briefly just to blend. Season with salt and pepper.
- Cook the ravioli and, when tender, lift from the water with a large strainer. Drain the ravioli well and slide out onto a large warmed serving platter. Loosen the pesto with about a tablespoon of hot pasta water and spoon over the ravioli. Garnish with whole parsley sprigs.

Scallion and Ricotta Ravioli with Tomato-Bay Leaf Sauce

Scallions as a Savory Filling for Ravioli

I love the flavor of scallions. Though they're not used much in traditional Italian cooking, they complement many Italian seasonings and are a refreshing taste change from the more commonly reached for onion. Ricotta, a classic ingredient in so many filled pastas, is very well complemented here by the subtle and mysterious flavor of fresh bay leaves.

[Makes 4 main-course or 6 first-course servings]

For the filling:

A few tablespoons unsalted butter

3 bunches scallions (about 20), cut in
    very thin rounds, with some of
    the tender green

2 cups fresh ricotta cheese, well drained

1 large egg

About 1 cup freshly grated Grana
    Padano cheese

Salt

Freshly ground black pepper

For the pasta:

1 recipe Three-Egg Pasta (page 365),
    cut for ravioli

For the sauce:

About 3 tablespoons unsalted butter

2 garlic cloves, very thinly sliced

5 or 6 fresh bay leaves

One 35-ounce can Italian plum
    tomatoes, drained and
    well chopped

Salt

Freshly ground black pepper

A splash of balsamic vinegar

A few scallions, sliced in thin rounds,
    for garnish

- To make the filling, melt the butter in a medium skillet over medium heat, add the scallions, and sauté until tender but still holding their shape, 3 or 4 minutes. Place the ricotta in a mixing bowl. Add the egg, a large handful of Grana Padano (save a small handful to sprinkle on top of the ravioli), and the scallion mixture. Season with salt and pepper and mix well. Let this cool completely.
- Lay out the pasta sheets on a floured surface and fill and form into ravioli (see page 370 for instructions).

- To make the sauce, heat the butter with the garlic and bay leaves in a large skillet over low heat about 1 minute to extract the flavors. Add the tomatoes and turn the heat to high. Cook 2 to 3 minutes. Turn off the heat. Season with salt and pepper and add the balsamic vinegar.
- Cook the ravioli in a large pot of boiling water until tender. Lift from the water with a large strainer and drain briefly, either by resting the strainer on a few paper towels or kitchen towels to absorb the water or by gently sliding the ravioli into a colander. Transfer to a large warmed serving platter. Top with the sauce and a sprinkling of Grana Padano. Garnish with scallions.

Ideas

The classic addition to ricotta for pasta fillings is spinach, but here I've used scallions. Chopped sautéed leeks can replace the scallions. Ricotta is also a sweet mild base for fresh herbs. A cup of lightly chopped mixed herbs (marjoram, fennel tops, parsley, and basil, for instance) plus a handful of grated mild Pecorino will give you a wonderful herb ravioli to serve either with the tomato–bay leaf sauce or simply with melted butter and a scattering of the same herbs you chose for the filling.

You can also make a bay leaf sauce with a base of butter instead of tomato. Let a half-dozen fresh bay leaves simmer gently in a stick of unsalted butter until the butter is melted and infused with flavor, 2 or 3 minutes. Pour the butter over ravioli.

Sauce of Plum Tomatoes, Shallots, and Butter (page 21) is lovely with these ravioli.

STORE-BOUGHT RAVIOLI

Store-bought ravioli can be very good if you find a reliable source that turns out high-quality pasta and has a good turnover. The simple ricotta-and-spinach-filled kind commonly sold can be dressed up for a special dinner with a sauce of sautéed wild mushrooms, asparagus tips, sliced artichokes, or tomato. For more elaborately stuffed ravioli containing mushrooms, pesto, squash, salmon, and such, try any of the simpler sauces suggested in the following recipes. The bay leaf sauce, for instance, goes well with squash filling. A sauce of truffle oil and a bit of chicken broth is satisfying on mushroom ravioli. Try the fontina cream on store-bought pesto or sun-dried-tomato ravioli. Heavy cream or unsalted butter can be gently heated along with a single chopped herb, making a quick rich sauce for many types of ravioli; also try adding sage, rosemary, or basil.

Potato and Cabbage Ravioli with Poppy Seeds

Ravioli with Winter Vegetables

Potato and cabbage is a common stuffing for ravioli in the Veneto and parts of Emilia-Romagna. Poppy seeds are used to flavor lasagne in the Trieste region. They also add texture to a dish of ravioli, blending well with butter and herbs.

[Makes 4 main-course or 6 first-course servings]

For the filling:

2 medium baking potatoes (about
    1 pound)

A few tablespoons olive oil

1 strip slab bacon, cut in small dice

6 or 7 scallions, sliced into thin rounds,
    with some of the green

½ head small Savoy cabbage, cored and
    finely chopped (about 1 cup)

1 or 2 garlic cloves, finely minced

Salt

Freshly ground black pepper

A tiny splash of sherry vinegar

For the pasta:

1 recipe Three-Egg Pasta (page 365),
    cut for ravioli

For the sauce:

About ½ cup (1 stick) unsalted butter

About a dozen sage leaves, cut in
    thin strips

A palmful of poppy seeds

Salt

Freshly ground black pepper

- To make the filling, boil the potatoes in water to cover until very tender.
- Meanwhile in a large skillet, heat 1 tablespoon olive oil over medium heat. Add the bacon and cook until crisp. Add the scallions and sauté until soft, about 2 minutes. Add the cabbage and garlic, season with salt and pepper, and sauté about 5 minutes. Stir in the sherry vinegar and a splash of water, cover the pan, and finish cooking over low heat until the cabbage is tender, about 10 minutes. Uncover for the last few minutes of cooking to evaporate any excess liquid (the cabbage should be moist but with no liquid on the bottom of the pan). Let the mixture cool a bit.
- Peel the potatoes and put them through a ricer directly into the skillet. Mix well. Check the seasoning. Let the mixture cool completely. The filling should hold together well when squeezed with your fingers.

- Lay out the pasta sheets on a floured surface and fill and form into ravioli (for instructions, see page 370). I like making these particular ravioli very large and slightly irregular because I think that look goes with the rustic character of the filling.
- To make the sauce, melt the butter in a small saucepan over low heat. Add the sage and poppy seeds. Season with salt and pepper.
- Cook the ravioli until tender. Lift from the water with a large strainer and drain. Gently transfer the ravioli to a large warmed serving platter and pour the sauce on top.

Ideas

Potato can be the backdrop for many ravioli fillings. Just remember to keep the finished filling reasonably dry.

Roasted garlic and potato make a highly flavored ravioli filling; simply add roasted garlic (page 49) from 3 or 4 heads of garlic to a base of well-seasoned mashed potatoes. You can also replace the garlic with chopped fresh chives. Try this ravioli with a sauce of warmed cream simmered with more chopped chives.

Another good replacement for the cabbage in this recipe is about ¾ cup of sautéed finely chopped wild mushrooms. Fold this into the mashed potatoes along with a small handful of grated Pecorino.

Use a purée of white beans instead of the potatoes.

Big Shells with Radicchio Filling and Fontina

Stuffed Shells Revisited

In this country stuffed shells have always meant one thing: ricotta filled, tomato-sauce drenched, and baked far too long to have much life left in them. But the stuffed shells concept has merit and is easily updated by choosing fresh vegetable fillings and cooking the dish briefly at high heat to preserve the texture of the pasta and to keep both filling and sauce moist.

[Makes 4 main-course or 6 first-course servings]

1 pound large shell pasta

About 3 tablespoons olive oil

1 large onion, cut in small dice

1 small cacciatorini sausage (about ¼ pound) or another dry Italian sausage such as soppressata, skinned and cut into very small cubes

2 medium heads radicchio, cored and thinly sliced

Salt

Freshly ground black pepper

¾ cup fresh ricotta cheese

A large handful of freshly grated Asiago cheese, plus a little extra to sprinkle on top

A few gratings of nutmeg

For the fontina cream:

1 cup heavy cream

About ½ pound fontina cheese, cut in small cubes

1 clove, ground

A pinch of cayenne pepper

A pinch of salt

- Cook the shells until very al dente (a bit less tender than usual because they will cook further in the oven). Run under cold water and drain well, making sure to give the colander a few shakes to remove any water trapped inside the shells. Toss with a little olive oil to keep them from sticking together.
- Preheat the oven to 425°F.
- In a large skillet, heat the olive oil. Add the onion and sausage and sauté until the sausage starts to brown slightly. Add the radicchio and season it with salt and pepper. Sauté until it just starts to wilt but still retains some dark red color, 5 or 6 minutes.

Remove the pan from the heat and let the mixture cool a bit. Stir in the ricotta, Asiago, and nutmeg. Mix well. Check the seasoning.

- To make the fontina cream, simmer the cream with the fontina in a small saucepan over low heat, stirring often, until the sauce is thick and smooth. Season with the clove, cayenne, and salt.

- Lightly oil a large, shallow baking dish. Fill the shells with the radicchio mixture and place them close together in the dish. Pour the fontina cream over the shells and top with a sprinkling of Asiago and some freshly ground black pepper. Bake, uncovered, until the top is lightly browned and the sauce is bubbling, about 20 minutes.

Ideas

For another way to flavor radicchio, see Garganelli with Roasted Radicchio, Anchovies, and Black Olives (page 118); this also makes a fine filling for shells. Try it with Oven-Roasted Tomato Sauce (page 38) instead of the fontina cream.

Just about any filling you might use for cannelloni is also good in stuffed shells. The watercress, prosciutto, and goat cheese filling for ravioli (page 147) is delicious in shells. So is the filling for Crespelle with Zucchini, Anchovies, and Mozzarella (page 156).

Cannelloni with Escarole, Asiago, and Tomato-Basil Cream

Three Cannelloni Recipes Combining Green Vegetables and Cheese

This is really a variation of Crespelle with Zucchini, Anchovies, and Mozzarella (page 156), using pasta instead of crespelle, escarole instead of zucchini, Asiago for the mozzarella, and pancetta instead of anchovies. It's a formula with interchangeable components. Asiago is a slightly tangy yet subtle-tasting cheese from the region around Venice. I often look for reasons to cook with it.

[Makes 4 main-course or 6 first-course servings]

For the filling:
About 3 tablespoons olive oil

5 thin slices pancetta, cut in
    small dice

1 medium onion, cut in
    small dice

A few garlic cloves, finely minced

2 large heads escarole, cored,
    chopped, and washed but not dried

Salt

Freshly ground black pepper

½ cup ricotta cheese

A handful of pine nuts, toasted

Freshly grated Asiago cheese

For the tomato-basil cream:
1 cup crème fraîche

3 ripe tomatoes (about 1½ pounds),
    peeled, seeded, and cut in small dice
    (see Tomato Concassé, page 43)

A dozen basil leaves, cut in thin strips

Zest of 1 lemon

Salt

Freshly ground black pepper

1 recipe Three-Egg Pasta (page 365),
    cut for cannelloni

A handful of pine nuts, toasted

- To make the filling, heat the olive oil in a large skillet over medium-low heat. Add the pancetta and sauté until crisp. Add the onion and cook until soft and fragrant, 3 to 4 minutes. Add the garlic and sauté briefly, just until it gives off aroma. Add all the escarole, turn the heat up a bit, and cook, uncovered, stirring frequently, until it is wilted and all the water has evaporated from the pan. Season with salt and pepper. Let cool about 5 minutes and then add the ricotta, pine nuts, and a handful of Asiago, reserving some Asiago to sprinkle over the cannelloni. Mix well and taste for seasoning.

- Preheat the oven to 425°F.
- To make the tomato-basil cream, heat the crème fraîche in a small saucepan over low heat just until it is a pourable consistency. Add the tomatoes, basil, and lemon zest. Season with salt and pepper and mix well. Turn off the heat.
- Cook the cannelloni in small batches, drain under cold water, and lay out on paper towels or kitchen towels. Spread each one with a layer of filling, roll loosely, and place in a lightly oiled 13 x 9 x 2-inch baking dish, seam side down. Pour the tomato-basil cream on top and finish with a light layer of grated Asiago. Bake, uncovered, until brown and bubbling, about 20 minutes. Scatter pine nuts on top for a garnish.

Ideas

Cream is an excellent conduit for flavoring. Try simmering different herbs or mixtures of herbs in cream to make highly perfumed but simple sauces for filled pasta. Oily herbs like rosemary work very well. So do sweet ones like basil or parsley. Herbs that tend to be somewhat bitter, like oregano, however, can become even more so with long simmering. Citrus zest adds good flavor, but it, too, can become bitter if you're not careful to remove all the white pith before simmering. Spices such as whole cinnamon sticks, bay leaves, saffron, or a few whole cloves infuse cream sauces with their essence. Add assertive accents such as tomatoes or capers just before dressing the pasta.

MAKING CANNELLONI

Good cannelloni are very easy to make. They are meant to be delicate, though, so try not to overstuff them or they'll taste heavy and dull. I usually roll out long sheets of thin pasta on my hand-cranked machine and cut them into roughly 5- or 6-inch squares. Boil them, a few at a time, in salted water until tender, run them under cold water, and lay them out on damp towels. I spread the filling out in a thin layer, covering all but the edges of the pasta sheets, instead of placing a lump of it only in the center. This way, you get a good balance of pasta to filling with every bite. Then roll up the cannelloni loosely and place in a single layer, seam side down, in a lightly oiled baking dish. Stuff the pasta soon after boiling it, before it begins to dry out. The cannelloni can also be stuffed, refrigerated, and baked the next day, if need be, without too much damage to taste or texture.

Crespelle with Zucchini, Anchovies, and Mozzarella

Here are cannelloni made with crespelle, the Italian version of crêpes. This easy batter (which I make with olive oil instead of the more usual butter) is wonderful for making spur-of-the-moment filled pasta. The filling idea comes from the fried zucchini blossoms filled with mozzarella and anchovies that Romans make in early summer.

[Makes 4 main-course or 6 first-course servings]

For the crespelle:
1 cup unbleached all-purpose flour
3 large eggs, at room temperature
1½ cups whole milk
3 tablespoons olive oil
Salt

For the filling:
About 3 tablespoons olive oil
1 large onion, cut in small dice
2 garlic cloves, finely chopped
8 small young zucchini, cut in
    small dice

Salt
Freshly ground black pepper
8 anchovy fillets, chopped
1 pound mozzarella cheese, cut in
    small dice
A small handful of mint leaves, chopped
A handful of basil leaves, chopped

1 recipe Sauce of Plum Tomatoes,
    Shallots, and Butter (page 21)
About ½ cup freshly grated Montasio
    cheese

- To make the crespelle, put all the ingredients into a food processor and process until you have a smooth batter. Pour the batter into a bowl and let it rest for about 30 minutes.
- I make crespelle in a 7-inch nonstick omelet pan. Heat the pan and brush it lightly with olive oil. Pour in enough batter (about 3 tablespoons for a 7-inch pan) to lightly coat the pan. Tilt the pan, lifting it off the heat for a moment, until the surface is completely covered with batter. Cook over medium heat until the edges of the crespelle just begin to turn golden, usually less than 1 minute. Turn the crespelle with a metal spatula and cook for a few seconds on the other side. The first few have a tendency to stick and tear, but the process becomes much easier once the pan is well seasoned and the heat is regulated. You can stack the crespelle on a large plate as you make them. Add more oil to the pan

as you need it. (Crespelle can be made ahead of time, stacked, covered with plastic wrap, and refrigerated 2 days before being filled and baked.)

- Preheat the oven to 425°F. Lightly oil a 13 x 9 x 2-inch baking dish.
- To make the filling, heat the olive oil over medium heat in a large skillet. Add the onion and sauté a few minutes to soften. Add the garlic and sauté 1 minute, just until it gives off aroma. Add the zucchini and season with very little salt (you will be adding anchovies later) and more liberally with pepper. Sauté until the zucchini is tender and lightly browned but still holds its shape. Turn off the heat. Add the anchovies and mix well. Let the mixture cool a bit, then add the mozzarella and herbs and mix again.
- Spread the crespelle with a few tablespoons of the zucchini filling and roll them loosely. Place them next to each other, seam side down, in the baking dish. Pour the tomato-shallot sauce down the middle of the dish, letting it run down between the crespelle a bit, and top with a sprinkling of grated Montasio and freshly ground black pepper.
- Bake, uncovered, until the top is lightly browned, 15 to 20 minutes.

Ideas

Crespelle batter can be flavored with citrus zest, chopped herbs, or a ground spice such as nutmeg or fennel seed.

Zucchini is used extensively in southern Italian cooking. Its taste is very mild, so especially when using it as a filling, make sure it's well seasoned. I like zucchini sautéed and then tossed with a few tablespoons of basil pesto. Traditional French ratatouille makes a splendid filling for crespelle. Also see the zucchini recipes on pages 64 and 65 for more ideas on how to flavor zucchini.

Crespelle with Spinach and Lemon-Parmigiano Sauce

Tagliatelle tossed with a lemon- and Parmigiano-flavored sauce has been a very popular restaurant dish in Italy for the last decade. It is subtle and delicious. I use a variation on that sauce as a topping for the familiar spinach and ricotta filling, updating a classic dish. This filling also makes very good ravioli, topped either with the lemon and Parmigiano sauce or simply with melted butter and a few chopped sage leaves.

[Makes 4 main-course or 6 first-course servings]

Ingredients for 1 recipe crespelle (page 156)

For the filling:
3 large bunches fresh spinach, stemmed, washed, blanched, and roughly chopped (about 1 ½ cups)
½ cup ricotta cheese
1 large egg
A few gratings of nutmeg
Salt
Freshly ground black pepper
A large handful of freshly grated Parmigiano-Reggiano cheese, plus a little extra to sprinkle on top of this dish

For the sauce:
1 cup heavy cream
2 tablespoons unsalted butter, plus extra butter for coating the baking dish
Zest of 4 lemons
Juice of 1 lemon
A few lemon thyme sprigs, leaves chopped
About ½ cup freshly grated Parmigiano-Reggiano cheese

- Make the crespelle batter and cook the crespelle (see page 156).
- To make the filling, be sure most of the water is squeezed from the blanched spinach and place it in a mixing bowl along with all the other ingredients for the filling. Mix well and taste for seasoning. Set aside.
- Preheat the oven to 425°F. Butter a 13 x 9 x 2-inch baking dish.
- To make the sauce, place the cream and butter in a small saucepan. Bring to a boil and add the lemon zest, lemon juice, and thyme. Continue boiling until the sauce is reduced

by almost half, stirring all the while, 3 to 4 minutes. Turn off the heat and add the Parmigiano. Stir to blend.

- Spread each crespelle with a thin layer of filling and roll up loosely. Place the crespelle, seam side down, in the baking dish. Pour the sauce evenly on top. Sprinkle with the remaining parmigiano.
- Bake, uncovered, until the top is brown and bubbling, 15 to 20 minutes.

Ideas

Ricotta can be flavored in many ways to create your own customized pasta filling. Here I've used the standard spinach addition, but try chopped fresh herbs or pureed vegetables such as asparagus, carrots, or artichokes. Also try other cooked chopped greens like escarole, green chard, arugula, or dandelion. Chopped prosciutto, bresaola, salami, or roasted chicken can be added (see Cannelloni Filled with Chicken, Capers, and Ricotta, page 335). Black olives add vibrant taste and texture. Try sautéed leeks or onions or roasted garlic purée. Ground or chopped hazelnuts, pine nuts, or almonds are worth experimenting with.

Nutmeg is traditionally used to flavor ricotta, but also try cinnamon, allspice, or a few drops of orange flower water or brandy. A seasoning added to ricotta should add just a hint of flavor. A small pinch of ground spice or a tiny splash of a liqueur should do it.

A very delicate pasta stuffing can be made from ricotta mixed with lemon zest and a pinch of nutmeg. Try this sauce with nothing but a little melted unsalted butter.

Pasta
and Fish

I've always had an upbeat feeling about combinations of seafood and pasta. My mother made spaghetti with clam sauce on Christmas Eve, and the dish is still one of my absolute favorites. As a child, I always asked for spaghetti with mussels on my birthday, and to this day I order pasta and seafood on every birthday. When I invite friends for dinner and want to make something impressive but easy, some combination of pasta and fish is usually on the menu. The result feels elegant and refined to me. Seafood is always a highlight of summer vacations too—pasta with razor clams in Ischia in Italy or squid grilled for a pasta salad in a friend's backyard.

If some of my fish and pasta dishes don't seem obviously Italian, it's because many of our American fish varieties don't exist in Italy. If they did, Italians would have found ways to combine them with pasta, just as I have here.

Fish can be expensive, but when you cook it with pasta, you can buy less and feed a group lavishly. And look for special values. You may not think of fish as seasonal, since you can always find farm-raised salmon, clams, and mussels, but in spring, look for tilefish, wild Alaskan salmon, and shad. During the year, seek out imports such as Portuguese sardines or true Mediterranean black mussels (both of which make exquisite classic pasta sauces). I like to buy fish I've never cooked before and substitute it in a dish I make all the time. Bucatini with fresh tuna and capers or olives is a favorite combination. Salmon instead of tuna produces a completely different dish, suaver and more buttery. But so does mako, in a subtler way. Skate adds a sweet taste and clingy texture.

When devising a seafood and pasta combination, think about what kind of pasta will work best. Many olive oil–based dishes such as pasta with traditional clam sauce pair well with dried long pasta. But tinker subtly with the flavorings, adding a bit of unsalted butter and a mild herb like chervil or tarragon, for instance, and you will create a richer dish that complements a fresh egg pasta well. Seafood with a spicy sauce always gets a dried pasta when I make it, but take out the spice and add a splash of cream, and tagliatelle would be superb.

Since most seafood sauces cook within minutes, adding just a few simple seasonings, especially to mild fish, is the wisest rule of thumb. Sometimes the fresh fish itself, a box of pasta, some olive oil, and salt will combine into a gorgeous meal.

With a little imagination, you can make just about any fish into a good pasta sauce. The most important thing to remember is not to overcook any fish. The recipes here are all for fast sauces that can be started and completed while the pasta is cooking. If you need to wait for the pasta to finish cooking, pull the sauce off the heat. Don't let shrimp or clams simmer for more than a few minutes. If you must reheat the sauce, do so very gently. Sometimes the heat from the pasta is enough to heat the entire dish.

Some Good Fish to Cook with Pasta:
Using Anchovies and Sardines to Add Big Flavor to Pasta Sauces

Anchovies and sardines can add subtle flavor to many vegetable, fish, or even meat sauces, and in southern Italy both are often the main ingredient in a pasta sauce. Sicilians especially love combining pungent small fish with pasta. In Siracusa, Sicily, cooks toss a sauce of lightly sautéed anchovies, garlic, and olive oil with spaghetti and finish it with a scattering of toasted bread crumbs. This makes a delicious first course. In many recipes throughout this book, I've used one or two anchovies as a flavoring. In this section I offer recipes in which the fish is the main ingredient.

I think of both anchovies and sardines as concentrated fish; you get a lot of flavor from very few. Fish containing an abundance of healthy fish oil take well to strong flavorings and a good shot of acidity. Sicilians typically season anchovies and sardines with orange juice, lemon juice, and fennel; with rosemary and garlic; or with raisins, almonds, and pine nuts. Tomatoes are always a good choice with them. When you're thinking about ways to use these fish with pasta, think about contrasts. A splash of sherry vinegar or a scattering of fresh mint leaves added at the last minute can work wonders with either of these robust little fish.

Good preserved anchovies are available in this country packed in oil or salt. You can also find fresh anchovies marinated in vinaigrette in Italian and Spanish markets. (For an in-depth discussion of how to select and cook with all the various types of anchovies available, see the anchovy section in "The Improviser's Pantry," page 338.)

One thing to remember when cooking any anchovies in a pasta sauce is that they burn easily, and burned anchovies have a rank smell and taste. So when sautéing garlic or onions for a sauce, be sure to add the anchovies *after* the onion or garlic has started to sauté, and turn the heat down a bit. Once you add liquid to a pasta sauce containing anchovies, you can simmer it indefinitely without worrying about burning.

Fresh sardines have become easier to find. They are usually flown in from Portugal. Sardines are dark, oily fish that can go bad quickly when not properly iced, so make sure you smell and touch them before you buy them. They should be firm and shiny and have a pleasant, light sea aroma. Canned sardines don't take well to heating; they easily turn to mush and also develop a strong fishy flavor. If I use them at all with pasta, I add them to a cold pasta salad.

Anchovy and Fennel Seed Sauce for Spaghetti

Pasta con le sarde (pasta with sardines) is the most famous pasta dish in Palermo, Sicily, and many sauces from there are designed to mimic its taste—which includes wild fennel, saffron, raisins, pine nuts, and onion—without the sardines. These are whimsically referred to as "pasta with sardines still in the sea." Here is a good example of one; the anchovies are not a replacement for the sardines but rather another standard ingredient in the dish. This recipe illustrates how you can pick apart a complicated dish and reduce it to a simple form without sacrificing any enjoyment. The result is completely improvisational. The fennel taste is provided by ground fennel seeds, which are strong and fragrant and make an interesting substitute for the wild fennel used in Italy, which is not easy to find here.

[Makes 4 main-course or 6 first-course servings]

Extra-virgin olive oil

1 large onion, cut in small dice

About 1 teaspoon of fennel seeds, lightly toasted (see Note) and ground with a mortar and pestle

Coarsely ground black pepper

About 12 salt-packed anchovies, filleted and rinsed (see page 338)

A splash of Pernod or other anise-flavored liqueur

½ cup bread crumbs (see page 340)

Salt

1 pound spaghetti

- In a large skillet, heat about ⅓ cup olive oil over medium heat. Add the onion, ground fennel, and coarse black pepper (coarse-ground pepper gives a rustic touch to the dish). Sauté until the onion is soft, about 5 minutes. Add the anchovies and cook until they soften and dissolve into the sauce, about another 3 minutes. Add a splash of Pernod and let it boil away.
- In a small sauté pan, heat 1 tablespoon olive oil over medium heat. Add the bread crumbs, season with salt and pepper, and sauté until crisp and golden, about 2 minutes.
- Cook the spaghetti until al dente (southern Italians eat their pasta very al dente). Drain, leaving some water clinging to the strands, and place in the skillet with the onion. Sauté briefly with the sauce, adding more olive oil, if needed, to coat the pasta sufficiently. Transfer to a large serving bowl and sprinkle with the toasted bread crumbs. Give the pasta a brief toss and serve hot.

A note on toasted fennel seeds: I lightly toast whole spices in a small sauté pan over low heat just until they start to give off their aroma, 1 to 2 minutes. Grind one toasted fennel seed with a mortar and pestle and taste the powder to see how strong it is. That way, you can judge how much of the taste you would like on your pasta. And remember that the flavor will open up a bit during sautéing.

Ideas

Aside from being a lovely, fragrant dish on its own, this is also an excellent starting point for elaborations. Try adding a handful of toasted pine nuts, soaked and drained raisins, or a chopped fresh fennel bulb. Blanched cauliflower or broccoli makes for a full-bodied dish; add either vegetable along with the anchovies.

Rosemary is another good flavoring for anchovies. Try it in place of the fennel seeds, using only about 1 small chopped sprig because its flavor is very strong. Or mix a small sprig of chopped rosemary with a generous handful of chopped flat-leaf parsley.

This sauce is also delicious with tomato. Seed and chop 2 large, ripe tomatoes and add to the sauce after you've sautéed the anchovies. Let the tomatoes cook over medium heat for about 5 minutes, then add the Pernod.

The addition of about ½ cup cream changes the character of this sauce completely. If you would like to make this an anchovy cream sauce, add the cream after sautéing the anchovies and let it simmer over low heat for 2 to 3 minutes to blend the flavors and to thicken the cream a bit. Try this sauce on fresh egg tagliatelle, leaving off the bread crumbs and instead adding a small handful of chopped flat-leaf parsley right before serving.

I also love pasta dressed with nothing but mashed anchovies, olive oil, and a little garlic. You don't even have to cook this sauce; simply mince the garlic and anchovies and let them sit in ⅓ to ½ cup olive oil while your spaghetti is cooking. Toss the hot pasta with this mixture, adding a generous amount of black pepper.

Penne Salad with Marinated Anchovies, Grilled Red Onions, Dandelions, and Black Olives

I find fresh filleted anchovies marinated in vinaigrette in many of the fancy food shops in my neighborhood. I refresh them by patting them dry and sprinkling them with fresh lemon juice and extra-virgin olive oil. They're wonderful in pasta salads.

Raw onions left to sit in a salad may turn acidic, spoiling the salad completely; grilling takes care of that problem. If you don't want to go to the trouble of grilling onions, use raw shallots instead. They are strong in flavor but less acidic and can be used uncooked more readily.

In my unspacious New York City apartment, I've found that a stovetop grill plate is one of the most useful kitchen gadgets. I've used it here for the onions, but the onions can be cooked just as well on an outside grill.

[Makes 4 main-course or 6 first-course servings]

About a dozen marinated anchovy
    fillets, patted dry

Juice of 1 lemon

Olive oil

1 pound penne

2 large red onions, cut in thin rings

Salt

Freshly ground black pepper

2 red bell peppers

A large bunch of very young, tender
    dandelion greens, washed,
    stemmed, and well dried

A large handful of black olives, pitted
    and halved (I use black Nyons)

A few large oregano sprigs,
    leaves chopped

A few large marjoram sprigs,
    leaves chopped

A large handful of flat-leaf parsley
    sprigs, leaves chopped

Zest of 1 lemon

- In a small ceramic bowl, marinate the anchovies in about half of the lemon juice and a few tablespoons of olive oil.
- Cook the penne until al dente, rinse under cold water, and drain. Transfer to a large serving bowl and toss with a little olive oil to prevent the pasta from sticking together.
- Preheat a stovetop grill plate or outdoor grill. Toss the onion slices with a little olive oil, season with salt and pepper, and grill them on both sides until they are tender and

have brown grill marks. Add them to the pasta. Oil the red bell peppers lightly and place them on the grill. Grill, turning, until all sides are blistered and lightly charred. Peel and seed the peppers and cut them into thin strips. Add them to the pasta bowl.

- Roughly chop the anchovies and add them and their marinating liquid to the pasta. Add the dandelions, olives, and all the herbs. Add a drizzle of good olive oil, the rest of the lemon juice, and the lemon zest. Season with salt and pepper and toss. Serve right away.

A note on grilling onions on an outside grill: To prevent onion slices from becoming too black or from falling into the fire, I like to grill them on sheets of aluminum foil that I've punctured with several small holes (a shish kebab skewer makes perfectly sized holes). Grill over medium-hot coals, turning once after they become brown. This is also an effective method for grilling sliced zucchini, tomatoes, eggplant, or peppers.

Ideas

Pasta salads are a good way to use leftover grilled seafood. Try making one with grilled salmon, tuna, shrimp, or squid. In this case, I would use anchovies as a flavoring, adding only 2 or 3 marinated or salt-packed ones. (When I talk about using leftover grilled or other cooked fish, I mean fish that was cooked for lunch and the leftovers eaten for dinner, not cooked fish that has been sitting in the refrigerator for a couple of days.)

I love smoked fish in pasta salads. Smoked trout, herring, tuna, or bluefish will produce a salad with robust flavor. For a delicate dish, add instead a few slices of chopped smoked salmon.

If you don't have dandelions, try another raw green, but one that can stand up to a soaking in olive oil. Arugula becomes flabby very quickly when tossed with oil, but escarole, chicory, and frisée retain their texture longer. Or use lightly cooked greens such as spinach, chard, or kale.

If you can't find marinated anchovies, use 4 or 5 anchovies packed in salt; they'll need to be filleted, soaked to remove excess salt, and well drained before you marinate them.

Bucatini with Fresh Sardines, Dill, Capers, and Almonds

I have flavored this dish differently from the classic *pasta con le sarde* (pasta with sardines), which blends saffron, wild fennel, pine nuts, and raisins. Instead, I've chosen some of the other common tastes of Sicily—capers, almonds, and tomatoes. I've also substituted dill for the fresh fennel usually used with sardines. It isn't an herb used much in Italian cooking, but in small doses it blends very well in some fish sauces. In fact, it is sometimes used in this country as a substitute for the hard-to-find wild fennel of the Mediterranean. Almonds give the dish a rich taste and balance well with the sharpness of capers.

This dish is wonderful followed by an orange and fennel salad garnished with red onion and black olives.

[Makes 4 main-course or 6 first-course servings]

About ½ cup bread crumbs (see page 340)

About ⅓ cup olive oil

Salt

1 large onion, cut in small dice

3 or 4 anchovy fillets, chopped

1½ pounds fresh sardines (12 to 14), boned and filleted (see Note)

About ¼ cup dry white wine

4 large ripe tomatoes (about 2 pounds), peeled if desired, seeded, and chopped

About ½ cup blanched almonds, lightly toasted and roughly chopped

A handful of salt-packed capers, soaked in several changes of water and drained (see page 343)

A few dill sprigs, chopped

A handful of basil leaves, chopped

Freshly ground black pepper

1 pound bucatini

- In a small sauté pan, toast the bread crumbs with a little olive oil and a pinch of salt over medium heat until very lightly browned.
- In a large skillet, sauté the onion over medium heat in about 3 tablespoons olive oil until soft and fragrant, 3 to 4 minutes. Add the anchovies and sardines and cook until tender, about 4 minutes. Add the wine and let it bubble away. Add the tomatoes and cook over medium-high heat until they start to give off liquid, only 3 to 4 minutes. The tomatoes

should remain almost raw, keeping their ripe tomato taste and texture, which contrast well with the richness of the sardines. Add the toasted almonds, capers, and fresh herbs. Add a good drizzle of olive oil to enrich the sauce and hold it together. Season with black pepper and, if needed, salt.

- Cook the bucatini until al dente, drain, and transfer to a serving bowl. Add the sardine sauce and toss. Top with the toasted bread crumbs.

A note about cleaning and boning fresh sardines: You can certainly ask your fish seller to bone sardines, but it is surprisingly easy to do yourself. Open the fish up on the underside with a small knife and, with your fingers, pull out the insides. Cut off the head. Rinse the fish under cold water while rubbing away all the scales. To pull out the backbone, lay the fish open, skin side down, on a cutting board and flatten it out with your fingers. You'll be able to feel the backbone jutting out. Lift it out at the head end with your fingers. The tiny side bones should come up with it. Now pull the entire backbone up and toward the tail end. Snap it off at the tail.

Ideas

Citrus is another good flavoring for sardines; orange or lemon juice can be added to a sardine sauce, along with some of the zest. Orange, pine nuts, and raisins are the flavorings in a famous Sicilian dish of stuffed sardines called *sarde a beccafico*. This trio of seasonings also makes a wonderful sardine sauce for pasta.

Dill is used in this dish as a substitute for wild fennel, which is easy to find on the West Coast but appears only occasionally in the New York markets I frequent. This fragrant herb is used primarily for its sweet, anise-flavored, feathery tops. The tops of the more readily available bulb fennel are not as interesting. If you have wild fennel tops, do what they do in Sicily: Chop them well and blanch them for about a minute in the boiling salted pasta water. Pull them from the water and drain well before adding them to the sauce. Chopped bulb fennel tops can be added without blanching to a pasta sauce for a mild fennel taste.

If you can't find fresh sardines, make this sauce with fresh tuna, cut into small cubes and sautéed just until tender.

Spaghetti with Braised Mackerel, Tarragon, and Capers

Mackerel takes well to pasta. Its suave, rich taste blends beautifully with acidic flavorings such as tomato, lemon, wine, or vinegar. Here I've paired it with tomatoes, tarragon, and sherry vinegar. A sauce of lemon juice and olive oil can also highlight the slightly oily but sweet flavor of this special fish. I think it tastes best on dried pasta.

[Makes 4 main-course or 6 first-course servings]

A few tablespoons olive oil

Salt

Freshly ground black pepper

1 whole large mackerel or 2 small ones (about 1½ pounds; see Note), gutted (I use Spanish mackerel, which is sweeter and less oily than Boston mackerel)

1 large red onion, thinly sliced

3 or 4 garlic cloves, thinly sliced

A splash of sherry vinegar

One 35-ounce can Italian plum tomatoes with juice, roughly chopped

1 or 2 bay leaves

A generous handful of fresh tarragon leaves, chopped

1 pound spaghetti

A handful of salt-packed capers, soaked and drained (see page 343)

- Preheat the oven to 400°F.
- Choose an ovenproof skillet large enough to hold the fish (if you have a problem finding a large enough skillet, cut the tail and head off the fish).
- Heat the olive oil in the skillet over medium-high heat. Salt and pepper the mackerel on both sides and add it to the pan. Brown it on one side and then gently turn it over with a spatula. Lower the heat and add the onion, sautéing for a minute to start it softening. Add the garlic and sauté a minute. Add a splash of sherry vinegar and let it bubble away. Add the tomatoes, bay leaves, and half of the tarragon and mix all the ingredients around well. Season lightly with salt and pepper. Place the skillet, uncovered, in the oven to finish cooking the fish. This should take about 30 minutes. The fish should be tender and flake easily, and the sauce should be slightly thickened.
- Let the fish cool a bit in its sauce. When it is cool enough to handle, lift the fish out of the sauce onto a clean plate. Pull off the skin and flake the fillets into bite-size pieces, making sure to remove all the bones. Discard the bones and skin. Return the flaked fish to the sauce in the skillet. While the spaghetti is cooking, reheat the sauce gently over

low heat, adding the capers. Add the remaining tarragon and another very small splash of vinegar. Taste for seasoning. The sauce should have a pleasant acidity.

- Cook the spaghetti until al dente, drain, and add to the skillet. Toss well and transfer to a serving bowl.

Note: If you buy mackerel fillets, make the recipe the same way, but cut the oven time down to about 10 minutes.

Ideas

Gremolata, a mix of grated lemon zest, minced garlic, and parsley (and sometimes sage) is often sprinkled over ossobuco (veal shank) right before serving. This mix is also appealing on mackerel. Sauté mackerel fillets in olive oil. When tender, add a splash of white wine and let it bubble away. Flake the fish into bite-size pieces and toss with spaghetti, adding about ½ cup gremolata and a handful of toasted bread crumbs.

I chose tarragon as a flavoring because it lightens up the rich fish. But I also love rosemary with mackerel. It produces a deeper, earthier sauce, ideal for a fall or winter meal. Use about 1 small chopped sprig.

This tomato and vinegar braising liquid works wonders on many types of rich, oily fish. Substitute 1 pound of thick tuna steaks for the mackerel.

Linguine with Salmon, Black Olives, and Summer Savory

Salmon is such a versatile fish that it pairs just as well with dried pasta as it does with delicate egg pasta and a little cream. Here is a bold treatment with bright Provençal flavorings.

[Makes 4 main-course or 6 first-course servings]

2 to 3 tablespoons olive oil

1 to 1 ½ pounds skinless salmon fillet, pin bones removed

Salt

Freshly ground black pepper

A generous splash of cognac or brandy

1 large onion, chopped

A few garlic cloves, finely chopped

About ½ cup dry white wine

4 ripe tomatoes (about 2 pounds), peeled, seeded, and chopped in medium dice

2 long strips of orange peel

Several summer savory sprigs, leaves chopped (plus a few whole sprigs for garnish, if you like)

2 whole cloves, ground with a mortar and pestle

¾ cup black olives, pitted and halved (Niçoise are perfect here)

1 pound linguine

A few large flat-leaf parsley sprigs, leaves chopped

- Heat about 2 tablespoons olive oil in a large skillet over medium-high heat. Season the salmon with salt and pepper and sear it quickly on both sides until browned but not completely cooked through. Add the cognac and let it bubble away. Transfer the salmon to a plate. Turn the heat to medium, add the onion to the skillet, and sauté until soft, 3 to 4 minutes. Add the garlic and cook a minute, just until it gives off aroma. Add the wine and let it bubble away to almost nothing. Add the tomatoes, orange peel, savory, and cloves, season with salt and pepper, and simmer about 5 minutes over lively heat. The tomatoes should be giving off a little juice but still remain rather firm. Add the salmon and olives and continue simmering just until the fish starts to flake (2 to 3 minutes), breaking it up with your spoon into bite-size pieces. Taste for seasoning.
- Cook the linguine until al dente, drain, and transfer to a serving bowl. Add the salmon sauce and parsley and toss well. Garnish with savory sprigs.

Ideas

Grilled salmon is also great with pasta, especially in a pasta salad. Break pieces of grilled salmon into cold cooked ziti, add a small bunch of stemmed arugula, and toss with Uncooked Tomato Sauce (page 34).

A very good but unexpected combination is salmon and eggplant. This is a variation on a modern pasta dish I ate in Rome. Grill salmon alongside rounds of sliced eggplant (skin left on). When both are tender and have a nice crust, chop them up and add to hot spaghetti, finishing the dish with a cup of diced raw tomatoes, a drizzle of quality olive oil, minced fresh garlic, and a generous amount of chopped basil or parsley.

Roasted red peppers go beautifully with salmon. Roast, peel, seed, and thinly slice 2 red bell peppers. Add them to the sauce in place of the olives.

FISH STEAKS AND FILLETS MAKE EXCELLENT PASTA SAUCES

*M*any of the fish we find in our markets make superior pasta sauces. Southern Italians often combine swordfish and tuna with pasta. Both have a strong flavor and a texture that stands up well to dried pasta. Mackerel and bluefish, two of the most common American fish, also make boldly flavored accompaniments for pasta. I love experimenting with the many types of milder fish as well. Halibut, fresh cod, monkfish, flounder, and even catfish make for fine pasta sauces and fillings for stuffed pasta.

Your choice of flavoring ingredients should reflect the delicacy or assertiveness of the fish. You'll want to respect a subtle white fish and not overwhelm it with hot red pepper or too much acid. On the other hand, tuna, swordfish, bluefish fillets, or mackerel will really shine when matched with ripe, juicy tomatoes, dry wine, strong herbs such as oregano, rosemary, or savory, or a generous amount of fresh garlic. I also enjoy a note of sweetness in some fish sauces. A handful of currants or a splash of sweet red vermouth can round out the flavor, especially if you have included a sharp seasoning such as green olives, lemon zest, or capers.

Think about texture. Fish usually cooks up soft. An uncooked summer tomato sauce adds sparkle and refreshing bite to a fish sauce. A handful of toasted pine nuts or a scattering of crunchy bread crumbs can make a fish sauce texturally more interesting and add another layer of flavor.

Cavatappi Salad with Grilled Swordfish, Corn, Mint, and Tomato

I have divided feelings about mint. I dislike it in desserts, but I love it with fish and with tomatoes (an uncooked tomato sauce with fresh mint leaves is a marvelous thing on a summer evening). In southern Italy a type of wild mint called *mentuccia* (its proper name is *nepitella*) is used to flavor vegetables and fish. It tastes like a mix of mint and oregano. If you use half fresh oregano and half spearmint, you will come close to this wonderful flavor.

The taste of the grill brings out the best in swordfish, and the strong, direct flavors of fresh mint, tomato, and anchovy round out this summer pasta.

Make sure your grilling rack has closely spaced bars so the tomatoes and scallions won't fall through the cracks. You can use hinged grill trays that hold the pieces securely. Or grill small pieces of food on aluminum foil poked with a few tiny holes to let smoke through.

[Makes 4 main-course or 6 first-course servings]

1 to 1½ pounds swordfish steak
   (about 1 inch thick), skinned
About 5 spearmint sprigs, leaves
   chopped
Chopped fresh oregano leaves, equal
   in amount to the mint
Salt
Freshly ground black pepper

Olive oil
1 pound cavatappi
3 ears sweet, tender corn
About 10 plum tomatoes (about
   1½ pounds), cut in half lengthwise
A dozen scallions, ends trimmed
2 or 3 young garlic cloves, minced
4 or 5 anchovy fillets, chopped

- Preheat a grill.
- Place the swordfish in a shallow bowl. Add about half of the mint and oregano leaves, season with salt and pepper, and drizzle with a few tablespoons of olive oil. Let marinate, unrefrigerated, for a few minutes before grilling.
- Cook the pasta until al dente, run it under cold water, and drain well. Place in a serving bowl and toss with a little olive oil to prevent sticking.
- When the grill is ready (a medium-hot grill with low flames is ideal), wrap the corn in aluminum foil. Toss the tomato halves with a little olive oil, salt, and pepper. Do the same with the scallions. Grill the ingredients in any order you are comfortable with. If

you have a big grill, you can do them all together. The tomatoes need to be just slightly charred on their skin side. When they start to become soft (after 2 or 3 minutes), pull them off the grill and add them to the pasta bowl without losing any of their juices. Grill the scallions until lightly browned, turn them once, and grill the other side. Chop them into small pieces and add to the pasta. The corn should be turned once or twice and will probably take about 8 minutes, depending on the heat of your grill. Turn the swordfish once and cook until it loses its pinkness. It should take only a few minutes per side.

- Flake the cooked swordfish into the pasta bowl. Remove the corn kernels with a sharp knife and add them, along with the garlic, the anchovies, and the rest of the mint and oregano. Toss well and taste for seasoning. You will probably need to add a little olive oil to help pull the flavors together. Let the pasta stand, unrefrigerated, for about 10 minutes to blend flavors and to cool a bit. It is best served just slightly warm. Give it a good toss before serving.

Ideas

One thing I love about adding just-grilled ingredients to pasta is that all the juices from the fish (or meat) and vegetables slowly emerge, adding great fresh flavor and a light sauce to your dish. That's why it's best to let the dish stand 5 to 10 minutes before serving.

You can really pull this dish apart, taking out ingredients. For instance, try it with just swordfish, scallions, and tomatoes, without the corn. For a vegetarian version, leave out the swordfish and anchovies.

If you can't find fresh, top-quality swordfish but happen upon a pound of sweet-smelling shrimp, use them instead. Grill them on skewers, turning once. They should take only a minute or two per side.

In the winter you can make versions of this dish on a stovetop grill plate using winter vegetables. Grilled radicchio is wonderful with swordfish. So is grilled endive.

Making Italian Food in the United States

*E*ven the most traditional regional Italian dishes are constantly being adapted to changing times and changing people. In Puglia the local specialty of baked pasta with tiny meatballs was once cooked in the baker's oven; now it is made in a stainless-steel restaurant oven (now that Puglia *has* restaurants). Of course, it tastes different, having none of the wood smoke or bread-baking aromas sealed into it. But times change. It is easier to find a good cut of meat now, so the meatballs taste fresher and richer because they don't need to be stretched with as much stale bread.

If a cuisine is changing in the country where it was born, imagine what is happening to it an ocean away—say, in New York City. Sometimes these changes are for the better, sometimes for the worse. Recall the red sauces of Italian restaurants in the 1960s, attempts to replicate southern Italian cooking stymied by inferior ingredients. Italian American cooking has come a long way since then. Now you can find exquisite regional and inventive dishes that use authentic Italian ingredients prepared by American chefs who not only have re-searched Italian cooking but who have, in the process, created their own style.

When devising Italian dishes in your own kitchen, the more knowledge you have of what good Italian cooking tastes like, the easier it will be for you to create those flavors. But the most important thing—always—is to make the food taste good. I occasionally run across strange old regional recipes in new cookbooks in which the writer has hunted down an ancient dish and presented it to his readers verbatim, without the subtle changes needed to make the dish palatable to modern tastes. Historical recipes are important to learn from, but if they taste terrible, they're nothing more than a curiosity.

The ethereal beauty of Mediterranean cooking is partly a myth made real by city chefs (here and in Italy) with an affluent clientele and an endless variety of ingredients to play with. Many regional Italian dishes were originally very spare, typically containing nothing more than dried pasta and one vegetable fried in oil (and not necessarily olive oil, which has always been expensive). To an American, such a dish cries out for embellishment: a scattering of fresh herbs, some roasted shallots, a little cream, a bit of meat, a shot of cognac. And this is what adaptive cooking is all about—this is what will make your own cooking exciting and forward moving. It's what I've done throughout this book.

To avoid using American ingredients when cooking Italian-inspired dishes strikes me as counterproductive. I constantly try to reproduce seafood dishes I've had in Italy with varieties of fish available here. Freshly caught Long Island bluefish is absolutely delicious marinated in the Italian *agrodolce* style with vinegar, pine nuts, and raisins. When transporting a recipe across country lines, you want to preserve the spirit, adapting it when necessary to the ingredients you have to work with. Make creative use of our excellent and abundant seafood and meats. Take advantage of our green markets, buying our amazing spring asparagus and morels and our unsurpassed late-summer tomatoes and other Mediterranean vegetables such as eggplant, broccoli rabe, fresh young garlic, and local basil, mint, and marjoram. Use avocados in a pasta sauce, by all means—Italian chefs do so all the time now—but return to the Italian palate for seasoning and accents. Learn the flavor range you want to work with and limit your seasonings. Cilantro has no place in a dish of Italian pasta, but a bit of lemon verbena, not a traditional Italian pasta herb, blends extremely well with peperonata or sautéed eggplant and will not make a diner say the dish doesn't taste Italian. Learn what works.

Seeking out authentic Italian flavoring ingredients, such as prosciutto, olives, balsamic vinegar, and preserved anchovies, not only is important but is also easy. If you want the best ragù sauce you can make, season it with imported Parmigiano-Reggiano cheese, not some soapy supermarket substitute. Use our fine local catfish to stuff a dish of cannelloni, but sauce it with the flowery salt-packed capers of Pantelleria, Sicily. Because of the huge popularity of Italian food in the United States, fine Italian ingredients such as top-notch olive oil and regional cheeses are now widely available, and enticing new imports appear all the time. And keep a critical eye open to American-made Italian-style ingredients, some of which can be quite wonderful. The more you cook and learn to use ingredients, the more you will discern what is good and what isn't. Locally made cow's milk mozzarella from your corner Italian market can be excellent and much fresher than any import. But American-made prosciutto can't hold a candle to the subtle, sweet, silken-textured cured ham from Parma. A shop in my neighborhood makes first-rate fresh pappardelle as delicious as any I've had in Italy. But dried pasta made by American companies is so inferior to the firm, nutty versions imported from southern Italy that it is not even worth considering.

The most important thing to remember about being an interpreter of Italian style is to keep moving ahead. I'm always reading new cookbooks and food articles in English and Italian. I try to eat at every new Italian restaurant that sounds interesting. I travel to Italy not only to sample traditional regional cooking but also to see how new Italian chefs are modernizing their own cooking. Which I guess is the main point: every good cook wants and needs to create. This is one of the main reasons no regional cuisine ever stands still.

Orecchiette with Mako and Cranberry Beans

I love this combination of fish, beans, and pasta; it's *pasta e fagioli* (pasta and beans) with seafood. Beans and fish are a very Italian combination. The classic trattoria salad of white beans and shrimp can be easily transformed into a main-course pasta with the addition of penne and a little bean cooking liquid. Here I've chosen mako shark for its solid, firm meat that won't flake and disappear into the sauce. Borlotti beans (an Italian variety of cranberry bean) are often paired with fish in Italian cooking.

[Makes 4 main-course or 6 first-course servings]

About 1 cup dried cranberry beans,
 soaked overnight in water to cover
 if very dry (see page 339), drained
Salt
1 pound orecchiette
Olive oil
1 large onion, peeled and chopped (save
 trimmings to cook with the beans)
2 celery stalks, cut in small dice, plus a
 handful of celery leaves, chopped
 (save trimmings to cook with the
 beans)

2 small carrots, cut in small dice (save
 trimmings to cook with the beans)
1 to 1½ pounds mako, skinned and cut
 in small cubes
4 anchovy fillets
2 garlic cloves, thinly sliced
Freshly ground black pepper
A handful of flat-leaf parsley leaves,
 chopped (save stems for cooking
 the beans)
A few savory sprigs, leaves chopped

- Put the soaked beans in a pot with fresh cold water to cover by about 2 inches. Add all the vegetable and herb trimmings. Bring to a boil. Turn the heat to low, cover, and simmer until the beans are tender, at least an hour, depending on the dryness of the beans. Season with salt halfway through cooking. Remove the vegetable and herb trimmings, but keep the beans soaking in their cooking liquid.
- Start cooking the orecchiette.
- In a large skillet, heat about 3 tablespoons olive oil over medium heat. Add the onion, diced celery stalks, and carrots and sauté until soft and fragrant, 5 to 6 minutes. Add the mako, anchovies, and garlic. Season with salt and pepper and sauté until the fish is just tender, 2 to 3 minutes. Add the beans and as much of the cooking liquid as needed

to form an ample sauce (about ½ cup or a little more). Heat through gently, being careful not to overcook the fish. Add the parsley, savory, and celery leaves. Check the seasoning.

- When the orecchiette are al dente, drain them and add to the skillet. Toss well, adding a drizzle of fresh olive oil to add body to the sauce. Transfer to a large serving bowl.

Ideas

The marriage of fish and beans is worth exploring. Cannellini beans and salmon are a lovely combination. I also love tuna or mussels with chickpeas, and squid with French flageolets. Lentils with shrimp are delicious.

FRESH CRANBERRY AND OTHER FRESH SHELL BEANS

*F*resh shell beans come into season at the end of summer. If you see fresh cranberry beans in your market, buy some; they have superb flavor. They need to be shelled but take only about 20 minutes to cook. Cook them as you would dried beans, but don't worry about holding off the salt to the end—fresh beans won't toughen when salted, the way dried beans do.

Baccalà with Ditali, Sweet Onion, Chickpeas, and Rosemary

The taste of salt cod *(baccalà)* is unique, something like fresh cod but richer and more tightly textured. It has always been a classic companion for pasta in southern Italy. This all-white pasta dish is a Neapolitan treatment for salt cod. Try it this way, then experiment with red versions containing tomato and various other piquant additions (see Ideas, page 181).

[Makes 4 main-course or 6 first-course servings]

About 1 pound salt cod, cut in large chunks

1 cup dried chickpeas, soaked overnight in cold water

2 bay leaves

2 Vidalia, Walla Walla, or other sweet onions, peeled and thinly sliced (save the peels and ends for flavoring the beans)

1 dried red chile, broken in half

Salt

Freshly ground black pepper

Olive oil

A large rosemary sprig, left whole

A small piece of cinnamon stick

3 garlic cloves, thinly sliced

1 pound ditali

- Place the salt cod in a large pot of cold water in your sink and let it soak for at least 24 hours, changing the water frequently, until the fish has lost most of its saltiness. I usually set the bucket (or pot) under the tap and, from time to time during the day, just turn on the cold faucet and let the water run over the fish. After soaking, taste a little piece of the fish. It will always taste slightly salty, but it shouldn't be unpleasantly so after being properly soaked. Drain the salt cod, remove any bones or skin, and cut into large chunks.
- Drain the chickpeas and place them in a pot. Cover the beans with fresh cold water. Add 1 bay leaf, the trimmings from the onions, and the red chile, and simmer, covered, until tender—anywhere from 1 to 2 hours, depending on the beans—adding more water if necessary to keep the beans covered. Salt and pepper the beans about halfway through cooking.
- In a large skillet, sauté the onions over low heat in several tablespoons of olive oil until very soft and just starting to brown, about 30 minutes. Add the salt cod, rosemary, cinnamon stick, garlic, and a bay leaf and sauté until the garlic gives off its aroma and

turns lightly golden, about 3 minutes. Drain the chickpeas, reserving about 1 cup of cooking liquid. Add enough of the cooking liquid to the skillet to just barely cover the fish. Simmer, uncovered, until the salt cod is tender and flakes easily, about 15 minutes (see Note, below). Break the fish up into small pieces with the back of your spoon and season with plenty of ground black pepper. Taste to see if it needs salt. It may not if the cod is still quite salty.

- Start cooking the ditali. While the pasta is cooking, add the chickpeas to the sauce and let it continue to simmer over low heat for a minute or two. This will give the liquid a chance to reduce and thicken a bit. Add a fresh drizzle of olive oil. You can remove the cinnamon stick, rosemary sprig, and bay leaf for a tidier dish, but I enjoy the way they look and usually leave them in.
- When the pasta is al dente, drain it and add to the pan. Toss well and serve.

A note on cooking salt cod: Some cooks think that since salt cod is dried, they can just keep cooking it indefinitely, but that's not the case. It is, after all, still fish and can easily toughen if cooked too long or over very high heat. When the fish starts to flake, usually after about 15 minutes, it's done.

Ideas

For a red version of this sauce, add 3 chopped fresh tomatoes to the dish when you simmer the salt cod and cut the bean soaking liquid down by about half (the tomatoes will throw off their own liquid, and you don't want an overly soupy sauce).

In Sicily cooks often flavor *baccalà* with black olives and orange zest. In Rome the fish is seasoned with tomatoes, raisins, and pine nuts—it sounds Sicilian, but it's actually a very old Roman preparation. A mix of tomatoes, salt cod, potatoes, and black olives makes a great pasta sauce as well.

You can make this pasta with fresh cod, cooking the fish the same way. It will be delicious but much lighter.

See also Large Shells Filled with Baccalà Mantecato and Baked with Red Pepper and Garlic Purée, page 246.

Spaghetti with Poached Skate and Caper and Almond Pesto

Skate's ropy yet mild and tender meat clings beautifully to spaghetti. I usually cook it with the thick cartilage attached. The meat pulls off easily and can be shredded for use with pasta. Brown butter with capers is a classic French bistro treatment for this fish. Here's the same idea with an Italian accent.

[Makes 4 main-course or 6 first-course servings]

For the pesto:

About ½ cup whole blanched almonds

2 garlic cloves, peeled

About 1 cup loosely packed flat-leaf
    parsley leaves, plus a few whole
    parsley sprigs for garnish

A few thyme sprigs, leaves only

A handful of capers (about ¼ cup)

Zest of 1 lemon

Salt

Freshly ground black pepper

A few tablespoons olive oil

A few tablespoons unsalted butter,
    softened

For the skate:

Zest and juice of 1 lemon

Salt

Freshly ground black pepper

1 ½ pounds skate, cartilage attached

1 pound spaghetti

- To make the pesto, place the almonds and garlic in a food processor and grind to a rough consistency. Add the parsley leaves, thyme, capers, and lemon zest. Season with salt and pepper and process to a rough paste. Add a generous drizzle of olive oil and a few tablespoons butter and process until the mixture has loosened a bit but still has some texture.
- In a sauté pan or shallow saucepan, combine the lemon zest and juice. Add about 2 inches of water and season with salt and pepper. Bring to a boil. Turn the heat to low, add the skate, and poach until tender, about 5 minutes. The meat should pull away easily from the cartilage. Lift the fish from the liquid, reserving the liquid, and when cool enough to handle, remove the meat from the cartilage and separate it into long, thin strips along its natural dividing lines (it should pull apart with no effort).
- Cook the spaghetti until al dente and drain. Place in a large serving bowl. Add the pesto and a few tablespoons of the skate poaching liquid. Toss. Add the skate and a little more poaching liquid if needed to create a creamy consistency. Garnish with parsley sprigs.

Ideas

For pasta with poached skate and brown butter, melt a stick of unsalted butter until lightly browned. Add the juice of 1 lemon and a handful of capers. Toss spinach tagliatelle with the butter and add shredded poached skate and a handful of chopped parsley.

In Rome a popular pasta soup is made with a skate broth and the local green cauliflower. Make a fish stock using the skate and aromatic vegetables, simmering them for about 15 minutes. Strain the broth and add cauliflower florets (or green Romanesco broccoli, the traditional ingredient for this dish; it looks and tastes more like cauliflower than broccoli and has a brilliant light green head with spiral florets), a chopped tomato, a bit of hot red pepper, the shredded cooked skate meat, and a handful of broken spaghetti. Simmer until the vegetables and pasta are tender, about 5 minutes.

Shrimp and Pasta

Pasta cooked with a shrimp sauce always strikes me as a luxury. A dish of fresh tagliatelle sauced with shrimp, white wine, a splash of cream, and asparagus tips is heaven. But I love shrimp even more cooked simply, with olive oil, garlic, and a little tomato, and tossed with bucatini.

Shrimp are really best made at home, where you can watch the cooking and bring them right out to the table, tender and hot. Shrimp and pasta dishes are by nature quick work. Shrimp don't benefit from long simmering in a sauce the way squid does; they become tough. And remember that shrimp will continue to cook in the pan after you remove them from the heat. If you're not sure shrimp are cooked through, taste one. A cooked shrimp is firm but very tender to the bite. The minute they start turning uniformly pink, I whisk them off the stove.

Shrimp can be peeled or left unpeeled for pasta sauces. I enjoy pulling shrimp from a dish of spaghetti and peeling them with my fingers. Shrimp are often served this way in Italy. And shrimp cooked in their shells are more flavorful and less likely to overcook. Grilled shrimp are especially good this way and are wonderful right from the grill on top of spaghetti tossed, perhaps, with a cool Uncooked Tomato Sauce (page 34).

Shrimp for a pasta salad stay firmer if you briefly blanch them in salted water rather than sauté them. Once you dress shrimp with acid, such as vinegar or lemon juice, they will start to become mushy, actually cooking a bit from the acid, so only add lemon juice right before serving the salad. If you need to hold a pasta and shrimp salad for any length of time, add citrus zest instead of juice. Fresh lemon verbena, incidentally, is a wonderful summertime herb for shrimp.

Baked Saffron Tagliarini with Shrimp and Fennel Soffritto

I like baked pasta dishes that are very lightly cooked and creamy, as opposed to the cheese-heavy versions often served in Italian restaurants. This dish has no cheese, but it firms up on top when baked. The inside remains loose and moist. The trick to achieving moist baked pasta with a crispy top is to cook it in a hot oven.

[Makes 4 main-course or 6 first-course servings]

A few tablespoons unsalted butter

1½ pounds medium shrimp, peeled (save the shells)

A splash of Pernod or other anise-flavored liqueur

A large pinch of saffron threads, ground to a powder with a mortar and pestle (see page 352)

A few tablespoons olive oil

Salt

Freshly ground black pepper

3 thin slices pancetta, chopped

1 large white onion, cut in fine dice

1 large fennel bulb, trimmed and cut in fine dice

1 or 2 garlic cloves, finely minced

About 1 tablespoon all-purpose flour

1 cup heavy cream

1 pound Saffron Pasta (page 368), cut for tagliarini

A generous handful of basil leaves, cut in thin strips

About ½ cup bread crumbs, lightly toasted (see page 340)

- Make a quick shrimp broth by melting a tablespoon or so of butter in a small saucepan over medium heat. Add the shrimp shells and sauté until they turn pink. Add a generous splash of Pernod and let it cook down to nothing. Cover the shells with water and cook at a lively simmer for about 10 minutes. Strain.
- Return the shrimp broth to the saucepan, add the saffron, and simmer over medium heat until it's reduced to about ½ cup.
- In a large skillet, heat about 1 tablespoon each of olive oil and butter. Salt and pepper the shrimp and sear them quickly over high heat, just until they turn pink. They don't need to be cooked through at this point because they will cook further in the oven. Transfer the shrimp to a bowl. Set aside.
- Preheat the oven to 425°F.

- In the same skillet, heat another tablespoon of olive oil. Add the pancetta and sauté over medium-low heat until crisp. Add the onion and fennel and sauté until tender and fragrant and lightly browned, about 5 minutes. Add the garlic and sauté 1 minute longer, just until it gives off aroma. Add the flour and cook, stirring it into the vegetables, until well dissolved and creamy. Cook the mixture 3 to 4 minutes to lose the raw flour taste. Add the cream and shrimp broth and simmer until slightly thickened and smooth. Check the seasoning.
- Cook the tagliarini until tender and drain well. Add it to the pan with the sauce. Add the shrimp and basil and toss well.
- Butter a 12-inch round or oval baking or gratin dish. One that is about 3 inches deep is ideal. Pour the dressed pasta into the dish, scatter the bread crumbs on top, and bake, uncovered, until lightly browned and bubbling, about 20 minutes. This pasta should still be loose when you dish it out.

Ideas

Many substantial pasta sauces can be baked briefly in the oven to give them a crunchy top and a slightly firmer consistency. Spaghetti or bucatini tossed with tomatoes and fish or vegetables is often given this treatment in Sicily, where they are very fond of bringing formal baked pastas to the table for special occasions. *Pasta con le sarde* (pasta with sardines) is traditionally served this way. Pasta sauced with cream and lightly cooked seasonal vegetables works well when topped with bread crumbs or a high-quality grated cheese. Pasta dressed with tomato sauce and tossed with cubed mozzarella or a large dollop of ricotta for added body and great flavor is one of my favorite childhood baked pasta dishes, especially when made with rigatoni or another large tubular pasta. Top with grated Grana Padano or toasted bread crumbs and bake in a 425°F oven until bubbling and crisp on top. Many meat ragùs make wonderful baked pasta dishes as well, and this is a delicious way to use up leftover ragù or even a stew.

To make a pink shrimp sauce, mix a tablespoon of tomato paste or a few pureed sun-dried tomatoes into the cream and omit the saffron.

Mussels are an excellent substitute for the shrimp. They blend well with cream and saffron. You'll want to steam open about 2 pounds of mussels in a small wineglass of dry white wine (or white wine mixed with a little splash of Pernod). Shell the mussels and use the strained mussel liquid in place of the shrimp broth.

Grilled Paprika Shrimp on Spaghetti with Summer Tomato Sauce

The nice thing about this dish is that you don't have to cook the pasta sauce and can prepare it ahead, so while you grill the shrimp you don't have to worry about finishing or heating the sauce. This is another recipe based on a formula: uncooked sauce with cooked topping. It can be varied in many ways (see Ideas, page 187).

[Makes 4 main-course or 6 first-course servings]

1 pound large shrimp (or figure on 2 or 3 per serving for a first course, 4 or 5 for a main course), peeled and butterflied (see Note)

2 or 3 garlic cloves, finely sliced

About 1 teaspoon of Spanish or Hungarian paprika (see Note)

Freshly ground black pepper

Salt

Olive oil

For the tomato sauce:

About 5 large ripe summer tomatoes (2½ pounds), seeded and chopped in medium dice (if the tomatoes are very watery, drain them in a strainer for about 15 minutes)

3 or 4 anchovy fillets, chopped

A handful of slivered almonds, toasted

1 large red onion, very thinly sliced

2 or 3 garlic cloves, finely minced

Several flat-leaf parsley sprigs, leaves removed and left whole

A few marjoram sprigs, leaves removed and left whole, plus several whole sprigs for garnish

About 4 tablespoons extra-virgin olive oil

A splash of balsamic vinegar

Salt

Freshly ground black pepper

1 pound spaghetti

- Place the shrimp in a shallow bowl. Add the garlic, paprika, black pepper, salt, and several tablespoons of olive oil to coat the shrimp. Mix with your hands and let marinate, covered and refrigerated, about 30 minutes.
- Meanwhile, preheat a grill.
- In a large serving bowl, mix together all the ingredients for the uncooked tomato sauce except the whole marjoram sprigs and let stand, unrefrigerated, for about 30 minutes to develop flavor.

- When the grill is hot, start cooking the pasta.
- Remove as much garlic as you can from the shrimp (it can burn when grilled). Grill the shrimp on both sides, just until they turn pink, about 3 minutes total, depending on the size of the shrimp and the heat of the grill.
- When the pasta is al dente, drain it well and add to the bowl with the tomato sauce. Toss well. Taste for seasoning. Place the grilled shrimp on top. Or dish out bowls and place a few shrimp on each portion. Garnish with marjoram sprigs.

A note about butterflying shrimp: I butterfly the shrimp in this case because it creates more surface space for absorbing the seasoning. All you do is cut a little deeper with a sharp knife to make a long slit while removing the vein. The shrimp will open up during cooking.

A note about paprika: The type of paprika you choose will determine how this dish tastes. Spanish paprika comes in different flavors, some sweet, some spicy, some smoky. Hungarian can be sweet or spicy. So taste before using. And make sure the paprika is fresh and not musty tasting. I prefer Spanish paprika and use a sweet one for this dish.

Ideas

Ground fennel seed and orange zest make a particularly complementary marinade for grilled shrimp and blend beautifully with a fresh tomato sauce. Toast and grind to a powder a handful of fennel seeds and mix with the zest of 3 oranges. Add a few table-spoons olive oil, salt, pepper, and a pinch of cayenne—toss with the raw shrimp. Chopped fresh tarragon, sliced shallots, olive oil, and lemon zest make another excellent marinade. Crushed green peppercorns can replace the paprika in the above recipe.

A simple *aglio e olio* (garlic and oil sauce), page 54, can replace the uncooked tomato sauce for a winter version of this dish.

If you like green tomatoes, try a sauce of them lightly cooked; they taste extremely good with shrimp. Green tomatoes need a quick sautéing over high heat with a little olive oil and garlic to form a pleasant-tasting sauce. Basil is a great herb with green tomatoes.

For another recipe using uncooked sauce with hot toppings, see Spaghetti Nest with Genoese Pesto and Goat Cheese–Stuffed Tomatoes (page 102).

Bivalves and Pasta: Clams, Mussels, Scallops, and Oysters

When I make pasta with clam sauce, I don't want to detract from the beautiful sea taste of clams by adding too many other ingredients, but I've learned that you certainly can play with the standard white and red sauces to create subtle differences in the results.

I make pasta sauces with all types of hard-shell clams (soft-shells such as steamers are too sandy for a pasta sauce). Small clams are best because they are more tender. I love the little green New Zealand cockles I find all the time at my market; they're small and sweet and look pretty in a pasta sauce. Because littlenecks throw off such a wonderful, briny broth I think they make the best clam sauce.

Sandy clams can ruin a pasta sauce. Scrub them well. If you think there is a chance they are still sandy, heat them to open them in a little white wine, lift out the clams, and strain the juice. Then you can gently reheat the clams and their juice in your olive oil and garlic or tomato base. I try to pull the clams out one by one as they open so there won't be any overcooked ones.

Black Prince Edward Island mussels from Canada are cultivated and need very little cleaning and no bearding. Their taste is mild and sweet but a little bland. I usually buy Maine or local Long Island mussels, which need a bit more attention but have better flavor. Occasionally I see true Mediterranean black mussels in my market. If you find them, buy them. They have a deep, sweet mussel flavor and their cooking juices add magnificent flavor to a pasta sauce. The green-lipped New Zealand mussels look gorgeous nestled in a plate of spaghetti, but their quality, I've found, is inconsistent. Sometimes they're sweet and briny, sometimes harsh and fishy.

Look out for mussels that are open. One spoiled mussel can taint an entire pasta dish. Run the batch under cold water. They should all close up. If they don't, throw them out.

Linguine with Clams, Pancetta, and Marjoram—Elaborating on a Classic

Cured pork products (in this case, pancetta) can highlight seafoods in an appealing way—think of how the Spanish use smoked sausages with shrimp and shellfish. The more pancetta you add, the less you will taste the clams, so decide which flavor you want to dominate and adjust the quantities. Marjoram, a strong, flowery herb, blends well with the two other assertive tastes in this dish. But taste a leaf before adding it—you might prefer basil or parsley.

About 2 pounds small clams (I use
   green New Zealand cockles)

A small wineglass of dry white wine

1 pound linguine

4 thin slices pancetta, cut in small cubes

Olive oil

5 garlic cloves, thinly sliced

1 fresh red chile, finely chopped,
   with seeds

A few marjoram sprigs, leaves chopped

A large handful of flat-leaf parsley
   leaves, chopped

Salt, if needed

- Place the clams in a large pot and pour the wine over them. Include any garlic skins or herb stems you have on hand. Cook over high heat, stirring occasionally, until the clams open (cockles usually start opening after a few minutes; littlenecks take a bit longer). Lift the clams from the pot with a large strainer and place in a bowl. Pour the cooking broth through a fine-mesh strainer into a small saucepan and set aside.
- Start cooking the linguine.
- In a large skillet over low heat, sauté the pancetta in about 3 tablespoons of olive oil until it is crisp, about 3 minutes. Add the garlic and red chile and sauté until they give off a strong aroma and the garlic turns very lightly golden, about 1 minute. Add the strained clam cooking juice and a drizzle of olive oil; boil this down a few minutes to concentrate the flavor (you'll need enough liquid to amply coat the pasta, so don't boil it too much). Add the clams in their shells, the marjoram, and parsley. Taste to see if the broth needs salt.
- When the pasta is al dente, drain it and place in a large serving bowl. Pour the clam sauce on top and toss.

Ideas

Add chopped, seeded fresh tomatoes to the sauce at the end of cooking for a fresh but not overtly tomatoey sauce. The tomatoes will warm up but not cook through, giving you a modern red clam sauce, as opposed to the usual thick, long-simmered tomato sauce.

For an interesting smoky flavor, use American bacon in place of the pancetta.

Use browned sausage (try chorizo) instead of pancetta for a taste reminiscent of paella.

Try clams tossed with caper and almond pesto (page 182) or clams with corn and hot pepper, tossed with pasta. Make this by sautéing the kernels from 2 sweet ears of corn in a few tablespoons olive oil until tender and adding them to the recipe.

For a classic white clam sauce, leave out the pancetta and replace the marjoram with Italian parsley.

Make a clam and pasta soup by adding a quart of Light Fish Broth (page 376) or Chicken Broth (page 374) to the clam sauce. Add a handful of greens to this, along with orzo or broken spaghetti.

Tagliatelle with Mussels and Chervil Bread Crumbs

Pasta with mussels was a dish I always begged my mother to make, and I've never tired of the combination. I've chosen a fresh egg pasta here because of the delicate flavor of the sauce.

[Makes 4 main-course or 6 first-course servings]

Olive oil

Unsalted butter

½ cup bread crumbs (see page 340)

About ¼ teaspoon anise seeds, ground

Zest of 1 lemon

Salt

Freshly ground black pepper

1 large bunch of chervil, finely chopped

1 large fennel bulb, cut in small dice, plus some of the feathery tops, chopped

1 large white onion, cut in small dice

2 or 3 garlic cloves, thinly sliced

2 pounds small mussels, scrubbed well and bearded if necessary

A small wineglass of white Cinzano or other dry white vermouth

Juice of 1 lemon

1 pound Plain Egg Pasta (page 364), cut for tagliatelle

- In a small skillet, heat 1 tablespoon each of olive oil and butter over medium heat. Add the bread crumbs, half of the ground anise, the lemon zest, salt, and pepper and sauté until just lightly golden, about 2 minutes. Add half of the chopped chervil and mix it in. Set aside.
- In a large, heavy-bottomed pot, heat 4 tablespoons olive oil over medium heat. Add the fennel and onion and sauté until tender and fragrant, 3 to 4 minutes. Add the garlic and remaining ground anise and sauté until they give off aroma, a minute or so. Add the mussels, Cinzano, lemon juice, and a liberal amount of black pepper and cook, stirring frequently, until the mussels open. Taste for saltiness and add salt if needed. Add the remaining chervil and a drizzle of fresh olive oil to give body to the sauce.
- Cook the tagliatelle until tender, drain well, and transfer to a large serving bowl. Pour on the mussel sauce, reheat gently over low heat for a moment if necessary, and toss well. Add the bread crumbs, toss again briefly, and serve.

Ideas

I feel I have a little more leeway with mussels than with clams. Their taste is not as direct, and it's easier to play with the seasonings. Many classic French and Italian mussel preparations translate well into pasta dishes. Mussels Provençal, traditionally made with white wine, tomatoes, garlic, and herbs, makes a great pasta sauce. Mussels with shallots, white wine, fresh tarragon, and a splash of heavy cream added at the end are wonderful tossed with tagliatelle. Mussels with tomatoes, hot pepper, saffron, and a few slices of chopped prosciutto creates a Spanish-tasting dish that works well with sturdy pasta such as penne or orecchiette; add the prosciutto right before serving so it doesn't cook and lose its delicacy. A delicate pasta sauce is made with onions sautéed with a handful of chopped wild mushrooms, white wine, and mussels; add chopped chives and parsley just before tossing with tagliatelle or spaghetti. In all of these variations, the cooking technique is the same. Sauté the onion, shallot, or garlic first. Add your choice of vegetable (tomato, mushroom, or other). Add the wine or liquid and the mussels and cook, uncovered, until they open. Toss with hot, drained pasta.

Cavatelli with Mussels, Potatoes, and Rosemary

This treatment for mussels produces a hearty, rich dish with bold, direct flavors.

[Makes 4 main-course or 6 first-course servings]

1½ pounds mussels, scrubbed well
  and bearded if necessary

A small wineglass of dry white wine

A generous pinch of saffron threads,
  ground to a powder with a mortar
  and pestle (see page 352)

8 or 9 small red-skinned new potatoes,
  cut in quarters

1 pound cavatelli

Olive oil

1 medium red onion, thinly sliced

4 garlic cloves, thinly sliced

A few small rosemary sprigs,
  leaves chopped

Salt

Freshly ground black pepper

2 ripe tomatoes (about 1 pound), peeled,
  seeded, and chopped

A few flat-leaf parsley sprigs, leaves
  chopped

- Place the mussels in a large pot. Add the wine and saffron and cook, uncovered, over high heat until the mussels open. Lift out the mussels and let them cool a bit. Strain the cooking broth and set aside. Remove the mussels from their shells, discarding any that haven't opened.
- Set up a large pot of salted water to cook the pasta. Bring to a boil and add the potatoes. Blanch for about 2 minutes, leaving the potatoes a bit firm but tender. Lift them from the water with a large strainer.
- Start cooking the cavatelli.
- In a large skillet, heat 3 to 4 tablespoons olive oil over medium heat. Sauté the onion until soft, 3 to 4 minutes. Add the garlic and sauté until it gives off its aroma but does not color, about 1 minute. Add the potatoes and rosemary, season with salt and pepper, and sauté briefly. Add the tomatoes and cook only a few minutes (the pieces should stay firm and juicy). Add the mussel cooking liquid and let the sauce boil a minute or two to concentrate the flavors.
- When the pasta is al dente, drain it and add to the pan. Add the mussels and parsley and toss well. Taste for seasoning and transfer to a serving bowl.

Twisted and Rolled Shapes

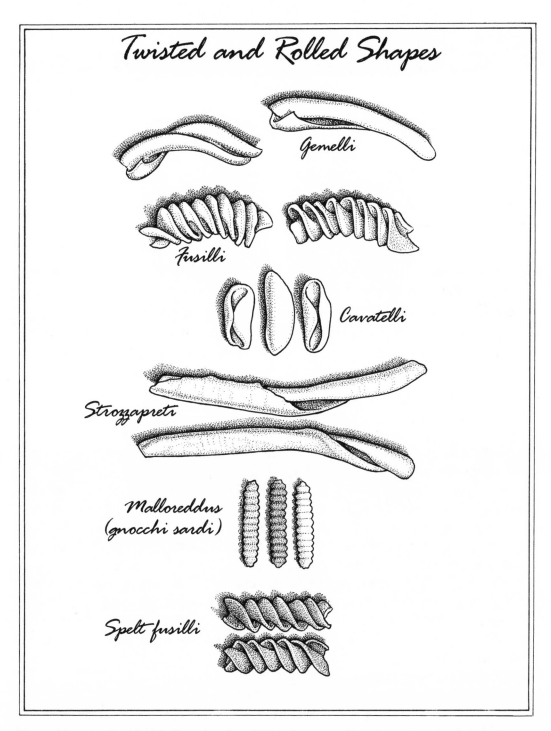

Gemelli

Fusilli

Cavatelli

Strozzapreti

Malloreddus
(gnocchi sardi)

Spelt fusilli

These work extremely well with thin strips of zucchini, bell pepper, or prosciutto—ingredients that willingly wrap around the pasta. Pesto clings beautifully to these elegant forms.

Black Pepper Tagliatelle with Seared Scallops, Lemon, and Basil

This is an incredibly simple and fast sauce that illustrates an uncluttered approach to seasoning delicate shellfish.

[Makes 4 main-course or 6 first-course servings]

1 to 1½ pounds sea scallops, side
  muscle removed

Olive oil

Zest of 2 lemons

Freshly ground black pepper

Salt

Unsalted butter

7 or 8 shallots, thinly sliced

A generous splash of dry sherry

About ¼ cup low-salt canned
  chicken broth

1 pound Black Pepper Pasta (page 368),
  cut for tagliatelle

A large handful of basil leaves, cut in
  thin strips, plus a few whole leaves
  for garnish

Juice of 2 lemons

A handful of unsalted pistachios,
  skinned and coarsely chopped

A large handful of capers, rinsed

- Dry the scallops well and place them in a small bowl. Toss them with a few tablespoons olive oil, half of the lemon zest, and a sprinkle of pepper.
- Heat a large skillet until it is almost smoking. Season the scallops with salt and place them in the skillet, leaving some space between them so they will brown and not steam (brown them in 2 batches if they are too crowded). Sear the scallops quickly on both sides, leaving them slightly undercooked in the middle. They should be nicely browned. Remove the scallops from the pan and set aside.
- Add a few tablespoons each of butter and olive oil to the skillet. Turn the heat to medium and sauté the shallots until soft, about 4 minutes. Add the sherry and let it cook away. This will deglaze the pan, loosening all the scallop cooking particles so they can flavor the sauce. Add the chicken broth and let it simmer for about a minute over low heat.
- Start cooking the tagliatelle.
- Return the scallops to the pan along with the chopped basil, the lemon juice, remaining lemon zest, pistachios, and capers. Add a tablespoon of butter and a generous drizzle of olive oil to the pan. Season with pepper and additional salt if needed. Reheat the

scallops gently for a minute or two to finish cooking. Drain the tagliatelle and add it to the pan. Toss well, getting up all the pan juices. Transfer to a large serving bowl and garnish with whole basil leaves.

Ideas

Another very good flavor combination for scallops, one that emphasizes their sweetness more than their sea taste, is pancetta, leeks, and fresh sage. Sear the scallops and remove them from the pan. Add a few slices of chopped pancetta and 3 or 4 thinly sliced leeks. Sauté until the pancetta is crisp and the leeks are tender. Deglaze the pan with a splash of white wine and add a small handful of thinly sliced fresh sage leaves. Toss with pasta, adding extra olive oil to coat the pasta.

A beautiful addition to this dish is sautéed escarole. Wash and roughly chop a small head of escarole. Blanch it briefly in the pasta cooking water, squeeze it dry, and sauté it along with the shallots, adding a few sprigs of lemon thyme instead of the basil. I would omit the pistachios in this case.

I like a mix of seared scallops, blanched fava beans, and toasted pine nuts for a pasta sauce. Toss this with green penne.

Squid and Eel Add Mellow Sea Flavor
To Pasta Sauces

Squid is wonderfully versatile in pasta sauces. You can quick-sauté small ones with a hand-ful of chopped fresh tomato for a fresh, bright sauce for tagliatelle, or you can long-simmer larger squid with wine, onion, and herbs for a deep, rich sauce to dress penne or rigatoni. The availability of precleaned squid makes cooking this sweet, mild fish a pleasure (although cleaning squid is easy to do yourself). Eel, another delicious mild, white-meat fish, has unfortunately not caught on with Americans, maybe because it's best bought live. But eel are plentiful in our waters and very easy and rewarding to cook with. They're always in Italian markets around Christmastime and usually available by special order or frozen at other times of the year. You can have your fish seller clean them for you.

Ziti with Grilled Squid, Red Onions, Black Olives, and Mint

Grilling is one of the best fast-cooking methods for small, tender squid. In the winter I make this inside on my stovetop grill. It smokes up the house a bit, but the flavor is worth it.

[Makes 4 main-course or 6 first-course servings]

1½ pounds small squid, cleaned and left whole, tentacles left whole

Olive oil

Salt

Freshly ground black pepper

About 3 dozen cherry tomatoes, stemmed

2 large red onions, sliced in thin rounds

1 pound ziti

A small handful each of mint, marjoram, and parsley leaves

Zest and juice of 1 large orange

A handful of black Niçoise olives, pitted and halved

2 small garlic cloves, minced

- Preheat a grill.
- Dry the squid well and place in a bowl. Add a few tablespoons olive oil and sprinkle with salt and pepper. Mix well and let stand, unrefrigerated, while proceeding with the recipe.
- Coat the tomatoes in a little olive oil and season with salt and pepper. Thread the toma-toes on metal grill skewers. Brush the onion slices with olive oil.
- Start cooking the ziti.

- When the grill is hot, place the onion slices on the rack and cook until they show grill marks, turning once. Place in a serving bowl big enough to hold all the pasta and other ingredients.
- Place the tomato skewers on the grill and cook until lightly browned. Turn and grill the other side. This should take only about 3 minutes. Slide the tomatoes off the skewers into the pasta bowl.
- Grill the squid quickly on both sides, just until it shows grill marks, probably only about 1 minute on each side. If you are not sure it's cooked through, taste a bit—it should be tender to the bite but firm. Its color will be opaque white. You might want to skewer the tentacles so they don't fall through the rack. If the squid are very small, leave whole. If they are a little bigger and you would rather cut them for easier eating, grill them whole and then hold the grilled squid over the serving bowl and cut it into bite-sized rings with kitchen scissors. That way, you won't lose any of the juices. Juices from all your grilled ingredients will collect in the bowl and, when combined with olive oil and the other seasonings, produce a very flavorful sauce.
- When the ziti are al dente, drain them well and add to the serving bowl. Add all the fresh herbs, the orange juice and zest, black olives, and garlic. Add a generous drizzle of olive oil. Season with salt and pepper. Toss. Serve hot.

Ideas

Hot grilled squid is absolutely delicious tossed with basil pesto and a pasta such as penne.

Let the grilled ingredients come to room temperature and toss with pasta that has been cooked al dente and rinsed under cold water. This makes an excellent summer salad that can be created from leftover grilled vegetables.

Try grilling other vegetables. Bell peppers, eggplant slices, zucchini, scallions, and whole mushrooms take well to grilling and can be mixed with squid or other fish for endless variations on this summertime pasta.

Pappardelle with Eel, Chickpeas, White Wine, and Saffron

This is a pasta sauce I adapted from a Neapolitan eel dish typically served as part of the Christmas Eve fish feast. I've flavored it with saffron, which is not traditional but tastes lovely with chickpeas.

[Makes 4 main-course or 6 first-course servings]

1 cup dried chickpeas, soaked overnight in cold water to cover

1 large onion, cut in small dice (save trimmings to cook with the chickpeas)

1 bay leaf

2 whole cloves

2 garlic cloves, finely minced, plus a few whole cloves, lightly crushed to cook with the chickpeas

A large handful of flat-leaf parsley leaves, chopped (save stems to cook with the chickpeas)

Salt

Freshly ground black pepper

Olive oil

Flour for dredging the eel

About 2 pounds small eels, skinned, cleaned, and cut in small chunks (it should still be on the bone)

A few thin slices pancetta, chopped

A small wineglass of dry white wine

1 pound Plain Egg Pasta (page 364), cut for pappardelle

A large pinch of saffron threads, ground to a powder with a mortar and pestle (see page 352)

About 4 savory or thyme sprigs, leaves chopped

A tiny splash of tarragon white wine vinegar

- Place the drained chickpeas in a pot of fresh cold water, covering them by at least 3 inches. Add the onion trimmings, bay leaf, cloves, whole crushed garlic cloves, parsley stems, and any other vegetables or herbs you might have on hand (such as celery leaves, leek greens, or a carrot). Bring to a boil. Turn the heat to low, cover the pan, and simmer until the chickpeas are tender, at least 1 hour, probably longer, depending on the dryness of the beans. Check the pot from time to time to see if it needs additional water. Salt and pepper the chickpeas about halfway through cooking. Drain the chickpeas, saving about 1 cup of the cooking water. Remove and discard all the vegetables.
- In a large skillet, heat 2 to 3 tablespoons olive oil over medium-high heat. Flour the eel pieces and season with salt and pepper. Brown them on both sides. They should cook

quickly, a few minutes on each side. When cooked through, the meat will pull away easily from the bone. Remove the eel pieces and bone them.

- In the same skillet, sauté the onion and pancetta until browned. Add the garlic and cooked chickpeas and sauté a minute or so, just until the garlic gives off aroma. Add the wine and let it boil down to almost nothing.
- Start cooking the pappardelle.
- Return the eel to the pan. Add the saffron, the savory or thyme, and a small ladle of the bean cooking water. Season with salt and pepper and let the eel simmer while the pasta is cooking. But remember, eel toughens if cooked too long, so don't let it simmer more than a few minutes.
- When the pappardelle are tender, drain them well and transfer to a large serving bowl. Pour on the eel sauce. Add the parsley, vinegar, and a drizzle of fresh olive oil. If you like a looser sauce, add a bit more of the bean cooking liquid. Check the seasoning. Toss well.

Ideas

In France and Italy, eel is often simmered in red wine, which produces a rich dark sauce. For a hearty pasta sauce with this flavoring, cook the eel pieces as in the above recipe and remove from the pan. Sauté a large chopped onion and a few slices of chopped pancetta. Add a small wineglass of Chianti and let it reduce to almost nothing. Return the eel to the pan along with 2 or 3 chopped fresh tomatoes and a little chopped rosemary. Simmer a few minutes and toss with penne. If you like, finish the dish with a splash of balsamic vinegar.

A delicious pasta dish I ate in Rome consisted of chunks of eel cooked with spinach, olive oil, garlic, and white wine.

Mushrooms go very well with eel, enhancing its delicate qualities. I would include a handful of sliced sautéed wild mushrooms and omit the chickpeas and saffron.

If you can't locate eel, this sauce is very good made with slow-simmered calamari, mussels, or chunks of cod or monkfish.

Pasta with Crab and Lobster

Spaghetti with lobster is a dish my mother occasionally made on Christmas Eve, usually in a tomato sauce. I loved it. I now make versions of this dish for holidays. Over the years of cooking lobster sauces for pasta, I've found I like delicate and sweet sauces best. I love tarragon and basil with lobster. Slightly sweet white wine works well too. I almost never add hot chile to the sauce, finding it drowns out the flavor of the lobster.

Crabmeat is another exquisite partner for fresh and dried pasta. It is a bit gutsier in flavor than lobster and, I think, can stand up to stronger seasonings such as garlic, capers, a splash of dry white wine, or a pinch of hot red chile.

Bucatini with Crab, Parsley, and Lemon Verbena

I hardly ever find live hard-shell crabs in New York markets. I sometimes see blue crabs in their hard-shell phase, but unlike the large West Coast Dungeness crab, their meat is very difficult to remove. Here is an easy and really delicious crab sauce using lump crabmeat, which is readily available.

I'm always looking for new ways to add sparkle to sauces. Lemon verbena adds brightness to rich seafood. Here I've mixed it with parsley to give a subtle lemony tone to the dish.

[Makes 4 main-course or 6 first-course servings]

A large handful of flat-leaf parsley leaves, coarsely chopped

About a dozen fresh lemon verbena leaves, coarsely chopped

A handful of capers, rinsed

A handful of pine nuts, toasted

1 or 2 garlic cloves, minced

Extra-virgin olive oil

Salt

Freshly ground black pepper

1 pound bucatini

1 pound lump crabmeat, picked over to remove any small bones (see Note)

A splash of dry white wine

About ½ cup bread crumbs, toasted and seasoned with a pinch of cayenne (see page 340)

- Place the chopped parsley and lemon verbena in a small bowl. Add the capers, pine nuts, garlic, and about 4 tablespoons olive oil. Season with salt and pepper and mix well. Set aside.

- Start cooking the bucatini.
- In a large skillet, heat 2 to 3 tablespoons olive oil over medium heat. Add the crabmeat and sauté for about 1 minute (see Note, below). Add the wine and let it evaporate. Season with salt and pepper.
- When the bucatini are al dente, drain them, leaving a bit of water clinging to the pasta, and transfer to a serving bowl. Add the parsley and lemon verbena sauce and the crabmeat. Toss. Top with a sprinkling of toasted bread crumbs.

Note: When buying lump crabmeat, remember that you are buying cooked crab, so don't let it simmer too long in any sauce.

Ideas

Crabmeat can be briefly warmed in a simple tomato sauce and tossed with ziti or penne. It also makes a nice addition to A Puttanesca Sauce (page 27), which is basically a tomato sauce flavored with capers, olives, and sometimes anchovies.

Also try adding crab to *aglio e olio* (garlic and oil sauce), page 54, and tossing it with linguine or capellini. A soffritto of onion, garlic, fennel, and celery makes a good base for a crab sauce; simply add crabmeat and a splash of white wine to this sautéed base and let it warm through.

This sauce of parsley and lemon verbena makes a good pasta sauce on its own, with no fish at all.

Soft-Shell Crab over Linguine with Arugula Almond Pesto

Oone of the pleasures of East Coast living is the soft-shell blue crab season. I love a sautéed soft-shell crab over salad, which gave me the idea for this recipe. If you choose small soft-shell crabs, this will make a good first-course pasta.

[Makes 4 main-course or 6 first-course servings]

For the arugula almond pesto:
2 large bunches of arugula
 (reserve a few leaves for garnish)
¾ cup whole blanched almonds
2 or 3 small garlic cloves, peeled
About ⅓ cup fruity olive oil
1 tablespoon unsalted butter,
 softened
¾ cup grated Pecorino Toscano cheese
Salt
Freshly ground black pepper

A handful of blanched almonds,
 finely ground
Salt
Freshly ground black pepper
2 large eggs
1 pound linguine
About 2 tablespoons unsalted butter
Olive oil
4 to 6 soft-shell crabs (1 per person)
Juice of 1 lemon
1 lemon, cut into wedges, for garnish

½ cup finely ground cornmeal

- To make the pesto, place the arugula, almonds, and garlic in a food processor and grind to start breaking up the nuts. While the machine is still running, start adding the olive oil through the feed tube, adding enough to achieve a thick paste. Add the butter and process a few seconds longer to blend. Add the Pecorino and season with salt and pepper. Process a few seconds longer to blend. Taste for seasoning.
- In a shallow bowl or plate, mix together the cornmeal, ground almonds, salt, and pepper. In another shallow bowl, beat the eggs lightly.
- Start cooking the linguine.
- In a large skillet, heat the butter and a drizzle of olive oil over medium-high heat. Dip the crabs in egg and then in the cornmeal mix. When the butter and oil are hot and bubbling, add the crabs and brown them on both sides. They will cook in 3 to 4 minutes. Squeeze lemon juice over the crabs.

- When the pasta is al dente, drain it, reserving about ½ cup of the cooking water, and place in a large bowl. Toss with the pesto, adding a tablespoon or so of cooking water to loosen the sauce. Divide the linguine among individual pasta bowls and top each with a crab. Garnish with arugula leaves and a lemon wedge.

Ideas

The best way to cook soft-shell crabs for pasta is to sauté them. Deep-frying is, I believe, too rich for this purpose.

For a lighter version of this dish, try dressing the pasta with parsley and capers (a classic Italian green sauce) or a briefly cooked tomato sauce punctuated with chopped fresh basil or mint.

Sautéed sardine fillets are sometimes draped across dishes of pasta in Sicily. You can use them here in place of the crabs.

Saffron Tagliatelle with Lobster, Tomato, and Cognac

Fresh egg pasta with a lobster sauce is one of the most delicious of all pasta dishes. There are many good ways to prepare it, but I think simple is best. The charm of lobster fra diavolo has always escaped me. I don't understand the appeal of overpowering a sweet, subtle fish with hot pepper. Try experimenting with various gentle flavorings (see Ideas, page 205).

[Makes 4 main-course or 6 first-course servings]

2 live lobsters (about 1½ pounds each)

½ cup homemade Chicken Broth
(page 374) or low-salt canned

A generous pinch of saffron threads,
ground to a powder with a mortar
and pestle (see page 352)

Unsalted butter

4 or 5 shallots, finely diced

About ¼ cup cognac

4 large, ripe tomatoes (about 2 pounds),
peeled, seeded, and cut in
medium dice

2 bay leaves, fresh if possible

Salt

Freshly ground black pepper

1 pound Saffron Pasta (page 368), cut
for tagliatelle

½ cup mascarpone cheese

A handful of basil leaves, chopped
(plus extra whole leaves for garnish)

A large handful of pine nuts, toasted

- In a large pot of rapidly boiling salted water, cook the lobsters for 5 minutes (this will be enough to allow you to easily remove the meat from the shell, but will leave the meat slightly underdone). Remove the lobsters from the water, saving the cooking water. When the lobsters are cool enough to handle, remove the meat over a large bowl to catch any juices that run from the shells. Chop the meat into thick pieces and place in the bowl with the lobster juices. Break the shells into large pieces.
- In a small saucepan, heat the chicken broth with the saffron until the saffron dissolves. Remove from the heat.
- In a large skillet, melt about 2 tablespoons butter over medium heat. Add the shallots and sauté until soft, about 3 minutes. Add the reserved lobster shells and the cognac and cook until the cognac evaporates. Add the tomatoes, bay leaves, and saffron-scented chicken broth and simmer over low heat for a few minutes. Remove the lobster shells and discard them. Season the sauce with salt and pepper.

- Start cooking the tagliatelle in the same water in which you boiled the lobsters.
- Turn the heat to very low and add the lobster meat and all its juices to the skillet, along with the mascarpone, basil, and pine nuts. Check the seasoning. The mascarpone should melt easily. The lobster will warm through and finish cooking in less than a minute.
- Don't cook the lobster any longer or it will toughen. Turn off the heat.
- When the tagliatelle are tender, drain them and transfer to a large serving bowl. Toss with a tablespoon or so of butter and then pour on the lobster sauce and toss again. Garnish with whole basil leaves.

Ideas

Lobster pairs extremely well with all sorts of mushrooms; try simmering a handful of reconstituted dried porcini along with the tomatoes. Fresh chanterelles are especially wonderful; sauté them in a little unsalted butter and add them to the sauce at the end of cooking.

Tarragon is another excellent herb for lobster and can replace the basil in this recipe. A mix of chervil and fresh chives is another very good choice.

Dry Marsala wine instead of cognac gives the sauce a sweeter, more haunting flavor.

Partially cooked lobster meat (as in this recipe) can be added and simmered to finish cooking in a tomato sauce for a southern Italian–style lobster dish, which would classically be tossed with spaghetti. You can purchase precooked lobster meat at many fish markets; sometimes it's juicy and tender, but most times it is a little overcooked for my taste. I don't advise using precooked lobster in a pasta sauce in which it will need to warm through and cook further, but it's fine for a pasta salad, providing it is moist and tender.

See also Lobster with Small Diced Fall Vegetables and Pappardelle (page 238).

Spaghetti with Shad Roe

Shad roe is a delicacy as interesting as sturgeon roe when mixed with pasta. It never occurred to me to cook shad roe with pasta until I tried a wonderful recipe for it from Giuliano Bugialli's book, *Classic Techniques of Italian Cooking* (he uses fresh tuna roe, but he suggests shad roe as a good American alternative).

[Makes 4 main-course or 6 first-course servings]

1 pound spaghetti

Olive oil

Unsalted butter

1 pair shad roe, separated and trimmed
    of any tough membrane

Salt

Freshly ground black pepper

Juice of 1 large lemon

A large handful of salt-packed capers,
    soaked and rinsed (see page 343)

A large handful of flat-leaf parsley
    (about ½ cup), leaves coarsely
    chopped, plus a few whole sprigs
    for garnish

A few chervil sprigs, leaves coarsely
    chopped

- Start cooking the spaghetti.
- In a large skillet over medium heat, heat about 2 tablespoons olive oil and 1 tablespoon butter. Add the shad roe, season liberally with salt and pepper, and sauté quickly on both sides, breaking it up with a spoon as it cooks so the roe can be released. This will take only a minute or two on each side. Don't overcook it; it will toughen. It should be slightly pink at the center when you start breaking it up. Squeeze on the lemon juice and add the capers.
- When the pasta is al dente, drain it, leaving a bit of water clinging to the strands, and add it to the pan. Add the parsley and chervil and toss quickly just to coat. Transfer to a serving bowl. Garnish with parsley sprigs.

Ideas

This makes a good pasta salad. I've also made it with tarragon in place of the parsley.

To make a simple but lovely pasta with sturgeon or salmon caviar, toss hot tagliatelle with crème fraîche, ricotta cheese (thinned with a few tablespoons of heavy cream or pasta cooking water), or mascarpone, adding the zest of 2 or 3 lemons and a handful of lightly chopped mild herbs like chervil, basil, parsley, fennel tops, or tarragon. Top each serving with a tablespoon of sevruga or osetra caviar. Or use salmon roe, which looks beautiful and tastes wonderful, especially with crème fraîche. Garnish with capers, chopped chives, or very thinly sliced raw shallots.

Bottarga, a pressed dried tuna or mullet roe from Sicily and Sardinia, is served shaved over long, thin pasta that has been simply dressed with either butter or olive oil. My favorite version is one from Palermo, where fresh tagliatelle were tossed with butter, olive oil, and fresh mint leaves, with *bottarga* grated over the top. For more information on caviar and *bottarga,* see "The Improviser's Pantry" (page 343).

Fish Soups and Stews

I approach mixed-fish stews for pasta in two nearly opposite ways. One is to use very few seasonings and let the blend of fish make its own sauce. The other is to add many seasonings to the same pot, creating a complex sauce. Both can work wonderfully.

Among my favorite ingredients: dried porcini mushrooms blend especially well with fish stews made with nonoily fish; black olives can add depth but can overpower milder fish. Sausage, pancetta, and bacon can have a surprisingly gentle effect in a fish stew, particularly one made with freshwater fish; also try them with clams. Fresh mint can add brighten a rich fish stew made with tuna and swordfish, while pine nuts or almonds can mellow a tomato-based stew. Bay leaves impart lovely flavor to mild fish; try them with squid or fresh cod.

Add vegetables to fish stews. Roasted red peppers give sweetness and depth; they're especially good with clams or mussels. Fresh peas, artichokes, spinach, and other cooked greens can stretch a stew while adding another layer of flavor. I like a squid stew simmered with fresh spinach, white wine, and tomatoes and tossed with penne. And if you like hot chile, go ahead and use it, dried or fresh. I think it works best with strong-flavored fish like swordfish, and with clams and mussels. Spanish or Hungarian paprika has a sweeter flavor than dried cayenne. You can find both mild and hot varieties.

Fish that need long cooking to become tender, such as squid and octopus, make especially lovely, full-bodied sauces when left to simmer slowly in wine with aromatic vegetables. Don't overlook octopus; it's actually very easy to cook, and its rich taste will surprise you.

Try experimenting with different mixes of fish. I like an all-shellfish sauce containing clams, mussels, shrimp, and maybe scallops. But a stew of several types of mild white fish can be wonderful too, especially if cooked in white wine and unsalted butter and accented with lemon and maybe a handful of capers and basil or tarragon. Or try an all-freshwater fish sauce with tagliatelle.

All the following dishes are suitable for main-course meals. In fact, I think of them as celebration or special-occasion pastas that should be served family style in large bowls in the middle of the table. You can easily double any of these recipes to serve a larger group.

Penne with Squid Simmered in White Wine and Cinnamon

Simmered Sauces for Squid and Octopus

Sicilians occasionally use cinnamon to flavor fish stews. In very small amounts, it contributes a subtle, unexpected perfume. Try adding a little to different fish sauces to see how it alters them. It goes especially well with sauces containing white wine and tomatoes. I use a whole stick of cinnamon here to enhance the sweetness of the squid.

[Makes 4 main-course or 6 first-course servings]

Olive oil

4 or 5 garlic cloves, thinly sliced

About 1½ pounds squid, cleaned and cut in thick rings, tentacles left whole

1 cinnamon stick

1 or 2 bay leaves, fresh if possible

Salt

Freshly ground black pepper

About ½ bottle dry white wine (try a Vernaccia di San Gimignano)

One 35-ounce can Italian plum tomatoes, chopped and well drained (see Note)

1 pound penne

Several flat-leaf parsley sprigs, leaves chopped

- In a large flameproof casserole, fitted with a lid, heat a generous amount of olive oil over low heat (I like a lot of oil in this dish, at least ¼ cup and probably a little more). Add the garlic and sauté slowly until it is just turning golden and gives off a sweet aroma. Add the squid, cinnamon stick, and bay leaves and sauté for several minutes, seasoning with salt and pepper. Add the wine and tomatoes and bring to a boil. Turn the heat to low, cover, and simmer until the squid is very tender, about 1 hour. If the sauce is very liquid, you can cook it uncovered for the last 15 to 20 minutes. Taste for seasoning. The sauce should have a sweet but well-rounded taste.
- Cook the penne until al dente, drain, and add to the casserole. Add a generous amount of chopped parsley, a drizzle of olive oil, and serve from the pot if desired.

A note on draining canned tomatoes: When do you drain tomatoes? If you want to sear or roast them on high heat, you don't want a lot of liquid or they'll just stew. In this recipe I wanted the wine taste to prevail. I didn't want a lot of tomato juice diluting the wine, so I chose to use only the tomatoes. And even though this sauce simmers for so long and leaches juice from the tomatoes themselves, it still ends up wine rich and less tomatoey.

Ideas

Fresh ginger in place of the cinnamon is another unlikely but delicious flavoring sometimes used for seafood in southern Italy. Try simmering squid with tomatoes, white wine, and a few thin slices of fresh ginger.

You can easily add vegetables to this very simple sauce. Peas are a classic with squid, but also try lettuce or more assertive greens like escarole. Or add a handful of raw arugula to the sauce at the last minute and allow it to briefly wilt.

For a sweet and spicy sauce, add a generous pinch of slightly hot paprika or a pinch of cayenne.

For an even simpler version—a purer version—leave out the tomatoes, but make sure to use ample olive oil so the sauce will cling to the pasta.

If you want to make squid stewed in its own ink, replace the cinnamon stick with a package of commercially available cuttlefish ink (if you can buy squid with ink sacks attached, use the fresh ink instead). Add it about halfway through the cooking. The result will be a dark, rich, inky, winy sauce that will be wonderful with spaghetti.

Squid Stuffed with Pistachios and Greens, Served over Bucatini

In this recipe large squid are filled with green chard and ground pistachios and braised in a broth scented with coriander seed, bay leaf, fennel seed, and saffron, giving the effect of a light, elusive curry.

You can offer the squid as a second course, or place thick slices on top of each serving of pasta.

[Makes 4 main-course or 6 first-course servings]

For the squid:
Olive oil
2 leeks, washed, white part cut in
    small dice
1½ to 2 pounds large squid, bodies
    cleaned (see Note) and left whole,
    tentacles finely chopped
2 garlic cloves, minced
A large bunch of green chard, washed
    and well chopped (if center ribs are
    thick, cut away before chopping)
Salt
Freshly ground black pepper
4 or 5 anchovy fillets
2 large handfuls of unsalted pistachios,
    coarsely ground in a food processor
    (half is for the stuffing, half is to
    sprinkle on top of the pasta)
About ⅓ cup bread crumbs, toasted
    (see page 340)
1 large egg

For the sauce:
Olive oil

3 leeks, washed, white part cut in
    small dice
Salt
Freshly ground black pepper
3 garlic cloves, minced
A large pinch of saffron threads, ground
    to a powder with a mortar and
    pestle (see page 352)
A small handful of coriander seeds,
    ground
A small handful of fennel seeds, ground
2 bay leaves, fresh if possible
A small wineglass of semidry white
    wine (a fruity Chardonnay is fine)
1 cup homemade Chicken Broth
    (page 374) or low-salt canned
One 35-ounce can Italian plum toma-
    toes, drained and chopped

For the pasta:
1 pound bucatini
Unsalted butter
A handful of flat-leaf parsley leaves,
    stemmed but left whole

- To prepare the squid, heat a few tablespoons of olive oil in a large skillet. Add the leeks and sauté a few minutes to soften. Add the chopped squid tentacles and the garlic and cook until the squid is opaque, about a minute longer. Add the chard, season with salt and pepper, and sauté until wilted and soft but still bright green, about 5 minutes. Add the anchovies and mix in well. Let this cool a few minutes, then add half of the ground pistachios, all the bread crumbs, and the egg. Mix well and taste for seasoning. The stuffing should be highly seasoned.
- Loosely stuff the squid bodies with this filling and close the ends with toothpicks. (Don't overstuff; squid tend to shrink during cooking.)
- To make the sauce, choose a skillet large enough to hold all the squid and sauce. Heat about 2 tablespoons olive oil over medium heat. Add the leeks and sauté until tender and fragrant, about 4 minutes. Salt and pepper the stuffed squid and add it to the pan. Sauté to brown very lightly on all sides. Add the garlic and all the spices and the bay leaves and cook a few minutes to release their perfume. Add the wine and let it bubble a few minutes to release some of the alcohol. Add the chicken broth and tomatoes and bring to a boil. Turn the heat to low, cover the pan, and let the squid simmer until very tender, about 1 hour. Turn the squid once or twice during the cooking.
- Start cooking the bucatini.
- While the pasta is cooking, remove the squid from the skillet and cut into thick slices on the diagonal. Check the sauce; it should be chunky from the tomatoes but still slightly brothy. If you feel it is too thin to coat the pasta, reduce it over high heat for a few minutes. Check the seasoning.
- When the bucatini are al dente, drain them and add to the skillet. Add a few tablespoons of butter and the parsley leaves and toss well. Check for seasoning. Transfer to a large serving bowl. Place the squid slices on top and sprinkle with the remaining ground pistachios. Or you can make up individual bowls of pasta with the squid arranged on each portion.

A note about cleaning squid: Squid are actually very easy to clean. If you run them under cool water, the purplish outer skin peels right off. Then all you need to do is reach inside and pull out the insides, including the translucent white quill. Rinse the bodies under water to remove any sand that might be trapped inside. If you feel the tentacles, you'll notice a hard, round head at the root. Cut right below that to free the tentacles. And that's it.

Ideas

A classic stuffing for squid and one that I enjoyed often as a child is made from toasted bread crumbs mixed with hard-boiled egg yolks, blanched peas, and onion. Think about other flavorings that go well with squid and you can come up with numerous alternatives. Spinach teams well with squid and can easily replace the chard in this recipe. Just make sure to chop all ingredients into small pieces and either sauté them until soft enough to hold together or add a binder such as bread crumbs or an egg.

A soffritto of aromatic vegetables (page 31) mixed with bread crumbs and an herb such as thyme, savory, or parsley makes a delicate stuffing. Sautéed leeks alone can be mixed with a small amount of bread crumbs and a raw egg to hold the stuffing together. One of my favorite stuffings is a mix of sautéed wild mushrooms, onion, and bread crumbs. Basil, thyme, rosemary, and marjoram all go well with squid. Olives or bits of ham or anchovy can be included for deeper flavor. Or try a sweet stuffing of currants, fennel seeds, and pine nuts.

Sauces for stuffed squid can be very simple (a little chopped garlic and a wineglass of wine) or a bit more involved. Here I've added broth, tomatoes, and spices. I've eaten stuffed squid with sauces that contained sliced mushrooms, artichoke hearts, fava beans, and even little cubes of potato. In general, a simple sauce is best with a rich filling, and a more elaborate sauce works well with a very simple filling, such as one of bread crumbs and herbs.

Cavatappi with Octopus, Red Wine, Star Anise, and Red Peppers

This is an adaptation of a dish I discovered at a Sicilian restaurant in New York. It came not with pasta but as an octopus served whole (it was a small one), bathed in a fragrant dark red sauce that contrasted beautifully with the mild taste of the simmered meat. The star anise is my own addition. It highlights the sweet flavor of the bell peppers.

[Makes 4 main-course or 6 first-course servings]

One 2- to 3-pound octopus (see Note)

2 bay leaves, fresh if possible

Salt

About 2 tablespoons olive oil

2 red bell peppers, roasted over a flame
    until charred, peeled, seeded, and
    cut in thin strips

1 large onion, cut in medium dice

4 garlic cloves, thinly sliced

1 star anise

A splash of brandy or cognac

A large wineglass of dry red wine
    (a Chianti is good here)

4 ripe tomatoes (about 2 pounds),
    seeded and chopped

Freshly ground black pepper

A pinch of cayenne pepper

A few tarragon sprigs, leaves chopped

A small handful of basil leaves, chopped

1 pound cavatappi

- Place the octopus in a large pot and cover it with cold water. Add the bay leaves and season the water liberally with salt. Bring to a boil. Once the octopus starts to cook, it will curl up and you may need to add extra water to keep it covered. Turn the heat to low, cover the pan, and simmer until the octopus is partially cooked (at this point it will still be somewhat chewy), about 45 minutes.
- Lift the octopus from the water, saving the cooking liquid (which will have become dark pink), and let cool a few minutes. Rub off some of the skin (it should be soft and come off easily). Slice the octopus into bite-size pieces.
- In a large skillet, heat the olive oil. Add the red peppers and onion and sauté until just starting to soften. Add the chopped octopus, garlic, and star anise and sauté a minute longer. Add the brandy and let it cook out. Add the wine and let it boil a minute or two. Add the tomatoes and a generous ladle of octopus cooking liquid. Season with salt, black pepper, and the cayenne. Simmer over medium-low heat, partially covered, until the octopus is very tender and the sauce has thickened, about 1 hour. Add more cooking liquid if the sauce becomes too thick. Add the fresh herbs and check the seasoning.
- Cook the cavatappi until al dente, and transfer to a serving bowl. Add the octopus sauce and toss.

Note: If you buy a frozen octopus, thaw it overnight in the refrigerator (set the octopus in a pan so the water doesn't drip all over the place).

Ideas

In Puglia, cooks often add potatoes to octopus sauce; use them in place of bell peppers. You can also substitute a cup of cooked chickpeas.

Mushrooms, especially strong-tasting ones such as porcini or portobello, are excellent in place of bell peppers. Sauté them in olive oil and add them to the sauce in the last 5 minutes of cooking.

A teaspoon of Spanish paprika (called *pimentón*) can be added to the sauce. And if you like a little acidity, try adding a splash of sherry vinegar right before serving.

Toss the pasta with ricotta before adding the octopus sauce. This treatment is especially good with fusilli: the ricotta becomes caught in all the grooves of the pasta, adding taste and texture to the finished dish.

Octopus with red peppers is essentially a Sicilian dish, and it is very richly flavored. If you would like a lighter sauce, make the dish with a dry white wine, leave out the red peppers, and increase the amounts of fresh herbs. The result is wonderful with Saffron Pasta (page 368), cut for tagliatelle.

Add a dollop of aioli (see page 107) to each serving, to be mixed in by each guest.

Spaghetti with Snails Simmered in Tomatoes, Marsala, and Mild Herbs

Try Snails with Pasta

In Rome and parts of southern Italy, snails are slow-simmered with tomatoes, wine, garlic, and herbs to produce a heavenly perfumed sauce that is wonderful tossed with pasta.

[Makes 4 main-course or 6 first-course servings]

Unsalted butter

4 shallots, minced

Two 7-ounce cans snails
(about 2½ dozen snails)

A few generous gratings of nutmeg

3 or 4 garlic cloves,
finely minced

Salt

Freshly ground black pepper

A generous splash of dry Marsala

5 ripe tomatoes (about 2½ pounds),
peeled, seeded, and chopped

A handful of flat-leaf parsley leaves,
chopped

A few tarragon sprigs, leaves chopped

A few thyme sprigs, leaves chopped

A handful of basil leaves, chopped

1 pound spaghetti

- In a large skillet, heat about 3 tablespoons butter. Add the shallots and sauté until soft and fragrant. Add the snails, nutmeg, and garlic, season with salt and pepper, and sauté until the garlic gives off aroma but has not taken on any color. Add a generous splash of Marsala and let it boil away. Add the chopped tomatoes, cover the pan, and let the sauce simmer over low heat until the snails are tender and the flavors are well blended, about 20 minutes. Add all the herbs and taste for seasoning.
- Cook the spaghetti until al dente, drain well, and add to the pan. Add a generous pat of fresh butter and toss well. Transfer to a serving bowl.

Ideas

In Italy, the Sienese like to simmer snails in tomato sauce flavored with the local salami. Try browning finely diced capocollo or soppressata before adding the garlic to the pan.

Snails also go very well with spinach, which you can use here in place of the herbs.

Snails sautéed in garlic, unsalted butter, and olive oil make an excellent pasta sauce if you add a little white wine and parsley. I also like to throw in a handful of green peppercorns.

Try cooking snails in Simmered Tomato Sauce (page 28). Let them simmer for about 20 minutes. This is a classic southern Italian approach—uncomplicated and delicious.

Fish Stew with Couscous, Black Olives, and Bay Leaves

Two Mixed-Fish Stews

In Trapani, in western Sicily, fish stews are served with couscous seasoned with Arab-influenced spices, such as saffron and cinnamon, and with bay leaves. I like the addition of thyme and orange zest.

[Makes 4 main-course or 6 first-course servings]

About 4 cups Light Fish Broth (page 376)
  or homemade Chicken Broth
  (page 374)

Juice and zest of 1 large orange

2 whole allspice, ground

5 bay leaves, fresh if possible

A splash of orange flower water
  (about 2 teaspoons)

1½ cups couscous (not quick-cooking)

A large pinch of sugar

Salt

Freshly ground black pepper

Olive oil

1 large onion, cut in medium dice

3 garlic cloves, crushed

3 or 4 anchovies, chopped

A few thyme sprigs, leaves chopped

2 pounds mixed fish fillets, such as cod,
  monkfish, flounder, sea bass,
  halibut, or orange roughy, skinned
  and cut into large chunks (a mix of
  4 types of fish is best, but a good
  stew can also be made using 2 or
  3 kinds)

A large handful of whole unpitted
  black olives (I use black oil-cured
  Moroccan olives)

- In a large saucepan, heat the fish or chicken broth (or use half of each) with the orange juice and zest, allspice, bay leaves, and the orange flower water. Bring to a boil, turn the heat to low, and simmer for about 5 minutes, just to infuse the broth with the flavorings.
- Place the couscous in a large, shallow bowl. Season it with the sugar, salt, and pepper. Pour on about 1½ cups of the hot seasoned broth, making sure to add a few of the bay leaves. Add a drizzle of olive oil and stir to distribute the broth evenly.
- Cover the bowl with aluminum foil and let stand while you continue with the recipe.
- In a large flameproof casserole, heat about 3 tablespoons olive oil over medium heat. Add the onion and sauté until soft, 3 to 4 minutes. Add the garlic, anchovies, and thyme. Sauté a few minutes to release the flavors. Season the fish with salt and pepper

and add it to the pan. Sauté, turning the pieces once, until the fish just becomes opaque, a few minutes at the most. Add the remaining warm broth and simmer about 5 minutes, just to finish cooking the fish and to blend the flavors. Transfer to a shallow serving bowl. Add the olives. Check the seasoning.

- Fluff the couscous with a fork. If it seems dry, add a few tablespoons of stew broth or a little hot water. Bring both platters to the table. Have the diners serve themselves couscous and then ladle the stew on top, making sure they have ample broth and a few olives.

Ideas

Other seasonings traditionally used in Sicilian fish couscous include cinnamon, saffron, and sometimes nutmeg. Tomatoes and pine nuts are often added. Sometimes almonds. Sicilians also boil lobster, chop it up with its shell, and garnish the couscous with it. If you want to include squid in the stew, add it about a half hour before the fish so it has a chance to become tender. Shrimp or scallops can be added in the last few minutes of cooking.

Peas and strips of roasted bell pepper are another traditional garnish for this dish. Substitute them for the olives.

Try an all-freshwater fish stew. Keep the seasonings simple. Maybe choose one herb, such as thyme or basil. Sauté a little pancetta along with the onion and then boil down a wineglass of white wine in the pan before adding the fish and the broth. Good fish to try are trout, carp, catfish, eel, and perch.

Orzo is a good substitute for the couscous. Cook it al dente and dress it with olive oil, chopped herbs, and maybe a little garlic. Serve it in a separate bowl, as you would the couscous.

Zuppa di Pesce with Ground Almonds and Spaghetti

Ground nuts are used in African and Spanish cooking to thicken stews. They also work well here, helping the sauce cling to the strands of spaghetti.

The quantities of seafood I list below are only suggestions for a good balance of flavors and textures. You might want to be more generous with the clams or leave out the mussels completely. Maybe sea scallops are too expensive at the market and you'd rather add a few more mussels and small shrimp instead. The idea here is simply to have a mix of shellfish.

[Makes 4 main-course or 6 first-course servings]

Olive oil

1 large red onion, cut in small dice

1 fresh red chile, with seeds, finely minced

4 young garlic cloves, minced

⅓ cup whole blanched almonds, finely ground, plus a handful left whole for garnish

About ½ teaspoon sweet Spanish paprika

Salt

Freshly ground black pepper

A small wineglass of dry Spanish sherry

5 ripe tomatoes (2 to 2½ pounds), peeled, seeded, and chopped

About a dozen small clams, scrubbed well

About a dozen mussels, scrubbed well and bearded if necessary

1 pound spaghetti

½ pound medium shrimp, shells left on

½ pound sea scallops

A few marjoram sprigs, leaves chopped, plus a few whole sprigs for garnish

A tiny splash of sherry vinegar

- In a large flameproof casserole, heat several tablespoons of olive oil over medium heat. Add the onion and chile and sauté until soft and fragrant, 3 to 4 minutes. Add the garlic, ground almonds, and paprika and season with salt and pepper. Sauté a minute to lightly toast the almonds. Add the sherry and let it bubble a few minutes. Add the tomatoes and let the sauce simmer for about 5 minutes.
- Add the clams and cook until they just start opening. Add the mussels. Remove each mussel and clam as it opens and place in a large bowl.
- Start cooking the spaghetti.

- In a small sauté pan, heat 1 tablespoon olive oil over medium heat. Add the whole almonds you will use for garnish and sauté until just starting to turn golden, about 2 minutes. Season lightly with salt and pepper and set aside.
- Add the shrimp and scallops to the casserole and simmer until cooked through—2 to 3 minutes should do it. Put the mussels and clams back into the pot, along with any juices they've released. Add the chopped marjoram leaves, sherry vinegar, and a generous drizzle of olive oil. Taste for seasoning.
- When the pasta is al dente, drain it and place in a large serving platter or bowl. Pour on the shellfish sauce and toss briefly. Garnish with the whole toasted almonds and marjoram sprigs.

Ideas

Another excellent sauce for shellfish can be made by making a soffritto (see page 31) of onion, garlic, fennel, abundant parsley, and lemon zest. Add a wineglass of white wine to the soffritto and then add the shellfish and let them open in the broth. Toss with bucatini or spaghetti, adding a little fresh olive oil.

Simplifying it further, you can make a classic white sauce by sautéing garlic in olive oil and adding parsley, white wine, and clams or mussels. I love this sauce with shrimp.

Tuna Ragù with Fusilli Lunghi

Braising Tuna for a Pasta Sauce

In this dish fresh tuna is braised in one piece and served as a second course after the pasta, which has been dressed with the braising liquid. Serve the fish with an arugula salad or asparagus dressed with olive oil and lemon.

[Makes 4 main-course or 6 first-course servings]

4 or 5 garlic cloves, peeled

8 anchovy fillets

A few oregano sprigs, leaves chopped

A large handful of mint sprigs, leaves chopped

2 pounds tuna steak

Roughly cracked black pepper

Salt

3 to 4 tablespoons olive oil

1 large onion, cut in medium dice

4 or 5 tender inner celery stalks, cut in small dice, with leaves

A small wineglass of dry white wine

One 35-ounce can Italian plum tomatoes with juice, chopped

1 bay leaf

1 pound fusilli lunghi

- Put the garlic cloves, anchovies, oregano, and mint in a food processor and grind to a rough paste.
- With a thin knife, make deep incisions all over the tuna steak and push the paste into them, using about half of the paste. Press cracked black pepper onto the surface of the tuna and salt lightly.
- In a large flameproof casserole fitted with a lid, heat the olive oil over medium heat. When the pan is very hot, add the tuna steak and brown well on both sides. The tuna should not be cooked through, just well seared. Remove the tuna from the casserole.
- Add the onion and celery and sauté until fragrant, about 4 minutes. Add the remaining garlic-herb paste and sauté briefly. Add the wine and let it bubble for a minute or so. Add the tomatoes and bay leaf and season with salt and pepper. Let the sauce simmer over medium heat for about a minute. Return the tuna to the casserole, spooning some sauce on top of it. Turn the heat to low, cover the casserole, and let the fish cook slowly until just tender, 15 to 20 minutes. The sauce should be slightly thickened. Check the seasoning.
- Meanwhile, cook the fusilli lunghi until al dente, drain, and transfer to a serving bowl. Remove the tuna from the sauce, ladling a bit of sauce on top, and keep warm. Pour the rest of the sauce over the pasta and toss well. If you like, you can flake a little of

the tuna into the pasta sauce for texture. Serve the fish as a second course along with a salad or vegetable. This fish is also very good served cold the next day, along with a vegetable in vinaigrette.

Ideas

Instead of the garlic-herb stuffing, try a mix of ground fennel seed, garlic, and parsley. Or basil or arugula and almond pesto (page 102 or 202).

For a substantial one-dish meal, flake the tuna and add it to the pasta sauce instead of making it a second course.

Monkfish and Escarole Soup with Toasted Orzo and Mint Pesto

Monkfish soup is very popular in Provence, where cooks generally flavor it with fennel, orange, and saffron; I've opted here for a basil-and-mint pesto.

[Makes 4 main-course or 6 first-course servings]

For the broth:
One 2-pound piece of monkfish, with bone (see Note)
About 2 tablespoons olive oil
About 1 tablespoon unsalted butter
1 large onion, chopped
1 large carrot, chopped
2 bay leaves
2 whole cloves, ground
A long strip of lemon peel
About 1 pound fish bones from nonoily fish
2 or 3 garlic cloves, lightly crushed
A small wineglass of dry white wine
2 large, ripe tomatoes (about 1 pound), roughly chopped
About 5 cups light homemade Chicken Broth (page 374)
Salt
Freshly ground black pepper

For the pesto:
A large handful of pine nuts
2 garlic cloves, peeled
About 1 cup basil leaves
A few mint sprigs, leaves removed
Zest of 1 lemon
Olive oil
Salt
Freshly ground black pepper

For the soup:
About 2 tablespoons olive oil
1 cup orzo
1 large head escarole, washed, chopped, and left slightly wet
2 large, ripe tomatoes, peeled, seeded, and cut in small dice

- Fillet the monkfish and remove all the membrane. Cut the fish into thin slices and set aside.
- To make the broth, chop the monkfish bone into a few pieces. In a large soup pot, heat the olive oil and butter over medium heat. Add the onion, carrot, bay leaves, ground cloves, and lemon peel and sauté until the onion starts to soften, about 5 minutes. Add the monkfish bones and other fish bones and the garlic and sauté a few minutes longer. Add the wine and let it boil for a few minutes. Add the chopped tomatoes, chicken

broth, and about 1 cup of water, enough to just cover the bones. Bring to a boil. Turn the heat to low and let this simmer, partially covered, for about 30 minutes, skimming occasionally. Season with salt and pepper. Remove the fish bones, lemon peel, and bay leaves. Pour the broth through a fine-mesh strainer into a bowl, reserving all the vegetables. Puree the vegetables with about 1 cup of the fish broth in a food processor. Stir the purée into the remaining broth. The broth will still be rather thin.

- To make the pesto, place the pine nuts and garlic in a food processor and grind to a rough paste. Add the basil, mint, and lemon zest and process a minute, just to chop the herbs. Add a generous drizzle of olive oil and process a minute longer, just to achieve a smooth consistency, but leave some texture to the sauce. Season with salt and pepper.

- To make the soup, heat the olive oil in a clean soup pot. Add the orzo and sauté, stirring frequently, until very lightly golden (this gives the pasta a nice nutty taste). Add the escarole and sauté until wilted. Add the broth and diced tomatoes. Bring to a boil, turn the heat to medium, and cook at a low boil until the orzo is cooked through, about 5 minutes. Add the monkfish and simmer until the fish is just tender, about 3 minutes. Taste for seasoning.

- To serve, ladle the soup into large soup bowls. Top each with a large dollop of pesto.

Note: If you can't find monkfish with the bone in, buy a pound of monkfish fillets and purchase fish bones from other white-fleshed fish. If you're short on fish bones, you can make this soup with homemade chicken broth.

Ideas

If you would like to make a monkfish soup with the flavors of a Marseilles-style bouillabaisse, add garlic, orange peel, fennel seeds, thyme, tomato, a pinch of cayenne, and a shot of pastis to the broth base. The appropriate pasta for this dish is broken vermicelli or capellini.

Fish and Vegetables with Pasta

This is an opportunity ripe for improvisation. Experimenting can result in untold new and un-expected flavors that go far beyond the usual southern Italian pairings of fish with tomatoes. Sicilian cooks like pasta sauces that combine tuna, swordfish, or fresh sardines with their beautiful eggplant, zucchini, fava beans, or fennel. An exquisitely flavored pasta dish of swordfish, eggplant, and fresh mint is a Sicilian classic with a taste that's a revelation. Coming up with my own fish and vegetable combinations is one of my favorite areas of exploration. I love a sauce of pan-roasted scallops with zucchini, or squid braised with artichokes and roasted pep-pers. Salmon is rich and delicious with baked eggplant or with oven-braised endive or radicchio. I love tagliatelle tossed with sautéed chanterelle mushrooms and shrimp.

Work on keeping each dish simple. One type of fish plus one or occasionally two seasonal vegetables should suffice. You want to taste each component in the dish and avoid chaos on the tongue, becoming aware of the texture of each cooked ingredient and contemplating how those textures will fit together. Eggplant, which cooks up rather soft and creamy, is wonderful with firm tuna but might not be so wonderful with a soft white fish that breaks apart in the sauce. I love the silken texture of gently cooked salmon matched with a lightly crunchy green veg-etable such as fava beans or asparagus. Choose herbs and flavorings that won't overshadow del-icate fish. Think about how much oil a fish contains, and choose complementary ingredients for their acidic or mellow qualities. Lemon or tomato works well with oily fish; cream or unsalted butter and gentle herbs blend better with delicate fish.

I'd feel comfortable offering any of these well-balanced dishes as a main course, but if you'd rather, serve them Italian style as a first course (each recipe make six small servings), following in the same vein with another seafood dish.

Fresh Cod, Yellow Peppers, and Thyme with Ziti

This has the feel of a stew, offering a loose sauce with large chunks of fish and vegetables.

[Makes 4 main-course or 6 first-course servings]

Olive oil

4 ripe yellow bell peppers, seeded and cut in very thin strips

1 large onion, thinly sliced

3 garlic cloves, thinly sliced

3 or 4 anchovies

A few thyme sprigs, leaves chopped

About 1 pound cod fillets, cut in bite-size chunks

Salt

Freshly ground black pepper

A pinch of cayenne pepper

A generous splash of dry white vermouth

About ¼ cup low-salt canned chicken broth

A handful of green olives, pitted and cut in half (picholine is my choice for this dish)

1 pound ziti

½ cup bread crumbs, toasted (see page 340)

- In a large skillet, heat a few tablespoons of olive oil. Add the peppers and onion and sauté slowly over medium-low heat until they are very soft, about 20 minutes. Add the garlic, anchovies, and thyme and sauté about 2 minutes longer, just to release their flavors. Add the cod. Season with salt, black pepper, and cayenne and sauté on both sides until just cooked through (the fish will start to break up a bit). Add the vermouth and let it boil away to almost nothing. Add the chicken broth and a drizzle of fresh olive oil and let the sauce simmer a few minutes. Add the olives. Check the seasoning.
- Cook the ziti until al dente, drain, and transfer to a large serving bowl. Add the cod sauce and toss. Top with a sprinkling of toasted bread crumbs.

Ideas

Sweet peppers and fish are a time-honored southern Italian combination. The peppers can be roasted, grilled, or slow-sautéed to bring out their sweetness and blend well with mild- and strong-tasting fish. In my travels in Italy I've enjoyed everything from roasted red pepper and octopus with penne to tuna or swordfish with red peppers, spaghetti, and mint.

Cavatelli with Swordfish and Eggplant

This is a fairly straightforward Sicilian recipe that I've jazzed up a bit with herbs and wine. The pairing of fish and eggplant may seem unlikely, but the taste is incredible.

[Makes 4 main-course or 6 first-course servings]

Olive oil

About 6 scallions, cut in thin rounds,
   with some of the tender green

1 large eggplant, cut in small cubes

Salt

Freshly ground black pepper

2 or 3 garlic cloves, thinly sliced

About 2 dozen cherry tomatoes,
   cut in half

A large handful of capers

1 pound cavatelli

1½ pounds swordfish steak, cut in
   small cubes

A splash of dry white wine

A few marjoram sprigs, leaves chopped

A few mint sprigs, leaves chopped

- In a large skillet, heat about 4 tablespoons olive oil over medium heat. Add the scallions and eggplant, season with salt and pepper, and sauté until the eggplant is just tender but not falling apart, about 10 minutes. Add the garlic and sauté until it gives off aroma. Add the cherry tomatoes and cook until they soften a bit and give off juice, about 4 minutes. Add the capers.
- Start cooking the cavatelli.
- In another skillet, heat 2 tablespoons olive oil over high heat. Salt and pepper the swordfish, and when the pan is very hot, add the fish and sauté it quickly until just starting to brown. This should take only a few minutes. Loosen the cooking juices with a splash of white wine and add the fish to the eggplant sauce. Simmer very gently about 1 minute, just to heat through. Check the seasoning.
- When the cavatelli are al dente, drain them and transfer to a serving bowl. Toss with a generous drizzle of fresh olive oil and the marjoram and mint. Add the fish sauce and toss again.

Ideas

Tuna, squid, and sardines are often cooked with eggplant with excellent results. When deciding on a fish to cook with eggplant, think rich and meaty. Delicate fish like flounder will be overwhelmed by the sauce.

In season, substitute zucchini for the eggplant. Cook this dish exactly the same way, but add a few chopped anchovies to the skillet when the zucchini is just tender, and leave out the capers.

The sauce can also be tossed into cold cooked rice for a very good Sicilian-style rice salad.

Scallops and Shrimp Cooked with Vegetables

Scallops are so expensive, it's a good idea to think about ways to cook them with pasta, which lets you buy less but still feed a group lavishly. Add a vegetable to the sauce and you stretch the dish even further without losing the beautiful fragrance of the fresh seafood.

I love scallops with any kind of sautéed mushrooms, in either a butter or an olive oil base. Ripe summer tomatoes barely cooked, abundant fresh basil, and seared scallops make a memorable pasta sauce that takes about 5 minutes to prepare. Asparagus, artichokes, and all sorts of cooked greens, especially ones with a slightly bitter edge, mix well with scallops, helping to highlight their sweetness. Try arugula, mustard greens, escarole, or endive.

There are several types of scallops in our markets. The large North Atlantic sea scallops are a favorite of mine for pasta sauces. Look for sea scallops labeled "dry." This means they have not been pumped up with phosphates to make them look juicier and prolong freshness. Dry scallops are easier to brown because they don't release as much liquid. In winter months, look for tiny, sweet bay scallops. I love them tossed into an *aglio e olio* (garlic and oil) sauce with spaghetti. They cook in about a minute. The relatively inexpensive calico scallops, which resemble bay scallops in appearance but not in flavor, are often sold in supermarkets. Although never as delicious as bay scallops, calicos can be good with pasta if you cook them very briefly over high heat and pull them off the flame quickly so they don't have a chance to toughen.

Garganelli with Scallops, Chanterelles, and Fava Beans

This is an elegant summer pasta to make when chanterelles and fresh fava beans are in the market at the same time.

[Makes 4 main-course or 6 first-course servings]

1 pound sea scallops, side muscle removed

Salt

Freshly ground black pepper

Olive oil

Unsalted butter

2 medium spring onions, cut in small dice

About ½ pound chanterelles, sliced in half lengthwise

½ to 1 cup homemade Chicken Broth (page 374)

A few gratings of nutmeg

About ¾ cup fresh fava beans, peeled (see page 95)

1 pound garganelli

1 lemon

A bunch of chervil, tough stems removed, leaves coarsely chopped

- Season the scallops with salt and pepper and toss them in a little olive oil.
- In a large skillet, heat about 2 tablespoons butter and the same amount of olive oil over medium heat. Add the onions and sauté until fragrant and soft, 3 to 4 minutes. Add the chanterelles, season with salt and pepper, and sauté until the mushrooms are tender and just starting to give off some juice, about 5 minutes. Add about ½ cup of the chicken broth, the nutmeg, and the fava beans and let the sauce simmer over low heat, uncovered, for a minute or two, until the beans and mushrooms are tender.
- Start cooking the garganelli.
- In a separate large skillet, heat 1 tablespoon each of butter and olive oil over high heat. When very hot, add the scallops, leaving some space between them. Sear them quickly on both sides until browned but not completely cooked through. This should take only a minute or two. Add a generous squeeze of lemon juice and loosen up all the cooked pan juices so they will form part of your sauce. Turn off the heat.
- When the pasta is just about cooked, add the scallops to the mushroom and fava bean sauce and simmer over low heat for a minute to finish cooking, adding a little more chicken broth if the sauce has become too thick. Be careful not to overcook the scallops. (If your scallops weren't thick to begin with, they might already be cooked and need only to be added to the mushroom sauce at the last minute, so cut one in half to check.) Taste for seasoning.

- Drain the pasta well and transfer it to a large bowl. Toss with a tablespoon each of fresh butter and olive oil. Pour the sauce over the pasta. Add the chervil and toss well.

Ideas

This mix of fresh fava beans and chanterelles makes an excellent all-vegetable sauce if you omit the scallops. You can replace the chicken broth with vegetable broth or water.

Fish and mushrooms are a popular combination in European and Asian cooking. Add another vegetable, and you create a rich but clear group of flavors that do not overwhelm a pasta sauce if you've selected your ingredients well. Here are a few suggestions for matching flavors: cremini mushrooms, artichokes, and squid; morels, monkfish, and fresh peas.

Fusilli with Rock Shrimp, Pureed Onions, and Peas

The pureed onions give this dish a wonderfully creamy texture.

[Makes 4 main-course or 6 first-course servings]

2 large sweet onions, such as Vidalia or Walla Walla, chopped in coarse chunks

Olive oil

2 garlic cloves, minced

A few thyme sprigs

1 bay leaf

Salt

Freshly ground black pepper

A few splashes of dry white wine

½ cup low-salt canned chicken broth

About 1 cup freshly shucked peas (the fresher, the better)

1 pound fusilli

1 pound rock shrimp

A handful of flat-leaf parsley sprigs, leaves chopped

- Place the onions in a food processor and process until they are just pureed but not mushy.
- Heat about 3 tablespoons olive oil in a large skillet. Add the onions, garlic, thyme, and bay leaf, season with salt and pepper, and sauté over medium-low heat, stirring frequently, until the onions are soft and very lightly golden, about 15 minutes. Add a splash of white wine and let it boil away. Add the chicken broth and peas and let the sauce simmer until it is thick and creamy and the peas are tender, about 4 minutes longer.
- Start cooking the fusilli.
- When the fusilli are almost cooked, heat 2 tablespoons olive oil in a clean large skillet over high heat. When the pan is just about smoking, add the shrimp, season with salt and pepper, and sauté quickly until they are just pink, less than a minute. Add a small splash of wine to the pan just to loosen any cooking juices. Add the shrimp, along with any pan juices, to the onion sauce. Add the parsley.
- When the pasta is al dente, drain it and add to the pan. Toss well and transfer to a large serving bowl.

Ideas

Using the pureed onion as a base, you can alter this sauce in many ways, changing the fish or the vegetable or both.

If you don't have fresh peas, instead of substituting frozen, try thinly sliced asparagus (peeled if the skin is tough), fava beans, or thinly sliced artichoke hearts.

Any fish that cooks quickly and doesn't fall apart can work in this recipe. Small sliced squid is delicious here. So are bay scallops. Cook them in the same manner as you did the shrimp—in a separate pan, quickly, over high heat—before adding them to the onion sauce. I also like little bits of anchovy studding the sauce in place of the squid. Try anchovies with tiny broccoli florets; blanch them in boiling water until tender and add them to the onion sauce, along with 3 or 4 anchovy fillets, letting this simmer for about a minute before tossing with pasta.

Farfalle with Shrimp, Celery Root, and Celery

Celery root is a thick-skinned vegetable with a strong aroma—like celery but more earthy. Here I've mixed it with stalk celery for a two-celery sauce.

[Makes 4 main-course or 6 first-course servings]

Unsalted butter

1 pound medium shrimp, shelled, (save the shells), deveined, and chopped into small pieces (cut each shrimp into thirds)

4 medium leeks, washed, trimmed, and thinly sliced (save a handful of trimmings)

A small wineglass of dry white wine

Olive oil

1 small celery root, peeled, thinly sliced, and cut in small dice (see Note)

3 tender inner celery stalks, cut in small dice, plus the leaves, coarsely chopped

Salt

Freshly ground black pepper

1 pound farfalle

Juice of 1 lemon

A small handful of flat-leaf parsley leaves, coarsely chopped

- In a saucepan, melt about 2 tablespoons butter over medium heat. Add the shrimp shells and leek trimmings and sauté until the shells turn pink and give off a sweet shrimp smell. Add the wine and let it cook down to almost nothing. Add enough water to just cover the shells and let it simmer, uncovered, until the broth is concentrated and has good flavor, about 15 minutes. Strain. You should have about 1 cup of broth. Put the broth in a clean pan and reduce over high heat by about half.
- In a large skillet, heat 1 tablespoon each of butter and olive oil over medium heat. Add the leeks, celery root, and celery stalks and season with salt and pepper. Sauté until soft and fragrant, about 10 minutes.
- Start cooking the farfalle.
- When the farfalle are almost cooked, add the chopped shrimp to the skillet and sauté until they turn pink, about 1 minute. Add the shrimp broth to create a loose consistency (this dish should be a little brothy). Add lemon juice to taste, the celery and parsley leaves, and extra salt and pepper if needed.

- When the farfalle are al dente, drain them well and place in a large serving bowl. Add the shrimp sauce and toss well, adding a drizzle of fresh olive oil to help the sauce cling to the pasta.

A note about cutting celery root: Celery root has thick, bumpy skin that needs to be removed before cooking. I've found the easiest way to deal with it is by cutting off a slice at one end of the root so that it sits flat on the counter. Then, starting at the top, I cut the skin off, working downward, with a sharp knife.

The easiest way to julienne celery root is to make very thin slices on a mandoline or with the slicing blade of a food processor. Then stack a few slices at a time and cut them into thin strips with a sharp knife.

Remember, celery root is one of those vegetables (like artichokes and avocados) that turn brown when exposed to air. So if you cut it ahead, drop the pieces into a large bowl of cold water acidulated with the juice of a lemon.

Ideas

If you want to make an all-vegetable sauce, leave out the shrimp and simmer the celery root in a little water and olive oil until tender. Finish with grated Pecorino Toscano or another mild Pecorino.

Penne Salad with Mussels and Braised Artichokes

Ever since I tried a recipe cookbook author Marcella Hazan wrote for pasta with clams and zucchini, I've been captivated by the idea of pairing bivalves with green vegetables and have discovered many excellent variations on this theme, using both cooked and raw vegetables. Such pairings can make extremely interesting pasta salads with real flavor and integrity. Both clams and mussels taste wonderful cold.

1 [Makes 4 main-course or 6 first-course servings]

½ pounds small mussels, scrubbed well
  and bearded if necessary

A large wineglass of dry white wine

A small handful of coriander seeds,
  lightly toasted and ground (use a
  mortar and pestle or an electric
  spice grinder)

A small handful of fennel seeds, lightly
  toasted and ground

About 4 garlic cloves, minced

Olive oil

About 15 baby artichokes (a few more if
  they're very tiny), trimmed and cut
  in half (see Note)

Salt

Freshly ground black pepper

1 pound penne

2 medium round tomatoes (about 1
  pound), peeled, seeded, and cut in
  medium dice

A handful of unsalted pistachios,
  coarsely chopped

A generous bunch of flat-leaf parsley
  leaves, coarsely chopped

Juice of half a large lemon

- Place the mussels in a large pot. Pour in the wine, about half of the ground coriander and fennel seeds, and about half of the minced garlic. Cook over high heat, uncovered, until the mussels open. Stir them around a few times to make sure they cook evenly. Lift out the mussels and place in a bowl. Boil the cooking liquid down to about ¼ cup. Strain. Remove the mussels from their shells and set aside, discarding any that haven't opened.
- In a large skillet, heat about 3 tablespoons olive oil over medium heat. Add the artichokes and sauté until they just start to turn golden. Add the rest of the garlic, season with salt and pepper, and cook 1 minute longer, just to gently release the flavor of the

garlic. Add a splash of water to the pan and finish cooking the artichokes until tender, about 5 minutes. By this time the water should have cooked away.

- Cook the penne until al dente, run them under cold water, and drain well. Transfer to a large serving bowl. Add the mussels, artichokes, tomatoes, pistachios, and parsley.
- Add about 3 tablespoons fresh olive oil to the mussel cooking liquid, along with the lemon juice and remaining ground spices. Pour this over the pasta and toss well. Correct the seasoning. Serve the salad warm or let it cool to room temperature.

A note about baby artichokes: These tender vegetables are picked before their fuzzy chokes form, so they're completely edible without much trimming. Simply remove a layer or two of outer leaves until you reach the light, bright green leaves. Trim the stem. The artichokes can be left whole if very small, or can be cut into halves or quarters. Drop trimmed artichokes into a large bowl of water with the juice of 2 lemons. This keeps them from turning dark.

Ideas

You can borrow good ideas for seafood pasta salads from recipes for Italian seafood salads made without pasta. Many contain squid, shrimp, conch, mussels, or octopus. Sometimes they're accented with celery or tomatoes or black olives. When composing a seafood pasta salad, exercise a light hand with the vinegar and lemon. A seafood salad can be bracing; a dish of pasta should be a bit more mellow.

Try substituting roasted red peppers for the artichokes. Peas and roasted red peppers cooked with mussels will give you a dish that tastes and looks a little like Spanish paella. Chopped escarole sautéed in olive oil and garlic is an excellent alternative to the artichokes.

Grilled Squid and Mushroom Skewers over Rosemary Tagliarini

Squid with Vegetables

Rosemary and mushrooms are a Ligurian flavor combination that I find enjoys the addition of squid.

[Makes 4 main-course or 6 first-course servings]

2 pounds cleaned small squid, left whole (if you have large squid, cut it in thick rings and leave the tentacles whole)

About 20 small cremini mushrooms, stemmed and wiped clean

Olive oil

Zest of 2 lemons

A few large rosemary sprigs, leaves chopped

Salt

Freshly ground black pepper

4 garlic cloves, finely minced

About ½ cup pine nuts

Juice of 1 large orange

1 pound Plain Egg Pasta (page 364), cut for tagliarini

- Preheat a grill.
- Thread alternating pieces of squid and mushroom onto metal grill skewers (I like skewers with square edges because they hold the food better during cooking, preventing it from spinning around as much). Make 1 skewer per person, 6 short (6- to 8-inch) ones for a first course, 4 longer (about 10-inch) ones for a main course. Lay them in a shallow glass or ceramic dish. In a small bowl, mix together about ⅓ cup olive oil, half of the lemon zest, half of the chopped rosemary, salt, and pepper. Pour this over the skewers, turning them over so they are evenly coated with the marinade. Let stand unrefrigerated, while you continue with the recipe.
- In a large skillet, heat about ⅓ cup olive oil over low heat. Add the garlic, pine nuts, and the rest of the rosemary and lemon zest and sauté until the nuts are very lightly golden and the rosemary and garlic give off strong fragrance, 2 to 3 minutes. Add the orange juice and stir it into the sauce. Season with salt and pepper. Turn off the heat.
- When the grill is very hot, grill the skewers, turning once, until just browned and tender, about a minute or so on each side, depending on the heat of the grill (a very hot grill works best with squid because it sears the outside, leaving the inside tender and moist).

- Cook the tagliarini until tender, drain well, and add to the sauté pan. Toss well over low heat with the rosemary sauce, adding more olive oil if needed to coat the pasta. Check the seasonings and transfer to a large serving bowl. Place the squid skewers on top. Or dish out individual servings of pasta and place a skewer on top of each bowl.

Ideas

This recipe is more an embodiment of a style than a set piece. Many different combinations of fish and vegetables can be skewered and grilled and placed on top of a simply dressed pasta, among them shrimp with zucchini, chunks of fresh tuna with green peppers, large sea scallops with yellow cherry tomatoes, and chunks of salmon skewered with red onion.

I've chosen to dress the pasta in a simple rosemary, oil, and pine nut sauce, but other simple sauces work well for this type of dish; basil pesto is wonderful with a swordfish and tomato skewer, or try *aglio e olio* (garlic and oil sauce) with shrimp and shiitake mushroom skewers. Uncooked Tomato Sauce (see page 34) is great with squid or fast-grilled baby octopus.

Instead of tossing the pasta with a rosemary-infused sauce, make Herb Pasta flavored with rosemary (page 368). Dress it with garlic and olive oil. The flavor will be a bit more subtle.

Lobster with Small Diced Fall Vegetables and Pappardelle

Here is a fragrant and beautifully colored dish to make in the fall, when lobster is at its best.

[Makes 4 main-course or 6 first-course servings]

2 lobsters, 1½ to 2 pounds each

2 small carrots, peeled (save trimmings for lobster broth)

2 medium leeks, washed and trimmed (save trimmings for lobster broth)

3 tender inner celery stalks (save trimmings for lobster broth)

2 small parsnips, peeled (save trimmings for lobster broth)

About a dozen medium chanterelle mushrooms, wiped clean, stems trimmed and saved for lobster broth (if you can't find chanterelles, substitute a dozen shiitake mushrooms)

Olive oil

1 cup homemade Chicken Broth (page 374) or low-salt canned

Salt

Freshly ground black pepper

Unsalted butter

A few thyme sprigs, leaves chopped

1 bay leaf

A few gratings of mace

A small wineglass of dry Spanish sherry

1 pound pappardelle

A few flat-leaf parsley sprigs, leaves coarsely chopped

- Cook the lobsters in a very large pot of rapidly boiling salted water for 4 minutes. Remove them from the water, saving the water for cooking the pasta. When cool enough to handle, remove the lobster meat from the shells and cut it into thick slices, making sure to save any cooking juices that come from the lobsters. (It's easiest to do this over a large low-sided pan so the juices will fall into it as you shell the lobsters.) The meat should be just slightly underdone but still cooked enough to pull away from the shell easily. This way, you can afford to reheat it gently in the sauce without it becoming overcooked and rubbery. Save the shells.

- Cut all the vegetables into very small, uniform dice. Save all the peels and trimmings for the lobster broth. Making the vegetables all the same size is important not just for appearance but so they will finish cooking at the same time.

- Break the lobster shells into large pieces. Put them in a large saucepan along with a drizzle of olive oil and all the vegetable trimmings. Sauté over medium heat for a few minutes, just to release the flavors from the vegetables. Add the chicken broth and about ½ cup of water and let this simmer over medium-low heat for about 15 minutes. Remove the shells and strain the broth through a fine-mesh strainer. Transfer the broth to a clean saucepan. Boil it down to about 1 cup. Season with salt and pepper.

- In a large skillet, heat 2 tablespoons each of butter and olive oil over medium heat. Add all the vegetables, the thyme, bay leaf, and mace, season with salt and pepper, and sauté until the vegetables are just tender but still firm enough to keep their shape, 6 to 7 minutes. Add the sherry and let it cook out to nothing. Add about ½ cup of the lobster broth and simmer for 2 to 3 minutes.
- Start cooking the pappardelle.
- Add the lobster and any juices that have collected to the vegetables. Gently heat the sauce over low heat for about 1 minute, being careful not to overcook the lobster. Check the seasoning.
- When the pappardelle are al dente, drain them well and place in a large serving bowl. Toss with a generous dollop of butter. Add the lobster sauce and parsley and toss again, adding a bit more of the lobster broth if needed to loosen the sauce. Serve right away.

Ideas

Another good cold-weather lobster pasta combines lobster meat, a cup of tender simmered white beans, and raw arugula tossed with tagliatelle. This is especially lovely garnished with a scattering of salmon roe. For a fragrant dish of lobster and wild mushrooms, parboil the lobster as directed in this recipe and slice the meat, reserving any juices. Sauté a variety of wild fall mushrooms (sliced if large) and a few cloves of sliced garlic in a generous amount of good olive oil. Add the lobster meat, its juices, a squeeze of lemon juice, and a handful of chopped parsley and cook gently for about 1 minute before tossing with spaghetti.

For a spring version of this dish, combine the lobster with peas, shallots, and a splash of heavy cream.

For a summer version, use bell peppers, zucchini, tomato, basil, and young garlic, cut in small dice.

Scallop Mousse Ravioli with Shiitake Mushroom Sauce

This is a variation of an appetizer that was very popular with New York caterers a few years back. It was a scallop mousse wrapped in lettuce leaves and then steamed. I always found it delicious and discovered that the filling works well in ravioli. I've used a pasta made with white wine because its light texture cuts the richness of the filling.

[Makes 4 main-course or 6 first-course servings]

For the filling:

About 1½ pounds sea scallops, side
   muscle removed

1 large egg

A tiny splash of heavy cream

A small bunch of chives, finely chopped,
   plus extra chopped for garnish

A few gratings of nutmeg

Salt

Freshly ground black pepper

For the pasta:

1 recipe Three-Egg White Wine Pasta
   (page 367), cut for ravioli

For the sauce:

About 3 tablespoons unsalted butter

3 shallots, thinly sliced

About 15 medium shiitake mushrooms,
   stemmed, wiped clean, and
   thinly sliced

A tiny splash of cognac

½ cup Light Fish Broth (page 376)
   or Chicken Broth (page 374)

Salt

Freshly ground black pepper

Zest of 1 lemon

- To make the filling, place the scallops in a food processor and grind to a paste. Add the egg, cream, chives, nutmeg, salt, and pepper. Process again for a few seconds, just to blend the ingredients. Transfer the filling to a bowl and refrigerate for about 30 minutes (this firms it up a little so it's easier to work with).
- To make the ravioli, roll out the pasta dough and fill the ravioli with the scallop mixture (see page 370 for helpful hints on filling ravioli). Set the ravioli on a pasta drying screen or on a baking sheet dusted with a little flour. If you need to refrigerate them, leave them uncovered so they won't get soggy.
- To make the sauce, heat the butter in a small sauté pan over medium heat. Add the shallots and sauté until soft, 3 to 4 minutes. Add the mushrooms and sauté until soft and fragrant, about 5 minutes. Add the cognac and let it boil away to nothing.

- Add the broth and let it simmer for a few minutes. Season with salt and pepper and the lemon zest.
- When you're ready to eat, drop the ravioli into a large pot of boiling salted water and cook until tender. Scoop the ravioli from the water with a large strainer and place in a colander to drain for a minute. Gently slide the ravioli onto a large serving platter. Reheat the mushroom sauce briefly if necessary and pour it over the ravioli. Top with chopped chives.

Ideas

This white wine pasta dough, excellent for rich fillings, is very easy to work with, being a bit sturdier than all-egg pasta. So think about using it when you have a moist or very rich filling.

Scallops make a sweet base for many simple vegetable sauces. A variety of vegetables can be thinly sliced and sautéed in unsalted butter or olive oil and then loosened with a little broth or wine. Try substituting sliced baby artichokes, asparagus tips, peas, grated zucchini, or a few peeled, seeded tomatoes, cut in small dice and quickly sautéed.

Trout Cannelloni with Pancetta and Sage Sauce

Farm-raised trout can be a little bland, so they're often much improved by strong flavorings. Here is a very easy but elegant way to prepare them for cannelloni.

[Makes 4 main-course or 6 first-course servings]

For the filling:

3 thin slices pancetta, chopped

3 or 4 shallots, cut in small dice

A few tablespoons unsalted butter

4 trout fillets, skinned and cut in chunks

Salt

Freshly ground black pepper

A splash of dry white wine

A generous squeeze of lemon juice

For the sauce:

1 cup crème fraîche

About 6 fresh sage leaves, cut in thin strips

Zest of 1 lemon

A handful of blanched almonds, lightly toasted and roughly ground (see page 345)

For the pasta:

1 recipe Three-Egg Pasta (page 365), cut for cannelloni

- To make the filling, sauté the pancetta in a large skillet over medium-low heat until just starting to crisp, 3 to 4 minutes. Add the shallots and butter and sauté until the shallots are soft. Season the trout with salt and pepper and add it to the pan. Sauté, turning once, until it flakes easily. Add the wine and let it boil away to nothing, then add the lemon juice. Break the trout up a bit with a spoon (you can leave it in small bite-size pieces).
- Preheat the oven to 425°F.
- To make the pasta, cook the cannelloni squares until tender in a large pot of boiling salted water. Lift them from the water with a large strainer and transfer to a colander. Run them under cold water and drain. Lay them out on kitchen towels or paper towels.
- Fill each cannelloni with the trout filling (2 heaping tablespoons for each should do) and roll them loosely. Place them in a single layer in a lightly buttered baking dish, seam side down. They should fit fairly snugly. (For more information on filling cannelloni, see page 155.)

- To make the sauce, heat the crème fraîche in a small saucepan over low heat for a few seconds, just to get it to a pourable consistency. Scatter the sage leaves and lemon zest over the cannelloni. Pour on the crème fraîche, season with salt and black pepper, and top with the toasted almonds. Bake, uncovered, until bubbling and lightly browned on top, about 20 minutes.

Ideas

Trout, although a freshwater fish, can really stand up to aggressive seasoning. Italians love it with strong herbs like rosemary and sage. For a robust variation on this dish, make your filling by sautéing the trout with a few small sprigs of chopped rosemary and topping the cannelloni with Oven-Roasted Tomato Sauce (page 38). Bake until hot and bubbling.

I really love sautéed trout with a dollop of traditional basil pesto on top. This combination also makes tasty cannelloni. Sauté and flake the fish (omitting the pancetta), spread it with a thin layer of pesto, and roll as usual in the precooked cannelloni squares. Pour on about ½ cup warmed heavy cream laced with a few chopped basil leaves. Top with pine nuts and bake until lightly golden on top.

Paprika Ravioli with Shrimp in a Shrimp and Tomato Broth

The paprika in the pasta dough imparts a sweet taste that brings out the natural sweetness of shrimp. I love all kinds of fish ravioli served in a light broth. Shrimp are especially good for this, as you can save their shells to make a quick little shrimp stock.

[Makes 4 main-course or 6 first-course servings]

For the filling:
Olive oil
3 tender inner celery stalks, cut in fine
    dice, plus the leaves, chopped
    (save trimmings for the broth)
2 shallots, cut in fine dice
    (save trimmings for the broth)
1 pound medium shrimp, shelled
    (save the shells) and deveined
    if you like (see Note)
Salt
Freshly ground black pepper
A few tarragon sprigs, leaves chopped
    (save stems for the broth)
A few basil leaves, chopped
A few drops of tarragon white wine
    vinegar
1 large egg

For the broth:
Unsalted butter
3 plum tomatoes, roughly chopped

2 cups homemade Chicken Broth
    (page 374)
A splash of pastis, such as Pernod
2 or 3 garlic cloves, unpeeled and
    crushed
A few fennel seeds
Salt
Freshly ground black pepper

For the ravioli:
1 recipe Three-Egg Paprika Pasta
    (page 368), cut for ravioli

4 plum tomatoes, peeled, seeded, and
    cut in small dice
A handful of basil leaves, cut in thin
    strips
A few tarragon sprigs, leaves chopped
Olive oil

- To make the filling, heat a few tablespoons of olive oil in a large skillet. Add the celery and shallots and sauté over medium heat until soft, about 3 minutes. Season the shrimp with salt and pepper and add them to the pan, sautéing over medium-high heat until pink and just cooked through, about 2 minutes. Add the herbs and a few drops of tarragon vinegar. Chop the shrimp mixture roughly in a food processor and transfer to a bowl. Let it cool a few minutes and then mix in the egg. Let the filling cool completely (refrigerate it if you prefer, but don't let it be icy cold when you fill your ravioli).
- To make the broth, sauté the shrimp shells until pink in a few tablespoons of butter in a medium saucepan over medium heat. Add the celery trimmings, shallot peels, tarragon stems, and all the other ingredients for the broth. Simmer over medium-low heat for about 20 minutes. Strain the broth through a fine-mesh strainer into a clean pot. Taste to make sure it is sweet tasting and well seasoned. If not, boil it down for a few more minutes. You should have about 1½ cups.
- Fill and seal the ravioli according to the directions on page 370.
- Drop the ravioli into a large pot of boiling salted water and cook until tender. Lift from the water with a large strainer and place in a colander to drain for a few seconds.
- Divide the hot ravioli among each pasta bowl. Garnish with chopped tomatoes and herbs. Ladle about ½ cup of hot broth over the top. (The broth serves as a sauce, not a soup, so pour on just enough broth to moisten the ravioli as you eat them.) Drizzle with olive oil and serve hot.

A note on deveining shrimp: I devein shrimp for esthetic reasons only. If the top vein looks particularly thick and dark, I remove it. There is no health or flavor hazard in leaving the vein in.

Ideas

All sorts of ravioli can be served in a bit of broth. Try veal ravioli with a veal broth enriched with a little unsalted butter and an herb. Make a rich chicken broth studded with bits of mushroom for mushroom- or chicken-based ravioli. A light fish broth made with bones and trimmings is wonderful with any type of fish ravioli; you can accent it with lemon or orange zest, pastis, or white wine, or with a chopped vegetable that corresponds to your fish filling, such as a little chopped sautéed shallot or carrot.

Large Shells Filled with Baccalà Mantecato and Baked with Red Pepper and Garlic Purée

Ín my family we always stuffed giant shells with fresh ricotta and spinach and baked them in tomato sauce. I loved this dish, but a strongly flavored fish filling also goes beautifully into shells and can stand up to a more robust sauce, like this one of sweet peppers and garlic.

Baccalà mantecato—whipped salt cod—is a specialty of Venice and often served in wine bars there, usually as a topping for crostini. It is almost identical to the French *brandade de morue* and makes a great filling for pasta.

[Makes 4 main-course or 6 first-course servings]

For the filling:
1 pound dried salt cod, broken into
    several large pieces
2 bay leaves
1 thyme sprig
1 large baking potato, boiled until
    tender and peeled
3 garlic cloves, finely chopped
About ¼ cup olive oil
Freshly ground black pepper
About ½ cup whole milk
Salt, if needed

4 red bell peppers, roasted over a flame
    until charred, peeled, seeded, and
    chopped
A pinch of sugar
One 15-ounce can Italian plum toma-
    toes, drained and chopped
4 or 5 anchovies, chopped
A few thyme sprigs, leaves chopped
Salt
Freshly ground black pepper
About ¼ cup heavy cream
Zest of 1 lemon

For the sauce:
2 heads of garlic
About 2 tablespoons olive oil
1 medium onion, cut in small dice

For the pasta:
1 pound large shell pasta
About 1 cup bread crumbs, toasted
    (see page 340)

- Soak the salt cod in a large pot of cold water for at least 24 hours. Change the water frequently. I usually leave the pot under the tap and run new water into it every once in a while. You can keep the bowl in the refrigerator while it's soaking, but it is not necessary for freshness. After soaking, taste a piece of the fish to make sure enough salt has been leached out of it. It should be just very lightly salty, not unpleasantly so.
- Drain the cod, place in a shallow saucepan, and cover with cold water. Add the bay leaves and thyme sprig. Bring to a simmer and poach until you are able to flake the cod with a fork, about 15 minutes. Don't cook it much longer or it will toughen. Drain and break it up into small pieces, removing any pieces of skin.
- In a food processor, place the cod, potato, garlic, olive oil, and a few grindings of black pepper. Pulse the machine until you have a rough purée. Now add enough milk to smooth it out to a thick purée. Pulse just to blend. Taste to see if it needs salt. Take care not to overblend the *mantecato* or it may become gluey.
- Preheat the oven to 425°F.
- To make the sauce, wrap the heads of garlic in aluminum foil and roast until tender and fragrant, about 30 minutes.
- In a large skillet, heat the olive oil. Add the onion and sauté until soft, about 4 minutes. Add the roasted peppers and a pinch of sugar and sauté until the peppers are very tender, about 5 minutes. Add the tomatoes, anchovies, thyme, salt, and black pepper and sauté until the tomatoes give off juice and soften, about another 5 minutes. Cut off the root end of the roasted heads of garlic and squeeze the softened cloves into the pan. Puree the sauce in a food processor. Check the seasoning. Return the pureed sauce to the pan and add the cream and lemon zest. Let the mixture simmer a few minutes to thicken and to blend the flavors.
- Cook the large shells until al dente, run under cold water, and drain well, making sure you drain out any water that is trapped inside the shells (I do this by giving the colander a few good shakes).
- Ladle a little sauce into a 12 x 10 x 2-inch baking dish. Fill the shells with a generous amount of *baccalà mantecato* and place them snugly in the dish in a single layer. Pour on the remaining sauce and top with the bread crumbs. Bake, uncovered, until the sauce is bubbling and the top is nicely browned, about 20 minutes.

Ideas

Any addition that is bold or bright makes sense with salt cod. What you want to stay away from is richness (too much cream or heavy cheese). Tomato, with its pleasant acidity, makes good sense. So do green olives or capers.

Salmon Lasagne Provençal

This is an improvisation I came up with when I had some mismatched produce in my refrigerator. Sometimes this works; sometimes it doesn't. This one turned out very well. I recommend making the dish in the summer with fresh ripe tomatoes. And since it contains no cheese or béchamel, the texture remains loose when it's cold; it's a pleasure to eat it served that way with a green salad and a glass of rosé wine.

[Makes 4 main-course or 6 first-course servings]

1½ pounds salmon fillets, skinned and cut in very thin slices (see Note)

Sea salt (see Note)

Freshly ground black pepper

Juice of 1 orange

Olive oil

8 or 9 scallions, cut in thin rounds, with some of the green

5 or 6 young garlic cloves, thinly sliced

About 7 large, ripe tomatoes (about 4 pounds), peeled, seeded, and chopped

A few thyme sprigs, leaves chopped

A handful of basil leaves, chopped

A large handful of black olives, pitted and halved (little black Niçoise olives are especially good here)

Zest of 1 orange

1 recipe Three-Egg Herb Pasta flavored with thyme (page 368), cut for lasagne

About 1 cup bread crumbs, toasted (see page 340)

- Place the salmon slices in a shallow bowl. Season them with sea salt, pepper, orange juice, and about 3 tablespoons olive oil. Let stand, unrefrigerated, for 20 minutes. Since this salmon is put into the lasagne raw, to ensure proper cooking, it's best if it's not too cold when it goes into the oven.
- To make the tomato sauce, I use 2 large skillets because I don't want to crowd the tomatoes. They should cook quickly over high heat and not stew. You can either cook them in batches or use the two-pan method.
- In both skillets, pour about 2 tablespoons olive oil. Over medium heat, sauté the scallions, distributing them more or less evenly between the pans. Divide the garlic between the pans and sauté until it is aromatic but doesn't color. Add the tomatoes to both pans and season with sea salt and black pepper. Turn the heat to high and sauté quickly. The tomatoes should start giving off juice. Sauté until some of the juice has evaporated but the tomatoes are still chunky, about 5 minutes. Mix the tomatoes

together in one bowl and add the thyme, basil, olives, and orange zest. Check the seasoning.

- Preheat the oven to 425°F.
- Cook the lasagne sheets in batches until tender. Run under cold water, drain, and lay them out on kitchen towels or paper towels.
- In a large baking pan (about 12 x 10 x 2 inches), ladle out a thin layer of the tomato sauce. Arrange a layer of pasta on top. Make a layer of salmon slices and cover with tomato sauce. Put down another pasta layer, another layer of salmon, and then tomato sauce. Continue until all the ingredients are used up. The top should be a layer of pasta topped with tomato sauce and sprinkled with bread crumbs. Cover the pan with aluminum foil and bake the lasagne about 20 minutes. Uncover and bake until bubbling and the bread crumbs are crisp and browned, about another 20 minutes.

A note on how to cut salmon: Place the skinned fillet on a flat surface and hold the knife almost horizontally over the fish. Starting at the thick end, cut thin diagonal slices. This way, you will get wider pieces than by simply cutting down into the fish.

A note about sea salt: Sea salt goes so well with both tomatoes and salmon, it's a pity not to use it here. Sprinkle a little sea salt on a tomato wedge and taste how it brings out the acidity and sweetness in a special way (for more on choosing sea salt, see page 351 in "The Improviser's Pantry").

Ideas

Since the salmon is cut very thin and the lasagne is cooked at a high temperature, using uncooked fish works well here. This method doesn't work as well with thick cuts of fish. I've also made this lasagne with thinly sliced scallops and a similar lasagne using thin slices of lightly marinated fresh tuna.

Basil Lasagne with Scallops and Zucchini

This is a light lasagne that contains no béchamel or cheese. It's wonderful in the summer, when both young zucchini and fragrant basil are in abundance. A good winter version can be made by substituting the same amounts of Belgian endive for the zucchini and parsley for the basil.

[Makes 4 main-course or 6 first-course servings]

1½ pounds sea scallops, side muscles removed

Salt

Freshly ground black pepper

Olive oil

2 large white onions, thinly sliced

8 or 9 medium zucchini, sliced in thin rounds

3 or 4 anchovy fillets, chopped

For the basil sauce:

A large bunch of basil leaves (about 2 packed cups)

2 or 3 garlic cloves, peeled

Salt

Freshly ground black pepper

Olive oil

1½ cups heavy cream

2 large eggs

1 recipe Three-Egg Herb Pasta flavored with basil (page 368), cut for lasagne

About 1 cup bread crumbs, toasted (see page 340)

- If some of the scallops are very thick, cut them in half horizontally; otherwise, leave them whole. Season the scallops with salt and pepper and toss with a few tablespoons of olive oil. Heat a large skillet until it is almost smoking and sear the scallops on both sides (this should take no more than a minute or so). They should be lightly browned on both sides but slightly underdone in the center. Remove them from the pan and set aside.
- In the same skillet, add a few more tablespoons of olive oil and sauté the onions over medium heat until they just start to soften, 3 to 4 minutes. Add the zucchini, a bit of salt and pepper, and sauté until lightly browned and tender, about 8 minutes. Add the anchovies and cook 1 minute to blend.
- To make the sauce, place the basil leaves and garlic in a food processor. Season with salt and pepper and add a healthy shot of olive oil. Grind to a rough paste. Add the cream and eggs and process a few seconds, just to blend the ingredients.
- Preheat the oven to 425°F.

- Cook the lasagne sheets in batches until tender. Run under cold water, drain, and lay them out on kitchen towels or paper towels.
- Ladle a thin coating of the basil sauce over the bottom of a large baking pan (about 12 x 10 x 2 inches). Add a layer of pasta. Top with a layer of zucchini and dot with a layer of scallops. Add a thin coating of basil cream. Add another layer of pasta, another coating of basil sauce, then zucchini, scallops, and so on. End with a layer of pasta coated with a layer of basil sauce. Top with a thin but even coating of toasted bread crumbs.
- Cover the pan with aluminum foil and bake the lasagne for 20 minutes. Uncover and bake until the sauce is bubbling and the top is lightly browned, about 15 minutes more. Let rest a few minutes before cutting.

Ideas

Other vegetables combine well with scallops. I've made a scallop and escarole lasagne that was wonderful. Try sautéing sliced leeks until very soft and using a layer of them instead of zucchini; omit the onion. Spinach, too, goes well with scallops.

I've made a great lasagne by alternating layers of traditional basil pesto (page 102), a lightly cooked tomato sauce, and seared scallops.

Another interesting lasagne can be made from scallops grilled with lemon and oregano and layered with sautéed green chard.

This lasagne is also excellent if you leave out the scallops for an all-vegetable version.

Lasagne with Fresh Tuna, Caciocavallo, and Marjoram

In Sicily, cooks combine firm strong fish with bold cheese.

[Makes 4 main-course or 6 first-course servings]

Coarsely ground black pepper

Salt

About 6 large marjoram sprigs, leaves coarsely chopped

1 pound tuna steak, cut in several medium chunks

Olive oil

4 or 5 garlic cloves, minced

A large handful of pine nuts

6 or 7 anchovy fillets

Two 35-ounce cans Italian plum tomatoes, drained and chopped

1 recipe Three-Egg Pasta (page 365), cut for lasagne

About 1 cup freshly grated caciocavallo cheese

About ½ cup bread crumbs, toasted (see page 340)

- Place a generous amount of coarsely ground black pepper, salt, and about half of the chopped marjoram on a large plate and combine well. Press the tuna chunks into this mixture, turning them until they are lightly coated on all sides.
- In a large skillet, heat about 3 tablespoons olive oil over high heat. Add the tuna chunks and sear them on both sides until browned. Remove from the pan. They should be pink in the center. When cool enough to handle, cut the tuna into thin slices.
- In a separate large skillet, heat a few tablespoons of olive oil. Turn the heat to low and add the garlic, pine nuts, and anchovies. Sauté a few minutes to toast the pine nuts and garlic lightly. Break up the anchovies with a spoon. Add the tomatoes, turn the heat to high, and cook at a lively simmer for about 5 minutes. Add the remaining marjoram. Season with pepper and add salt if needed (it might not be if the anchovies are very salty).
- Preheat the oven to 425°F.
- Cook the lasagne sheets in batches until tender. Run under cold water, drain, and lay them out on kitchen towels or paper towels.
- Ladle a thin layer of tomato sauce in a large baking pan (about 12 x 10 x 2 inches). Add a layer of pasta. Top with tuna, tomato sauce, and a generous sprinkling of caciocavallo. Continue until you have used everything up. End with a layer of pasta topped with tomato sauce, cheese, and the bread crumbs.
- Cover the pan with aluminum foil and bake the lasagne about 20 minutes. Uncover and bake until hot and bubbling, 15 to 20 minutes more.

Filled Fresh Pasta

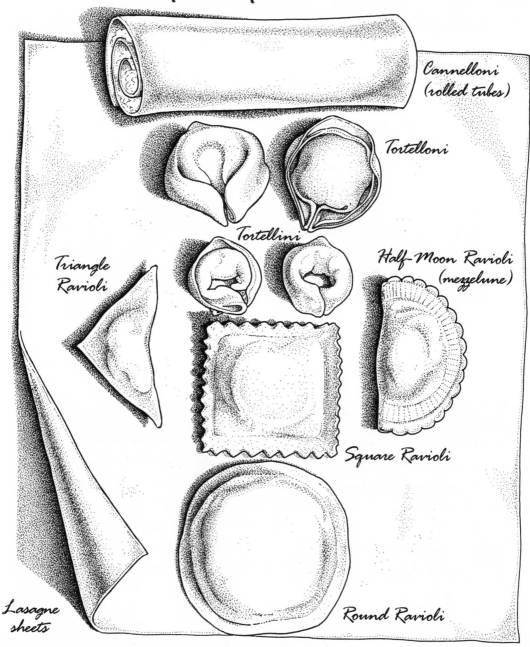

Cannelloni (rolled tubes)

Tortelloni

Tortellini

Triangle Ravioli

Half-Moon Ravioli (mezzelune)

Square Ravioli

Lasagne sheets

Round Ravioli

Simple butter sauces or homemade broths highlight the filling of these delicate pastas. Cream or mascarpone can be added for richness. There is nothing more delicious than ricotta-filled ravioli in a lightly cooked tomato sauce.

Fazzoletti over Cod Baked with White Wine and Shallots

azzoletti are large squares of very thin pasta meant to lie in folds the way a dropped handkerchief might (for information on cutting, see page 370). They are commonly served topped with a sauce, but they can also be draped over many types of stews to form a tent over the dish. This recipe reflects how they were always served by Alan Tardi, the chef at Le Madri, a restaurant in New York, when I cooked there. The great thing about presenting fazzoletti this way is that it gives the illusion of a fancy stuffed pasta without the trouble of stuffing anything.

I've chosen a variety of seasonings—rosemary, fennel seeds, thyme, garlic, and anchovies—to flavor the cod (along with white wine and shallots). It adds up to a bold and delicious blend of tastes, a little more complicated than I usually like. Make it this way once, and then if you decide you don't care for one aspect of the mix, leave it out or substitute. You can replace the rosemary with parsley for a more toned-down flavor.

[Makes 4 main-course or 6 first-course servings]

Olive oil

4 shallots, cut in small dice

2 or 3 garlic cloves, thinly sliced

4 or 5 anchovy fillets, chopped

About 4 thyme sprigs, leaves chopped

2 or 3 small rosemary sprigs, leaves
    chopped

A small handful fennel seeds, lightly
    toasted and ground with a mortar
    and pestle

2 pounds cod fillets, cut in large chunks

Salt

Freshly ground black pepper

A small wineglass of dry white wine

3 ripe round tomatoes (about 1½
    pounds), peeled, seeded, and cut
    in small chunks

A small handful of capers

1 recipe Three-Egg Pasta (page 365),
    cut for fazzoletti

- Preheat the oven to 425°F.
- In a large skillet that can go from stovetop to oven, heat a few tablespoons of olive oil over medium heat. Add the shallots and sauté until soft, 2 to 3 minutes. Add the garlic, anchovies, about half of the thyme and rosemary, and all the ground fennel and sauté until they give off aroma, about 2 minutes.

- Season the cod with salt and pepper and add it to the pan. Turn the heat up a bit and brown the fish lightly on one side. Turn the fish once, add the wine, and let it bubble a minute. Add the tomatoes and capers and put the skillet in the oven, uncovered. Cook for about 10 minutes, or until the fish flakes easily.
- Divide the fish among 4 warmed serving plates.
- Cook the fazzoletti until tender. Lift them from the water with a large strainer, let the water drain off, and drape 2 or 3 fazzoletti over each fish serving. Finish each dish with a drizzle of fresh olive oil and the remaining chopped herbs. Serve very hot.

Ideas

Cod is a fish that can be flavored in many ways. Try it poached in red wine with a few juniper berries. Olive oil, garlic, and parsley together are simple but surprisingly rich and go very well as a fragrant stew base for fazzoletti. Or try basil, tomatoes, and black olives.

Pasta
and Meat

Pasta flavored with meat has a long tradition in both southern and northern Italian cooking. Pappardelle with hare sauce from Tuscany, the sophisticated ragù sauces of Emilia-Romagna, and the long-simmered mixed-meat and pasta stews of Campania are a few examples of these glorious, richly flavored labors of love. In this section, I've created modern interpretations of classic meat dishes, including lasagne and ragù sauces, incorporating some traditional American ingredients such as turkey, parsnips, and hot peppers. In Italy rich dishes used to be served in small servings as first courses. Times have changed, and even Italians eat them as a full meal. Americans tend to like pasta as a main course, and it's a perfectly acceptable way to serve most of the meat recipes in this section. I've noted the few exceptions.

I love the Italian custom of braising meat in an aromatic sauce, using the sauce to dress pasta, and then serving the tender meat as a second course or at the next meal. This continuity of flavor makes a lot of culinary sense to me, and I've included several recipes in this style.

I am always experimenting with quick-cooked meat sauces to toss with pasta. Prosciutto, fresh and dried sausage, thinly sliced veal, beef, duck breast, and chicken livers are good meats to keep in mind for spur-of-the-moment main-course pasta dishes with satisfying flavor. I especially like mixing such meats with a seasonal vegetable. There are so many wonderful sausages available in our markets now, it is exciting to pick ones to pair with pasta, updating favorite old sauces traditionally made with Italian pork sausage, such as orecchiette with sausage and broccoli rabe. In the following recipes I've chosen several different types of sausages, cooking some with vegetables or Italian cheeses to create modern, quick-cooked dishes that retain strong Italian style. If you can't, for instance, find the fresh veal sausage I suggest in a recipe, substitute a chicken sausage you love. Take my recipes as suggestions to get you thinking about ways to use newly available ingredients with pasta.

Conchiglie with Veal Sausage, Radicchio, and Cream

This recipe was inspired by a preparation of loin of veal with braised radicchio I ate at an Italian restaurant in New York many years ago. I still remember it well for its subtle mix of flavors.

[Makes 4 main-course or 6 first-course servings]

1 pound veal sausage, casings removed and crumbled

3 thin slices pancetta, chopped

4 garlic cloves, thinly sliced

1 large round head of radicchio, cored and chopped

A splash of cognac

1 cup heavy cream

A few thyme sprigs, leaves chopped

A few small rosemary sprigs, leaves chopped

Salt

Freshly ground black pepper

1 pound conchiglie (medium shell pasta)

About 1 cup freshly grated Pecorino Toscano cheese

- In a large skillet, brown the crumbled sausage along with the pancetta over medium heat, breaking the sausage up into little bits with your spoon as it cooks. Add the garlic and let it soften a minute. Add the radicchio and sauté until it has wilted and turned a deep burgundy color, about 6 minutes. Add the cognac and let it cook away. Add the cream, thyme, and rosemary. Simmer gently for a few minutes to blend the flavors. Season with salt and pepper.
- Cook the conchiglie until al dente, drain well, and add to the pan. Add a handful of the cheese and toss well over low heat until the pasta is well coated. Transfer to a large serving bowl. Serve extra cheese at the table.

Ideas

This recipe offers an easy formula for a quick but robust pasta sauce: sausage, cream, and an assertive vegetable. Sliced endive, roasted bell pepper strips, and sliced fennel can all replace the radicchio for very successful variations on this recipe.

Chicken Sausage and Parsnip Soup with Acini

I've been finding great chicken sausages in the market lately, some seasoned with sage, some spicy with chiles. I often reach for them when devising quick pasta sauces. Keep in mind, however, that most chicken sausages have much less fat than pork sausages, so cook them briefly to keep them juicy.

The parsnip in the recipe lends a sweetness that I love in meat-based soups; for a more assertive flavor, turn to celery root or half parsnip and half turnip. If you want an even sweeter taste, mix sweet potatoes with carrots. Soup was devised partly as a way to use leftovers and feed large families, so you're staying true to its spirit when you keep your recipes flexible.

[Makes 4 main-course or 6 first-course servings]

About 2 tablespoons olive oil

1 pound chicken sausage, casings removed and crumbled

1 medium white onion, cut in small dice

2 medium leeks, washed and cut in small dice (discarding most of the green)

3 medium carrots, cut in small cubes

3 medium parsnips, cut in small cubes

A few gratings of nutmeg

Salt

Freshly ground black pepper

About 6 cups homemade Chicken Broth (page 374)

About ½ cup acini, cooked until al dente and tossed with a little olive oil

About 6 sage leaves, chopped

Freshly grated Grana Padano cheese

- In a large soup pot, heat the olive oil over medium-high heat. Add the sausage and brown well, breaking it up into bits with your spoon. Add the onion, leeks, carrots, and parsnips and sauté along with the sausage until just starting to soften, 3 to 4 minutes. Season with the nutmeg, salt, and pepper. Add the chicken broth and bring to a boil. Turn the heat to medium-low and simmer until the vegetables are tender and the flavors are well blended, 10 to 12 minutes. Add the acini and sage. Taste for seasoning. Serve with grated Grana Padano sprinkled on top.

Ideas

Sometimes the chicken sausage I buy has red bell pepper in it. In that case I make a soup using the sausage plus roasted red peppers, onion, celery, and some small pasta. I season it with basil.

Smoked chicken sausages can be very good. If you find them, try them here. Chop them into small pieces and brown them the same way you do fresh sausages.

THE FINAL TOUCHES

The time to make last-minute adjustments to a dish is when you are tossing the pasta with the sauce. Does it need more olive oil? Does the sauce seem too thick or too dry? Should you add a little of the pasta cooking water? Check the seasoning. Maybe you need to add more salt, pepper, or a grating of cheese, or you want to freshen the sauce with newly chopped herbs. Take this opportunity to put the finishing touch on your pasta. If you think you've made too much sauce, don't use it all. Save it to use in frittata or as a topping for baked fish, sautéed chicken breasts, or polenta.

Ziti with Merguez Sausages, Goat Cheese, Tomato, and Parsley

Merguez is a spicy Moroccan lamb sausage sold at many specialty markets. I've tempered its spiciness here by blending it with a mild, creamy goat cheese. The tomatoes provide a contrast for the spicy sausage. If you don't have ripe summer tomatoes, use canned Italian plum tomatoes, well drained.

[Makes 4 main-course or 6 first-course servings]

Olive oil

1 pound merguez sausage

1 pound ziti

2 or 3 garlic cloves, thinly sliced

4 ripe tomatoes (about 2 pounds), seeded and chopped, or one 35-ounce can Italian plum tomatoes, drained and chopped

Salt

1 small log (about 6 ounces) unaged goat cheese, crumbled (Montrachet is perfect for this)

A small bunch of flat-leaf parsley, stemmed, leaves left whole (about ½ cup whole leaves)

- Heat a skillet over high heat until it is very hot. Add 1 tablespoon olive oil and the merguez and brown the sausages on all sides, leaving them slightly undercooked in the center. Remove them from the pan and cut them in thin slices.
- Start cooking the ziti.
- In the same skillet, heat 2 tablespoons olive oil over medium heat. Return the sausages to the pan and finish cooking, about 1 minute. Add the garlic and sauté just for a minute, not letting it color. Add the tomatoes, season with salt, and sauté until they release their juices but retain their bright red color, no longer than 3 to 4 minutes.
- When the ziti are al dente, drain them, add to the skillet, and toss well. Taste for seasoning and transfer to a large serving bowl. Add the cheese and parsley and toss until the cheese is slightly melted and the pasta is well coated.

Ideas

This is really a variation on the classic southern Italian pasta sauce that combines ricotta and tomato with pork sausage. But goat cheese melts even more beautifully than ricotta and adds a tang similar to that of the buffalo milk ricotta you find in southern Italy and now in many specialty food shops in this country. If you think of the tomato and goat cheese as your base flavors, you can vary the meat by choosing different fresh or dried sausages.

LEARNING HOW TO TASTE

*M*ost chefs have their tasting spoons (usually a clean teaspoon they keep in their back pocket). I find, especially when cooking sauces, that a small piece of white Italian bread dunked in the pot can provide a neutral and appropriate background against which to accurately tell what the sauce really tastes like. Let the sauce cool a bit on the bread before tasting it so the heat doesn't interfere with the flavor. The balance will be immediately apparent, and so will the saltiness. Spiciness comes on slowly, so let the sauce sit on your tongue a few seconds for the pepper to present itself.

When you cook, always taste as you add ingredients. Concentrate on remembering how each addition to a dish alters its character. You may find yourself, somewhere in the middle of your cooking, tasting the dish and deciding, this is the way I want it to be, so I won't bother adding those olives or that additional butter called for in the recipe.

Penne with Boudin Blanc, Escarole, and Capers

Boudin blanc is a French white sausage traditionally made with chicken, veal, or sweetbreads and bound with egg white. In France it is served with sautéed apples and onions or with cabbage, but its smooth texture and delicate, herby taste are wonderful with pasta, as long as you provide a counterpoint to its smooth mildness, in this case escarole and the acidity of capers.

[Makes 4 main-course or 6 first-course servings]

1 large bunch of escarole, cored and coarsely chopped

Olive oil

1 pound boudin blanc sausage

5 medium shallots, thinly sliced

3 garlic cloves, thinly sliced

A few thyme sprigs, leaves chopped

Salt

Freshly ground black pepper

1 pound penne

A generous splash of medium-dry white wine

A handful of capers

About ½ cup freshly grated Gruyère cheese

- Set up a large pot of salted water to cook the pasta. Bring to a boil, add the escarole, and blanch for about 1 minute. Remove the escarole from the water with a large strainer, run it under cold water to preserve its green color, and squeeze it dry. Give it an extra chop to make sure there are no large pieces.
- In a large skillet, heat about 2 tablespoons olive oil over medium heat. Add the sausages and brown well on all sides. Remove them from the pan, cut in thin slices, and set aside.
- Add about 2 more tablespoons olive oil to the same skillet. Add the shallots and sauté over medium heat until soft and tender. Add the garlic and thyme and sauté for a moment, just to release their aroma. Add all the escarole, season with salt and pepper, and sauté a minute or two to blend the flavors.
- Bring the water back to a boil and start cooking the penne.
- Return the sausages to the skillet, add the wine, and let it cook away. Add the capers. Let this simmer while the pasta finishes cooking.
- When the pasta is al dente, drain, leaving some water clinging to it, and transfer to a large serving bowl. Add the sauce and toss, adding a drizzle of fresh olive oil to help coat the pasta. Top with the Gruyère.

Ideas

Since cabbage is traditional with *boudin blanc,* the combination is a natural for pasta sauce: Brown the sausage in a large skillet. Remove and cut into slices. Sauté onions and cabbage in the same pan until tender. Return the sausage to the pan and simmer it in a little white wine. Toss with a sturdy dried pasta. Top with freshly grated Pecorino cheese.

Another excellent combination for pasta is *boudin blanc,* lentils, and tomato, seasoned with simmered onions and basil.

I like *boudin blanc* cooked with mushrooms and parsley and tossed with penne. Add sliced mushrooms when you would add the escarole in this recipe and sauté until tender. Add a generous amount of chopped flat-leaf parsley at the last minute.

In spring and summer, when fresh fava beans are available, I like matching them with *boudin blanc.* Sauté the beans in pancetta or prosciutto fat, then add browned sliced sausage, a splash of chicken broth, and lemon zest and toss with hot pasta.

Cavatappi with Capocollo, Yellow Peppers, and Provolone

Capocollo is a rich Italian sausage made of pork shoulder and seasoned with white wine and nutmeg. I often buy paper-thin slices of this delicious sausage to serve with provolone as an antipasto. This highly flavored combination also makes a winning pasta sauce.

[Makes 4 main-course or 6 first-course servings]

Olive oil

1 large onion, very thinly sliced

3 garlic cloves, thinly sliced

A few small rosemary sprigs

5 yellow bell peppers, roasted over a flame until charred, peeled, seeded, and cut into very thin strips

Salt

Freshly ground black pepper

A small wineglass of dry white wine

About ½ cup low-salt canned chicken broth

1 pound cavatappi

About 10 pieces of thinly sliced capocollo, cut in thin strips (use either the sweet or the spicy pepper-coated variety)

A tiny splash of balsamic vinegar

A small chunk of provolone cheese, thinly shaved with a vegetable peeler

- In a large skillet, heat about 3 tablespoons olive oil over medium heat. Add the onion and sauté until soft, about 4 minutes. Add the garlic, rosemary sprigs, and roasted peppers, season with salt and pepper, and sauté a few minutes longer, just until the peppers are very tender and redolent with garlic. Add the wine and cook until it boils away. Add the chicken broth and turn the heat to low. Simmer the sauce gently while the pasta is cooking.
- Cook the cavatappi until al dente and drain well. Add them to the skillet. Turn off the heat. Add the capocollo and balsamic vinegar and toss well. Remove the rosemary sprigs and transfer to a serving bowl. Add the shaved provolone and give the pasta a light toss.

Ideas

Like many of my dishes, this one is really a formula recipe in which the components can be varied widely to explore different tastes. Use any cured meat, any assertive vegetable that will stand up to a strong cured-meat flavor, and a piquant Italian grating cheese.

Roasted green bell peppers, Pecorino Romano, and soppressata make an excellent combination, as do artichokes, Pecorino Toscano, and prosciutto.

In the Tuscan town of Siena, capocollo is sometimes served with a tarragon sauce. Picking up on this idea, I created a pasta dish tossed with a tarragon-seasoned tomato sauce and, right before serving, added sliced capocollo and a handful of crumbled fresh goat cheese. The flavors blend beautifully.

Tagliatelle with Saucisson à l'Ail, Green Olives, and Savory

Everyone has foods that they're absolutely crazy about. For me, one of those foods is *saucisson à l'ail,* French garlic sausage, which is now available at many specialty food shops in this country. Since this sausage is customarily served with a warm potato salad, I knew it would be excellent with another starch: pasta. I've cut its richness with lightly cooked tomato and Cerignola olives, a sweet, fresh-tasting variety from Bari, Italy.

[Makes 4 main-course or 6 first-course servings]

½ pound garlic sausage, casing removed
    and cut in thin strips

Olive oil

1 medium onion, cut in small dice

3 tender inner celery stalks, cut in
    small dice, plus leaves

Salt

Freshly ground black pepper

About ¼ cup dry white wine

1 pound Plain Egg Pasta (page 364), cut
    for tagliatelle

About ¼ cup low-salt canned
    chicken broth

3 ripe round tomatoes (about
    1½ pounds), seeded and cut in
    small dice

A handful of green olives, pitted and
    cut in thin strips (I use Cerignola)

A handful of flat-leaf parsley leaves,
    chopped

A few savory sprigs, leaves chopped

About ½ cup freshly grated
    caciocavallo cheese

- In a large skillet, brown the sausage over high heat. Lower the heat and stir in about 2 tablespoons olive oil to the pan. Add the onion and celery and sauté until tender and fragrant, about 4 minutes. Season lightly with salt and more generously with pepper (remember, you'll be adding olives, and the saltiness from the sausage will present itself more as you continue with the sauce).
- Deglaze the skillet with the wine, scraping up any browned sausage bits from the bottom. Let the wine boil away.
- Start cooking the tagliatelle.
- Add the chicken broth, tomatoes, olives, and herbs to the pan. Let the sauce simmer over low heat while the pasta is cooking.

- When the pasta is tender, drain it and add to the pan. Toss well, adding a drizzle of fresh olive oil. Check the seasoning. Transfer to a large serving bowl. Top the pasta with grated caciocavallo.

Ideas

Garlic sausage goes so well with pasta, it is worth experimenting with. I love it browned and then simmered in a tomato sauce (an especially good choice is Sauce of Plum Tomatoes, Shallots, and Butter, page 21). Garlic sausage and string beans make another excellent combination. Brown the sausage pieces in olive oil, add blanched string beans, a little chicken broth, and a handful of flat-leaf parsley, and toss the mixture with pasta.

If you happen to have some leftover meat gravy or reduced meat stock, add it to the sauce for richness.

Adding Prosciutto, Pancetta, and Bresaola to Pasta Sauces for Big Flavor

It's amazing how a few slices of chopped pancetta, bacon, or prosciutto can pull together all the flavors in a pasta dish, rounding it out and making it taste complete. I've experimented with adding these meats to recipes much the way cooks do in Italy. Pancetta is the main flavoring in several classic Roman pasta preparations, among them *pasta alla gricia,* a dish of pancetta, Pecorino, and black pepper; and pasta carbonara, a more elaborate variation that includes eggs. Prosciutto and butter alone are a favorite pasta sauce in the Emilia-Romagna region. Bresaola, an air-dried salted beef, is delicious tossed with cream and peas or added to a pasta salad. In northern Italy smoked prosciutto is called speck and is often incorporated into pasta dishes. American bacon can be very good, imparting a smoky taste that blends well with green vegetables and tomato.

Fusilli Lunghi with Prosciutto, Lemon, and Artichokes

This is one of those you-can't-go-wrong pasta sauces—as long as you buy good prosciutto di Parma (see page 350 of "The Improviser's Pantry" for more information about imported Italian ham). It's another formula recipe: choose any seasonal vegetable that will not overwhelm the delicate taste of the ham. I've used artichokes, but asparagus, peas, or leeks can fit just as easily.

[Makes 4 main-course or 6 first-course servings]

About 15 baby artichokes

Olive oil

Unsalted butter

About ¼ pound (6 or 7 slices) thinly sliced prosciutto di Parma (see Note), cut in thin strips, excess fat trimmed and saved

About 12 scallions, cut in thin rounds, with some of the tender green

4 garlic cloves, thinly sliced

A few gratings of nutmeg

Salt

Freshly ground black pepper

About 1 cup homemade Chicken Broth (page 374)

1 pound fusilli lunghi

Zest and juice of 1 lemon

A generous handful of pine nuts, toasted

A handful of flat-leaf parsley leaves, chopped

Freshly grated Parmigiano-Reggiano cheese

- Snap off the outer leaves from the artichokes until you reach the light green tender ones. Trim the stem and cut the artichokes in half lengthwise (or in quarters if they are large). Baby artichokes should have no chokes, but if you see any fuzzy choke starting to develop on any of your artichokes, cut it away with a small knife. Drop the cut artichokes into a bowl of cold acidulated water so they don't darken (see Note, page 271).
- In a large skillet, heat 2 tablespoons each of olive oil and butter over medium heat. Chop the prosciutto fat and add it to the pan. Drain the artichokes well and add them to the skillet. Sauté until the artichokes just start to turn golden. Add the scallions, garlic, and nutmeg and season the artichokes very lightly with salt (remember, you will be adding prosciutto and chicken broth) and more liberally with black pepper. Sauté until the garlic gives off aroma, about 1 minute. Add the chicken broth and simmer,

uncovered, over medium-low heat until the artichokes are fork tender, about 5 minutes. You should still have some liquid left at this point.

- Start cooking the fusilli lunghi.
- Add the lemon zest and juice to the sauce and taste for seasoning.
- When the pasta is al dente, drain it and add to the pan. Turn off the heat. Add the pine nuts, prosciutto, and parsley. Add a lump of fresh butter and toss well. Transfer to a large serving bowl. Serve with grated Parmigiano-Reggiano at the table.

A note about acidulated water: Acidulated water can keep vegetables such as artichokes from turning dark once they've been cut. To make acidulated water, squeeze the juice of one lemon into 2 cups cold water.

A note about prosciutto in pasta sauce: Prosciutto is a cured raw ham. Its delicate taste and texture are diminished by cooking, so when you want to highlight it in a pasta sauce, add it at the last minute. Its fat, on the other hand, is very good for sautéing and adding flavor to a sauce. You can use fatty end cuts the same way you would use pancetta or fatback to add a meaty flavor to many sauces. But thinly sliced prosciutto di Parma or any other good Italian prosciutto should not be allowed to stew in a sauce.

Ideas

Prosciutto and unsalted butter make one of the world's loveliest pasta sauces. Do as they do in Parma, Italy: leave out the artichokes and toss the pasta with prosciutto, unsalted butter, and freshly ground black pepper.

I think slightly crisp green vegetables make the best match with prosciutto. String beans or haricots verts, the thin French string beans, can replace the artichokes. Peas, asparagus, and fava beans are all excellent with prosciutto as well. Any of these vegetables can be briefly blanched and added to the sauce along with the scallions (you'll need only about ¼ cup of the chicken broth called for in this recipe).

Cavatelli with Mozzarella, Bresaola, and Roasted Fennel

Bresaola is an air-dried salt-cured raw beef from the Lombardy region of Italy. I love it in a pasta sauce. It creates a rich, meaty sauce without cooking any meat. Try substituting it in recipes that call for prosciutto; the result is a less delicate, beefier taste. But remember that, like prosciutto, it should be added at the last minute and not allowed to cook.

I like the contrast between the roasted fennel and the slightly cooked cherry tomatoes. Try experimenting with combining foods at different stages of doneness. Here I use raw cured meat, roasted fennel, seared tomatoes, and mozzarella melted only by the heat of the pasta. I like tarragon with dried beef, so I've included it too.

[Makes 4 main-course or 6 first-course servings]

2 medium fennel bulbs, cored and thinly sliced, plus some of the feathery tops, finely chopped

1 large onion, thinly sliced

Salt

Freshly ground black pepper

Olive oil

1 pound cavatelli

5 or 6 anise seeds, ground to a powder with a mortar and pestle

About 2 dozen ripe cherry tomatoes, halved

About 10 thin slices (about ¼ pound) bresaola, cut in thin strips

½ pound mozzarella, cut in small cubes

A few tarragon sprigs, leaves chopped

A handful of basil leaves, cut in thin strips

- Preheat the oven to 400°F.
- Place the sliced fennel bulbs and onion on a large baking sheet. Season with salt and pepper and toss with about 3 tablespoons olive oil until the vegetables are evenly coated. Roast until tender and lightly browned, 35 to 40 minutes. You will need to stir the vegetables once or twice so they cook evenly.
- When the fennel has finished roasting, start cooking the pasta.
- In a large skillet, heat about 3 more tablespoons olive oil over medium heat. Add the ground anise seeds, and sauté a minute just to release the flavor. Add the tomatoes, season with salt and pepper, and sauté quickly, turning the heat up a bit. The tomatoes should just start giving off liquid but not lose their shape.

- When the cavatelli are al dente, drain them and transfer to a large serving bowl. Add the roasted fennel, tomatoes, bresaola, mozzarella, tarragon, basil, and fennel tops. Toss well to allow the cheese to melt slightly. Taste for seasoning. Serve right away.

Ideas

The tomatoes in this recipe serve to create liquid and add sparkle, but the dish is very good without them too. You can add a little chicken broth or pasta cooking water to loosen up the sauce if you leave them out.

Escarole goes very well with bresaola, and so does broccoli or cauliflower. A sauce of bresaola and broccoli rabe, seasoned with plenty of garlic, olive oil, and black pepper, makes a welcome change from the usual pork sausage and broccoli rabe pairing.

FEAR OF SALT

*W*hy does food usually taste so vibrant and special at good restaurants, and why can't I get that taste at home? Is it the genius of some fabulous chef, or is it that he understands salt and how to use it? A lot of home cooks seem to be afraid of salt, but if you have no medical problem that requires a reduced salt intake, there is no reason not to salt food enough to realize its full potential. Season as you go, and taste every time you add salt to make sure you aren't overdoing it.

Certain foods need ample salting to bring out their flavor. I find that most green vegetables taste better with a little more salt. Meats and fish have more natural salt in them, but they still profit from seasoning. I usually salt chicken and veal a little more heavily than I do duck or beef, especially when including them in a pasta sauce; mild meats can get lost amid all that starch. On the other hand, certain sweet foods, like fresh cream or carrots, lose appealing character when oversalted. There is a tendency, especially in health food cooking, to make up for lack of salt by overdoing it with spices, herbs, and garlic. This kind of thinking results in food with no balance of flavors and little natural integrity.

Cold pasta salads (and cold foods in general) need more salt than hot pasta because chilling diminishes flavor a bit.

Food that sits overnight in the refrigerator and is reheated might need to be resalted. Even if it was perfect the day before, taste it again.

I use sea salt for all my cooking, keeping several types in my pantry. Sea salts from Sicily and from various areas in France, especially along the Mediterranean, are all wonderful for Italian cooking. (For a discussion on what types of sea salt to buy, see page 351 in "The Improviser's Pantry.")

Farfalle with Gruyère, Eggs, and Broiled Pancetta

This is a cross between a carbonara and an Alfredo sauce. I've added shallots, sage, parsley, and a bit of nutmeg to give depth to the sauce, and I've grilled the pancetta for a crunchy texture. You'll probably like this rich pasta best as a first course.

[Makes 4 main-course or 6 first-course servings]

About 10 thin slices pancetta	**2 egg yolks**
1 pound farfalle	**About ½ cup freshly grated Gruyère**
Olive oil	**cheese**
4 shallots, finely diced	**4 or 5 large flat-leaf parsley sprigs,**
1 cup heavy cream	**leaves chopped**
A few gratings of nutmeg	**Salt**
A few sage leaves, chopped	**Freshly ground black pepper**

- Place the pancetta in one layer on a broiler pan and broil until crisp and slightly shriveled, about 2 minutes. Break the pancetta up into pieces.
- Start cooking the farfalle.
- In a large skillet, heat about 2 tablespoons olive oil. Add the shallots and sauté until soft, 3 to 4 minutes. Add the cream, nutmeg, and sage and simmer gently over low heat for a few minutes while the farfalle finishes cooking.
- In a large warmed serving bowl, combine the egg yolks and Gruyère. Mix well. Add the cream sauce and mix.
- When the pasta is al dente, drain it well and add to the bowl. Add the parsley and chopped pancetta. Season with a little salt and a generous amount of black pepper and toss well. Serve very hot.

Ideas

To make a classic carbonara, sauté pancetta until crisp and add a splash of white wine to loosen the browned pan particles. In a large bowl, whisk together 3 whole eggs with a large handful of grated Pecorino. Add drained spaghetti, the pancetta with the pan juices, and a generous amount of freshly grated black pepper and toss well.

Fresh Egg Pasta

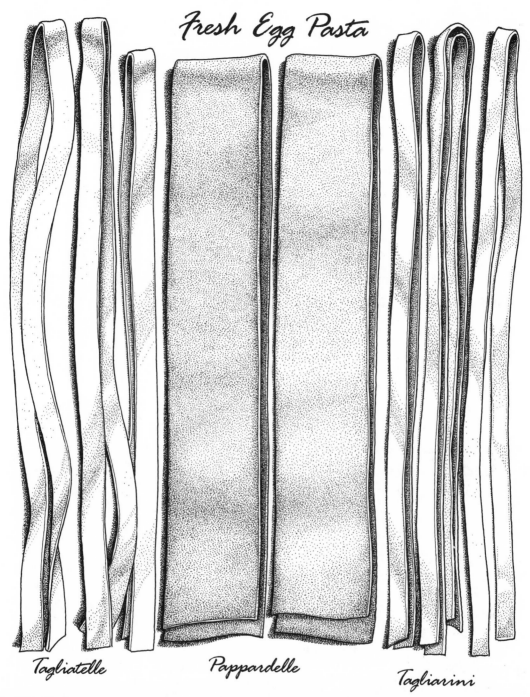

Tagliatelle

Pappardelle

Tagliarini

Traditionally these delicate pastas are reserved for butter- and cream-based sauces, game, and complex ragùs. They are also superb with wild mushrooms or spring asparagus. I think tagliatelle is an exquisite complement to sweet shellfish, such as lobster, scallops, or shrimp, especially when prepared with butter, wine, or a touch of cream.

Rigatoni with Spanish Ham, Potatoes, and Celery

Tue Serrano ham from Spain has just begun to be imported into this country. It's a bit less delicate in texture than prosciutto but has a delicious sweet-salty taste that combines beautifully with pasta, especially sturdy, bold shapes like rigatoni. Here I've paired the ham with potatoes, celery, and leeks, which contribute to the well-rounded flavor of the dish. In keeping with the Spanish theme, I've added a splash of Madeira to the sauce. I think this subtle mix of flavors tastes best without cheese.

I have a particular fondness for the forthright texture of rigatoni, and I love using it with chunky sauces such as this one. Also try it with any of the southern Italian–inspired meat ragùs in this chapter.

[Makes 4 main-course or 6 first-course servings]

4 small waxy potatoes (I use Yukon
    gold), cut in small chunks
1 pound rigatoni
4 or 5 tender inner celery stalks, includ-
    ing leaves, cut in small dice
3 medium leeks, washed, white part
    cut in small dice
Olive oil
1 allspice, ground to a powder with a
    mortar and pestle

A few thyme sprigs, leaves chopped
A generous splash of Madeira
½ cup homemade Chicken Broth
    (page 374)
About ¼ pound Serrano ham, thinly
    sliced and cut in thin strips
Freshly ground black pepper
Salt

- Set up a large pot of salted water to cook the pasta. Bring to a boil, drop in the chopped potatoes, and cook until they are tender but still quite firm (they'll cook further in the pasta sauce). Lift them from the water with a large strainer and let drain in a colander.
- Bring the water back to a boil and start cooking the rigatoni.
- In a large skillet, sauté the celery and celery leaves together with the leeks in a few tablespoons of olive oil until soft and fragrant, about 5 minutes. Add the potatoes and sauté until they are well coated with oil. Add the allspice and thyme and sauté a minute to blend the flavors. Add the Madeira and let it all cook away. Add the chicken broth and let the sauce simmer while the pasta finishes cooking.

- Drain the rigatoni and add to the pan. Add the ham and a generous amount of black pepper. Toss well. Taste for salt and add some if needed.

Ideas

I love potatoes and ham with pasta, but for a lighter version of this dish, substitute about ¾ cup shelled fresh peas for the potatoes, blanching them only about a minute in the pasta cooking water. Ham, peas, and roasted red peppers are a particularly Spanish combination that also makes an excellent pasta sauce.

Also try this with the same amount of cooked ham: prosciutto cotto, Westphalian, or Smithfield.

HOW TO READ A RECIPE

*E*laborate, detailed recipes can be intimidating. Even with my years of cooking experience, I tend to get stupefied trying to follow long, involved directions. If I feel I'm cooking with the brakes on, I don't enjoy it. But I've worked out my own way of dealing with the problem. First I read through the list of ingredients and break it up in my head into two groups: main ingredients and flavoring ingredients. This gives me a visual picture of what the pieces of the dish will look like. Since ingredients are almost always listed in order of use, not in order of importance, it is sometimes hard to figure out what you are supposed to be making.

Say a recipe calls for 2 tablespoons olive oil, 1 red bell pepper, ½ cup white wine, a small onion, a garlic clove, 1 pound medium shrimp, 1 tablespoon capers, 4 pounds chopped tomatoes, and a few sprigs of chopped parsley. If you pull out the ingredients called for in large amounts (in this case the shrimp and the tomato), you can see this is mainly a shrimp dish cooked with a lot of tomato. The ingredients specified in small amounts can be logically categorized as seasonings. This is a shrimp dish cooked with a lot of tomato and flavored with a bit of bell pepper, garlic, white wine, and parsley.

I then note what the ingredients are to be cooked in—olive oil, butter, vegetable oil, or some other fat; this gives me a feel for the dish's style. Next I read the body of the recipe carefully to see exactly what it asks me to do. Do I need the oven? Will I be sautéing or grilling? How long will this take to cook? Then, if I feel comfortable enough, I close the cookbook and begin the recipe, but in a way I'll be comfortable with. Of course, this becomes easier to do with more experience, but even if you're a beginning cook, evaluating and breaking down a recipe beforehand can give you control, making you more confident and stronger in the kitchen. Even if you go back to the recipe for exact measurements and directions, it will only be to check yourself.

Tagliatelle with Sweetbreads, Green Peppercorns, and Watercress

Tender Meat Cooked Quickly for Elegant Pasta Sauces

Sweetbreads are a delicacy. Their tender white meat and mild taste are complemented by many different flavorings. Wild mushrooms such as chanterelles or morels are exquisite with them. So are many types of cooked greens, such as the wilted watercress I chose for this dish. Sweetbreads blend well with butter or olive oil and take well to hints of acidity from a little vinegar, white wine, capers, or citrus juice. In Italy sweetbreads often become a filling for stuffed pasta such as ravioli or cannelloni. Here they grace fresh egg pasta, which is their perfect match.

[Makes 4 main-course or 6 first-course servings]

1 pair sweetbreads (about 1 pound)

Salt

A splash of white wine vinegar

About 1 tablespoon unsalted butter

About 1 tablespoon olive oil

Freshly ground black pepper

Flour for dredging

5 medium shallots, thinly sliced

A few thyme sprigs, leaves chopped

A small handful green peppercorns,
    rinsed and crushed

A splash of cognac

About ½ cup homemade Chicken Broth
    (page 374) or low-salt canned

About ½ cup heavy cream

2 bunches watercress, thick stems
    removed

1 pound Plain Egg Pasta (page 364),
    cut for tagliatelle

About ½ cup freshly grated Parmigiano-
    Reggiano cheese

- Soak the sweetbreads in cold water for about an hour to remove any blood (the sweetbreads will turn from light tan to a milky white after soaking). Remove from the water.
- Place the sweetbreads in a shallow pot of fresh cold water to cover. Season with about 1 teaspoon salt and the vinegar. Bring slowly to a boil. Turn the heat to low and let them simmer for about 5 minutes. Lift them from the pot and run under cold water. Now remove as much of the thin membrane coating as you can (it will pull off easily). Slice the sweetbreads in thin strips and dry well.
- In a large skillet, heat the butter and olive oil over high heat. Season the sweetbreads with salt and black pepper and coat them lightly with flour, shaking off any excess. Add

the sweetbreads to the skillet and brown quickly on both sides. Turn the heat down a little and add the shallots, thyme, and green peppercorns. Cook a few minutes to soften the shallots. Add a splash of cognac and let it cook away. Add the chicken broth and cream and let the sauce simmer a few minutes to thicken slightly. Add the watercress and let it wilt in the sauce, about 30 seconds.

- Cook the tagliatelle until tender, drain well, and transfer to a serving bowl. Pour on the sweetbread sauce. Add a handful of grated Parmigiano-Reggiano and toss well.

Ideas

Sweetbreads are wonderful flavored with dry Marsala, which makes a fine substitute for the cognac I've used here, creating a slightly sweeter, richer sauce.

Arugula and capers can replace the watercress and green peppercorns.

Chanterelle, fresh porcini, or morel mushrooms marry well with sweetbreads; when in season, substitute them for the watercress. Simply slice a handful of wild mushrooms and add them to the skillet when you add the shallots.

Gemelli with Chicken Livers, Leeks, Tomato, and Sage

This is a dish I created while learning to cook for myself as a teenager. I loved pasta, and I adored chicken livers. One night I decided to combine them for dinner, adding canned tomatoes and Marsala, two items always on hand at our house. Over the years I've refined this recipe to reflect my changing tastes. Chicken livers with pasta still remains a favorite dish—and it is also a Tuscan classic.

[Makes 4 main-course or 6 first-course servings]

1 pound chicken livers, cleaned, quartered, and well dried

Olive oil

Unsalted butter

Salt

Freshly ground black pepper

About ¼ cup dry Marsala

3 thin slices pancetta, chopped

4 large leeks, washed, white part cut in small dice

2 garlic cloves, thinly sliced

One 35-ounce can Italian plum tomatoes, drained and chopped

About ½ cup low-salt canned chicken broth

1 pound gemelli

6 or 7 fresh sage leaves, chopped

About 1 cup freshly grated Pecorino Toscano cheese

- Dry the chicken livers with paper towels (wet meat will lead to steam in the pan, which inhibits browning). In a large skillet, heat about 1 tablespoon each of olive oil and butter over high heat. When very hot, add the chicken livers, season with salt and pepper, and sauté quickly until browned (they should be well browned but still quite pink in the center). Add a small splash of dry Marsala and let it boil away. Remove the livers from the pan and set aside.
- Lower the heat to medium. Add another tablespoon of olive oil to the skillet. Add the pancetta and sauté until crisp. Add the leeks and sauté until soft (you can't sauté the leeks with the chicken livers because they would burn at the high heat needed to sear the livers). Add the garlic and sauté a minute until it gives off aroma. Add another small splash of Marsala and let it boil away. Add the tomatoes and chicken broth and season with salt and pepper.
- Start cooking the gemelli.
- Cook the sauce over medium heat for about 5 minutes. It should have thickened slightly.

When the pasta is about a half minute away from being done, return the chicken livers to the pan. Add the sage leaves and heat the sauce gently over low heat. Taste for seasoning. Don't cook the sauce more than about a minute or the livers will toughen.

- When the pasta is al dente, drain it and transfer to a serving bowl. Add the chicken liver sauce, a fresh tablespoon of butter, and a small handful of Pecorino. Toss well. Serve additional cheese at the table.

Ideas

I frequently make a chicken liver and pasta dish in the style of chicken cacciatore, by adding mushrooms and sliced green bell peppers to the sauce. Add sliced mushrooms and one thinly sliced green bell pepper to the skillet along with the onion and sauté until all the vegetables are just tender, about 4 minutes. I usually make this sauce without tomatoes, and you can omit them here.

If you happen to have duck livers, by all means use them in place of the chicken livers. For a really rustic dish, cook a few chicken hearts along with the livers.

ABOUT COOKING CHICKEN LIVERS

If you don't like chicken livers, it may be because you haven't had them cooked properly. A splash of brandy or grappa (or dry Marsala in this case) adds much to their appeal, taking away the slightly iron taste they can have. They should be cooked over high heat to brown nicely while remaining slightly pink in the center. Butter helps them brown. Cook them quickly in a large pan so they are not crowded (this also helps them brown). Add the alcohol after they've browned and boil it away quickly, leaving only its essence.

Fusilli with Veal, Capers, and Lemon

Innumerable classic Italian dishes can be effortlessly adapted for pasta. The sauce here is essentially veal piccata, the beloved Italian American standard, updated with fresh herbs and arugula. Another traditional favorite that makes a great pasta sauce is Veal Marsala. It's basically prepared the same way but flavored with Marsala wine instead of white wine and lemon.

[Makes 4 main-course or 6 first-course servings]

1 pound fusilli

Flour for dredging the veal

1 pound veal scaloppine, pounded, thinly sliced, and cut in strips

Salt

Freshly ground black pepper

A pinch of cayenne pepper

Unsalted butter

Olive oil

12 scallions (about 2 bunches), cut in thin rounds, with some tender green

3 garlic cloves, thinly sliced

About ¼ cup dry white wine

About ½ cup homemade Light Veal Broth (page 376) or Chicken Broth (page 374)

A generous handful of salt-packed capers, soaked and drained (see page 343)

Zest of 2 lemons

A large bunch of arugula, washed, stemmed, dried, and coarsely chopped

A few large marjoram sprigs, leaves chopped

A few large oregano sprigs, leaves chopped

A few flat-leaf parsley sprigs, leaves chopped

Juice of 1 lemon

- Start cooking the fusilli.
- Flour the veal and shake off any excess (I like doing this job in a strainer so I can just shake it off into the garbage). Season it with salt, black pepper, and the cayenne.
- In a large skillet, heat about 2 tablespoons each of butter and olive oil over high heat. When very hot, add the veal and brown it quickly on both sides. Remove the veal from the pan and set it aside on a plate covered with aluminum foil to keep warm.
- In the same skillet, heat about 1 more tablespoon olive oil. Add the scallions and cook over medium heat until tender and fragrant, about 2 minutes. Add the garlic and sauté a minute to release its flavor. Add the wine and simmer until it has almost all cooked away. Add the veal or chicken broth, capers, and lemon zest and let this simmer a few minutes.

- When the pasta is al dente, drain it well and place in a large serving bowl. Add the veal (and any juices the pieces have released), the broth with the capers, the arugula, all the fresh herbs, and the lemon juice to the bowl. Add a drizzle of fresh olive oil and toss well. Season with salt and pepper. The arugula should start to wilt slightly with the heat of the pasta.

Ideas

Rosemary and garlic together are another typically Italian treatment for veal; add 1 or 2 thinly sliced garlic cloves to this dish when the scallions are tender, and replace the thyme with a few small sprigs of chopped rosemary. I also love orange zest with scaloppine recipes (orange zest and juice can replace the lemon in this recipe). Basil, tarragon, and rosemary all blend wonderfully with orange.

Veal is delicious seasoned with saffron. Dissolve a generous pinch of ground saffron (see page 352) in the broth used in this recipe (warm it in a small saucepan so the saffron dissolves completely). Add this in place of the plain broth, and add a splash of heavy cream or crème fraîche to the pan right before adding it to the cooked pasta.

THE IMPORTANCE OF BROWNING MEAT FOR SAUCES

*B*rowning gives meat texture and deep, caramelized flavor. And browned pan juices, when loosened with wine or other liquid, add depth to meat sauces. Make sure the surface of the meat is dry before getting ready to brown it. The pan should be hot enough to sear the meat on contact. Crowding the pan causes meat to steam rather than brown, so if you are preparing a large amount of meat, brown it in batches. Try not to become impatient and start stirring the pieces around too quickly after you put them in the pan. Too much stirring will release juices from the meat, causing it to steam. Let the meat sit undisturbed until you can see the edges brown. Give it time to form a crisp crust. When a piece of meat is well seared, it will move easily in the pan and not stick to the bottom.

Butter, which has a lower burning point than oil, browns meat quickly. A mix of half butter and half olive oil works very well and doesn't burn as readily as straight butter, since the higher burning point of the oil tempers the butter. Olive oil alone can work well if you let the oil get very hot before adding the meat. Dredging the meat in flour will help it form a crisp crust and will lightly thicken your sauce as well, but if you want a very loose, brothy sauce, leave off the flour.

Veal Bracioline Stuffed with Yellow Raisins and Capers, Served on Pasta

Stuffed beef rolls long-simmered in tomato sauce is a classic southern Italian dish my mother often made on weekends. I loved the rich, dark, beef-scented sauce but disliked the texture and flavor of the falling-apart meat, which seemed to have given up every bit of its integrity to the sauce.

Here is a modern version of that recipe made with veal. The meat rolls are browned and returned to a lighter sauce to simmer for only a few minutes. The combination of raisins, prosciutto, and capers might seem strange, but as a filling for these veal rolls it echoes the sweet-and-sour taste of southern Italian cooking, which I always find imaginative and unexpected.

[Makes 4 main-course or 6 first-course servings]

For the filling:
A large handful of golden raisins
A large wineglass of dry
    white wine
A small handful of capers
3 thin slices of prosciutto,
    coarsely chopped
Freshly ground black pepper

For the meat:
8 slices veal, cut for scaloppine
    (about 1½ pounds)
Salt
Olive oil

For the sauce:
Olive oil
4 shallots, finely diced
One 35-ounce can Italian plum
    tomatoes, drained and chopped
About ¼ cup homemade Mixed-Meat
    Broth (page 375) or Chicken Broth
    (page 374)
A few mint sprigs, leaves chopped
A small handful of capers

1 pound fusilli
Freshly grated Asiago cheese

- To make the filling, soak the raisins in the wine until plump. Drain, saving the wine. Put the raisins, capers, and the prosciutto in a food processor and grind to a rough paste. Season with pepper.

- To stuff the meat, lay the veal out flat on a counter. Season with salt and pepper. Spread a thin layer of filling on each piece of meat and roll them up widthwise, starting with the thinner end. Close each piece with a toothpick.
- In a large skillet, heat about 2 tablespoons olive oil over medium heat. Add the meat rolls and brown them on all sides. Remove the meat to a plate.
- To make the sauce, in the same skillet that you browned the veal, sauté the shallots over medium heat until soft. Add the raisin soaking wine and let it boil a minute, scraping up any browned cooking juices from the skillet bottom so they can become part of your sauce. Add the tomatoes and the meat or chicken broth and cook over lively heat for about 8 minutes. Season with salt and pepper and add the mint and capers.
- Start cooking the fusilli.
- When ready to serve, return the meat rolls to the sauce, bring to a gentle simmer, and reheat for 1 to 2 minutes (longer cooking will make them tough).
- When the fusilli are al dente, drain them and place in a large serving bowl. Add the sauce and toss well. Either thickly slice the rolls and place them on top of the pasta, or serve them on a separate plate, topped with sauce. Don't forget to remove the toothpicks.
- Pass a bowl of grated Asiago at the table.

Ideas

When thinking of your own ideas for fillings here, think strong flavors. Remember that the filling not only is wrapped in meat but also has to compete with a sauce.

The traditional filling for beef or veal bracioline is grated Parmigiano, chopped parsley, and a few bread crumbs. Here are ideas for other fillings: dried figs, prosciutto, and Parmigiano; pine nuts, raisins, and orange zest; anchovies, marjoram, and bread crumbs; black or green olive tapenade; basil pesto; and roasted garlic purée.

Long-Simmered Meat Sauces for Pasta

These are the sauces that fill the kitchen with those incredibly deep, rich smells that make people's mouths water in intense anticipation of dinner. I like to imagine I've turned my apartment into a restaurant and I'm preparing a sauce so lush and spectacular people will come in off the street and pay anything just to get a taste.

And since long-simmered sauces take a while to cook, I have time to tinker with their flavoring, perfecting it along the way. I can add herbs or vegetables at the beginning of cooking for a mellowed, slow-blended result, or I can make additions toward the end for brightness, emphasis, or texture. A few anchovies, a shot of vinegar, a fresh dose of herbs, or a few chopped tomatoes can break right through that long-simmered complexity with a burst of flavor.

When you take this approach, just remember that anything you add toward the beginning of cooking—for instance, a half bottle of strong red wine—will remain the backbone of the dish, and you must work with that. But always taste your sauce along the way, because you have much room for spur-of-the-moment decisions. Maybe you just remembered that dish of sautéed artichokes in your refrigerator or the fresh string beans you bought at the farmers' market. You can add either, if you choose, to a slow-simmered chicken sauce.

The richness that develops from long cooking gives you a pasta sauce well suited for a main course.

Cavatelli with Chicken, Saffron, and Green Olives

I don't usually like boneless chicken breast in pasta sauces. Its mild whiteness seems to get lost, and it dries out easily. But here the flavor of the dark chicken meat braised with the saffron and green olives comes together in the rich cooking liquid to make a wonderful pasta sauce.

[Makes 4 main-course or 6 first-course servings]

1 cup homemade Chicken Broth (page 374) or low-salt canned

A generous pinch of saffron threads, ground to a powder with a mortar and pestle (see page 352)

Olive oil

2 thin slices pancetta, chopped

1 large onion, cut in small dice

Salt

Freshly ground black pepper

3 whole chicken legs, with thigh attached

A small wineglass of dry white wine

A few marjoram sprigs

A few thyme sprigs

1 pound cavatelli

A handful of pine nuts, toasted

½ cup green olives, pitted and cut in
**   half (picholine are good here)**

A pinch of cayenne pepper

- Heat the chicken broth in a small saucepan and add the ground saffron to it.
- In a large skillet or flameproof casserole fitted with a lid, heat 1 tablespoon olive oil over medium heat. Add the pancetta and cook until it is just starting to get crisp. Add the onion and sauté until tender, 3 to 4 minutes. Salt and pepper the chicken legs and add them to the pan. Brown them lightly on both sides. Pour off the excess fat. Add the wine and let it boil for a minute or two. Add the marjoram, thyme, and saffron-flavored chicken broth. Bring to a boil and then turn the heat to low. Cover the pan and let the chicken simmer until very tender, about 45 minutes, turning it once or twice.
- Remove the chicken from the skillet, skin it, and with your fingers, shred the meat into small pieces.
- Start cooking the cavatelli.
- Skim the excess grease from the sauce if necessary. Remove the herb sprigs. Return the shredded chicken to the sauce. Add the pine nuts and olives, and simmer a few minutes to blend the flavors. Check the seasoning. You probably won't need to add more salt because of the saltiness of the olives, but add a little more black pepper and the cayenne.
- When the cavatelli are al dente, drain them well and add to the pan. Toss very well. I think this sauce is best without cheese.

Ideas

My mother always made wonderful chicken stews. She referred to all of them as chicken cacciatore, but each one was different. Sometimes she'd add mushrooms or green pepper, sometimes just tomato, occasionally a few capers. I sometimes add chunks of pork sausage. I think the key to making this type of dish interesting is to choose vibrant flavorings that lift the delicate taste of the chicken; therefore, I stay away from heavy cream sauces and favor instead wine-based ones.

Coq au vin, the classic French dish of chicken simmered in red wine with mushrooms, onions, and herbs, makes a wonderful sauce for pasta. Serve the chicken pieces as a second course.

Chicken with saffron and fennel is another good combination. Sauté a sliced fennel bulb along with the onion and add a few toasted fennel seeds to intensify its flavor.

This can easily be turned into a red sauce with the addition of a can of chopped plum tomatoes in place of the chicken broth.

Orecchiette with Turkey and Wild Mushroom Cacciatore

Dark-meat turkey takes wonderfully to a braise, becoming tender and succulent and leaving behind a rich, flavorful sauce for pasta. Lately I've been thrilled to see whole turkey legs in my supermarket. Now I can enjoy my favorite part of the turkey without buying the whole bird. Here I've braised a turkey leg with red wine, leeks, and porcini mushrooms, seasoning the sauce with a bit of juniper berry for a deep, woodsy taste.

[Makes 4 main-course or 6 first-course servings]

Olive oil

1 turkey leg (about 1½ pounds)

3 thin slices pancetta, chopped

Salt

Freshly ground black pepper

3 medium leeks, washed, white part cut
  in small dice

1 medium carrot, cut in small dice

3 garlic cloves, minced

1 bay leaf

A few fresh sage leaves

About 4 juniper berries, lightly crushed

A large wineglass of dry red wine (I use
  a Merlot)

1 cup homemade Chicken Broth
  (page 374) or low-salt canned

½ pound fresh porcini mushrooms
  (cultivated cremini mushrooms
  work well too and are a fraction
  of the cost)

A splash of brandy

1 pound orecchiette

About 1 cup freshly grated Grana
  Padano cheese

- In a large flameproof casserole, fitted with a lid, heat 2 tablespoons olive oil over medium heat. Add the turkey leg and pancetta, season with salt and pepper, and brown the leg on one side. The pancetta will brown along with the turkey. Turn the leg over, add the leeks and carrot, and cook until the turkey is browned on the other side and the vegetables are tender. Add the garlic, herbs, and juniper berries and sauté a minute to release their flavors. Add the red wine and cook until it has boiled down to a few table-spoons. Add the chicken broth, cover the pan, and braise over low heat, turning the turkey leg occasionally, until tender, 1 hour or a little longer.
- Remove the turkey leg and let it cool a bit. Reduce the sauce over high heat until it is slightly thickened (the sauce will remain brothy). Skim off the excess fat if necessary.

- In a small sauté pan, heat 1 tablespoon olive oil. Add the mushrooms and sauté over high heat until just starting to brown. Season with salt and pepper. Add a splash of brandy and let it evaporate.
- Remove the meat from the turkey and cut it in small cubes about the same size as the orecchiette. Discard the skin and bones. Add the turkey and mushrooms to the sauce and heat gently.
- Cook the orecchiette until al dente, drain well, and place in a large serving dish. Add a handful of grated Grana Padano and toss it with the pasta. Pour the sauce on top and toss again. Serve extra cheese at the table.

Ideas

Here I've added the turkey meat to the sauce because I wanted to create a chunky dish for dried pasta. But braised turkey adds good flavor to any simmering liquids, which then make a flavorful pasta sauce without the meat, especially if a little butter and grated cheese are added to the pasta before it is tossed with the sauce (try tagliatelle with this elegant sauce).

To make a quick turkey sauce using already cooked turkey, sauté the pancetta, leeks, carrots, and garlic. Add the mushrooms and cook until tender. Add a splash of brandy and let it boil away. Add ½ cup of the chicken broth and the chopped cooked turkey. Season with salt, pepper, and the fresh herbs. Simmer over low heat a few minutes to blend flavors. Leave out the juniper berries. Toss with pasta.

Lasagnette with Braised Duck and Black Olives

Central and northern Italy abound in recipes for pasta with duck, some flavored simply with tomatoes, others delicately seasoned with white wine, nutmeg, sage, and onion. The inspiration for this recipe comes from a classic Tuscan dish of duck braised with olives, which I've adapted for a pasta sauce. Here duck liver, olives, and a rich duck braising liquid become the sauce for the pasta. Slice the duck and serve it as a second course, along with what's left of the sauce and a green salad.

[Makes 4 main-course or 6 first-course servings]

Olive oil

1 duck (about 4 pounds), separated into whole legs, wings, and breasts, with bones in (save the duck liver)

1 large onion, finely chopped

A few tender inner celery stalks, with leaves, finely chopped

A few slices prosciutto end, fat and meat chopped

A few rosemary sprigs

A few oregano sprigs

1 bay leaf

2 whole cloves, ground

Salt

Freshly ground black pepper

Brandy

1 large wineglass of dry red wine (Corbières is a good choice)

One 35-ounce can Italian plum tomatoes, drained and chopped

1 cup duck stock (see Note) or homemade Chicken Broth (page 374)

About ½ cup crème fraîche

A large handful of black olives, pitted and cut in half (black Nyons are good)

1 pound lasagnette (a dried curly-edged, long pasta)

Freshly grated Grana Padano cheese

- In a large flameproof casserole, fitted with a lid, heat about 2 tablespoons olive oil over medium-high heat. When hot, add the duck pieces and brown them well on both sides. Pour off all but a few tablespoons of duck fat. Lower the heat a bit and add the onion, celery, celery leaves, prosciutto, herb sprigs, bay leaf, and ground cloves. Season with salt and pepper and sauté until the vegetables are soft. Pour a splash of brandy over the duck pieces and let it boil away. Add the wine and let boil for a minute. Add the tomatoes and duck stock or chicken broth. Bring to a boil. Lower the heat, cover, and simmer until the duck is very tender, about 1½ hours. Remove the duck. Boil the sauce down until it is fairly thick. Skim off the excess fat.

- Heat 1 tablespoon olive oil in a small sauté pan over high heat. Add the duck liver and sauté it quickly on both sides until it is well browned. Add a splash of brandy to the pan and let it boil away. Season with salt. Chop the duck liver fine and add it to the sauce. Add the crème fraîche and olives and mix well. Pull out the herb sprigs. Taste for seasoning.
- Cook the lasagnette until al dente, drain, and transfer to a large serving bowl. Pour on enough sauce to coat the pasta and toss. Pass grated Grana Padano at the table.
- For a second course, if necessary, reheat the duck pieces gently in the remaining sauce. Remove the duck skin and slice the duck thinly. Place on a serving plate and top with the remaining sauce. Serve with a green salad.

Note: I usually make a simple duck broth with the back, neck, wings, and trimmings plus a few onion skins, parsley stems, and celery leaves. You can also enrich low-salt canned chicken broth by simmering it for about 10 minutes with duck trimmings. See page 373 for more on making broths.

Ideas

Red wine, rosemary, and black olives are a delicious flavoring trio, and I've used them together in this recipe. If you use dry white wine, fresh sage, and green olives instead, you can change the character of this dish dramatically, lifting it from warm and earthy to bright and piquant.

I enjoyed a penne with shredded duck confit, black olives, and chopped cornichons in a French bistro in Manhattan. It was a charming and unexpected concoction. If you ever have a few pieces of duck confit left over, you can make a great pasta dish in no time (I sometimes buy prepared duck confit just for this purpose). Make a soffritto base for your dish by sautéing chopped onion and celery in olive oil. Add the shredded confit, a splash of white wine, and a small glass of chicken or duck broth. Simmer a minute. Add a small handful of chopped olives and cornichons (a little less cornichons) and a handful of chopped parsley. Toss with penne.

For a simple but delicious duck sauce, simmer browned duck pieces in Tomato and Orange Sauce (page 25) until tender. Chop about half the duck meat into bite-size pieces and return it to the sauce. Toss with pappardelle.

Pappardelle with Rabbit, Chianti, and Chocolate

This is a rich sweet-and-sour sauce subtly flavored with unsweetened cocoa, a New World ingredient that made its way into Italian cooking long ago. More pungent versions of this rabbit dish are made throughout Italy, like one I ate in Siracusa, Sicily, which contained vinegar and sugar as well as wine, raisins, pine nuts, and a hint of cocoa. My version is only slightly tart and rich and mellow enough for a pasta sauce. I like this very fragrant sauce served without cheese.

[Makes 4 main-course or 6 first-course servings]

Flour for dredging the rabbit

One 3½- to 4-pound rabbit, cut in serving pieces

Olive oil

Salt

Freshly ground black pepper

1 large onion, cut in small dice

2 small carrots, cut in small dice

2 garlic cloves, minced

A large wineglass of Chianti or other hearty dry red wine

1 or 2 bay leaves

3 or 4 fresh sage leaves, chopped

2 or 3 long strips of orange peel

One 15-ounce can Italian plum tomatoes, drained and chopped

About 1 cup homemade Light Veal Broth (page 376), Mixed-Meat Broth (page 375), or Chicken Broth (page 374)

A pinch of cayenne pepper

1 tablespoon unsweetened cocoa powder

A large handful of pine nuts, toasted

A large handful of golden raisins

1 pound Plain Egg Pasta (page 364), cut for pappardelle

- Flour the rabbit pieces. In a large flameproof casserole, heat about 3 tablespoons olive oil over medium heat. Add the rabbit pieces and brown well on both sides, seasoning them with salt and pepper. Turn the heat to low and add the onion and carrots. Sauté until the vegetables are tender, about 5 minutes. Add the garlic and cook a minute longer. Add the wine, bay leaves, sage, and orange peel. Turn the heat to high and boil the wine down by about half. Add the tomatoes and enough broth to just cover the meat. Add the cayenne and bring to a boil. Turn the heat to low and simmer, partially covered, until the rabbit is tender, about 1 hour. In the last 15 minutes of cooking, add the cocoa, pine nuts, and raisins. Check the seasoning.

- Remove the rabbit pieces from the pot along with a ladle of sauce and serve as a second course or save for another meal.
- Boil the sauce down a few minutes to reduce and thicken slightly. Skim off the excess fat if necessary.
- Cook the pappardelle until tender, drain well, and place in a large serving bowl. Top with the sauce.

Ideas

Stemperata is another Sicilian sweet-and-sour sauce often used for rabbit. I sampled this dish in a tiny family-run restaurant in Noto, a town in southeastern Sicily. It is made by braising rabbit pieces with white wine, chicken broth, celery, green olives, sometimes capers, and a pinch of sugar. Add a splash of white wine vinegar, a pinch of hot red pepper flakes, and a few chopped fresh mint leaves at the end and toss the sauce with ziti or penne. Serve the rabbit as a second course.

This dish also works very well with chicken.

CREATING YOUR OWN STYLE

*E*arly on, I knew I wanted to learn to make good Italian food. My ancestors were from southern Italy, and I grew up exposed to their native palate. But even though my tastes ran toward the Mediterranean, I found myself using a lot of cream and Parmigiano-Reggiano when I first started experimenting with pasta sauces. I guess those ingredients seemed dressy, and they also seemed easy. I was also reacting against the ubiquity of tomato sauce in Italian American cooking at the time.

So I played with creamy sauces and created a fair number of gluey, indigestible disasters. It was my love of seafood that eventually pulled me in another direction, toward simple, direct flavors incorporating vegetables, herbs, and olive oil.

As a teenager, I became obsessed with linguine with white clam sauce, a dish my mother made very well with fresh Long Island clams and abundant flat-leaf parsley. I think of it as one of the inspired dishes of Italian cooking. I wanted life to be like this dish. I wasn't sure exactly what I meant by that, but it had to do with having a vibrant, bright existence, but one that was also strong and serious at the same time.

As I was forming my persona as a cook, I discovered that books on technique never helped me much. I needed romance to get me excited about learning. I preferred to plunge into an exciting, exotic recipe and fail miserably rather than start with very fundamental techniques.

I think observing how good cooks put flavors together (observing them by reading their books and eating at their restaurants) is an important part of learning how to cook; it will help you develop your own style. Studying a Matisse will get your mind going more than painting by numbers ever will. I'm not saying technique is unimportant, but for an accomplished home cook, the hours needed to learn the basics can be made a lot more enjoyable if you create a cooking fantasy that will little by little lead you to your own style.

Conchiglie (Shells)

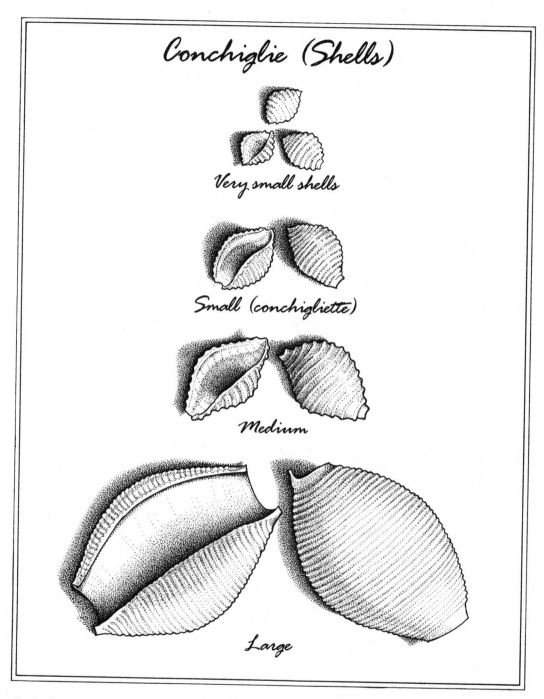

Very small shells

Small (conchigliette)

Medium

Large

For Southern-style ragùs and chunky broccoli or cauliflower sauces. Shells are wonderful for sauces containing small cubes of mozzarella. Large shells are perfect for stuffing and baking.

Ziti with Tripe, Prosciutto, and Rosemary

Romans make a wonderful stew of tripe cooked in tomato and white wine and served with a generous topping of grated Pecorino Romano cheese. I've eaten many versions of this dish in Rome, but my favorite is one tossed with pasta. Here I've added a mellow Grana and the strong, piney flavor of rosemary, which go extremely well with the sweetness of long-cooked tripe.

[Makes 4 main-course or 6 first-course servings]

Olive oil

3 or 4 thin slices prosciutto, fat trimmed and saved, meat cut in thin strips

1 large onion, cut in small dice

2 or 3 tender inner celery stalks, cut in small dice, plus leaves, chopped

2 or 3 garlic cloves, crushed

2 bay leaves

2 or 3 rosemary sprigs

About 1½ pounds honeycomb tripe, trimmed of thick membrane and cut in thin strips (see Note)

Salt

Freshly ground black pepper

A large wineglass of crisp Italian white wine (a Vernaccia is perfect here)

One 35-ounce can Italian plum tomatoes, drained and chopped

1 pound ziti

About 1 cup freshly grated Grana Padano cheese

- In a large flameproof casserole fitted with a tight lid, heat 2 tablespoons olive oil over medium heat. Add the prosciutto fat, onion, and celery, and sauté until the vegetables are tender, about 6 minutes. Add the garlic, herbs, and tripe, season with salt and pepper, and sauté a few minutes. Add the wine and let it bubble and reduce by about half. Add the tomatoes.
- Cover the casserole and simmer gently over low heat until the tripe is very tender, about 2 hours. The sauce should be thick and fragrant and the tripe should be tender to the bite. Check the casserole occasionally to make sure it isn't boiling hard. If the sauce is very liquid, uncover the casserole for the last half hour of cooking to reduce the sauce. Check the seasoning. The sauce should have a sweet, mellow taste. Remove the rosemary sprigs.
- Cook the ziti until al dente, drain, and place in a serving bowl. Add the tripe sauce and the chopped prosciutto and toss. Serve with the grated Grana Padano.

A note on buying tripe: Tripe is the stomach lining of a cow, and several cuts from different areas of the stomach are eaten. Honeycomb tripe has the most delicious sweet flavor and tender texture of all the cuts and is what you will usually find in our markets (it is distinguishable by its honeycomb-like surface). All the beef tripe I have seen here has been well cleaned and parboiled, but it still takes about 2 hours of gentle simmering to become tender. Uncooked tripe can take twice as long.

Ideas

Tripe is popular in central and northern Italian cooking. Some Tuscan versions are seasoned with hot red pepper. A Roman version is often flavored with fresh mint. Pine nuts are another common Roman addition.

Black olives, especially the small Niçoise type, go very well with rosemary and are excellent in this dish; add them during the last 5 minutes of cooking.

Capers and saffron are another excellent flavoring for tripe. Dissolve a generous pinch of ground saffron in a few tablespoons of warm water and add this, along with a handful of rinsed capers, to the casserole about 15 minutes before it has finished cooking. Omit the rosemary.

Lard is a traditional Provençal cooking medium for tripe. If you like, replace the prosciutto fat with a tablespoon of lard.

Instead of topping the dish with grated cheese, sprinkle on gremolata, a mix of finely chopped lemon zest, garlic, and parsley—the traditional garnish for ossobuco.

Using leftover meat gravy to flavor pasta sauces

Gravy and pan juices from roasts will last several days in the refrigerator, or they can be frozen. Use them the next day to flavor a dish of penne with sautéed mushrooms, in place of wine or canned broth. If a ragù calls for chicken broth, add the broth but enrich it with a few tablespoons of leftover juice from a veal roast of the night before. I like to add meat juices to hearty vegetable sauces. Pasta sauces containing cabbage, eggplant, cooked greens, tomatoes, or bell peppers often are helped considerably by a splash of meat sauce. Lamb gravy might overpower a zucchini sauce but could be just the thing to enrich a roasted red pepper sauce. Veal juices can add depth to a simmered tomato sauce. This is true improvisational cooking, making the best you can with what you have.

Baked Tagliatelle with Veal Juices and Parmigiano-Reggiano

It's always a good idea to save the braising liquid or extra sauce from a stew or roast to use in a pasta dish. Add a handful of grated cheese for body, and you'll have the sauce for a very flavorful, elegant baked pasta.

Here I braise a whole veal shank in wine, herbs, and mushrooms. The shank is the same cut of meat used for ossobuco. I've decided to cook the shank whole (ossobuco is traditionally cut into thick pieces). The cut, when very slowly braised, gives off a rich, flavorful sauce with lots of body. Thinly slice the meat for a light second course. Use any leftover meat to fill ravioli.

[Makes 4 main-course or 6 first-course servings]

½ cup dried porcini mushrooms

Flour for dredging the veal

1 whole veal shank (about 3 pounds)

Salt

Freshly ground black pepper

Olive oil

Unsalted butter

1 large onion, cut in small dice

2 small carrots, cut in small dice

A few tender inner celery stalks, cut in small dice, plus leaves, chopped

3 long strips of lemon peel, with as little white pith as possible

1 or 2 bay leaves

A few thyme or savory sprigs

A rosemary sprig

A large wineglass of fruity white wine (a Chardonnay is good here)

3 ripe tomatoes (1 to 1½ pounds), peeled, seeded, and chopped

About 2 cups homemade Light Veal Broth (page 376) or Mixed-Meat Broth (page 375)

1 pound Plain Egg Pasta (page 364), cut for tagliatelle

About 1 cup freshly grated Parmigiano-Reggiano cheese

- Preheat the oven to 350°F.
- Soak the mushrooms in water to cover for about 15 minutes or until soft. Lift the mushrooms from the soaking liquid and chop them. Strain the liquid and set aside.
- Flour the veal shank and season it with salt and pepper. In a large flameproof casserole fitted with a lid, heat a tablespoon or so each of oil and butter over medium-high heat. Add the veal shank and brown it well on all sides, about 8 minutes. Turn the heat down to medium and add the onion, carrots, celery, celery leaves, lemon peel, and herbs and sauté

until the vegetables are soft and lightly browned, about 5 minutes. Add the wine and let it boil and cook down by about half. Add the tomatoes, mushrooms, mushroom soaking liquid, and enough broth to cover the meat by three-quarters. Season with salt and pepper. Bring to a boil.

- Cover the casserole, place in the oven, and cook until the meat is very tender, about 2½ hours. Turn the shank several times during cooking. If you notice that the liquid has cooked down too much at any time, add a little more broth.
- Remove the veal shank and set it aside. Skim the sauce of excess fat if necessary. The sauce should be fairly liquid but have enough body to lightly coat the pasta. If you feel it is too liquid, boil it over high heat for a few minutes to thicken it. Check the seasoning. The sauce should have a rich flavor and deep color from the combination of meat juices and dried mushrooms.
- Turn the oven up to 450°F.
- Cook the tagliatelle, leaving it a bit firmer than usual. Drain it well and place in a baking dish about 12 inches wide (wider is better than deeper; you want more surface space so a crisp crust can develop). Ladle enough hot braising sauce over the pasta to coat it well, making sure to pull out any herb stems or bay leaves. Stick a chopstick into the cut end of the shank bone and wiggle it around to loosen all the marrow. Add this to the sauce (the marrow will add another layer of flavor and richness to the sauce). Add a handful of grated Parmigiano and toss. Sprinkle a thin layer of cheese on top and bake, uncovered, until the top is lightly browned and the dish is bubbling hot, about 15 minutes.
- Slice the meat thin and serve it with the remaining sauce as a second course (or reheated for another meal) with a vegetable (artichoke hearts or asparagus would be wonderful) and a salad.

Ideas

Any cut of veal that is good for roasting can be the base for this sauce; try top round or a boned shoulder. Just remember that you'll want to have enough liquid left after cooking to coat a pound of pasta, plus extra to serve with the meat, so check the casserole and add more broth if the juices seem to be getting low.

You don't have to bake this dish. Any pasta tossed with rich veal juices is wonderful.

In Trieste, braised veal shank is usually cooked in a sauce subtly flavored with anchovies. Substitute about 4 anchovy fillets for the dried porcini mushrooms. Add a handful of chopped fresh parsley while tossing the pasta. Omit the cheese and serve unbaked.

Lamb shank can be substituted for veal and cooked in the same manner. If using lamb, omit the mushrooms and include instead a few finely sliced garlic cloves (added after you cook the onion and carrot) and a bit more rosemary.

Proportions for Meatball Recipes

A recipe can give exact proportions of cheese, olive oil, and bread crumbs to add to a meatball recipe, but so much depends on the moistness of the meat, the size of the eggs, and the choice of any other moist ingredients, such as wine, milk, or broth, that you really need to think more about texture than about exact measurements. I usually combine all the ingredients in a large bowl except for the cheese and bread crumbs (most meatball recipes call for both). I mix everything together gently and see how loose the mixture is. I add small amounts of grated cheese and bread crumbs until the mixture holds together when I grab a handful but is still noticeably moist. Then I season it with salt and pepper. To keep meatballs light and tender, mix the meat as little as possible, just until the ingredients are well distributed.

I usually test one meatball for seasoning and texture by sautéing it in a small pan in a tablespoon of hot olive oil. Brown it quickly on all sides. Make sure it holds together. If it doesn't, add more bread crumbs or another egg to the rest of the mixture. Taste the cooked meatball and adjust the seasoning in the mixture, adding more cheese, mint, or salt and pepper if needed.

Here are some other good things to include in meatball recipes:

MEATS

Ground beef
Ground lamb
Ground turkey
A mix of ground meats, such as half veal and half turkey
Sweet or hot Italian pork sausage (use about one-fourth sausage meat
*   with ground beef, veal, or turkey for added richness and flavor)*
Chopped prosciutto (add 2 or 3 chopped slices per pound of ground meat)
Sautéed chopped pancetta (1 or 2 thin slices, chopped and sautéed until crisp)
Finely chopped mortadella or dry salami (a few slices)

AROMATIC VEGETABLES

Roasted garlic purée from 1 or 2 bulbs
Roasted red or yellow bell pepper, finely chopped
Very finely minced red onion, scallion, or shallot (2 or 3 tablespoons for
*   a pound of meat)*
Finely chopped sautéed wild mushrooms
Dried porcini mushrooms, soaked, drained, and finely chopped (about 1/4 cup
*   for a pound of meat). Strain the soaking liquid and add a*
*   few tablespoons to the meat mixture.*
Blanched spinach, well drained and finely chopped (about 1/2 cup for a pound of meat)

LIQUIDS

A splash of red or white wine
A splash of dry Marsala, vermouth, or sherry
A splash of milk
A drizzle of olive oil

SEASONINGS

A pinch of ground cinnamon, nutmeg, or mace
A ground clove or two
A pinch of cayenne pepper
Fresh herbs (tarragon for veal meatballs; rosemary or thyme for lamb;
        a few fresh, chopped sage leaves for turkey or chicken meatballs)
Green or black olives, pitted and finely chopped
Anchovies (1 or 2 fillets, well chopped, will subtly flavor a pound of ground meat)
Pine nuts, toasted and chopped
Ground pistachios (unsalted and skinned)
Currants or raisins (soaked in water or wine until plump, then drained
        and chopped—save the wine and add it to the meatball mixture)

CHEESE AND BINDERS

Grated provolone cheese
Grated dry aged goat cheese
Grated ricotta salata
Fresh ricotta, well drained (about ¼ cup can be added to pound of
        chopped meat to lighten the texture)
Stale Italian bread, soaked in milk and squeezed dry

Veal and Eggplant Meatballs with Cavatelli in a Tomato, Caper, and Cream Sauce

Two Meatball Recipes

Italians do serve pasta with meatballs, but usually the meatballs go on the side or become a second course, and the pasta is dressed with the meat-flavored braising sauce. I like pasta and meatballs served together in one dish, as long as the meatballs are very tiny. In Campania and Puglia one of the most popular dishes is tiny meatballs baked with pasta. It has a very enticing, old-fashioned taste—as long as it's not baked to death.

The pureed eggplant in this recipe makes these meatballs very light. I've included fresh mint and caciocavallo cheese—two Sicilian touches with assertive flavors.

[Makes 4 main-course or 6 first-course servings]

2 thin slices pancetta, cut in small dice

Olive oil

1 medium eggplant, peeled and
    cut in small cubes
    (about 1 cup or a little more)

2 garlic cloves, finely minced

Salt

Freshly ground black pepper

1 pound lean ground veal

1 large egg

A generous handful of fresh mint leaves
    (about ¼ cup), well chopped

About 1 cup untoasted bread crumbs
    (see page 340)

A large handful of freshly grated
    caciocavallo cheese, plus more for
    the table

1 pound cavatelli

For the sauce:

Unsalted butter

1 medium sweet onion, such as Vidalia
    or Walla Walla, finely chopped

3 or 4 garlic cloves, minced

5 or 6 ripe tomatoes (about 3 pounds),
    peeled, seeded, and chopped

Salt

Freshly ground black pepper

A large handful of capers

A splash of sherry vinegar

½ cup heavy cream

A pinch of cayenne pepper

A few mint sprigs, leaves lightly
    chopped

- In a large skillet, sauté the pancetta in a tablespoon of olive oil over medium-heat until crisp. Add the eggplant and sauté until soft and lightly browned. If the eggplant starts to brown too quickly before it is cooked through, cover the pan, lower the heat slightly, and let it steam until tender. In the last minutes of cooking, add the garlic. Season with salt and pepper. Puree in a food processor.
- Place the eggplant purée in a large mixing bowl. Add the ground veal, egg, and mint. Mix lightly. Add about ½ cup of the bread crumbs and about ¼ cup of the grated cacio-cavallo. Mix again lightly. Add more bread crumbs and cheese if needed to ensure the meatballs hold together (grab a ball of meat and squeeze it in your palm to test). Season generously with salt and black pepper.
- Form the meatballs into approximately ½-inch balls.
- In a large skillet, heat about ¼ inch olive oil and let it get hot before adding the meatballs, otherwise they might stick to the pan. Working in batches, brown the meatballs well on all sides over medium-high heat, turning them with kitchen tongs so you don't pierce them and allow the juices to run out. When the meatballs are browned, place them on paper towels to drain off the excess oil.
- Begin cooking the cavatelli.
- To make the sauce, choose another large skillet big enough to hold all the meatballs. Melt about 2 tablespoons of butter over medium heat. Add the onion and cook until soft and fragrant, about 4 minutes. Add the garlic and sauté a minute. Turn the heat up a bit and add the tomatoes, season with salt and pepper, and cook over lively heat for about 5 minutes, just until they start to soften and give off juice. You want the tomatoes to remain bright red and not break down completely. Add the capers and sherry vinegar and cook a minute longer. Add the cream and cayenne and stir to blend. Taste for seasonings.
- When the cavatelli are al dente, drain them and transfer to a warmed large serving bowl. Toss with a tablespoon or two of fresh butter and the extra chopped mint leaves.
- Add the meatballs to the sauce and warm through about a minute. They should be cooked through but still moist and tender. Add the meatballs with sauce to the pasta and toss. Serve with a bowl of grated caciocavallo.

Baked Cavatappi with Chicken-Arugula Meatballs

Chicken and arugula, a popular Italian combination, is not usually used for meatballs. But when it is, the meatballs come out light and tasty and cook quickly. In southern Italy, when meatballs are baked with pasta, they are always made very small—about ½ inch across—so the dish will be delicate. When you bite into one, it comes as a pleasant little surprise, not a big lump of meat.

[Makes 4 main-course or 6 first-course servings]

Olive oil

3 thin slices pancetta, well chopped

2 garlic cloves, minced

1 large bunch of arugula, stemmed, dried, and finely chopped (by hand or pulsed briefly in a food processor)

1 pound ground chicken (a mix of white and some dark meat is preferable to keep the meatballs moist)

1 large egg

1 large handful of capers, rinsed and chopped

About ½ cup untoasted bread crumbs (see page 340)

A handful of freshly grated Pecorino Toscano cheese for the meatballs, plus another large handful for the baking dish

A pinch of ground nutmeg

A few thyme or savory sprigs, leaves chopped

Zest of 1 lemon

Salt

Freshly ground black pepper

1 pound cavatappi

1 recipe Simmered Tomato Sauce (page 28)

- Preheat the oven to 425°F.
- In a large skillet, heat 2 tablespoons olive oil over medium heat. Add the pancetta and sauté until crisp. Add the garlic and sauté a minute, just until it gives off aroma. Add the arugula and cook until wilted, about half a minute.
- In a large mixing bowl, lightly mix the ground chicken, egg, and chopped capers. Add the arugula mixture, the bread crumbs, and a handful of grated Pecorino (use a little less cheese than bread crumbs). Add the nutmeg, thyme or savory, and lemon zest and season with salt and pepper. Mix gently (I always use my hands for this). Check the texture. The mixture should be dry enough to hold together in a ball when you grab it, but have a moist, glossy look to it. Roll into approximately ½-inch balls.

- Test one meatball for flavor and to make sure it holds together when cooked (see page 300).
- In a large skillet, heat about ¼ inch olive oil over medium heat. When hot, start browning the meatballs in batches to avoid crowding. Turn the meatballs gently with kitchen tongs so you don't pierce them and allow juices to flow out. As they brown, place them on paper towels to absorb the excess oil.
- Cook the cavatappi until al dente, drain well, and place in a large baking dish. Add the meatballs, the tomato sauce, and a handful of grated Pecorino. Toss to mix all the ingredients. Top with a sprinkle of the grated Pecorino and bake, uncovered, until bubbling and lightly browned, about 20 minutes.

Ragùs

Ragùs, the long-simmered meat sauces made exclusively to be served with pasta, are one of the glories of Italian cooking, north and south. For me, cooking these sauces, seeing and smelling them take shape during their lazy, gentle simmering, is a great pleasure and always a proud accomplishment.

When you cook a ragù, you always reach a moment when the meat comes together with the liquid you're cooking it in. The broth thickens and suspends the meat, almost like an emulsion. The ingredients bond to form a perfect consistency and mingling of flavors. You can see it when it happens, and you know your sauce is ready. That is why I cook ragù sauces on top of the stove—so I can watch the pot, watch the simmering process. You can finish cooking the sauce in an oven (which will cook a stew or ragù at a desirable even simmer), but you won't be able to watch your efforts come together the same way.

Northern Italian meat sauces, such as the classic Bolognese-style sauces using several meats, which are slowly simmered until silken and rich, are well loved, and recipes for them appear in many cookbooks. The recipes that follow are contemporary and, in some but not all cases, lighter. They reflect my love of southern Italian cooking and contain elements such as fennel, squash, red peppers, eggplant, pine nuts, raisins, and Marsala wine—ingredients not often found in a true Bolognese ragù. The cooking techniques are inspired by both southern and northern Italian methods, but the recipes reflect my own ideas about what I find tastes good.

All ragùs start with the browning of meat and aromatic vegetables such as onions, celery, and carrots—a soffritto. Prosciutto, pancetta, or a little smoked bacon is often added. This initial browning is what gives depth and sweetness to the finished sauce. Then liquids such as wine are added and reduced. The wine boils down and mingles with the browned meat and juices from the aromatic vegetables to form a rich base. Broth is added, and the ragù simmers—reducing further, concentrating flavors, and breaking down the meat's fibers to make it tender. In classic southern- and northern-style ragùs, broth is added several times in small amounts and allowed to reduce, in a way similar to adding liquid to a risotto. This provides depth of flavor. Milk is sometimes added to make the sauce smoother. And you can swirl in a pat of butter at the end for mellow sweetness.

Pork, beef, veal, lamb, chicken, venison, oxtail, or poultry giblets, alone or in combination, all produce ragùs of different character. Ideally, you use the same inexpensive cuts of meat you would choose for stews. Northern-style ragùs usually start with boneless chunks or sometimes ground meat. Southerners make this kind of sauce too, but the classic Neapolitan ragù, the Sunday supper sauce, is simmered with large bone-in cuts to be taken off the bone later and added to the sauce or served whole as a second course. You'll find ideas for both types here.

Because some of these sauces were inspired by southern Italian cooking, I've included many Mediterranean vegetables. When you choose vegetables to add to a ragù, bear in mind the meat you are using. If it is lamb, select a vegetable you like to eat with lamb—peas, for instance, or artichokes. If you want the vegetable to stand out as a separate taste, add it toward the end of cooking so it doesn't get a chance to soften too much. But if you want, say, the artichoke to break down into almost a purée, imparting body and subtle flavor to the sauce, add it toward the beginning of cooking. Fresh herbs or spices, depending on when you add them, will produce different end results. Vegetables and fresh herbs, aside from those in the soffritto mix, are not generally a part of northern Italian meat sauces.

Long-simmered meat sauces that fill the house with rich fragrance for hours are home cooking at its best. And home cooking cries out for improvisation. So absolutely do improvise with my recipes, taking aspects of one and including it in another and making substitutions for meat, vegetables, or flavorings according to availability and personal preference.

Flavoring Ragùs and Other Long-Simmered Meat Sauces

Salt pork, fatback, pancetta, bacon, prosciutto fat, anchovies: any one of these can be included in the soffritto of just about any long-simmered meat sauce. Keep in mind that each will impart its own character to the final taste.

Anchovies added at the beginning of cooking give meat ragùs depth and no recognizable fishiness. They're especially good with lamb and veal. Added at the end, perhaps with a shot of good vinegar, they can energize a mellow sauce.

Pancetta gives a subtle, sophisticated flavor. It should always be added at the beginning of cooking and allowed to slowly sauté so that the fat has a chance to cook out and flavor the sauce. American bacon, which comes from the same cut of meat as pancetta, has a pronounced smoky flavor that can add robustness to pork or beef sauces. If you want to minimize its smoky effect, blanch it first in boiling water for a few moments.

If a recipe calls for prosciutto, you can heighten that taste by trimming the fat from the prosciutto and using it to sauté the soffritto called for in the recipe. Add the lean meat of the prosciutto at the end of cooking so its delicate flavor and texture are not lost. You can sometimes buy fatty prosciutto ends inexpensively from Italian butchers. Store them in the refrigerator and cut off small chunks to sauté along with your soffritto or to let simmer in a broth.

Salted fatback and lean salt pork are, to my taste, very salty. They must be blanched for several minutes in boiling water before you sauté them. Fresh fatback is a good alternative.

Ziti with Lamb, Tarragon, and Anchovies
Two Lamb Ragùs with Different Seasonings

This is essentially a Roman lamb stew, which usually contains anchovies and a good amount of vinegar. I've gone light on the vinegar and added tarragon, which goes well with lamb. The anchovies add a kick that is not fishy.

[Makes 4 main-course or 6 first-course servings]

Olive oil

1½ pounds lamb shoulder, cut in ½-inch cubes (cut the meat a little smaller than you would normally for a stew to allow it to break up during cooking and thicken the sauce)

Salt

Freshly ground black pepper

1 large onion, cut in small dice

3 inner celery stalks, cut in small dice, plus leaves, chopped

3 or 4 garlic cloves, finely minced

A large wineglass of dry white wine (Frascati is a good choice)

1 cup homemade Mixed-Meat Broth (page 375) or Chicken Broth (page 374)

2 bay leaves

4 or 5 anchovy fillets, chopped

A generous splash of champagne vinegar

A handful of flat-leaf parsley leaves, chopped

A handful of tarragon sprigs, leaves chopped, plus a few whole sprigs for garnish

1 pound ziti

- In a large flameproof casserole fitted with a lid, heat about 2 tablespoons olive oil over medium heat. Season the lamb with salt and pepper and brown it on all sides. If the pan seems crowded, brown the lamb in batches. Remove the meat from the pan and set aside. Turn the heat down a bit, add the onion, celery, and celery leaves, and sauté until soft, adding an extra tablespoon of olive oil if the pan is too dry. Add the garlic and cook a minute, just until it gives off fragrance. Return the meat to the casserole, along with any juices it has released. Add the wine and let it boil a few minutes to cook off the alcohol. Add the broth and bay leaves and bring to a boil. Turn the heat to low, cover the pan, and let simmer until the meat is very tender, about 1½ hours or a little longer. At this point the meat will have started to break down a bit to thicken the sauce (test a piece; it should be very soft and very tender to the bite). Skim the sauce of excess fat if necessary.

- When the meat is very tender and the sauce thick, add the anchovies, vinegar, parsley, and tarragon. Let simmer, uncovered, a few minutes to blend the flavors. Add black pepper and, if needed, salt.
- Cook the ziti until al dente, drain well, and transfer to a large serving bowl. Pour on the lamb ragù. Garnish with whole tarragon sprigs.

Ideas

By substituting red wine and rosemary for the white wine and tarragon, you will produce a richer, deeply flavored ragù with a dark, burnished color. Omit the anchovies and add instead 2 or 3 strips of orange peel to the sauce when you add the broth.

Sauté about a half dozen sliced artichoke hearts in a little olive oil and then let them simmer in the ragù until tender during the last 15 minutes of cooking.

Lamb and fennel pair well; sauté a chopped fennel bulb along with the onion in your soffritto, and add a small handful of ground fennel seed to the sauce in place of the anchovy. A mixture of rosemary, fennel, and lemon peel make another good seasoning for this ragù.

When in season, spring peas added in the last 5 minutes of cooking make a delicious addition.

Lamb with mint is a Roman classic; mint can replace the tarragon in this recipe, but since Roman mint is a wild, mellow variety, I would make an herb mix of half mint leaves and half parsley leaves (American mint can be very strong).

Malloreddus with Lamb, Pork, and Roasted Red Peppers

I've chosen to season this pasta sauce after the fashion of Greek pastitsio, with a bit of cinnamon and marjoram (though the Greeks might choose oregano). Roasted red peppers long-simmered in the sauce almost disappear, leaving only their sweet essence.

Malloreddus is a Sardinian pasta made fresh without eggs. Dried versions are available in this country; if you can't find it, cavatelli or penne will do. In Sardinia it is often served with a sausage sauce. Also try it with any of the sausage recipes in this book.

[Makes 4 main-course or 6 first-course servings]

2 or 3 slices pancetta, chopped

1 large onion, cut in small dice

2 celery stalks, cut in small dice,
    plus a handful of celery leaves
    if you have them

Olive oil

1 cinnamon stick

2 or 3 garlic cloves, smashed with
    the side of a knife

2 bay leaves

1 pound ground lamb

1 merguez sausage, casing removed

1 sweet Italian pork sausage, casing
    removed

Salt

Freshly ground black pepper

A large wineglass of dry red wine
    (a Merlot is a good choice)

1 cup homemade Mixed-Meat Broth
    (page 375) or Chicken Broth (page
    374) (meat broth works best here, but
    if you don't have it, chicken is fine)

One 35-ounce can Italian plum toma-
    toes, chopped, drained of about
    half their juice

2 red bell peppers, roasted over a flame
    until charred, peeled, seeded, and
    cut in small dice

A few large marjoram sprigs, leaves
    chopped

1 pound malloreddus

Freshly grated caciocavallo cheese

• In a large flameproof casserole fitted with a lid, sauté the pancetta over medium heat until it is just starting to get crisp. Add the onion and celery and, if necessary, a little olive oil to sauté the vegetables. Sauté until soft and fragrant. Add the cinnamon stick, garlic, and bay leaves and sauté a minute to release their aromas. Add all the meat, seasoning it with salt and pepper and breaking it up with the back of your spoon. The meat will turn gray at first and release lots of liquid. Turn the heat up a bit and let these juices evaporate. Then the meat will start to brown. Add the wine and let it boil until it is almost completely evaporated. Add the broth and cook at a lively simmer, uncovered, until it is reduced by about half. Add the tomatoes, partially cover the pan, and let the sauce simmer over low heat until it is thick and the meat is tender, about 11/2 to 2 hours. In the last hour of cooking, add the chopped peppers and about half of the marjoram. When the sauce has finished cooking, skim off any excess fat on the surface. Remove the cinnamon stick and bay leaves if you prefer (I usually leave them in because I like the rustic touch it gives to the finished dish).

- Taste for seasoning. Add the remaining marjoram.
- Cook the malloreddus until al dente, drain, and transfer to a large serving bowl. Pour the sauce on top. Serve with plenty of the grated cheese.

Ideas

Eggplant with lamb is an exquisite flavor combination used in much of Mediterranean cooking, especially in Greece, Sardinia, southern Italy, and Provence. Sauté about 1 cup cubed eggplant in olive oil until partly cooked and add it to the stew in the last half hour of cooking instead of, or in addition to, the red peppers.

You can add cook chickpeas to this ragù, with or without the red peppers.

Add a handful of toasted pistachios at the end of cooking.

I also like this ragù with a wide fresh egg pasta such as pappardelle.

Baked Anellini with Beef, Currants, and Pine Nuts

A Beef Ragù with Sicilian Flavors

The combination of currants and pine nuts is one I always return to. It lends a sweet and exotic touch to many dishes, and I especially love it with meat. This is my version of a classic Sicilian-style meat sauce, which would more likely be made with pork or lamb. This updated, lighter version is made with ground sirloin but given a sweet touch with sweet wine, currants, and spices. Anellini is a Sicilian dried pasta cut into small, thin rings. If you can't find it, tubetti or ditali will do fine.

[Makes 4 main-course or 6 first-course servings]

Olive oil

A small chunk of soppressata (about ¼ pound), skinned and cut in small cubes

1 large onion, finely diced

2 tender inner celery stalks, finely diced

2 small carrots, finely diced

About ½ cinnamon stick

A generous grating of nutmeg

1 bay leaf

1½ pounds ground sirloin

Salt

Freshly ground black pepper

A small wineglass of semisweet white wine (a not-too-sweet Riesling works well here)

1 cup homemade Mixed-Meat Broth (page 375) or Chicken Broth (page 374)

A small wineglass of whole milk

One 15-ounce can Italian plum tomatoes, drained and chopped

A generous handful of currants

A generous handful of pine nuts, toasted

1 pound anellini

About ½ cup bread crumbs, toasted (see page 340)

About ½ cup freshly grated caciocavallo cheese

- In a large flameproof casserole fitted with a lid, heat 2 tablespoons olive oil over high heat. Add the soppressata and cook until it is just starting to brown. Turn the heat to medium and add the onion, celery, carrots, cinnamon stick, nutmeg, and bay leaf. Sauté until the vegetables are soft and fragrant, about 5 minutes. Add the ground beef, season with salt and pepper, and sauté until lightly browned. It will give off some juice at first. Let this evaporate and then let the meat brown lightly. Add the wine and let it boil away. Add the broth and let it reduce by about half. Add the milk and simmer, uncovered, for about 15 minutes. Then add the tomatoes, cover the pan, and simmer until the ragù is thick and tender, about 1½ hours. About 15 minutes before the ragù is done, add the currants and pine nuts. Skim off excess fat if necessary. Check the seasoning.

- Preheat the oven to 425°F.
- Cook the anellini until al dente, drain well, and mix into the ragù.
- Choose a large but relatively shallow round or oval baking dish (about 10 inches round and 4 inches deep). Brush the dish lightly with olive oil.
- In a small bowl, mix together the toasted bread crumbs and the caciocavallo and season it with a little black pepper. Scatter about half of this into the baking dish and press it against the sides as best you can. Add the sauced anellini. Top with the rest of the cheese and bread crumb mixture. Bake, uncovered, until it is hot and bubbling and the top is lightly browned, about 20 minutes.

Ideas

Any thick ragù sauce makes a good base for a baked pasta.

How Much Sauce Should I Use?

*E*specially with meat sauces, Americans tend to oversauce their pasta. If you find a lot of sauce left in the bowl after all the pasta is eaten, you probably used too much sauce. It should mix with the pasta and become one dish. Many pasta sauces, such as *aglio e olio* (garlic and oil), are tossed in the sauté pan with the pasta, coating it so completely you can't tell the sauce from the starch. In Italy this is called a *condimento:* The sauce is a condiment for the pasta. Even with thick meat sauces, the philosophy should hold. Toss the pasta very well and notice how the sauce blends and clings to the pasta, forming a union.

Fazzoletti with Pork Sausage and Prune Ragù

Pork Makes a Rich Ragù

I've always been fascinated by recipes for meat and fruit combinations, especially those in which the fruit is long-cooked and almost dissolved, suffusing the dish with a sweetness that is often hard to identify. You find this in many Moroccan dishes and in Arab-influenced Sicilian ones.

Fazzoletti, thin squares of fresh egg pasta, go very well with this elegant yet robust sauce. If you don't want to make your own pasta, substitute store-bought fresh pappardelle, which will provide a similar texture and surface area to show off this sauce.

[Makes 4 main-course or 6 first-course servings]

1 slice bacon, thinly sliced and cut in small dice

1 pound ground pork

2 sweet Italian pork sausages (about ½ pound), casings removed

Salt

Freshly ground black pepper

1 large onion, cut in small dice

2 medium carrots, cut in small dice

2 or 3 garlic cloves, minced

1 small fresh red chile, finely minced with some seeds

About half a bottle dry red wine (a Spanish rioja is wonderful here, but any assertive dry red wine can be used)

About 6 prunes, pitted and finely chopped

A large rosemary sprig, leaves chopped

1 cup homemade Mixed-Meat Broth (page 375)

2 medium round tomatoes (about 1 pound), peeled, seeded, and chopped

About 2 tablespoons unsalted butter

A handful of flat-leaf parsley leaves, lightly chopped

1 recipe Three-Egg Pasta (page 365), cut for fazzoletti

Freshly grated Parmigiano-Reggiano cheese

- In a large flameproof casserole fitted with a lid, brown the bacon pieces over medium-high heat. Then add all the meat, breaking the sausage up into little pieces with your spoon, and brown well. Season with salt and pepper. Turn the heat down a bit and add the onion and carrots and sauté along with the meat until soft, fragrant, and lightly browned. Add the garlic and chile and sauté a minute to release their aroma. When the meat and vegetables are brown and the liquids from the meat have cooked away, add the wine, prunes, and rosemary and simmer over lively heat until the wine is reduced. You should have about ½ inch of liquid left in the pan. Add the broth and tomatoes and bring to a boil. Lower the heat, cover the pan, and simmer until the meat is very tender and the sauce is thick, at least 1½ hours. Skim the surface of excess fat if necessary. Taste to adjust the seasoning. Add the butter and parsley and stir to blend.

- Cook the fazzoletti until tender and lift them from the water with a larger strainer. Drain well and place 3 or 4 on each plate, dropping them casually and letting them fall into natural folds. Top with a generous ladle of ragù and a sprinkling of Parmigiano-Reggiano.

Ideas

Dried fruit adds interesting taste and texture to sauces but should be added in conservative amounts for just a hint of sweetness. Raisins and currants stay whole when cooked and are often added to meat (and fish) sauces in central and southern Italy. I like prunes because they are not overly sweet and they dissolve into the sauce to contribute body and flavor. Dates, though very sweet, will disintegrate very quickly when heated, leaving a sweet essence in your sauce; include only one or two in a meat sauce. See also Simmered Tomato-Fig Sauce on page 30.

Baked Veal Ragù with Saffron and Artichokes

Veal and saffron make for an elegant, understated taste combination.

[Makes 4 main-course or 6 first-course servings]

A small chunk of fatty prosciutto end,
    cut in small pieces

4 medium shallots, finely sliced

2 or 3 celery stalks, finely diced

Olive oil

1 to 1½ pounds boneless veal shoulder,
    cut in ½-inch cubes

Salt

Freshly ground black pepper

A splash of cognac

About 2 cups homemade Light Veal
    Broth (page 376) or Chicken Broth
    (page 374)

A dozen baby artichokes, trimmed and
    cut in quarters (if you do this ahead,
    place them in a bowl of water acidu-
    lated with a cut lemon)

Zest of 1 lemon

About ¼ cup crème fraîche

A small palmful of saffron threads,
    ground to a powder (see page 352)
    and dissolved in a few tablespoons
    warm water

A squeeze of lemon juice

A few thyme sprigs, leaves chopped

1 pound dried garganelli

About 1 cup freshly grated Pecorino
    Toscano cheese

- In a large flameproof casserole fitted with a lid, cook the prosciutto end over medium heat until it renders its fat. Add the shallots and celery and, if necessary, a little olive oil to sauté the vegetables. When the vegetables are soft, add the veal. Season with salt and pepper and sauté. It will at first give off a fair amount of liquid, but continue cooking until the liquid has evaporated and the meat browns, about 20 minutes. Add the cognac and let it bubble and cook out a few minutes. Add enough broth to just cover the meat. Bring to a boil. Turn the heat to low, cover the pan, and let the ragù simmer until the meat is very tender and soft, 1½ to 2 hours. Skim off excess fat if necessary.

- Preheat the oven to 425°F.

- Meanwhile, in a small sauté pan, heat a few tablespoons olive oil over medium heat. Add the artichokes, season with salt and pepper, and sauté until just starting to become tender, about 5 minutes. Add the lemon zest. When the sauce has finished cooking, add the artichokes to the casserole. Add the crème fraîche, saffron water, lemon juice, and thyme and simmer, uncovered, for 3 or 4 minutes, just to blend the flavors and to finish cooking the artichokes. Notice how the addition of saffron perfumes the sauce, almost completely changing its aroma. Check the seasoning.
- Cook the garganelli until al dente (a bit firmer than usual) and drain well. Add the pasta to the veal sauce, along with a generous handful of grated Pecorino, and toss.
- Oil a large (about 2-quart) baking dish. Pour in the pasta and top with a sprinkling of Pecorino. Bake, uncovered, until brown and bubbling, about 20 minutes.

Ideas

There are essentially two types of traditional flavorings for veal stew. There is the white stew (called a blanquette in France), which can include white wine, cream, an egg yolk thickener, and sometimes mushrooms. The above recipe is a version of this type of stew. And then there are the red wine and tomato versions that are more highly seasoned with heavier herbs, garlic, and sometimes salt pork. Both can be either served over pasta or tossed with pasta for a hearty cold-weather meal.

Rigatoni with Oxtail and Chianti Ragù

Ragù Made with Oxtail

Stewed oxtail with pasta is a specialty served in the old Testaccio neighborhood of Rome. The gelatinous meat makes a thick, deeply flavored ragù you can season in many ways. Here I've chosen a strong red wine, a touch of ground cloves, and a little orange zest.

[Makes 4 main-course or 6 first-course servings]

Salt	A few savory sprigs, leaves chopped
Freshly ground black pepper	Zest of 1 orange
About 3 pounds oxtails	3 whole cloves, ground
Olive oil	About ¾ bottle of Chianti or other
3 thin slices pancetta, chopped	dry red wine
2 carrots, cut in small dice	One 35-ounce can Italian plum
1 large onion, chopped	tomatoes, drained and chopped
3 or 4 garlic cloves, minced	1 pound rigatoni
2 bay leaves	Freshly grated Pecorino Romano cheese

- In a large flameproof casserole fitted with a lid, salt and pepper the oxtails and brown them in olive oil over medium heat. Do this in batches if the pan seems crowded. Take out the oxtails, drain off the excess fat from the casserole if necessary, and add the pancetta. Sauté until the pancetta is crisp. Add the carrots and onion and sauté until the soffritto is soft and lightly browned. Add the garlic, bay leaves, savory, orange zest, and ground cloves and sauté a minute, just to release the flavors. Return the oxtails to the pot. Add the wine and let it reduce by almost half. Add the tomatoes and bring to a boil. Turn the heat to low, cover, and simmer until the meat is very tender. This can take about 3 hours. If you like, you can finish the cooking in a 325°F. oven.
- Let the casserole cool a bit. Skim off fat from the surface. Pull the oxtail pieces from the sauce and, when cool enough to handle, remove the meat (see Note, page 319). Skim the sauce again (oxtails give off a good amount of fat). Return the meat to the sauce. Taste for seasoning.
- Cook the rigatoni until al dente, drain well, and place in a large serving bowl. Pour on the oxtail sauce and toss. Pass a bowl of the cheese at the table.

Note on removing the meat from cooked oxtails: There is a lot of meat on these bones, but it's hard to get to with a knife. The best way is to go in there with your fingers. The meat is tucked away in the bone grooves, so just feel around for it and pull it out (if the oxtails are properly cooked, the meat will be very tender and will pull away from the bone easily).

Ideas

I like this pasta topped with fried capers (see page 111).

I like to throw in a few chopped anchovies and fresh marjoram in the last few minutes of cooking.

For an oxtail and mushroom ragù, add a handful of dried porcini mushrooms and their strained soaking liquid when you add the broth and the wine.

If you can't bear the thought of cooking oxtails, substitute about 2 pounds boneless beef chuck, cut into bite-size pieces. Cook them for about an hour and a half and you'll have a dark, rich sauce for tagliatelle.

Pasta with Meat Fillings

The urge to overload a meat lasagne can be strong. Resist it. Not every lasagne has to contain béchamel, ricotta, or mozzarella, let alone all three.

On the other hand, the end result should offer a hint of luxury. Try for rich but not complicated. Choose one or two elements. For example, any good ragù or stewed meat sauce is a perfect starting point for lasagne; just remember to take out the bones. You can then, if you like, add a layer of vegetables or a layer of cheese. A béchamel sauce is fitting for some meat lasagne, mellowing out the taste and helping to hold everything together, but a thin layer of fontina, or cream with a little Grana melted into it, can do the job just as well. It doesn't have to be all solid and dense. A good lasagne can have a little wobble and not be anchored to the pan by cheesy glue. I've tasted lasagne in Italy that was nothing more than sheets of pasta layered with rich pan juices from a roast and briefly baked to firm up the package ever so slightly.

Another thing to think about when putting together a dish from several components is seasoning. Make sure each sauce and each filling is well seasoned. It's very disappointing to work hard on a dish and have it come out flat tasting just because it lacks salt and pepper. And it's difficult to salt a lasagne after it has been assembled, for you can only salt the top layer and not get inside, where it really matters. First, remember to salt the pasta-cooking water. And season any cheese filling or cream sauce you layer in.

Lasagne with Chicken Livers, Wild Mushrooms, and Marsala

There is a famously rich lasagne called *vincigrassi* from the Marches region of Italy, which can include chicken livers, cream, Marsala wine, veal ragù, sweetbreads, and sometimes truffles and mozzarella. I've taken elements of it, specifically the Marsala and chicken livers, and created a lighter lasagne with the addition of wild mushrooms. Instead of a complex-tasting ragù, this lasagne features quickly sautéed ingredients, which account for its taste.

The Marches version traditionally includes Marsala or vin santo, a sweet wine, in the pasta dough. Marsala pasta is beautifully perfumed. I also make this lasagne with sage-flavored pasta, picking up another accent from the filling.

[Makes 4 main-course or 6 first-course servings]

Unsalted butter

Olive oil

3 thin slices pancetta, chopped

1 large onion, cut in small dice

About 1 pound wild mushrooms
(chanterelle, morel, hedgehog,
oyster, or other wild mushrooms) or
a mix of wild and cultivated mushrooms, wiped clean and cut in half if
very large

Salt

Freshly ground black pepper

3 or 4 garlic cloves, minced

A small wineglass of white wine

½ cup homemade Chicken Broth
(page 374) or low-salt canned

A handful of flat-leaf parsley leaves,
chopped

For the Parmigiano cream:

1 cup heavy cream

About ½ cup freshly grated Parmigiano-
Reggiano cheese

A pinch of salt

1 large egg

For the chicken liver layer:

About 2 tablespoons unsalted butter

1 pound chicken livers, tough
membranes removed, cut in small
pieces and well dried

Salt

Freshly ground black pepper

A small wineglass of dry Marsala

About 6 or 7 fresh sage leaves, chopped

1 recipe Three-Egg Herb Pasta flavored
with sage (page 368) or Marsala-
Flavored Pasta (page 368), cut for
lasagne

Freshly grated Parmigiano-Reggiano
cheese

- In a large skillet, heat 1 tablespoon each of butter and olive oil over medium heat. Add the pancetta and sauté until crisp. Add the onion and cook until soft, 3 to 4 minutes. Add all the mushrooms and season with salt and pepper. Let this cook over medium-high heat a few minutes. When the mushrooms just start to soften, add the garlic. Continue sautéing until all the mushrooms are tender but still firm and holding their shape. Add the wine and let it boil down to almost nothing. Add the broth and parsley and turn off the heat.
- Preheat the oven to 425°F.
- To make the Parmigiano cream, whisk the cream with Parmigiano in a small saucepan over low heat until the cheese is melted and the sauce is fairly smooth (there will probably still be a slightly grainy texture to it, but that's natural). Add the salt. Let this cool for a few minutes and then whisk in the egg.
- In another large skillet, melt the butter over high heat. Make sure you have patted the livers dry. Salt and pepper the livers and sear them quickly in the pan, browning all sides. Add the Marsala and let it boil for about a minute, just to cook off some of the alcohol. But let a bit of liquid remain. Add the sage leaves.
- Cook the lasagne sheets until just tender (do this in batches) and lift them from the water with a large strainer. Place in a colander and run under cold water. Drain and lay them out on kitchen towels or paper towels.
- Spread a thin layer of Parmigiano cream on the bottom of a 12 x 10 x 2-inch baking dish. Add a layer of pasta and a layer of mushrooms. Top with a layer of Parmigiano cream and another pasta layer. Make a layer using all the chicken livers and cover with a layer of pasta. Make a layer with the rest of the mushrooms. Make a pasta layer and top with the remaining cream. Sprinkle the top with grated Parmigiano-Reggiano.
- Cover the dish with aluminum foil and bake for about 20 minutes. Uncover the dish and bake until golden and bubbling, another 15 to 20 minutes. Let the lasagne stand for a few minutes before cutting.

Ideas

I love lasagne with layers of separate tastes. That's why I've treated the chicken-liver and mushroom mixes as different sauces. The chicken liver layer comes as a sort of surprise filling. This is a good way to envision your lasagne: Pick two ingredients that appeal to you, one vegetable and one meat. Then choose flavorings that will help bring the two together. In this case I feel the Marsala and the sage help pull together the components of this dish because both flavorings go well with my two principal ingredients.

The Marches version of this lasagne frequently contains sweetbreads as well as chicken livers. For instructions on how to prepare sweetbreads for pasta, see Tagliatelle with Sweetbreads, Green Peppercorns, and Watercress (page 278).

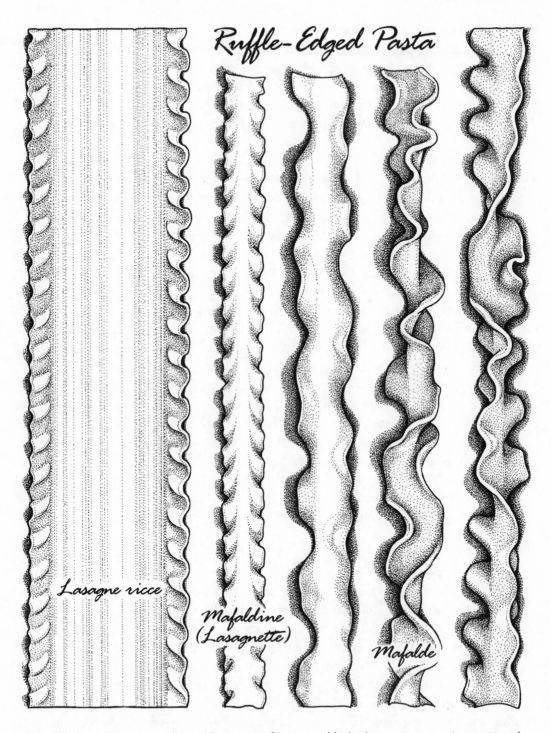

Ruffle-Edged Pasta

Lasagne ricce

Mafaldine
(Lasagnette)

Mafalde

These frilly long shapes are excellent with any type of pesto or with simple tomato sauces. Lasagnette pair well with tomato-based ragùs.

Lasagne with Tiny Chicken Meatballs, Mozzarella, and Tomato

This is an old-fashioned Neapolitan lasagne in concept, but I've lightened it by using Chicken-Arugula Meatballs and Simmered Tomato Sauce and pulled the whole thing together with a little mozzarella.

[Makes 4 main-course or 6 first-course servings]

1 recipe Three-Egg Pasta (page 365), cut for lasagne

A double recipe Simmered Tomato Sauce (page 304)

1 recipe Chicken-Arugula Meatballs (page 28)

About 1 pound fresh mozzarella cheese, thinly sliced

1 cup freshly grated caciocavallo cheese

- Preheat the oven to 425°F.
- Cook the lasagne sheets in batches until tender, lifting them from the water with a large strainer into a colander. Run under cold water and drain. Lay the sheets out on kitchen towels or paper towels.
- Ladle a thin layer of tomato sauce into the bottom of a 12 x 10 x 2-inch baking dish. Make a layer of pasta and then a layer of meatballs. Top with mozzarella and a sprinkling of caciocavallo. Repeat until you've used up all the ingredients. End with a layer of pasta topped with tomato sauce and caciocavallo.
- Cover with aluminum foil and bake 20 minutes. Uncover and bake until bubbling hot and lightly browned, another 15 to 20 minutes. Let the lasagne rest before cutting.

Ideas

This is a dish devised by pairing two recipes that already appear in this book. Here are a few other meat-lasagne recipes you can make by combining recipes in this book:

- Pork Sausage and Prune Ragù (page 314) with fontina cream (page 152)
- Veal and Eggplant Meatballs (page 302), a double recipe Sauce of Plum Tomatoes, Shallots, and Butter (page 21), and grated Grana Padano cheese
- Herb Pasta flavored with sage (page 368), Turkey and Wild Mushroom Cacciatore (page 288), and Parmigiano cream (page 321)
- Braised Duck and Black Olives (page 290) and grated Pecorino Toscano cheese
- Lamb, Pork, and Roasted Red Peppers ragù (page 310) and béchamel (page 140)

Green Lasagne with Capocollo, Roasted Peppers, and Tarragon

Sometimes I get good ideas for Italian food combinations by paying attention to what restaurants or take-out places put on top of pizza and focaccia or inside sandwiches and calzone. The idea for this lasagne came after I tried a calzone stuffed with salami, roasted red peppers, and ricotta. Not that that's a particularly unorthodox combination of ingredients, but I don't think I had ever had them together in a lasagne. I love tarragon with red bell peppers, so I've added it here for a touch of the unexpected.

[Makes 4 main-course or 6 first-course servings]

1 recipe Three-Egg Green Pasta (page 365), cut for lasagne

7 ripe red bell peppers, roasted over a flame until charred, peeled, seeded, and cut in thick strips

5 or 6 garlic cloves, thinly sliced

Salt

Freshly ground black pepper

A pinch of sugar

Tarragon white wine vinegar

A few large tarragon sprigs, leaves chopped

About 1½ cups fresh ricotta cheese

1 large egg

A few large flat-leaf parsley sprigs, leaves chopped

Olive oil

About ¼ pound thinly sliced sweet capocollo, chopped

1 cup freshly grated Pecorino cheese

½ cup heavy cream to pour over the top

- Cook the lasagne sheets in batches until just tender, lifting them from the water with a large strainer. Place in a colander and run cold water over them. Drain and lay them out on paper towels or kitchen towels.
- Preheat the oven to 425°F.
- In a shallow baking dish, place the roasted pepper strips and the garlic. Season with salt and pepper, a pinch of sugar, and a splash of tarragon vinegar. Roast until tender and fragrant, about 15 minutes. Add the fresh tarragon and an extra small splash of the vinegar and toss.
- In a small bowl, mix the ricotta with the egg and parsley. Season with salt and pepper.
- Coat a 12 x 10 x 2-inch baking dish lightly with olive oil. Arrange a layer of lasagne sheets on the bottom. Spread with a thin layer of ricotta. Make a layer of the roasted

peppers, including some of their cooking juices. Top with chopped capocollo and a sprinkling of grated Pecorino. Continue making layers in this fashion. End with a layer of pasta. Pour the cream over the top and sprinkle with grated Pecorino.

• Cover the dish with aluminum foil and bake about 15 minutes. Uncover and bake until bubbling hot and lightly browned, another 15 to 20 minutes. Let the lasagne rest a few minutes before serving.

Ideas

The huge variety of cured Italian meat products now available in this country range from delicate prosciutto di Parma to the highly spiced sausages of the south. Some are best eaten raw, but often a brief sautéing or heating can bring out subtle characteristics. They provide an easy way to add richness to a lasagne. When you see an unfamiliar cured meat or sausage at your Italian market, buy a small chunk of it. Take it home and give it a taste. Think of ways to work it into a pasta dish. This can really expand your cooking repertoire. Make sure to check for and remove the casing from any sausage you plan on cooking.

Here are some other good combinations pairing fresh herbs with vegetables to consider when putting together a lasagne: mint with artichokes, asparagus with lemon thyme, winter savory with canned plum tomatoes, eggplant with rosemary, basil with zucchini, and cauliflower and parsley.

Meat-Filled Ravioli and Cannelloni

Make sure the filling for meat ravioli is very dry, or it can make the pasta soggy. If you have a pasta-drying screen, use it for ravioli or any stuffed pasta that will need to be boiled after stuffing, such as tortellini. I sometimes lay the ravioli out on a floured baking sheet and turn them once after about 15 minutes to fully dry out. A trick I learned from working in Italian restaurants is to refrigerate ravioli uncovered (but not for more than a day). That way, moisture doesn't get trapped under the covering and make the pasta soggy.

Ravioli with Veal and Mild Fresh Herbs

The filling for these simple but highly flavored veal ravioli should be quite green from the herbs. I've suggested a mix of tarragon, basil, and chervil, and you might do best to get at least two of these. If you can't find chervil, you can use parsley, feathery fennel tops, or celery leaves.

[Makes 4 main-course or 6 first-course servings]

About 2 tablespoons unsalted butter

4 shallots, minced

1 pound ground veal

Salt

Freshly ground black pepper

A small bunch of tarragon, leaves chopped

A small bunch of basil, leaves chopped

A small bunch of chervil, leaves left whole

3 or 4 slices of prosciutto di Parma, finely chopped

1 large egg

Freshly grated Grana Padano cheese

About 1 tablespoon untoasted bread crumbs, if needed (see page 340)

1 recipe Three-Egg Pasta (page 365), cut for ravioli

For the sauce:

½ cup (1 stick) unsalted butter

A tiny splash of tarragon white wine vinegar

A pinch of salt

Freshly ground black pepper

A handful of chervil leaves

- In a large skillet, melt the butter over medium heat and sauté the shallots until soft. Turn the heat up and add the veal. Season the veal with salt and pepper and cook just until it loses all its pinkness, about 5 minutes. Add all the herbs and the prosciutto and mix well. Check the seasoning. Let this cool.

- When the meat has cooled, add the egg and a small handful of Grana Padano. Mix well. The stuffing should be fairly dry. If it seems too loose, add the bread crumbs and mix in. Make sure the filling is completely cool. You can put it in the refrigerator for about ½ hour to speed this up.
- Fill the ravioli (for instructions, see page 370).
- To make the sauce, melt the butter in a small saucepan. Add the tarragon vinegar. Season with a little salt and pepper and add the chervil.
- Cook the ravioli until tender and lift from the water with a large strainer. Drain well and slide onto a serving platter.
- Drizzle the butter sauce over the top. Serve a bowl of grated Grana Padano at the table.

Ideas

These ravioli are heavily perfumed by the herbs. The meat is really secondary. In fact, you can add a mix of fresh herbs to just about any tenderly cooked, chopped meat and come up with an interesting filling. I like using veal because it's mild and really shows off the herbs, but a stronger meat—ground lamb, for instance—will result in a bolder, more highly flavored filling. In that case, you might want to choose stronger herbs as well—maybe sage, parsley, and rosemary.

Making ravioli is also a good way to use up leftover meatballs, as long as they're not overcooked (the best meatballs for this purpose are those that have been browned and cooked through but haven't been allowed to simmer in a sauce, making them a little less moist).

Sausage Ravioli with Tomato and Olive Cream

Here commonly used Italian ingredients are cooked together in a slightly different way to produce a lush ravioli filled with sausage and ricotta and a suave tomato sauce finished with cream and black olives.

[Makes 4 main-course or 6 first-course servings]

½ pound mild Italian pork sausage, casings removed

1 medium onion, cut in small dice

1 tablespoon olive oil

1½ cups ricotta cheese, well drained

1 large egg

A pinch of ground allspice

A few marjoram sprigs, leaves chopped

Salt

Freshly ground black pepper

For the sauce:
2 garlic cloves, thinly sliced

2 tablespoons olive oil

One 35-ounce can Italian plum tomatoes, drained and chopped

About ½ cup heavy cream

A handful of black olives, pitted and cut in half (I use Niçoise)

A few marjoram sprigs, leaves chopped

Salt

Freshly ground black pepper

1 recipe Three-Egg Pasta (page 365), cut for ravioli

Freshly grated Pecorino Toscano cheese

- In a large skillet, cook the sausage and onion in the olive oil over medium heat until both are lightly browned. Break the sausage up with the back of your spoon as you cook so you wind up with small pieces. Drain off the excess fat if necessary (you can pulse the sausage in a food processor briefly to get a more uniform texture). Let this cool a few minutes and add the ricotta, egg, allspice, and marjoram. Season with salt and pepper and mix well. Let this cool completely.
- To make the sauce, sauté the garlic in another skillet over low heat in the olive oil until it gives off aroma, 1 to 2 minutes. Add the tomatoes, turn the heat to high, and cook for about 5 minutes. Add the cream, olives, and marjoram, season with salt and pepper, and cook a minute longer, just to blend the flavors.
- Lay out the pasta sheets and fill the ravioli (for instructions, see page 370). Boil the ravioli until just tender and lift from the water with a large strainer spoon. Drain well.

- Reheat the sauce gently.
- Slide the ravioli onto a large serving platter and pour the sauce on top. Finish with a sprinkling of grated Pecorino and pass additional cheese at the table.

Ideas

Ricotta is a beautiful filling stretcher. Recipes for meat- and ricotta-filled pasta abound; my all-time favorite is a mix of ricotta and chopped prosciutto, seasoned with a little nutmeg. You can also try chicken and spinach, a mix of mortadella and ground beef, or finely chopped bresaola.

Cannelloni with Spanish Ham and Spiced Leeks

Ｔrue Spanish Serrano ham has recently become available in this country, and I've been using it in Italian-style dishes with great success. Instead of prosciutto, I like this slightly heartier ham paired with strong flavors.

[Makes 4 main-course or 6 first-course servings]

About 2 tablespoons olive oil

9 leeks, trimmed of green, washed, and
   cut in short strips

2 allspice, ground

A few generous gratings of nutmeg

2 whole cloves, ground

1 bay leaf

A few thyme sprigs, leaves chopped

Salt

Freshly ground black pepper

2 garlic cloves, minced

1 cup homemade Light Veal Broth (page
   376) or Chicken Broth (page 374)

1 recipe Three-Egg Pasta (page 365), cut
   for cannelloni

About ½ pound thinly sliced Serrano
   ham, chopped into small bite-size
   pieces

For the sauce:

1 cup heavy cream

A large handful of freshly grated Comtè
   cheese

A pinch of ground nutmeg

A pinch of cayenne pepper

Salt

- In a large skillet, heat the olive oil. Add the leeks and all the spices and herbs and season lightly with salt and more generously with black pepper. Sauté a few minutes until the leeks give off aroma and start to soften. Add the garlic and sauté it a minute. Add the broth and cover the pan. Let this simmer until the leeks are very soft and tender, about 30 minutes. If there is still a lot of liquid, boil it down over high heat until you have about 2 tablespoons.
- Cook the cannelloni sheets in batches, lifting them from the water with a large strainer. Run them under cold water, drain, and lay them out on kitchen towels or paper towels. Fill the cannelloni with pieces of ham and the leeks and roll them loosely.
- Preheat the oven to 425°F.
- To make the sauce, gently heat the cream with the cheese in a small saucepan. Season with nutmeg, cayenne, and a little salt. Whisk over low heat until the sauce is smooth.
- Pour a thin layer of the cream mixture into your baking dish (a 14 x 9 x 2-inch dish or its equivalent is about right for this).

- Place the cannelloni, seam side down, in the baking dish. Pour on the rest of the sauce and grind a little black pepper over the top. Bake, uncovered, until bubbling hot and lightly browned, 15 to 20 minutes.

Ideas

The earthy flavor of cooked leeks can stand up to interesting seasoning. Instead of the spices I've chosen, flavor the leeks with a little ground saffron dissolved in the chicken broth and a pinch of cinnamon.

Comtè is a French cow's milk cheese in the Gruyère family. I love it with pasta. If you can't find it try Emmentaler, fontina, or any rich but mild cheese that melts nicely.

Cannelloni with Bresaola, Goat Cheese, and Radicchio with Tomato and Rosemary Sauce

Here is a good mix of the mellow, the tangy, and the pleasantly tart.

[Makes 4 main-course or 6 first-course servings]

About 3 tablespoons olive oil

1 large onion, thinly sliced

3 or 4 garlic cloves, minced

2 medium radicchio, cored and chopped
     into medium dice

Salt

Freshly ground black pepper

For the sauce:

About 2 tablespoons unsalted butter

2 garlic cloves, minced

2 small rosemary sprigs, leaves chopped

About 5 large tomatoes
     (about 2½ pounds), peeled,
     seeded, and cut in small dice

Salt

Freshly ground black pepper

A tiny splash of balsamic vinegar

¼ pound thinly sliced bresaola, cut in
     thin strips

One 11-ounce log of fresh goat cheese
     (Coach Farm is a good choice)

A handful of black olives, pitted and cut
     in half (Niçoise or Gaeta are good to
     try here, both lending different qual-
     ities to the dish)

A handful of flat-leaf parsley leaves,
     chopped

A splash of cognac or grappa

1 recipe Three-Egg Pasta (page 365), cut
     for cannelloni

Freshly grated Fiore Sardo cheese
     (about ¾ cup)

- In a large skillet, heat the olive oil. Add the onion and cook until soft, about 4 minutes. Add the garlic and radicchio, season with salt and pepper, and sauté until the radicchio is well wilted and tender, about another 5 minutes. Transfer this to a large mixing bowl and let it cool.
- Preheat the oven to 425°F.
- In the same skillet, start making the tomato sauce. Heat the butter over medium heat. Add the garlic and rosemary and sauté until they start to give off aroma, just about a minute. Add the tomatoes and cook over lively heat for about 3 minutes. Season with

salt and pepper and add the balsamic vinegar (maybe a teaspoon). Remove from the heat.

- Add the bresaola, goat cheese, olives, parsley, and cognac to the radicchio. Mix well and season with salt and pepper.
- Cook the cannelloni in batches, lifting them from the water with a large strainer. Drain well and lay out on kitchen towels or paper towels. Fill each one with a layer of the goat cheese mixture and roll it up loosely.
- Spread a thin layer of tomato sauce on the bottom of a 10 x 14 x 2-inch baking dish. Place the cannelloni, seam side down, in the pan. Top with the remaining sauce. Sprinkle a thin layer of Fiore Sardo on top and bake, uncovered, until lightly browned and bubbling, about 20 minutes.

Ideas

Fresh goat cheese is a tangy but still somewhat neutral base to layer with flavors. When using it as a filling for pasta, think of it as a bolder version of ricotta. It blends extremely well with assertive herbs such as bay leaf, savory, thyme, or the rosemary I've chosen here.

When adding meat, be conservative. Tiny bits of cooked sausage or chopped prosciutto are delicious here in place of the bresaola. Slightly bitter cooked greens can replace the radicchio. I especially like broccoli rabe or escarole with goat cheese.

Using Leftover Ragùs, Stew Meats, and Roasts to Make Fillings for Pasta

Most of us will never spend two hours cooking a ragù or stew just for a filling to make ravioli, but if you have leftover meat from a ragù or stew, you can easily transform it into a lush stuffing for ravioli, cannelloni, lasagne, or large shells. Meat stuffings for ravioli or tortellini need to be finely chopped and fairly dry; cannelloni or lasagne fillings can be left in larger pieces and a little moister. With a little doctoring, you can turn leftover cooked meatballs, pork loin, sausage, roasted chicken, or duck into wonderful stuffed-pasta fillings.

The amount of ravioli or cannelloni filling you make will depend on how much leftover meat you start with, but remember you can always stretch it by adding more vegetables, ricotta, or cheese. A chicken and spinach filling, if it needs to feed a few more people, can always become a spinach and chicken filling. From 1½ to 2 cups of filling is usually enough for ravioli or cannelloni for four as a main course or for six as a first course. Make sure any filling you use for ravioli is completely cooled before you start to fill.

Here are a few suggestions for stuffed pastas with fillings that use recipes from this book or leftovers as a starting point.

Oxtail Ravioli

Make these ravioli with leftover oxtail or Oxtail and Chianti Ragù (page 318). You can make the ragù, use the thick cooking broth to sauce spaghetti or tagliatelle, and save the meat to make these ravioli to serve the next day.

- Remove the meat from the oxtail pieces (page 319) and chop it fine. If it seems dry, mix in a very tiny amount of the stew broth. Add a small handful of freshly grated Pecorino or Grana Padano. You can prepare this in a food processor if you pulse the mixture and are careful not to puree it. The filling should be fairly dry. Check the seasoning. The meat may need extra salt and pepper, especially if it was cooked a day or two earlier. Fill the ravioli (page 370) and boil as usual. Dress them either with sauce from the ragù or with olive oil heated with a rosemary sprig, and top with freshly grated Grana Padano or Pecorino cheese.

Ideas

If you're short on leftover oxtail, an excellent stretcher is a handful of white mushrooms that have been sautéed in olive oil and finely chopped.

Cannelloni with Lamb and Orange

In Provence local cooks make a traditional ravioli out of their *boeuf à la Niçoise,* a beef stew flavored with orange zest. I make a similar filling for cannelloni by adding fresh orange zest to a lamb ragù with tarragon (page 308).

- Lift the meat from the sauce and place it in a large bowl. Chop it lightly into small pieces. Add the zest from an orange and a few sprigs of fresh herbs. The filling for cannelloni need not be finely chopped and can be a bit moist. Fill the cannelloni in the usual way and place in an oiled baking dish. Top with a handful of freshly grated Parmigiano-Reggiano cheese and a little of the stew juices. Or top with a thin béchamel (page 140). Bake as usual.

Ideas

For a lighter filling, lessen the amount of lamb and add a handful of sautéed, chopped spinach or cooked greens to it.

Duck and Artichoke Ravioli with Savory Butter and Parmigiano

Moist roasted duck legs or store-bought (or homemade) duck confit makes excellent ravioli filling. Here I've used a conservative amount of leftover duck meat and stretched the filling with artichoke hearts.

- Use leftover roast duck or duck confit. Remove the skin and chop it finely—you'll need about 1 cup. Add 3 or 4 blanched artichoke hearts sautéed in a little butter and finely chopped. Add a small handful of freshly grated Parmigiano-Reggiano cheese. The filling should be relatively dry. Taste for seasoning. Fill the ravioli as usual.
- For a simple sauce, melt a few tablespoons of unsalted butter with 2 or 3 savory sprigs. Add a splash of chicken broth for a lighter sauce. A light tomato sauce flavored with rosemary is also wonderful with this. Finish the dish with freshly grated Parmigiano-Reggiano cheese.

Cannelloni Filled with Chicken, Capers, and Ricotta

Leftover roasted chicken, especially moist dark meat, makes a superb filling for cannelloni.

- If you have meat from 2 whole cooked chicken legs, skin the chicken and pull the meat off the bone. Chop it into bite-size pieces and place in a bowl. Add 1 cup drained ricotta, a large handful of chopped capers, a handful of freshly grated Grana Padano, and a little chopped parsley. Make sure the filling is well seasoned.
- A Sauce of Plum Tomatoes, Shallots, and Butter (page 21) is good on these.

Ideas

Chopped cooked chicken can be mixed with any number of ingredients to make an interesting cannelloni filling. Chopped cooked greens such as kale, dandelions, or escarole are wonderful with chicken, but make sure they are squeezed dry.

Make these ravioli the day after Thanksgiving and substitute turkey for the chicken.

Large Shells Filled with Sausage, Escarole, and Lemon

Leftover grilled or pan-browned sausage is a wonderful ingredient to work with. If you have three leftover cooked Italian pork sausages (a little under a pound), you can add a vegetable or a little cheese and have a filling to make about four servings of cannelloni.

- Sauté a head of washed and well-chopped escarole with garlic and olive oil until just wilted. Chop the cooked sausage into small pieces and add it to the pan. Season with the zest from 1 lemon, a small sprig of chopped rosemary, salt, and black pepper. Heat through to blend the flavors. Check the seasoning. Cook the shells until al dente, drain well, and fill with this mixture. Place in a baking dish.
- Top with Simmered Tomato Sauce (page 28). Sprinkle with freshly Pecorino Toscano cheese and bake as usual.

Ideas

Broccoli rabe is traditional with sausage and makes a hearty substitute for escarole. For a rich, cheesy sausage stuffing, add about ½ cup young goat cheese or 1 cup well-drained ricotta. Omit the escarole if you wish.

Cannelloni with Beef, Rosemary, and Mushrooms

- If you have about a cup of beef stew left over, try mixing the meat with a handful of sautéed mushrooms and a few sprigs of chopped fresh rosemary. Add a ladle of stew broth for moisture. This will be especially delicious if your stew was cooked in red wine.
- A good sauce for this is Parmigiano cream (page 321) or a thin béchamel (page 140).

The Improviser's Pantry

Italians have a custom of inviting friends over for late-night pasta dinners, usually after an evening at the theater or the opera. The wine is opened, the water is put on to boil, and a sauce is started and usually finished by the time the pasta is cooked al dente. These impromptu sauces are generally put together from the ingredients most Italian households have in the pantry; extra-virgin, fruity olive oil, a few slices of prosciutto di Parma, salt-preserved anchovies, dried hot peppers, a chunk of Grana Padano or tangy Pecorino cheese. Use the following list as a guideline for stocking an improvisational pasta pantry. See pages 18–19 for a list of general quantities to keep in mind when shopping for pasta sauce ingredients.

Anchovies, canned or preserved in salt: One of the most useful preserved foods for spur-of-the-moment cooking, anchovies can elevate a flat, one-dimensional tomato sauce into something with real character. They add surprising depth to a chicken or lamb ragù without imparting a fishy taste. Dissolved in warm olive oil, they create a simple but utterly delicious sauce for spaghetti, one of the staple dishes of southern Italian cooking. A few chopped anchovy fillets heated with a cup of cream provide an exquisite base for an asparagus, artichoke, or primavera pasta sauce.

There are two types of preserved anchovies: the familiar oil-packed fillets in tins or small jars and whole (not filleted) salt-packed anchovies.

Oil-packed anchovies can be very good, but brands vary greatly in flavor; some have a slightly metallic taste (especially the ones packed in tins), and some are excessively salty. When oil-packed anchovies are old, they can become mushy. Unfortunately, the tins and jars are not dated, so you really have no way of knowing when they were packaged. I like to buy the ones in jars because at least I can see if they are falling apart. In general, I find that jarred oil-packed anchovy fillets imported from southern Italy have reliably good taste and texture, and I seek them out. Sometimes I notice that jarred anchovies packaged in Italy actually contain Spanish or Moroccan anchovies, but I have found most of these brands to be good as well.

You can't taste test canned or jarred anchovies before buying, but you can buy a few types and do comparison tastings at home. If you find a brand to be too salty, soak the anchovies for 2 or 3 minutes in cool water (hot water will cause them to break apart). Some Italian cooks soak them in milk, which helps remove any bitterness. Don't worry about opening a tin for just a few anchovies; they will keep their flavor for at least a month if you cover them with fresh olive oil, wrap them well with plastic wrap, and store them in the refrigerator.

The oil-packed anchovies wrapped around capers are generally used for presentation on antipasti platters. I don't generally buy them for cooking, but they can have fine flavor.

Whole salt-packed anchovies are available in upscale grocery stores and Italian food specialty stores. I usually find ones imported from Sicily, and they are almost always of very high quality. They need to be filleted, which is quite easy to do; the firm flesh pulls right away from the backbone. After filleting, they need to be soaked for 8 to 10 minutes in cool water or milk to remove excess salt. If they are very salty, change the water once during soaking. They usually have excellent flavor and a more substantial texture that doesn't break down during heating as oil-packed varieties may.

I find that the commercial anchovy paste sold in metal tubes, imported from Italy, is usually inferior in taste to oil-packed anchovies and certainly to the salt-preserved variety. You can make your own anchovy paste by pureeing anchovies in a food processor or grinding them with a mortar and pestle. Transfer the paste to a small jar and cover it with a thin layer of olive oil. Cover well and refrigerate. Make just enough to use up in a month.

Anchovy butter is delicious stirred into a tomato sauce or tossed with tagliatelle and gently cooked fava beans or spring peas. You can make it by mixing about a dozen well-chopped anchovy fillets, either oil packed or salt preserved, into a stick of softened unsalted butter (you can also blend this in a food processor). It is best used right away, but it will keep frozen in a well-covered plastic tub or rolled into a cylinder and wrapped in plastic; use it within two weeks for the best flavor.

Beans and lentils, dried and canned: *Pasta e fagioli* (pasta and beans) in all its regional variations is one of the delicious and simple glories of Italian pasta cooking. In Tuscany you'll find it made with cannellini beans; in Venice, with borlotti beans; in Puglia, with fava and ceci beans (chickpeas).

Ceci, cannellini, and fava are the dried Italian beans most commonly available in this country. Our native cranberry beans are very close in look and taste to the speckled tan and red borlotti beans used in central and northern Italian bean dishes, and they make a fine substitution. Imported borlotti beans are available at some Italian food shops. In New York I have occasionally seen and bought *fagioli di Lamon,* a brown streaked bean used in the traditional Venetian version of *pasta e fagioli.* Our brown pinto bean is a worthy replacement, although *fagioli di Lamon* have a richer, nuttier flavor.

Fava beans are usually dried with their skins on. They need to be soaked before cooking so you can remove their bitter skins; it is a tedious job and one I don't think worth the trouble. I occasionally find split, skinned dried favas; they tend to break during cooking, so they're best used as a pasta filling.

Many non-Italian varieties of dried beans available in the United States are fine to cook with pasta. Green flageolets, the delicately flavored French beans, are excellent in a mildly seasoned *pasta e fagioli.* Navy beans, red kidney beans, dried black-eyed peas (sometimes actually used in Italy), pintos, and dried lima beans (a bean almost never found in the traditional Italian kitchen) all make creative, delicious—if untraditional—*pasta e fagioli.*

Choosing the appropriate bean to suit the mood of your intended pasta dish takes a little familiarity with the different beans on the market, but in general, I pair a strong-tasting bean with an assertive sauce, and choose a delicate white bean to accompany gentle seasoning. For instance, the firm, nutty-tasting ceci (chickpeas) bean so prevalent in southern Italian pasta dishes blends well with hot chiles, garlic, tomatoes, olives, and oregano, savory, or thyme. I would also more often than not match it with a short, stubby dried pasta shape such as orecchiette or tubetti. Cannellini beans or great Northern beans go well with pasta dishes flavored with onion, celery, a light broth, or a light tomato sauce seasoned with basil or parsley. You can toss this type of sauce with fresh egg pasta such as tagliatelle and not be concerned that the sauce will overwhelm the pasta. White bean purée flavored with a little sage or fresh rosemary makes a wonderful filling for ravioli.

Pasta cooked with lentils is another fine variation on this theme. When pairing lentils with pasta, it's important to buy lentils that hold their shape and don't break down into a mush. French Le Puy lentils have a firmer texture than most lentils on the market. They also have a sweet taste and pretty green color. The Umbrian Castelluccio lentil that has just recently become available at several Italian markets in New York has a similar appearance and texture to the Le Puy and is worth seeking out.

Dried beans vary so much in cooking time that it's impossible to give anything but a rough estimate. You just have to test them often during cooking. It seems to me that improvements in commercial drying methods have resulted in beans needing a shorter time to cook these days. But it is still important to purchase beans from a store with good turnover so you're ensured freshness; old, hard beans take longer to cook and never taste as good as ones more recently dried. It's not easy to tell if dried beans are old, but in general, older beans feel lighter. Newly dried beans have more moisture, look slightly plumper, and feel a bit heavier. If you want to be completely sure you're getting freshly dried beans, buy them from a grower (for information on buying beans from bean growers, see page 379).

Drier, older beans benefit from soaking. They cook up creamier and tend not to burst if they are presoaked. I usually cook newly dried beans without soaking. Always give your beans a quick washing in cold water to remove any dirt. And check for little stones (in my experience, big bags of lentils almost always have a rock or two mixed in with them).

Beans that I know take a long time to cook, such as ceci or cannellini, I usually cook covered; it makes them creamier. Lentils and small beans that cook up faster, I generally cook uncovered; this seems to prevent them from becoming mushy or breaking apart. Cook all beans slowly, at a low simmer. And check the liquid often to make sure they haven't absorbed it all. Add hot liquid when necessary to keep the beans just covered.

When seasoning beans for cooking, remember not to add an acid such as lemon juice, wine, or vinegar to the water; this slows the cooking time considerably, and they can always be stirred in later for flavor. Adding salt during the first hour of cooking toughens the beans' skin, so add it toward the end.

To me, most canned beans taste like the can they come out of, and are packed in a slimy, salty liquid. Canned chickpeas beans are the only type that I find have much integrity (but they are no match for your own cooked dried beans). I always rinse them in cold water. It improves the flavor. So does a quick sautéing in olive oil, salt, and a little garlic.

Bread crumbs, homemade: To me, commercially packaged bread crumbs taste like cardboard, and the preseasoned ones taste like chemicals and stale herbs. If you routinely buy decent Italian bread, you can very easily turn leftover pieces of it into high-quality bread crumbs.

In the Italian kitchen, toasted bread crumbs (called *pangrattato* in Italian) are generally left unseasoned or seasoned only with salt, their usual purpose being to pick up flavors already present in the dish. I sometimes sauté bread crumbs (previously toasted or not) for about a minute in a hot skillet with a little olive oil and salt; this gives them extra flavor and a very crunchy, slightly fried texture. I use them right away. Chopped capers or olives, chopped chiles, minced garlic, herbs, or anchovies can be added while the bread crumbs sauté. Flavored bread crumbs are especially good sprinkled or tossed into an *aglio e olio* or olive oil and anchovy sauce.

I save pieces of thick-crusted white Italian bread, either from the large round peasant loaves or the long, thin loaves, letting them dry out for a day or two. I don't keep hard bread much longer than that because it just gets stale, and any bread crumbs made from it will have a musty taste. I wrap the dry pieces in a towel and then break them up with a hammer (or by smashing them a few times on the kitchen counter). Then I can easily grind them in a food processor. Sourdough and semolina bread (without sesame seeds) also make interesting-tasting bread crumbs.

I like bread crumbs to be ground not too finely; the slightly coarser texture holds up better when mixed with hot sauces. This is another problem with the packaged ones; they are ground almost to a powder, so they dissolve in contact with hot pasta, making it gummy. In Italian cooking, it is understood that bread crumbs will be lightly toasted (the untoasted insides of bread, called *mollica,* are used for different purposes, mainly in stuffings).

To toast bread crumbs, preheat the oven to 400°F. Spread the crumbs out evenly on a baking sheet and bake until just golden, about 10 minutes. I keep them unseasoned until I'm ready to use them; then I might add salt, pepper, garlic, or fresh herbs. Bread crumbs keep for about a week, stored in a covered glass jar and left unrefrigerated (refrigeration makes them mushy).

Toasted bread crumbs are sprinkled on or tossed into many pasta dishes in place of grated cheese when the latter is considered inappropriate—for instance, on fish-sauced pasta. The classic Sicilian *pasta con le sarde* (bucatini with sardines) is traditionally topped with a sprinkling of toasted bread crumbs before serving. Pasta dressed in *aglio e olio* (oil and garlic) is also frequently finished this way. So are pasta dishes based on olive oil with fresh herbs or hot chiles.

Toasted bread crumbs add texture and earthy taste to pasta dishes. They are best on dishes that do not contain too much of a loose sauce. I would not, for instance, add them to cream sauces, brothy sauces, or liquidy tomato sauces, where they would immediately be absorbed and turn to mush. Use them instead on olive oil–based vegetable- or fish-sauced pasta. Toss them in or sprinkle them on top just before serving so they don't have a chance to get soggy. Orecchiette tossed with cauliflower and black olives, a Pugliese specialty, is frequently topped with lightly sautéed bread crumbs. I also love adding a handful of hot chile–seasoned bread crumbs to spaghetti with a classic white clam sauce. They also elevate the flavor of pasta tossed with roasted pepper strips (grated cheese would distract from the pure pepper flavor). Bread crumbs are also an essential topping on many baked pastas, especially fish or vegetable lasagne. I sometimes mix half toasted bread crumbs and half grated Pecorino or Grana Padano cheese to brown on top of baked ziti for a crunchy, cheesy crust.

Broths and cooking juices: Chicken, fish, veal, and mixed-meat broths are invaluable improvisational aids. A few tablespoons added to a pasta sauce can sometimes be just the thing to pull all the flavors together (the reduced meat stocks used in classic French sauces are not generally used in the Italian kitchen). The problem for home cooks is that you would not necessarily have fresh broths on hand unless you've planned on making one—for a soup, for instance. Leftover braising liquid or slightly thickened meat gravies can serve the same purpose as homemade stocks.

If you've braised a piece of veal, try incorporating any of the leftover braising liquid into the next day's pasta sauce. A half cup of meat broth scented with wine and herbs is wonderful stirred into a ragù or a simmered tomato sauce. Gravies thickened with a lot of flour or cornstarch will make a pasta sauce gummy, but the thin pan juices from a roast chicken are excellent blended into a pasta sauce that contains chicken pieces, chicken livers, duck, or even vegetables. Liquid from a lamb or beef stew will add depth to pasta sauces containing little bits of meat such as lamb sausage or baby meatballs. If flavorful enough, the liquid can also serve as a pasta sauce in its own right (beef, lamb, or veal liquid left from a slow braise or a stew is often used to dress fresh egg pasta and ravioli in Italy and France).

Low-salt canned chicken broth is fine as a minor component in a sauce, but it's not delicious enough to use for a broth-based pasta soup or to add in large quantities to a ragù. I often add about ½ cup of canned broth to a vegetable-based pasta sauce as a liquid for the vegetables to finish cooking in.

A conservative amount of bottled clam broth, although very salty, can enhance a seafood pasta sauce, especially when diffused by herbs or vegetables and diluted with wine. Try not to boil down non-reduced-salt chicken broths; this will only concentrate its saltiness. I find every brand of canned beef broth, low salt or not, to have a metallic, salty taste, and I never use them for anything. When making a pasta sauce containing lobster or shrimp, I almost always make a quick little broth from the shellfish shells to give added sea flavor to my sauce.

Recipes for making your own broths for pasta sauces begin on page 373.

Butter: I always use unsalted butter for cooking because it doesn't conflict with my seasoning process. I use a brand called Keller's; it is sweet and concentrated, made in the European style with a lower water content and slightly higher fat, which makes it perfect for sautéing. Keller's is an American product now available in many supermarkets.

But when I want butter with real character—for an Alfredo sauce, for instance—I use butter from the Egg Farm Dairy in Peekskill, New York (see page 379 for mail-order information). It is less sweet than commercial butter and has an old-fashioned buttermilk tang to it. It is wonderful for sautéing wild mushrooms. And when I want a dish of pasta tossed with butter and Parmigiano-Reggiano cheese, this is what I choose.

You can add a generous lump of butter to a cooked tomato or meat sauce to sweeten it and pull all the flavors together for a sophisticated finish to the dish. You can also add a tablespoon or two of butter to the bowl while tossing pasta with pesto sauce, just to mellow out all the strong, contrasting flavor components. Butter carries the flavor of fresh herbs beautifully; cheese ravioli coated with a sauce of melted butter and fresh sage or rosemary is one of the genius dishes of the Italian table. Melted butter is also wonderful for sautéing pine nuts, walnuts, or almonds to make a quick, luscious sauce for ravioli or gnocchi. I occasionally add a little butter to an olive oil–based shrimp, scallop, or clam sauce when I want a sweeter, less direct flavor. Stirring butter into a hot but not boiling sauce will add thickening. A tablespoon of butter stirred into an overly salty sauce will make it taste a little less so.

Butter starts to turn rancid in your refrigerator sooner than you think. Buy only what you need and use it within a week. And remember that butter is one of those delicately flavored foods that pick up refrigerator odors very easily; keep it very well wrapped.

Capers: Capers are the flower buds of the caper shrub native to many parts of the southern Mediterranean. Grown in Spain, Morocco, Turkey, and Italy, they are preserved in either salt or vinegar. Often when I'm floundering around with a pasta dish, they turn out to be the perfect addition to pull all the ingredients together. I add them to tomato sauces and meat sauces, especially pork and beef. I often add a handful of capers to a veal ragù or to a pasta dish with chicken livers and herbs. You will appreciate how they cut right through an olive oil–rich sauce and give a touch of acidity. I love them with sautéed eggplant or roasted red peppers.

Capers grown in Pantelleria, an island off the coast of Sicily, have a reputation for being the best in the world. They have a floral taste that I have never noticed in any other capers. These large, aromatic, salt-packed capers are fortunately becoming easier to find in this country. Usually they're packaged in small plastic bags. Other types of Italian salt-packed capers are often sold loose in the appetizer section of Italian grocery stores. They can be very good, but you have to sample them to find out. When I can't find Pantelleria capers, my next choice is the vinegar-packed tiny French nonpareil capers. These are grown in Morocco by French companies and are available in many supermarkets. They have a sweeter taste than the large vinegar-packed ones. You'll also find tiny vinegar-packed capers from Spain and southern Italy.

Salt-packed capers need to be soaked for about 15 minutes in water and then rinsed to remove excess salt. If they still taste excessively salty after one soaking, change the water and soak them again. Use cool water; I find that soaking in hot water sometimes causes them to burst open. Vinegar-packed capers should be lightly rinsed to remove excess acidity. Once you've opened a package of salt-packed capers, you can store it, rewrapped, in the refrigerator for up to four months. Opened bottles of vinegar-packed capers should also be resealed and refrigerated and will last about the same length of time.

Caviar: For a spur-of-the-moment, elegant, late-night pasta dinner, there is nothing more sultry than spaghetti (or fresh tagliatelle) tossed with unsalted butter and chives and then sprinkled with a few tablespoons of good caviar. I also love a variation of this in which the pasta is instead tossed with ricotta thinned with a little heavy cream. For a special occasion, make this dish with sevruga or osetra caviar. It's also wonderful with large pink salmon roe. The only thing to bear in mind is that you mustn't toss the caviar with the hot pasta; that will cause the caviar to cook slightly, and black caviar will color the pasta in an unappetizing way. Just sprinkle the roe on top.

Also look for *bottarga*, a pressed roe made from tuna or mullet. It is exported from Sicily and Sardinia, where it is served shaved into thin strips and tossed, along with good olive oil and fresh mint, with hot spaghetti, making an intoxicating, beautifully perfumed dish of pasta that is best savored in small amounts, as a first course. You can find *bottarga* in many Italian food shops nowadays. The Sardinian mullet version is considered by most chefs to be choice. You will need very little (2 to 3 ounces) to flavor a pound of pasta, so buy small pieces. Leftover *bottarga* should be well wrapped and refrigerated. It will last about two weeks.

Cheeses: See "Good Italian Cheeses to Use with Pasta," page 357.

Chiles, dried: Hot chiles are used occasionally in southern Italian cooking, especially in the Abruzzo, Calabria, and in Basilicata, but usually with discretion and mostly dried. Because there are only a few varieties of hot chiles grown in Italy, there is no tradition of blending sophisticated, intricate chile flavors, as in the Mexican kitchen. Pasta with arrabbiata sauce, usually a relatively mildly spiced tomato sauce, is popular throughout the south. And pasta tossed with *aglio e olio* (garlic and oil sauce) spiked with hot chile is another common southern dish. In Naples and Puglia people like to sprinkle hot dried chile seeds over *pasta e fagioli* (pasta and beans). And olive oil infused with whole dried red chiles is drizzled conservatively over vegetable-sauced pastas and over fish and pasta soups.

I don't like introducing too many foreign tastes into my Italian dishes, so I usually use several types of dried hot chiles that are similar in taste to the ones found in Italy. I use fresh cayenne, fresh chiles d'arbol, and red peperoncini for pasta sauces. I do occasionally use fresh jalapeño chiles because the commercial ones I find are very mild and tend not to overwhelm most Italian sauces. The jars of dried red pepper flakes and seeds you see in every pizza parlor are a good authentic source of heat, but they need to be fresh to have any punch. I prefer buying dried whole chiles because I get both the skin and the seeds. If you want mild chile flavor, remove the seeds and grind the dried skins in a spice grinder; for strong heat, grind the whole chile or just crumble it with your fingers directly into your pasta sauce. For maximum flavor, I try to use ground chiles within two weeks. Store homemade chile powder in a covered jar, unrefrigerated.

Eggs: You can make fresh egg pasta in about an hour if you work fast, so if the urge strikes and you have a couple of eggs and some all-purpose flour on hand, let nothing stop you. Eggs add richness and thickness to pasta sauces too. I'll often mix a raw egg with a handful of grated cheese and toss it with hot spaghetti. The heat of the pasta cooks the egg perfectly, transforming it into a creamy sauce. If you add browned pancetta chunks and a generous amount of ground black pepper to this, you'll have a classic carbonara. As often as I can, I buy organic eggs from my local farmers' market. The taste really is superior to that of supermarket eggs. I can definitely taste the difference when I make fresh egg pasta, and maybe it's my imagination, but the texture even seems silkier. Always use room-temperature eggs when making fresh pasta; you'll get more elasticity in your dough.

Flour: Unbleached all-purpose white flour is perfect for making fresh egg pasta. It has the right amount of gluten to produce silky, thin pasta sheets with good elasticity. You can mix whole-wheat flour with white for a nuttier flavor and more rustic texture. Semolina flour, when blended with white, produces a sturdy pasta with good body. Buckwheat (which is technically not a type of wheat) can also be mixed with white for a tender texture but darkly colored, earthy taste. Chestnut flour mixed with white flour is used in Liguria to make special regional pastas, such as corzetti, a flat disk embossed with a design, but it also makes a lovely, slightly sweet-tasting tagliatelle. I buy chestnut flour imported from Italy at my Italian market. I've also seen it imported from France. Buy flour from a supermarket or a store that has a fast turnover so you know it will be fresh.

Garlic: See "Cooking with Garlic and Olive Oil," page 45.

Mushrooms, dried: Porcini are the best dried mushrooms for adding flavor to pasta sauces. They have a deep, woodsy taste that imparts a meaty quality to simmered tomato sauces and ragùs. I see a lot of different types of dried mushrooms in my markets, primarily Asian varieties, but these really don't have the right flavor for Italian sauces, although dried shiitakes blend very well with most Italian ingredients. Aside from imported porcini, I often like local dried mushrooms, especially from Washington State; look for local dried morels, oyster mushrooms, and black trumpets—I've cooked all of these into pasta sauces with very good results.

Soak all dried mushrooms in warm water to cover until they are soft, about 15 minutes. Lift the mushrooms from the water with your fingers so any dirt will stay on the bottom of the bowl. Strain the soaking liquid and use it to further flavor your sauce.

Nuts: When I have a sharp or assertive pasta sauce that I want to mellow out, I often reach for nuts. Their opulent richness is frequently just the thing to neutralize acidity in a sauce. The most widely used nuts in Italian pasta cooking are pine nuts (pignoli), almonds, pistachios, walnuts, and hazelnuts. Pine nuts, with their almost buttery taste and smooth texture, are used extensively in all sorts of pasta dishes, especially in pestos and in sauces containing strong fish, such as tuna, sardines, or swordfish. But they're also combined with vegetable sauces, particularly those involving cauliflower and broccoli, and I love them with artichokes and asparagus as well. Almonds can be substituted for pine nuts in many dishes. I like almonds in fish sauces, although they can sometimes produce a taste like Chinese food. Pappardelle with rabbit ragù is greatly enhanced by the addition of a handful of toasted chopped almonds. You can replace the usual basil and pine nuts used in pesto with parsley and walnuts. I like pistachios paired with mild meat sauces; you might include them in fillings for stuffed pasta.

Toasting brings out the flavor of nuts. If I'm going to add nuts as a garnish or in the last minutes of cooking, I usually toast them first. To toast nuts, preheat the oven to 400°F, spread the nuts out on a baking sheet, and toast them until golden, about 10 minutes. I also sometimes simply throw them into the skillet along with my onion or garlic and give them a light sauté to release their flavor and then proceed with the sauce. I also use them raw, especially in pesto sauces, where I am looking for a sweet, rich taste.

Hazelnuts usually need skinning. The easiest way to do this is by toasting them lightly and, while still warm, rubbing them with a kitchen towel; most of the dark, papery skin should come off. I love chopped hazelnuts sautéed in butter and poured over ricotta ravioli. I usually buy whole nuts and either use them that way or chop them by hand or grind them in a food processor.

All nuts must be very fresh to be worth using at all. Nut oil becomes rancid quickly. Walnuts and pine nuts can taste very bitter when stale. If possible, smell and taste nuts before you buy them. Purchase them in small quantities from a store with a healthy turnover and use them as soon as possible. Nuts tend to pick up refrigerator flavors too, so store them well sealed but unrefrigerated in a dry place. Use within a week.

Olive oil: To produce the best pasta dishes possible, always buy fresh, delicious, fruity, extra-virgin olive oil. You can be the most creative, heartfelt cook in the world, but if you skimp on that essential an ingredient, you'll never produce the flavor you dream of.

Extra-virgin olive oil, the highest-quality oil, is pressed from perfect, healthy olives soon after the olives are picked, so they don't develop acids. This first cold pressing is done without heat or chemicals (by law the acid content must not exceed 1 percent). Extra-virgin oils will vary in quality, depending on the olives and the conditions under which the oil was made. Below extra-virgin there are several other grades of virgin oil that are also cold pressed but whose acidity levels can be higher. There are then still lower grades, usually labeled simply *olio di oliva,* or olive oil, made from subsequent pressings that can involve both heat and chemicals, producing oils with higher acid and dull, heavy flavor.

I use extra-virgin olive oil for all my cooking, keeping two types in my pantry. I buy a midpriced extra-virgin oil for just about all my sautéing and use it in most oil-and-garlic-based pasta sauces and in my soffritto for tomato and meat sauces. I'm always trying new oils in this price range, which is usually $12 to $20 a liter. Since any grade of extra-virgin oil is expensive to produce, I would question a bottle labeled extra-virgin that is sold for a price much below this range. These midpriced oils tend to be brands bottled by large manufacturers. You can find very good oils from Puglia, Calabria, Sicily, Greece, and Spain in this category. You can also find very bad ones, and the only way to know for sure what you're getting is to try them.

One of the problems in selecting these oils is that the manufacturer doesn't provide much information on the bottle or package. Often the label on a bottle of oil will say "product of Tuscany" (a very desirable address for olive oil), but the olives may have actually come from Puglia or Greece or somewhere in the Mideast and only been bottled in Tuscany. Sometimes the oil is made from a blend of olives purchased by the company from different locations. That doesn't mean the oil is bad, but you have to sample and taste several brands before you find one that you like and is of consistently good quality. Also I've found that oils from large companies are hardly ever dated, which makes knowing if they're fresh very difficult. There is no law yet in Italy requiring olive oil producers to tell you where their olives were grown, when they were grown, or when they were pressed, so for now the best approach is to try several brands several times, stick with a few oils you know to be consistently good, and buy them from a shop with high turnover.

I reserve a top-quality extra-virgin oil for salads and for drizzling over cooked pasta dishes and for special sauces—for instance, when I have beautiful spring asparagus or baby artichokes to show off in a simple but elegant pasta dish. These prized bottles are usually produced on family wine estates, and in this country you'll find them in specialty food shops. These small producers usually date their bottles. You're likely to see only a year—for example, vintage 1998. Sometimes you'll be given an olive-harvest date and also an oil-release date. That's very thoughtful of the producer because it assures you that the olives weren't hanging around a year before pressing. Even when you buy top-of-the-line oils, you'll find that quality varies, but looking at these dates is a step in the right direction. And don't buy any olive oil that is more than two years old. Olive oil loses its bouquet after that long; it is best the year it is produced.

Cold-pressed extra-virgin oils come in different styles too; you can taste oils from various regions to see what you like. Tuscan oils from the Chianti region are made from underripe green olives that yield a fruity, bright green oil with a pleasant bite. Umbria, the area right below Tuscany, also produces green olive oils, but they tend to be a bit mellower. The Italian Riviera, in Liguria, presses riper olives that produce luscious, pale golden oils with a sweet note; good French oils from Provence have a similar taste. Two I love are Maussane les Alpilles, and Alziari brand. The Lake Garda area in northern Italy is another excellent area for fruity extra-virgin oils. Other superior Italian oils are made from riper olives. Puglia, the Abruzzo, Calabria, and Sicily all produce very high-quality, delicious oils with deep golden yellow color and rich, almondy taste. I'm just starting to find high-quality, extra-virgin Spanish oils in my market; I have tried one called Nuñez de Prado that reminded me of a southern Italian oil in its deep lushness.

The type of oil you choose for your pasta dishes will influence their style. Many cooks insist on Tuscan oils for Tuscan pasta dishes and Puglian oil for rustic vegetable-based southern Italian pastas, but I suggest you experiment with different oils and use what you like best. I buy olive oils from all over Italy and from other countries just for the pleasure of seeing how they alter the taste of my cooking. Currently my favorite Tuscan oil is Frescobaldi Laudemio, which has a sharp, grassy taste. For my more robust pasta sauces I love Biancolilla, a dark, golden, extra-virgin oil from Sicily. Another excellent Sicilian oil is Ravidà, with its herby taste. La Giara, a dark yellow oil from Calabria, is wonderful for bringing out the best flavor in broccoli, broccoli rabe, and cauliflower. When I'm feeling flush, I buy a bottle of Antonio Bianchi's pale yellow I Lecci oil, from Lake Garda. This sweet and delicate oil is wonderful drizzled onto a dish of tagliatelle and spring vegetables. It is available only at Zingerman's in Michigan (for mail-order information, see page 380). California now produces a small amount of extra-virgin olive oil, usually made in the Tuscan style.

I've found that the best way to sample olive oil is on a small piece of Italian white bread. You will taste the oil against a harmonious but somewhat neutral background that will not mask the true oil flavor.

I occasionally see midpriced olive oils labeled extra-virgin that are almost electric green. These oils have been colored with chlorophyll pressed from olive leaves. I don't buy brands with this coloring anymore because I just don't feel certain I'm getting real extra-virgin oil.

I use up olive oil so quickly that storing it is not a problem. If you think you won't finish a bottle within three months, buy smaller bottles. Always keep them away from high heat and direct sunlight. Storing oil in the refrigerator is, in my experience, a bad idea; water drops tend to form inside the bottle, actually accelerating spoilage.

Olives: Black and green olives are not interchangeable in pasta sauces (or in any dishes) unless you want to dramatically change the character of the dish. Green olives are picked underripe. They have a crunchy texture and a sharp, pleasantly tart flavor. Olives left on the tree to ripen can be blackish purple or pitch-black; they are softer than green olives and have a rich, more mellow taste. You'll find olives in all shades in between, from very dark green to deep purple to mahogany brown. Most high-quality Italian olives are treated in a saltwater-brine bath for about a month to remove bitterness. Then they are cracked or left whole. Sometimes they are packed in olive oil or flavored with herbs, garlic, or citrus zest. Other olives are salt-cured or oil-cured. The type you choose will strongly affect the flavor of your pasta sauce in its direction. Taste an olive before you use it, and know what you will taste in your sauce.

Some of the green olives I like with pasta are the French picholine; the large and very mild Cerignola and Baresi dolce olives from Puglia; and Castelvetrano from Sicily. Many of the herb-flavored green olives from Italy, Greece, and Spain are wonderful in a pasta sauce, but remember that anything they're flavored with will carry over into your sauce. Look for cracked Sicilian olives flavored with fennel seeds and lemon zest to use in pasta-and-fish dishes.

Niçoise are wonderful black olives to use for olive pesto and to mix with tomato sauces. The brownish French Nyons olives are also good pasta olives because they're mild and sweet and don't overpower most sauces. The Greek Kalamata olive, and to a lesser extent the Italian Gaeta, is a good strong black olive for mixing into sauces, but it does overwhelm delicate flavors. Also try the wrinkled oil- or salt-cured French and Moroccan olives. Greek Atalanta, a juicy light brown olive, blends well with meat sauces. A cocoa-colored olive from Calabria called Monachara is soft but has a gentle bite and is wonderful mixed into a tomato sauce; the Abequina, a light brown one from Spain, I liked in an olive pesto that I tossed with spaghetti and ricotta.

Taste any olive you plan on including in a pasta dish. If it is overly salty or bitter, blanch the batch in boiling water for a few minutes. Don't let any olives cook too long in a sauce; they can lose their perfume and sometimes make the sauce bitter. Add them in the last five minutes of cooking. The easiest way to pit a large quantity of olives—something I learned from my years working in restaurant kitchens making buckets of tapenade—is by laying them out on a counter covered with a kitchen towel. Give them a few quick whacks with the bottom of a heavy pot to crack them open slightly and you should be able to pull the pits out easily with your fingers. Olives are most luscious at room temperature, and since they are preserved, they don't need refrigeration. Store them unrefrigerated, covered with olive oil and well sealed, and try to use them within a month.

Onions: A pasta sauce made with nothing but slow-cooked onions in a mix of olive oil and butter is a perfect example of the purity of flavors central to much of Italian cooking. Onions sautéed in olive oil are the starting point and backbone of many pasta sauces. Keeping several members of the onion family in your pantry frees you to create pasta dishes at the spur of the moment. In fact, onions and good olive oil are the two most important ingredients for improvisational sauces—with these two, you can go almost anywhere. Leeks, shallots, scallions, red onions, yellow onions, and sweet white onions such as Vidalia all add different character to pasta sauces. They can be stored in a dry, airy place (I keep mine in an open wicker basket) for about two weeks. Don't buy onions that are soft and sprouting green shoots; they should feel firm and ooze juice when you cut into them. Cut onions don't keep well. Whenever I save a half onion, wrapped and refrigerated, I find its flavor has soured by the next day. Buy both large and small ones so you needn't have leftover halves.

Oranges and lemons, for juice and zest: You'll taste a jolt of orange or lemon in many Sicilian and southern Italian pasta dishes, especially those made with rich fish such as sardines, swordfish, tuna, or anchovies. The juice is used, but it's the fruit's zest that often adds the enticing bittersweet perfume. Lemon zest is my secret ingredient for picking up a heavy sausage sauce. Lemon zest also gives an unexpected lift to *aglio e olio* (garlic and oil sauce). Lemon zest, chopped prosciutto, and black olives combine to make a vibrant sauce for spaghetti. You can add orange zest to a tomato and beef ragù for a touch of sunny flavor on the tongue. I've found the best way to remove citrus zest without picking up too much bitter white pith is with a swivel-handled vegetable peeler. It takes the zest off in thin sheets so you can slice it very thinly with a sharp knife. A standard zester also works well.

Pancetta: Pancetta is unsmoked Italian bacon made from lightly spiced salt-cured pork belly. The only kind you will find here is American made, but it is generally very good. In this country it is sold rolled up into a large sausage shape instead of in slabs or strips like American smoked bacon. In Italy you will find it that way or flat. You can buy as much as you need thinly sliced, or you can purchase a chunk to slice yourself. Make sure you have a very sharp knife; because of its high fat content, pancetta can be slippery to cut. A well-wrapped chunk will last about a month in the refrigerator.

Pancetta is the main flavoring ingredient in carbonara and amatriciana sauces. A bit of chopped pancetta browned along with onion and other aromatic vegetables is a classic Italian starting point for any number of simple vegetable or tomato sauces, and it is one of the characteristic flavors of many Italian pasta dishes. Pancetta is fatty, so cut it into small dice and brown it slowly in a skillet to render the fat. (In Rome, however, a dish of spaghetti carbonara has huge chunks of fatty pancetta in it, and Romans like it just fine—that's the beauty of the dish.) I like a taste of pancetta in clam sauce and as an added dimension in cream sauces.

Pasta, dried: Try to have on hand at all times at least one long, thin pasta (spaghetti, for instance) and one short, fat one (penne or ziti). That way, no matter what type of sauce you come up with at the spur of the moment, you'll have a pasta that is more or less appropriate.

Imported dried Italian pasta is always better than commercial American brands. This is because American brands are designed to cook up softer. The technology and machinery are imported from Italy, and our wheat is superb, so there's no reason why our pasta can't have nutty wheat taste and firm texture. American companies just don't choose to make it that way because Americans supposedly prefer their pasta soft.

Recently I've noticed several imported brands of southern Italian artisanal pasta. These are dried pastas produced in small factories in an old-fashioned way. They are dried slowly and have a rougher surface texture than mass-produced brands. The slow drying gives the pasta a deeper, nuttier flavor, and the uneven texture enables sauce to cling to it more easily than to the more slippery commercial brands. Look for packages with the names Latini, Setaro, La Ruvida, and Laporta. Another high-quality artisanal dried pasta called Martelli is made in Tuscany (see pages 379 and 380 for mail-order information).

Dried pasta is supposed to last indefinitely, but I find that a half-used box of spaghetti or an unopened box I've had hanging around for three or four months tends to become brittle and dry looking and to break up while cooking.

Pasta, fresh: See "Making Fresh Pasta," page 363.

Prosciutto: *Prosciutto* is Italian for *ham*. Prosciutto crudo, the lightly salted air-dried ham typically served with melon, is the type most people are familiar with. Prosciutto di Parma and prosciutto di San Daniele are both exquisite Italian hams of this type available in this country. Both are fairly fatty and sweet—although Prosciutto di Parma is generally thought to be saltier. Prosciutto di San Daniele, from the Friuli region, is leaner, darker red, and more assertively flavored than prosciutto di Parma. Other varieties of prosciutto crudo are made in the Veneto, Tuscany, and the Marches in Italy; most are not exported, so you'll want to sample some of them while visiting Italy. One other ham I do see here often is prosciutto di Carpegna, from a town on the borders of Romagna, the Marches, and Tuscany. It has a flavor like the Parma variety but is less sweet. Since it is made in smaller quantities, it is more expensive than Parma ham. I like the Parma ham better. Prosciutto cotto is a cooked ham (usually steamed), and it is also exported to this country. Both types of prosciutto are wonderful in pasta sauces, but the crudo varieties should be added to the sauce at the last minute so their sweet taste and soft texture are not spoiled. Cooked ham can simmer in a sauce. I sometimes trim the excess fat from prosciutto crudo and use it as a cooking fat along with a bit of olive oil or butter to sauté onions or garlic.

Buy all these hams very thinly sliced and buy only what you will use right away, since sliced prosciutto dries out quickly. The center cut from prosciutto is the tenderest part. Many Italian pork stores sell the salty, fatty ends of prosciutto to flavor sauces.

Spain makes a salt-cured ham called Serrano; it is served in Spanish tapas bars simply sliced and drizzled with olive oil. It has just very recently become available in this country. It is a little less delicate than the Italian hams and has a slightly chewy texture. It is usually cut a bit thicker than prosciutto. I use it in pasta dishes when I want a heartier ham taste.

American versions of Italian and Spanish cured hams are made, but I always find them saltier and cruder in flavor. However, American cooked hams such as Virginia ham can work well with pasta, as long as they're not too sweetened with brown sugar or maple syrup.

Salt: Once you start cooking with sea salt, you'll never want to use overprocessed, chemically treated table salt again.

Several types of sea salt are now imported to the United States. The highly prized French *fleur de sel,* hand-harvested in coastal areas around Brittany, is one of the finest sea salts on earth. It has a flaky texture, pale ivory color, and soft saltiness that speaks of the sea with no bitter aftertaste. I've heard people say it suggests violets, but I can smell only a sweet, damp sea aroma when I put my nose to a jar. It should be added to a dish at the last minute to preserve its delicate taste. Try it sprinkled over a bowl of tagliatelle dressed with asparagus sauce—or put a small bowl of it on the table for your guests to serve themselves.

Sel gris, a gray, less fine salt from the same areas, is also exported. It has exquisite flavor but is not as precious and can be used more liberally. La Baleine, a brand of French Mediterranean sea salt, is available at many supermarkets reasonably priced. It comes in coarse or fine grain. Use the fine grain on cold foods, and the coarse grain, which needs to be heated to dissolve, for cooking. *Sel gris* has a saltier and bolder flavor than the finer *fleur de sel,* which you'll find only at specialty food shops.

Another wonderful Mediterranean sea salt is harvested in the salt beds of Trapani, in Sicily; it has a bright, iodine sea flavor and is wonderful seasoning for pasta and fish dishes. This is the salt I prefer for all my Italian cooking. It is available at some Italian food shops and can be ordered through a wholesaler who sells it to Italian restaurants in this country whose chefs won't use anything else (see page 379 for a mail-order source).

Coarse-grained kosher salt is not a substitute for sea salt. It has a comparatively harsh chemical taste.

Spices: Buy whole rather than powdered spices, and buy them in small quantities; whole spices stay fresh longer. Nutmeg, cinnamon, cloves, fennel seeds, hot red pepper flakes, black peppercorns, bay leaves, and saffron are traditional Italian spices for pasta sauces. Coarsely ground black pepper is the predominant flavoring for the Roman dishes *cacio e pepe* and *pasta alla gricia.* Saffron and fennel seeds are used in Sicilian-style fish dishes. Look for a date on the package when purchasing saffron. You should find something that indicates when it was harvested. Don't buy saffron that is more than two years old. It may be stale.

Grind small amounts of spices as you need them with a mortar and pestle, a hand grater, or a spice grinder. For softer spices such as saffron, use a mortar and pestle. Fresh saffron is usually slightly moist, which is a good sign. But for saffron to dissolve completely in a liquid, it's best to grind it to a powder, which is a little difficult if it is too moist. I usually place my saffron threads in a small pan and, over low heat, dry them out for a few seconds on the stove. I frequently throw whole spices such as cloves into a sauce, not worrying too much about retrieving them (you can always secure spices and herbs in a little bundle of tied cheesecloth for easy removal).

Tomatoes, canned: Any cook who prepares much Italian food often has heard about San Marzano tomatoes. For the most part, I think their fame is justified, but many Italian products are imported into this country with low quality despite familiar names. San Marzano is a farming town near Naples and the name of a particular plum tomato that's grown there. San Marzano is the only town that can label its tomatoes "San Marzano." The San Marzano tomato looks like a slightly longer, curvy Roma tomato (the variety of plum we most often find in the United States) with a pointed tip. It has a lower sugar content than the Roma and has less water in its fruit and fewer seeds, making it firm and meaty. This reduced sweetness and firm texture are what give a sauce made from the San Marzano variety its rich, noncloying flavor. Also, the skin slips off easily after only a very brief boiling, leaving the tomatoes just about raw when canned. Most other Italian canned tomatoes are of the Roma variety, which are mild, sweet, and juicy by comparison.

The San Marzano variety is a bit longer and skinnier than the Roma, so you can usually tell the difference by opening the can and looking at the tomatoes. In my experience, La Valle and La Bella San Marzano brands are the real thing and are of consistently good quality.

Some American canned tomatoes are excellent. When I want a very light, refreshing sauce, I often use Redpack tomatoes or Muir Glen organic whole tomatoes.

Transfer any canned tomatoes you've opened but can't use right away to a sealed plastic container or ceramic bowl before refrigerating. Tomatoes refrigerated in an open can will pick up a metallic taste.

Tomato paste, canned crushed tomatoes, and sun-dried tomatoes: I find I have no use these days for tomato paste. I used to routinely add a bit to simmered tomato sauces until I realized I didn't appreciate the heavy flavor it contributed. Canned "crushed" tomatoes are another product I've outgrown. They usually contain less-than-perfect tomatoes and acidic tomato purée, and I don't like the overly smooth texture they give to a sauce.

If I want rich, concentrated tomato taste, I oven-dry my own plum tomatoes (see page 38) or use store-bought sun-dried tomatoes, maybe adding a few to a fresh tomato sauce to deepen the flavor. Sun-dried tomatoes come either packed in olive oil or dehydrated and dry. Dehydrated tomatoes need to soak in warm water for about five minutes to revitalize. Both types are good. I usually buy ones imported from southern Italy because they have a sweet flavor, but local sun-dried tomatoes can also be excellent.

Tuna: Canned Italian tuna packed in olive oil is an ingredient you'll come to rely on for improvising. With it you can change a plain tomato or olive oil sauce into a healthy and delicious main-course pasta dish in a minute. It's also wonderful in pasta salads. Canned tuna should be drained before it is added to a sauce. For the best flavor and texture, add it at the last minute, just to warm it through. Canned tuna allowed to simmer in a sauce loses its flavor.

Vinegar: I'm not a huge fan of vinegar in pasta, but a small splash of good-quality vinegar can boost pasta salads and add sparkle to fish sauces, replacing the more common reach for a squeeze of lemon. Meat sauces, especially long-simmered ragùs, can also often benefit from a last-minute shot of acidity.

Balsamic vinegar is the kind most suited for pasta, especially sauces with eggplant and tomatoes, but also try it with a pork sausage sauce. This sweet, dark vinegar is made from the concentrated must of Trebbiano grapes—a white wine grape. True balsamic vinegars are made in the provinces of Modena and Reggio in central Italy. Very expensive long-aged vinegars are made by traditional artisan methods by small producers. They must be aged in wood for at least twelve years to develop their harmonious sweet-and-sour taste. But for cooking, choose a commercially made balsamic from this region. These industrial vinegars are not as fine and mellow as the artisanal bottles, but their flavors soften wonderfully when cooked briefly into a dish. The quality of these vinegars varies wildly, but two brands I've found consistently good are Fini and Cavalli. You'll see balsamic vinegar made in other parts of Italy in your markets, but they are rarely as good as the real thing.

Some chefs like to boil and reduce balsamic vinegar down to a syrup to use as a sauce for meats and fish. To my taste, this flavoring when added to a pasta sauce creates a flavor-like ketchup. I always add balsamic vinegar in the last few minutes of cooking to preserve its sweet-and-sour flavor.

Sherry vinegar is strong but sweet and worth experimenting with. Look for imported Spanish brands, and try adding a splash of it to roasted-vegetable sauces (see Orecchiette with Roasted Corn, Red Peppers, Ricotta Salata, page 108).

Champagne vinegar, red wine vinegar, and white wine vinegar can be used sparingly, but make sure the vinegar you use is not overly acidic or it will be too assertive for your sauce. I generally use a French brand called Dutour. I like to add a splash of tarragon white wine vinegar to a lamb or pork ragù at the last minute. You can also marinate the meat for a ragù in vinegar before browning it (be sure to pat it dry first). But too much vinegar, especially in a pasta salad, always makes pasta taste like it was brought home from a take-out deli.

Store all vinegars away from direct oven heat and strong sunlight.

Wine and good spirits to cook with: When I choose a wine to cook into a pasta dish, more often it will be the same wine I serve at the table with the dish. What's good inside the dish is good with it.

There are basically two ways to use wine in pasta cooking. The first is to add a splash of wine to deglaze the pan after sautéing onions or other aromatic vegetables for a soffritto. In this case you let the wine quickly boil away, leaving just a hint of its essence, before adding other ingredients such as vegetables. The other way, used when you make a long-simmered ragù or other meat sauce, is to employ a good amount of wine, usually a cup or more, to slow-cook and impart its flavor into the meat while its alcohol gradually boils away. When using wine for a long-simmered sauce, remember not to add more wine once the dish has started cooking. If the liquid starts boiling away too rapidly, add water or a light broth. Adding wine midway or toward the end of cooking will most likely sour the dish because the wine won't have enough time to cook out, releasing all its alcohol and becoming mellow.

I use so many types of wine in cooking that it's hard to recommend a few in particular, but in general, remember that the sweetness or dryness of your wine will be apparent in the finished taste of your dish. Also, I tend to avoid overly oaky wines in cooking, such as heavily oaked Chardonnays or Cabernets. They leave a leaden flavor that doesn't blend well with Italian seasonings. Occasionally, for authenticity's sake, I purposely choose a Chianti for a Tuscan pasta sauce, or a Sicilian wine for a Sicilian fish sauce, but in general, if I choose a wine that harmonizes well with my dinner, it means the wine will be a good one to cook into my dish as well.

I haven't had much luck adding rosé wine to pasta sauces; it seems to sour them. A semisweet or sweet dessert wine can be a good addition to long-simmered sauces, especially ones made with duck or pork. And it can also be delicious simmered with squid, emphasizing the fish's innate sweetness. I sometimes add a splash of vin santo or another sweet dessert wine to a shrimp, scallop, or lobster sauce. Use dry or sweet Marsala with lamb or pork sauces; sweet red or dry white vermouth for clam or fish sauces; and a splash of vodka or grappa to liven up a tomato sauce. Pastis—a French anise-flavored liquor (Pernod is the most commonly available in the United States)—is wonderful in many fish sauces. A shot of brandy or cognac is very important for removing an overly livery taste in sautéed chicken livers. Make sure to add all alcohol toward the beginning of cooking so it will have a chance to lose its raw taste and impart only its essence to the dish.

If you've had a half bottle of wine open for a few days and it starts to taste turned, don't use it for cooking. It will only make your dish taste of turned wine. If it's not good enough to drink, it's not good enough to cook with.

Good Italian Cheeses to Use with Pasta

Many varieties of Italian cheese are now exported to America. When I was a kid, it seemed all we could get was provolone, Pecorino Romano, and preground, fake Parmesan, even though I lived in an Italian neighborhood twenty miles from New York City. Now my local supermarket carries Gorgonzola dolce, robiola, and Sardinian Pecorino.

This is my list of good Italian cheeses to incorporate into or sprinkle on top of pasta dishes. They fall into two basic categories—grating cheeses and melting cheeses—with some overlapping.

The purpose of the list is to get you away from automatically thinking a Parmesan-type cheese should be on every dish. That creates a sameness in pasta sauces. Look for new imports you are unfamiliar with and ask your cheesemonger for a small taste. In the last few months my local shop has started carrying caprino, an Italian goat cheese, in fresh and aged varieties. I'd never previously seen this cheese outside Italy. If you are uncertain a cheese is right for your pasta dish, ask your cheese seller questions: Does it grate? Does it melt? Is it sharp or mild? Would it be better with tomatoes or asparagus?

Scattered throughout this book you'll find some recipes using cheeses that are not Italian but are nevertheless wonderful with pasta, such as American goat cheeses, Greek feta, French Gruyère and Comtè, and Spanish Manchego. I avoid non-Italian cheeses for use with pasta if I find they lend a very non-Italian taste. For instance, sharp English or American cheddar is, in my opinion, out of place in an Italian pasta dish, clashing with common Italian herbs and delicate ingredients like prosciutto. Some blue cheeses—English Stilton, for example—are too strong for any pasta sauce.

Asiago: A cow's milk cheese made in the Veneto region of Italy. It is slightly piquant but still has a delicate flavor. It is available in Italy young and as an older grating cheese. The Asiago I've purchased here is usually at the grating stage. I've also bought Asiago fresco, a slightly aged Asiago, which is soft like a fontina but has a subtle tang. If you can find this, it's wonderful melted into a pancetta- and onion-flavored tomato sauce. Older Asiago is slightly sharper and can be grated over pasta. Also use it thinly shaved and layered in a fall vegetable lasagne.

Bel Paese: This Italian cow's milk cheese, popular in the United States, is distinguished by its coating of yellow wax and very mild flavor. It melts easily and can be used in place of mozzarella in baked pasta dishes, although the result won't be as sweet and flavorful. Tiny cubes of Bel Paese tossed into a strongly flavored pasta salad will round it out, adding a mellow tone. I also like Bel Paese added to a pasta dish sauced with canned Italian tuna and black olives.

Caciocavallo: The ball-shaped cheese usually hung in pairs is caciocavallo. Its name, which means horse cheese, is thought to come from the practice of slinging the rope-tied cheeses over a pole the way you mount a horse, leaving them to ripen. This cow's milk cheese originated in Campania (the region of Italy that encompasses Naples) and is now made in Sicily as well, where it is sometimes made partly with goat's milk. It is soft when young (this type is used in cooking because it melts beautifully), but the type you'll find here is usually a little older and is best for grating. In southern Italy caciocavallo is grated over pasta as often as Parmigiano-Reggiano is in the north, but its flavor is very different. Caciocavallo is a variation of provolone, but it is usually less sharp. It is my choice for putting the finishing touch on a robust Sicilian-style eggplant-sauced pasta or a Neapolitan tomato and sausage ragù.

Caciotta: This is a generic term for a variety of small, farm-made cheeses from central Italy. They can be made from cow's, sheep's, or goat's milk, or sometimes combinations of all three, although all the caciotta cheeses I've seen in this country have been of sheep's milk. Large factory-made versions of these cheeses are also made, but they are not as distinctly flavored as the artisanal varieties. In this country you're likely to buy wedges of factory-made caciotta Toscana, a slightly creamy, sweet sheep's milk cheese that blends extremely well with delicate vegetable sauces and with complex but subtle ragù sauces. I have also bought caciotta di Siena, caciotta di Roma, and a small Tuscan farm cheese called caciotta d'oro, which has a creamy texture and sweet, grassy flavor. The taste of these cheeses varies from very mild and sweet to piquant, depending on the variety. All are fine pasta cheeses. *Cacio* is an old word for cheese in central and southern Italy.

Caprino: France is not the only country that produces great goat cheeses. Italian caprino (the name comes from *goat*) is available in our markets. You can find both fresh and aged versions. The fresh version is wonderful for melting into pasta dishes or in a dish of baked ziti. Use the stronger, aged cheeses for crumbling conservatively onto dressed pasta. Sardinia and the Abruzzo region are known for their goat cheeses, but I have yet to see these at my market. I recently bought a fresh goat cheese log from the Piedmont region, and it was tangy and wonderful tossed into penne with eggplant and olive sauce. All of the caprino I've tasted here has been on the pungent side. If your cheese tastes too strong, consider using half caprino and half ricotta in your sauce.

Crescenza: A soft cow's milk cheese from Lombardy, in the north of Italy, Crescenza has a taste like rich cream. The texture is soft and loose, and it melts beautifully when tossed with hot pasta, but its delicate taste would be lost in a baked pasta dish. Try to use this fresh cheese no later than a day or two after you buy it, as it goes off quickly. I once made ziti with a sauce of butternut squash, leeks, and this cheese; it was rich and delicious. Fresh Crescenza is one of several Lombardy cheeses under a category called Stracchino, and you might, in fact, see it labeled as Stracchino Crescenza in your market. Robiola, Taleggio, and Gorgonzola are aged varieties of Stracchino cheeses.

Fontina: A high-fat, semisoft cow's milk cheese with a pale yellow color, fontina comes from the Valle d'Aosta region, in northwest Italy. It has a sweet, slightly nutty taste and a creamy texture. It is one of the best Italian melting cheeses and makes a marvelous sauce for gnocchi or egg pasta. It can be melted into a vegetable sauce for richness, blending especially well with spinach, leeks, and asparagus. It's also wonderful baked in lasagne in place of the more commonly used mozzarella. There are American and Swedish cheeses marketed under the name Fontina, but I haven't found one that comes close to the suave creaminess of the original. Look for the words "Fontina dalla Val'Aosta" on the rind to make sure you're buying the real McCoy.

Gorgonzola: Produced near Milan, this famous Italian blue cheese is made from cow's milk and is sold either young (called Gorgonzola dolce) or aged. Both melt effortlessly into pasta sauces, but the dolce version is much milder. Add a dollop of either type to a plain tomato sauce or to a cream-based vegetable sauce. I like melting a few tablespoons of Gorgonzola dolce into an Alfredo sauce for unexpected flavor. Gorgonzola sauce is a classic for potato gnocchi, but try it on spinach ravioli and as a sauce for fresh egg pasta.

Grana Padano: Made in different parts of northern Italy, this hard, aged cheese is easy to find here and costs a few dollars less per pound than Parmigiano-Reggiano. It is not aged as long as Parmigiano-Reggiano, and its taste is less sweet and complex, but don't overlook it. It may lack the refinement of Parmigiano-Reggiano, but when it's purchased fresh and freshly grated, it can add a slightly nutty sweetness to ragù sauces, cream-based sauces, and delicate vegetable-sauced pasta dishes that a Pecorino might overpower. Like Parmigiano-Reggiano, it melts beautifully. Grana Padano will last several months in your refrigerator if kept well wrapped.

Mascarpone: A velvety textured, 90-percent-fat cow's milk cheese, mascarpone is excellent for enriching pasta sauces. Eating it is like eating solidified cream. Use it in place of cream, but add it at the last minute and heat it very gently; it can sometimes separate. I love a dollop of mascarpone in *penne alla vodka* in place of the usual cream. Freshly cooked tagliatelle tossed with toasted walnuts, mascarpone, and a little grated Parmigiano-Reggiano is a dish made in heaven. My cheese seller makes his own mascarpone, and it is wonderful; you can also buy a commercial product in 9- or 15-ounce containers. Mascarpone, like all fresh cheeses, is very perishable and should be used within a day or two after purchase.

Montasio: This semisoft cow's milk cheese from Friuli is now also made in the Venice area. When young it is sweet; as it ages, it becomes nutty tasting. When well aged and hard, it can have the piquant qualities of a Pecorino. I usually find the softer, younger variety in my cheese shop. I like young Montasio melted into a veal sauce or used in place of Grana Padano in a spinach- and ricotta-stuffed pasta filling.

Mozzarella (fresh or smoked): This soft, fresh cheese is made in this country from cow's milk. In southern Italy the best mozzarella is made from the milk of the water buffalo, which gives it a delicate tang (cow's milk mozzarella is also made in Italy, where it is called *fior di latte*). Buffalo-milk mozzarella is exported to the United States, but the several times I've tried it here it seemed sour and a little past its prime. All mozzarella is best the day it's made and acceptable a day or two after. Now I always ask my cheese seller when the cheese was made and shipped.

Supermarket-brand mozzarella is firmer and less moist than freshly made mozzarella and should be used only as a last resort. When heated, mozzarella becomes soft and stringy, imparting milky sweetness to baked ziti or lasagne. It's also delicious cut into tiny cubes and added to a dish of spaghetti while you are tossing it with a tomato sauce. I love adding little chunks to a pasta salad. Whenever I buy freshly made mozzarella, I try to use it right away and not refrigerate it, which corrupts its loose, milky texture.

Smoked mozzarella is a little too smoky for my taste and dominates most pasta sauces, but paired with other strong flavors, such as sausage or roasted peppers, it can blend well.

Parmigiano-Reggiano: This is the top-of-the-line aged cow's milk cheese made only in a defined zone within the provinces of Parma, Reggio nell'Emilia, Bologna, Modena, and Mantova. A true Parmigiano-Reggiano will have its name stamped on the rind. Use it on delicate pasta dishes such as stuffed *pasta in brodo,* or with tortellini or in cream sauces. For an exquisite treat, toss fresh tagliatelle with sweet butter, strips of prosciutto, and grated Parmigiano.

Authentic Parmigiano should have a soft, tannish yellow color and be firm but still slightly moist when cut. When really fresh, it smells to me a bit like ripe pineapple. Always buy it in small chunks and grate just as much as you need right before using it to preserve its special fruity sweetness. Save the rinds to flavor soups and stews.

Pecorino: Made throughout Tuscany and southern Italy, Pecorino is a sheep's milk cheese, although factory-made versions also include cow's milk. There are subtle differences in flavor depending on where the cheese is made. In general, Tuscan Pecorinos are milder than those from Rome and the south. Many good ones are exported to America. They are excellent for grating, shaving onto pasta, or melting into sauce. In Italy, Pecorino is one of the cheeses traditionally used in Genoese pesto. Look for cheeses labeled Pecorino Romano (Locatelli Romano—a common brand—is also a Roman Pecorino), Toscano, Senese (from Siena), or Sicilia. Tuscan Pecorino is especially delicate, and although most varieties are tangy, they never edge toward sharp the way Pecorino Romano does. Sicilian pepato, containing whole black peppercorns, is a spicy Pecorino good for grating over robust dishes such as penne with eggplant. Rome's famous *spaghetti alla gricia* is tossed with cooked pancetta, olive oil, black pepper, and grated Pecorino Romano. Fiore Sardo and Pecorino Sardo are names for Sardinian Pecorino, a cheese that can be sweet or piquant, depending on its age.

Provolone: In southern Italy this cheese is made from a variety of milks, including buffalo milk, but in this country you're likely to find the cow's milk version. It is always sharp and assertive, even when young. Aged versions will overpower any delicate pasta sauce. But pair provolone with a roasted pepper sauce or a bold lamb ragù and see how it complements strong flavors. I also like it shaved onto hot pasta; grating releases a strong aroma.

Ricotta: This milk product is made from the whey left over from making hard cheeses. In this country you're likely to find cow's milk ricotta, but around Rome and in Sicily, a sheep's milk version is preferred for its delicate tang (in Sicily cannoli are made with sheep's milk ricotta, and their taste is a revelation). I've bought imported sheep's milk ricotta at cheese shops in New York, and it has been excellent all but once, when it was definitely not at its freshest; ask for a taste before you buy it.

Just-cooked spaghetti tossed with fresh ricotta and an ample amount of black pepper is a dish I get cravings for. I also love a dollop of ricotta blended into a basil-scented tomato sauce. This is the cheese traditionally used to layer into lasagne and to fill ravioli and cannelloni. Try to find a cheese shop that makes its own ricotta; the supermarket brands sold in plastic tubs lack sweetness. Make sure to use this cheese a day or two after purchasing it, since it sours quickly.

Ricotta salata: This is salted, dried ricotta. It has a soft but crumbly texture and won't melt into creaminess but will instead soften when tossed with hot pasta, infusing your sauce with bits of salty tang. The taste and texture remind me of Greek feta. It's an excellent cheese for adding a piquant dimension to assertive vegetable or sausage sauces. It goes well with sun-dried tomatoes, olives, eggplant, and pork sauces. I almost always crumble ricotta salata on top of a sausage and broccoli rabe–dressed pasta before serving. It keeps for about a month, well wrapped, in your refrigerator.

Robiola and Taleggio: Robiola and Taleggio are both soft, lightly aged Stracchino cheeses from Lombardy with a buttery taste and a runny texture somewhat like Brie. They are rich and high in fat. The kind you'll find here are made from cow's milk, but in Italy cow's, sheep's, and sometimes goat's milk are also used. Both cheeses melt easily, making them perfect for cooking into a creamy pasta sauce. Robiola is aged less than Taleggio, so it has a softer texture and lighter, creamier taste, somewhat like good sweet cream. I like melting a few tablespoons into a wild mushroom sauce right before tossing with pasta. Taleggio has more body and a stronger taste than Robiola, which makes it a better choice to use in baked dishes. Both cheeses are quite fragile and should be used within a day or two of purchase.

Scamorza: This is a type of salted cow's milk mozzarella from the regions of the Abruzzo and Molise, where it is frequently cooked into pasta sauces. It is molded into a small pear shape and tied with cords. The fresh version is soft and delicately flavored. Scamorza is also sold in a lightly dried form that is good for shredding (it doesn't exactly grate). There is also a smoked scamorza, which is firm, with a tan rind and smoky flavor. I have never seen imported scamorza in this country, but a few Italian cheese shops in New York City make their own, and some of it is excellent. You will also find several very decent commercial brands in Italian grocery stores.

Making
Fresh Pasta

When homemade pasta comes out well, it's a thoroughly exciting and rewarding experience, and the taste is far better than anything you can buy. It's thinner, richer, and more delicate. It holds sauce better. I've found that most people need a few tries before they can make pasta with wonderful texture. Simple, clear instructions are very important, but no book can tell you exactly how a proper dough should feel in your hands. The size and moisture content of the eggs, the absorbency of the flour (usually determined by age and how it has been stored), and even the humidity in your kitchen will all affect the final results. You may find yourself using a little more or a little less flour than called for. Only after making pasta several times will you begin to recognize when you've got the dough exactly right: moist but not sticky, resilient but smooth and silky to the touch.

Fresh pasta should be delicate but elastic. You achieve this by slow kneading, giving the dough a chance to rest, and gradually stretching the dough out into sheets. Rolling the dough out with a rolling pin will give you a slightly finer-textured pasta sheet than if you stretch it with a hand-cranked pasta machine. But I must admit that more often than not I use my pasta machine, mainly because I have so little workspace. If you run the dough through the machine slowly, making it gradually thinner and thinner, you will achieve a very fine, velvety sheet of pasta, maybe a bit more compact and uniform in texture than by the hand-rolled method, but still a high-quality pasta, which can now be hand-cut into any of myriad lengths and shapes or passed through the pasta machine using the cutter blades to make tagliarini or tagliatelle.

Plain Egg Pasta

The following two recipes give the basic instructions for making the pasta used throughout this book.

Plain Egg Pasta

This pasta recipe makes enough dough for 4 moderate main-course servings or 5 or 6 first-course servings of tagliatelle, tagliarini, or pappardelle.

[Makes about 1 pound]

About 3½ cups unbleached all-purpose flour, plus extra for kneading

4 large eggs
A drizzle of olive oil

- Follow the directions on page 365 to make the pasta.

Three-Egg Pasta

This recipe makes enough dough for a 12 x 10 x 2-inch lasagne or for 4 moderate main-course or 5 or 6 small first-course servings of ravioli or cannelloni, all of which should be rolled very thin.

[Makes about ¾ pound]

About 2½ cups unbleached all-purpose flour, plus extra for kneading

3 large eggs
A drizzle of olive oil

- Place the flour in a mound on a large wooden or plastic surface, like a countertop or a cutting board. (Do not make pasta on a stainless steel or marble surface. These materials can be too cold and may reduce the elasticity of the dough.)
- Make a wide well in the middle of the mound of flour and crack the eggs into it. Add a drizzle of olive oil. Start beating the eggs with a fork, pulling a bit of flour in from the sides of the mound. As you do this, keep pushing the flour up around the well so the egg mixture doesn't spill out.
- When the dough forms a ball and becomes too stiff to work with your fork, start kneading the dough with your hands, incorporating as much additional flour as you can. You will inevitably have some flour left over that will be a bit lumpy. Push it to the side, scraping it up from the surface with a dough scraper or metal pastry spatula.
- Sprinkle some fresh flour on your counter and start kneading the dough by folding it in half with the palm of your hand. Push the dough down and away from you with your palm, stretching it out rather than compressing it. The dough will at first be sticky, but as you continue kneading it will become smoother. Keep folding it over and stretching it until you have a smooth ball. If the dough continues to be sticky, sprinkle it with a tiny amount of flour and continue kneading to incorporate the flour. Knead the dough for a total of about 10 minutes (a little longer if you are a beginning kneader). The kneading process is very important for achieving a light, smooth dough, so don't look for a shortcut here.
- Wrap the dough in plastic wrap and let it rest unrefrigerated for about 30 minutes. This allows the gluten in the flour to relax so the dough will be easier to stretch.
- Before rolling, cut the dough into 6 pieces to make it easier to work with. Keep the dough you are not immediately using wrapped in plastic.
- To hand roll, you will need a large, flat surface such as a wooden or plastic countertop or large cutting board. It is easiest to roll out large sheets of pasta if you have a long, thin pastry rolling pin (these are usually 23 or 24 inches long). Make sure that the

rolling surface is very clean and dry. Dust the surface with flour. With the palm of your hands, flatten a piece of dough out into a more or less round disk. Place it in the middle of your rolling surface and dust it with flour. Place the rolling pin in the center of the dough and start rolling it out toward the edge. Pick the dough up off the surface and give it a quarter turn. Place the rolling pin in the center of the dough and roll it out to the edge again. Keep turning the dough and rolling it out away from the center until you have a large, very thin, smooth, round sheet. You should be able to see your hand through it when you hold it up to the light. Turn the dough over once or twice during the rolling to make sure it isn't sticking to the surface. Flour it lightly if it is. Repeat with all the pieces of dough.

- To stretch the dough using a hand-cranked pasta machine, start running a piece of dough through the widest setting on your pasta machine. Do this a couple of times. Then start running it through on thinner and thinner settings. Don't jump from very wide to very thin. Gradual stretching is necessary to achieve a smooth sheet of dough. If the sheets get too long to comfortably handle, cut them in half. Repeat with all the dough pieces. If I'm making tagliatelle or pappardelle, I usually stop at the next-to-last setting (it is too hard to cut extremely thin pasta sheets into these long shapes). For lasagne or ravioli, I make the sheet as thin as possible.

- Lay the finished pasta sheets on a lightly floured countertop and let them dry a few minutes before cutting into the desired shape. This way, the strands won't stick together. Sprinkle the sheets very lightly with flour if they seem sticky.

- Now you are ready to cut the pasta into shapes (see page 369), either by hand or using the cutter blades on the hand-cranked pasta machine. I usually sprinkle a little flour over the cutter attachment to my hand-cranked machine before I run each set through so the strands won't stick together.

- Your pasta can be cooked right away. It can also be held in the refrigerator for up to 2 days. To do this, after cutting it into the desired lengths, let it dry for about 40 minutes (it should be leathery and flexible but not brittle) and then wrap it in plastic wrap or plastic bags and refrigerate. Fresh pasta can also be well wrapped and frozen for about 3 weeks.

A note about using the food processor: Don't try to knead the dough in a food processor; it works it too fast, so it doesn't develop the right amount of gluten, which allows the dough to stretch without tearing. Sometimes if I'm in a hurry, I'll begin the mixing in the food processor. The advantage of this approach is that it is very neat. The only problem I've found is that the machine pulls in every bit of flour, whether the eggs can absorb it or not, so if you use the usual portions, you can end up with a floury dough that doesn't hold together.

So what I do is start with about ¼ cup less flour than I would use if mixing by hand. I put the flour, eggs, and olive oil in the food processor and process them for a few seconds to mix them together until the dough just starts to form a loose ball. Stop the machine the minute this happens, dump the dough out onto a floured surface, and knead as usual. I've found there is no substitution for hand kneading. All the food processor can really do is blend the flour and eggs together in a neat, confined space.

Flavoring Plain Egg Pasta

Many Italian food purists think little of all the new flavored pastas, such as those with roasted garlic and jalapeño pepper, but traditional pasta flavoring can seem just as bizarre. Chocolate, beets, and green bell pepper pasta are all in the classic repertoire. I've had the best luck with herb, saffron, and black pepper pasta, in which the flavor can really come through. Throughout the book I've suggested different flavored pastas for several of my recipes. You'll find the recipes for these pastas here, but remember these are only suggestions. You can always substitute homemade plain egg pasta or high-quality store-bought fresh pasta.

The following flavored recipes are made with the Plain Egg Pasta recipe on page 364. For flavoring Three-Egg Pasta (page 365), use about half of the amount of any of the ingredients called for.

Green Pasta: This green pasta is made with spinach and watercress. Wash, stem, and leave slightly wet a small bunch of fresh spinach and a small bunch of watercress. Puree the greens in a food processor until you have a smooth paste. The little bit of water clinging to the leaves will help to give you a relatively smooth purée. You should have about ½ cup. Add this to the flour well, along with the eggs and oil, and mix into the dough. This mix of raw spinach and watercress produces a pretty, bright green pasta dough with a herby taste that is especially delicious layered into a ricotta-based lasagne with tomato sauce.

Note: Frozen spinach works well here instead of fresh. Simply thaw it out, drain it very well, and puree it. Use about ½ cup well-drained purée instead of the mix of fresh spinach and watercress. You can make other types of green pasta by adding the same amount of pureed raw arugula, borage, or young chard leaves (trimmed of stalks). Or use all fresh watercress or all spinach. A mix of half parsley and half spinach creates a gentle, sweet pasta perfect for rich seafood sauces.

White or Red Wine Pasta: The addition of white wine makes pasta very light but sturdy and a little less rich than straight egg pasta. Add about ⅓ cup to the well when you are making Plain Egg Pasta and leave out one of the eggs. This is especially good for rich fish fillings and fillings with a lot of cheese. Red wine can also be used to make a pink-tinted pasta that is beautiful and warming used in a meat lasagne.

Marsala-Flavored Pasta: This is wonderful with game, poultry, or mushroom sauces. Add about ⅓ cup dry Marsala to the flour well and omit one of the eggs. You can also make this with vin santo or another sweet white wine.

Vinegar Pasta: A tablespoon or so of high-quality white or red wine vinegar added to your dough will infuse a subtle brightness into your pasta. White wine vinegar gives the pasta a gentle acidity that is especially delicious when used to make seafood ravioli. Try red wine vinegar pasta for duck ravioli.

Herb Pasta: Any fresh herb or combination of herbs can be added to the basic pasta dough recipe to create subtle herb flavor. About ½ cup finely chopped stemmed herbs is enough to flavor a pound of dough. Rosemary, sage, parsley, basil, thyme, or marjoram works especially well. Basil-and-parsley pasta is wonderful with a white clam sauce. Half mint and half parsley pasta is delicious tossed with a ricotta-based sauce.

Black or Red Pepper or Paprika Pasta: Add about 1 tablespoon of finely ground black pepper or Spanish or Hungarian paprika to the eggs and mix it into the dough. If you like a spicy pasta, include a pinch of cayenne or use a spicy paprika. Paprika pasta is excellent with sausage or lamb sauce. I love black pepper pasta with Uncooked Tomato Sauce (page 34) or with a carbonara sauce (page 274). Remember to grind the black pepper fine so it doesn't tear the dough.

Nutmeg or Mace Pasta: Add about 1 tablespoon freshly ground spice to the pasta dough well and mix it into the dough. Try these with ragù sauces, with a cream and Parmigiano sauce, or with a meat ragù.

Fennel Seed Pasta: Especially delicious with seafood or sausage sauces. Grind about 1 tablespoon lightly toasted fennel seeds to a powder and incorporate it into the dough while you are working in the eggs.

Saffron Pasta: This looks and tastes beautiful in a fish stew or tossed with mussels and olive oil. I also like it with sauces containing black olives and tomatoes. Grind a large pinch of saffron threads to a powder and soak it in a small amount of hot water (a few tablespoons should be sufficient). Add this while you are working the eggs into the pasta dough.

Lemon or Orange Zest Pasta: Add the zest of 2 lemons or oranges to the basic dough. A little nutmeg is good mixed with the lemon zest. Try serving lemon zest pasta with a summer tomato sauce flavored with basil. Orange zest pasta will liven up an Alfredo sauce and is also wonderful with olive oil and fresh herb sauces.

Tomato Pasta: Add about 2 tablespoons tomato paste or an equal amount of well-pureed sun-dried tomatoes (previously soaked and drained if they are the dried version) to the Plain Egg Pasta dough recipe and work it into the dough.

Mushroom Pasta: Soak ½ cup dried porcini mushrooms in hot water until soft. Drain and puree in a food processor until smooth and add to the flour well while making your pasta (add the soaking liquid to your pasta sauce). Try this with a cream-based sauce or with a simple mushroom, garlic, and oil sauce. Mushroom-flavored pasta is also good simply tossed with butter and a chopped fresh herb like marjoram or basil.

Garlic Pasta: Very finely minced fresh garlic can be added to pasta dough, but make sure you use very young, fresh garlic or the taste may be a little strong. You can include garlic in tomato, herb (especially rosemary), mushroom, or green pasta as well.

Beet Pasta: Puree 1 medium cooked, peeled beet and add to the pasta. This will tint your pasta a beautiful bright pink. I love this slightly sweet pasta tossed with butter and grated Grana Padano or Parmigiano. In Italy beet pasta is frequently used for making ravioli filled with greens and ricotta. The taste of beet pasta is very subtle. I think the color is its main appeal.

Red and Green Bell Pepper Pasta: Stem and seed 1 bell pepper, any color you like, and cut it into small chunks. Puree in a food processor along with 1 or 2 garlic cloves (if you like) until very smooth. Add to the pasta dough when you are mixing in the eggs. Try bell pepper pasta with a lamb ragù (page 310) or with tomato and ricotta sauces.

Cutting Pasta Shapes

Here are some easy pasta shapes to make using fresh egg pasta.

Tagliatelle, Tagliarini, and Pappardelle: Tagliatelle (also called fettuccine in Rome but usually cut a bit thinner) and tagliarini can be cut using the two settings on your pasta machine (the thicker one is for tagliatelle). Or you can cut it by hand: Let the pasta sheets dry for about 5 minutes, depending on how moist they are. Wait until the sheets are slightly leathery but not brittle. Roll the sheets up into loose cylinders and cut them into strips with a sharp knife. Unroll the strips and dust them lightly with flour so they don't stick together. Since there is no pappardelle setting on most hand-cranked pasta machines, it needs to be cut by hand.

Tagliarini should be cut about ¼ inch thick, tagliatelle about ⅓ inch thick, and pappardelle about ¾ inch thick. The general length for all these pastas is about 10 inches.

Lasagne: I roll the dough out on a pasta machine to the last setting. This gives me a very thin, delicate sheet, which is really essential for light lasagne. You can cut the sheets the same length as your lasagne dish or make them a little longer if you like to fold the ends into the dish. If you have leftover short squares of pasta, that's okay—they work fine for layering lasagne. Any less-than-perfect or slightly ragged sheets can be hidden inside the layers, and no one will ever know. Hand-rolled pasta sheets can be cut into large squares to fit your lasagne dish, or into long, thick lengths as described above.

A note about store-bought lasagne sheets: If you're purchasing fresh pasta sheets for lasagne, make sure that you find a place that will roll it very thin for you. Most store-bought fresh pasta is just too thick and clunky to make very delicate lasagne, so shop around.

Cannelloni: A hand-cranked pasta machine will give you long pasta sheets about 5 or 6 inches wide. For cannelloni, cut these sheets into squares. I've found that the best way to fill them is by spreading an even but thin layer of filling over the entire square and rolling it up like a jelly roll, keeping it fairly loose.

Fazzoletti: These thin pasta handkerchiefs are usually about 4 inches square and rolled very thin so they can fall onto the plate in elegantly draped folds. They are especially wonderful made with white wine, which makes them very light but resilient (see White Wine Pasta, page 367).

Quadrucci: These are small soup pasta pieces made by cutting tagliatelle or pappardelle into squares.

Ravioli: For me, the easiest way to make ravioli is to make them large, about 2 inches square. I roll out a pasta sheet to the last setting and place it on a lightly floured surface. I dot the sheet at even intervals with about 1 tablespoon of filling. I wet the edges with a pastry brush and place another sheet of pasta on top. Then I press down around the packages to make sure there are no air bubbles. Finally, I cut the edges with a sharp knife.

You can make smaller ravioli by placing a teaspoon or so of filling at even intervals along one side of your pasta sheet and folding it over lengthwise.

Ravioli-type pasta comes in many variations and is known by several regional names. Keeping all these names straight is a challenge and is beside the point for the purposes of this book. But here are a few other commonly made shapes you can play with:

Round Ravioli: Make round ravioli with a round cookie cutter. A 2-inch cutter works well, but you can make them bigger if you like. Cut the pasta sheets into rounds with the cutter (dust the cutter edges with flour so the pasta doesn't stick). Place about 1 teaspoon of filling in the middle on half of the rounds. Wet the edges with a pastry brush and place another round on top. Press down with your fingers to seal them well.

Half-Moon Ravioli (Mezzelune): Half-moon shapes are made by cutting circles of any size you like with a cookie cutter, placing the filling on one side, brushing the edges with water, and folding the pasta in half. Make sure to press down around the edges to form a sturdy seal.

Triangle Ravioli: Cut 3- or 4-inch squares from your pasta sheet. Place 1 teaspoon of filling on one side, wet the edges with a pastry brush, and fold the square over into a triangle.

Ideas for Matching Sauces to Pasta

Long fresh egg pasta: Tagliarini, tagliatelle (fettuccine), pappardelle

Comments: Sophisticated, mellow, and rich are the seasonings I would strive for when pairing sauces with these types of fresh egg pasta. Direct, bold flavors such as olives or lots of garlic would overwhelm them.

Sauce ideas: Tomato sauce simmered with cream. Sophisticated ragù sauces such as *ragù alla Bolognese*. Rich game sauces; pappardelle with hare (or rabbit) sauce is a classic. Tagliatelle with chicken livers and mushrooms. Rich, sweet seafood, such as lobster, scallops, and salmon, complement egg pasta. Complex vegetable sauces, such as a primavera. Mushrooms sautéed in butter and broth. Unsalted butter, prosciutto, and Parmigiano. Unsalted butter and chopped gentle herbs. A sauce of Gorgonzola and cream.

Ravioli and other stuffed fresh pasta: Tortellini, tortelloni

Comments: Simple is best with stuffed pastas so the sauce doesn't compete with the stuffing and clutter the dish.

Sauce ideas: Unsalted melted butter and Parmigiano-Reggiano. Cream flavored with bay leaves. Mascarpone with thinly sliced leeks. Olive oil flavored with sage or rosemary. A simple tomato sauce. A light veal or chicken broth flavored with butter. Sautéed pine nuts in butter. A sauté of finely diced vegetables that have a relationship to the filling. Melted butter flavored with a small dice of fresh tomato.

Long, thin dried pasta: Capelli, spaghettini, spaghetti, linguine, bucatini (perciatelli), fusilli lunghi, lasagnette

Comments: Sharp, bold flavors are wonderful with spaghetti and its cousins. Olive oil–based sauces with small bits of vegetable are perfect for these shapes. These are the best pastas for tomato sauces punctuated with strong bits of flavor, such as anchovies, pancetta, olives, or capers. Most olive oil–based seafood sauces are best served with long, thin dried pasta.

Sauce ideas: Marinara sauce and other olive oil–based tomato sauces. *Aglio e olio* (garlic and oil sauce). Olive oil and chopped strong summer herbs. Puttanesca with its direct, bold olive and caper flavors. Pesto. Carbonara with Pecorino and pancetta. Linguine with clam or mussel sauce. Bucatini with sardines or *frutta di mare* with white wine. Spaghetti with simmered calamari and spicy tomato sauce.

Tube-shaped dried pasta: Penne, garganelli, cavatappi, ziti, rigatoni, tubetti, ditali

Comments: The idea here is to use the holes your pasta shape provides you with. Choose chunky sauces in which some of the pieces are just big enough to fit into the tubes, so you get flavor from inside and out.

Sauce ideas: Hearty sausage sauces. Chunky, boldly flavored vegetable sauces such as eggplant with ricotta salata. Broccoli sauce flavored with olives, hot pepper, and garlic. A Neapolitan ragù of mixed meats and tomatoes. Ziti with peperonata. *Boscaiola* sauces with chunks of mushrooms and herbs. *Pasta e fagioli* (pasta and bean) sauces. Tubetti and ditali are used not just for soup but also with small diced vegetable sauces such as zucchini with onion and mint.

Unusual short dried pasta shapes: Orecchiette, gemelli, fusilli, farfalle, conchiglie, radiatore

Comments: Here you have to judge your sauce by pasta shape and use an artistic eye. In general, the longer, thinner shapes like fusilli and gemelli look pretty with long strips of sauce that wrap around them—for instance, thin slices of bell pepper. Fusilli and radiatore ("radiators") are especially suited to thick tomato or pureed vegetable sauces that will cling to their curvy lines. Orecchiette and conchiglie have hollowed rounds to catch small chunks of sauce like bits of broccoli or sausage. Farfalle is a difficult shape; I like it with a tomato vodka sauce and also with tiny shrimp sautéed in olive oil and garlic.

Sauce ideas: Pesto. Uncooked summer tomato sauce. Pasta salads. Vegetable purées, such as asparagus or bell pepper. Spicy tomato sauce. Mushroom and tomato sauce. Roasted artichoke and garlic sauce. Olive oil and sautéed greens such as escarole, spinach, cabbage, or arugula. Try orecchiette with cauliflower florets sautéed with onion and anchovies.

Broths for Pasta Soups and for Enriching Pasta Sauces

When you want your pasta sauce to be the best

it can be, a simple homemade broth, used instead of water, canned broth, or bouillon cubes, can take your cooking to a higher level. Some sauces—a ragù, for instance—require a good amount of broth, usually at least a cup, and if that broth is a simple home-made one, it will improve the final results beyond measure. As with wine in cooking, the better the broth, the better the finished dish, especially in a long-cooked sauce in which the liquids are to be reduced, amplifying their flavor. If you will be using just a tiny amount of broth to loosen a sauce or to finish cooking vegetables, usually a low-salt canned chicken broth, possibly doctored up with a few aromatic vegetable ends or herbs, is sufficient.

Making a good chicken broth at home is a lot easier than you might think. What I often did in restaurant kitchens was order a few pounds of inexpensive chicken wings, chop them in a few pieces, and simmer them along with whatever vegetable and herb odds and ends we had in the walk-in refrigerator. You can make a flavorful soup base in a little over an hour that way. If you have a prosciutto end or can get your hands on a few beef bones, adding them will give you the kind of mixed-meat broth very popular in Italy for *pasta in brodo*.

Chicken Broth

- Buy about 2 pounds of chicken wings. Chop each one into 2 pieces with a sharp knife or a cleaver and put them in a large stockpot. If you want a dark, rich-tasting broth, brown the wings in a few tablespoons of olive oil over medium-high heat for a few minutes before adding other ingredients. The other ingredients you add can be determined by how you want the broth to taste or by what you have in your refrigerator. If you want a very sweet, oniony broth, add onions, leeks, or scallions generously. For a well-rounded full broth, add onions, celery, carrots, and a few herbs such as parsley and thyme. A spicier broth can be made by adding a few whole cloves, a cinnamon stick, or a few fennel seeds. Wine tends to sour a chicken broth.

- After choosing your ingredients, put them all in the pot, cover with cold water, and bring to a boil. Turn the heat to low and simmer, uncovered, for about 1½ hours. You'll probably need to skim the broth several times during cooking. Strain the broth, pressing on the bones and vegetables to extract all the flavor. The easiest way to remove the fat is by refrigerating the broth and then simply scraping the solidified fat off the top. If you don't have time for that, try to spoon off as much fat as possible. I like to leave a thin layer of fat on broth for flavor. Season with salt and black pepper. If your broth tastes a little weak, remember that you can always reduce strained broth by boiling it to concentrate flavors.

- It's best to chill hot broth rapidly by either putting the pot in an ice bath or placing the container uncovered in the refrigerator. This way it won't develop bacteria. If your broth has been sitting around the kitchen cooling down to room temperature all day, make sure you boil it for a few minutes before using it.

- Here are some additions for flavoring chicken broth:

Onion peels and trimmings or an unpeeled onion, halved	**Parsnip trimmings**
Scallion and leek trimmings	**Parsley stems**
Shallot trimmings	**A bay leaf**
Unpeeled garlic cloves, roughly chopped	**A few black peppercorns**
Unpeeled carrots, chopped	**A thyme sprig**
A few chopped tomatoes or tomato peels	**1 or 2 whole cloves**
Tough outer celery stalks, celery leaves, or root ends	**A can of low-salt chicken broth (if you don't have enough chicken wings)**
Trimmings from fennel bulbs, plus tops	**A chopped baking potato (to add body)**
	Mushroom stems

Doctoring up canned chicken broth: Any of the above items can be added to canned chicken broth to enrich it. Place the ingredients you want to add in a big pot, add the broth, simmer for about 30 minutes, and strain. I usually start with a low-salt broth, especially if it's going to reduce further by simmering. If you have a very salty canned broth, either dilute it with water or try not to reduce it too much (this will only concentrate the salt further).

Mixed-Meat Broth

This is a wonderful, light broth for pasta soups or to add to sauces. It is made by adding inexpensive cuts of other meat to the pot while you are making your chicken broth. Try including at least two of the following:

A prosciutto end	**A few chunks of veal stewing meat**
A few turkey wings	**(on or off the bone,**
Inexpensive pieces of beef (on and	**but a mix of both is best)**
off the bone)	**Veal and beef bones**

Light Veal Broth

- Substitute 1 pound stewing veal on the bone for the chicken and proceed with the recipe for chicken broth.

Shrimp Broth

- Whenever I have shrimp, I almost always make a quick broth with the shells. It enriches a shrimp and pasta dish immensely and takes about 15 minutes.
- In a medium saucepan, heat a few tablespoons unsalted butter or olive oil (depending on which taste goes best with the dish you will use the broth in). Add the shrimp shells (I usually have shells from about 1 pound of shrimp if I'm making a shrimp sauce for pasta) and sauté until they turn pink. Add a few crushed garlic cloves, an onion skin, some celery leaves, or a few fennel seeds if you like that flavor. I sometimes add a splash of white wine and let it cook out. Let the vegetables sauté a minute to give off flavor and then cover with water. Bring this to a boil, then turn the heat to medium and let it cook at a lively simmer. Seafood broth takes a much shorter time to cook than meat broth and doesn't benefit from long simmering, which can make the broth bitter. Let it reduce to about half, but don't cook it any longer than about 20 minutes. Strain. You will have a nice, sweet broth to enrich a shrimp sauce or another type of fish sauce. You can make a similar broth using cooked lobster shells.

Light Fish Broth

- Use as a base for pasta and fish soups, stews, or to add to quickly cooked fish and pasta dishes for enrichment. To make a quick fish broth, purchase about 2 pounds fish skeletons (2 medium fish skeletons should be enough) from nonoily fish such as monkfish, bass, or flounder (salmon, mackerel, and tuna produce a very strongly flavored broth that is not appropriate for pasta cooking). Break them up either with your hands or by chopping them with a sharp knife or cleaver. Place the bones in a large soup pot and cover with cold water. Add your chosen flavorings (see list page 377 for suggestions) and bring to a boil. Turn the heat to medium and cook at a lively simmer for about 40 minutes. Strain. Season with salt and pepper.

- Some suggested additions for flavoring light fish broth:

1 large onion, roughly chopped	**A few fennel seeds**
A large carrot, chopped	**A few whole cloves**
A few peeled garlic cloves, cut in half	**A small pinch of saffron threads**
A few celery stalks, plus leaves, roughly chopped	**A small glass of white wine**
1 or 2 plum tomatoes, roughly chopped	**A small glass of dry vermouth**
Parsley stems	**A lemon or orange peel**
A bay leaf	**A few shrimp shells**
A sprig of thyme	**A pinch of cayenne pepper**
	A can of low-salt chicken broth, for enrichment

Mushroom Broth

- You can make a mushroom broth with a chicken base or with a vegetable base. Simply add a large handful of mushroom trimmings to the pot when you are making a chicken or vegetable broth. The addition of a small handful of dried porcini mushrooms will give you a very rich mushroom flavor.

Vegetable Broth

- Roughly chop about 2 cups aromatic vegetables such as carrots, celery, an onion, leeks, shallots, a small fennel bulb, and a few mushroom stems if you have them. In a medium saucepan, heat a few tablespoons of olive oil over medium heat. Add all the vegetables along with a few herbs, such as parsley, a bay leaf, or a thyme sprig, and sauté for about a minute, just to release their flavors. Cover the vegetables with cold water and bring to a boil. Turn the heat to medium-low and simmer for about 1 hour. Strain and season with salt and pepper.
- Sometimes vegetable broths can cook up bitter. But if you add a few sweet vegetables, such as a Vidalia or Walla Walla onion, a small piece of sweet potato, or a small parsnip, the balance will improve. Wine tends to make vegetable broth very sour.

Mail-Order Sources

Balducci's, 424 Sixth Avenue, New York, NY 10011
(800) 225-3822
San Marzano canned tomatoes, *fleur de sel* French sea salt, Italian and Spanish olives, Italian cheeses, prosciutto di Parma, Spanish Serrano ham, Italian dried and fresh sausages, and many other specialty food items, with an emphasis on Italian products.

Buonitalia, 75 Ninth Avenue, New York, NY 10011
(212) 633-9090; fax (212) 633-9717
Artisanal southern Italian dried pasta (Setaro, Latini, La Ruvida, and Laporta brands), also many other hard-to-find Italian imports such as fresh porcini mushrooms, chestnut and semolina flour, Alba truffles, *bottarga,* and salt-packed capers and anchovies.

Egg Farm Dairy, Peekskill, New York
(800) 273-2637
Fine fresh butter. This product is also available at Citarella, 2135 Broadway, New York, NY 10023; (212) 874-0383.

Eurama Food, 210 North Tenth Street, Brooklyn, New York, 11211
(718) 782-3901
Sicilian sea salt, Sicilian olive oil, Pantelleria capers, *bottarga.*

Kitchen Arts and Letters, 1435 Lexington Avenue, New York, NY 10128
(212) 876-5550; fax (212) 876-3584
This wonderful, extremely well-stocked cookbook store also imports and sells by mail the exquisite Alziari olive oil from Provence.

Phipps Country Store and Farm, P.O. Box 349, Pescadero, CA 94067
(800) 279-0889; fax (650) 879-1622
This farm grows many varieties of beans and dries them on the premises. You'll always be assured delivery of the most recent crop. Some of the Italian beans they grow are cannellini, *ceci* beans (chickpeas), favas, *borlotti, piccolo morone* (a small, dark red bean), and *gigante* (a large white bean that cooks up very creamy).

**Vivande Porta Via, 2125 Fillmore Street, San Francisco, CA 94115
(415) 346-4430**
Salt-packed anchovies and capers, Italian cheeses, balsamic vinegar, and a wide range of other excellent Italian products.

**Zingerman's, 422 Detroit Street, Ann Arbor, MI 48106
(313) 769-1625**
Tuscan, Ligurian, Sicilian (Ravidà brand), and Lake Garda Italian olive oils of the highest quality. Also excellent Provençal, Spanish, and Greek extra-virgin olive oils. A good source for authentic balsamic vinegar. They also carry Martelli brand artisanal dried pasta from Tuscany.

Bibliography

Apicius. *La cucina dell'antica Roma*. Milan: La Spigna, 1994.

Artusi, Pellegrino. *La scienza in cucina e l'arte di mangiar bene*. Translated by Elisabeth Abbot. New York: Liverright, 1975.

Bettoja, Jo. *Southern Italian Cooking*. New York: Bantam, 1991.

Bettoja, Jo, and Anna Maria Cornetto. *Italian Cooking in the Grand Tradition*. New York: The Dial Press, 1982.

Bittman, Mark. *Fish*. New York: Macmillan, 1994.

Boulud, Daniel. *Cooking with Daniel Boulud*. New York: Random House, 1993.

Buonassisi, Vincenzo. *Pasta*. Translated by Elisabeth Evans. Wilton, Conn.: Lyceum Books, Inc., 1976.

Bugialli, Giuliano. *Bugialli on Pasta*. New York: Simon & Schuster, 1988.

———. *Foods of Sicily & Sardinia*. New York: Rizzoli, 1996.

Carrier, Robert. *Feasts of Provence*. New York: Rizzoli, 1993.

Castelvetro, Giacomo. *The Fruit, Herbs, and Vegetables of Italy*. New York: Viking, 1989.

Del Conte, Anna. *Gastronomy of Italy*. New York: Prentice Hall Press, 1987.

Correnti, Pino. *Il libro d'oro della cucina e dei vini di Sicilia*. Milan: Mursia, 1976.

De'Medici, Lorenza. *Lorenza's Pasta*. New York: Clarkson Potter, 1996.

Gray, Patience. *Honey from a Weed*. New York: Harper & Row, 1987.

Hazan, Marcella. *Marcella's Italian Kitchen*. New York: Knopf, 1986.

Jenkins, Nancy Harmon. *Flavors of Puglia*. New York: Broadway Books, 1997.

Johnston, Mireille. *Cuisine of the Sun*. New York: Vintage Books, 1979.

Jones, Louisa. *The New Provençal Cuisine*. San Francisco: Chronicle Books, 1995.

Kasper, Lynne Rossetto. *The Splendid Table*. New York: William Morrow and Company, 1992.

Lanza, Anna Tasca. *The Heart of Sicily*. New York: Clarkson Potter, 1993.

———. *The Flavors of Sicily*. New York: Clarkson Potter, 1996.

Middione, Carlo. *The Food of Southern Italy*. New York: Morrow, 1987.

Olney, Richard. *Lulu's Provençal Table*. New York: HarperCollins, 1994.

———. *Provence the Beautiful Cookbook*. San Francisco: Collins, 1993.

———. *Simple French Food*. New York: Simon & Schuster, 1970.

Penta de Peppo, Marinella. *L'arte della cucina Napoletana*. Milan: Mondadori, 1994.

Pupella, Eufemia Azzolina. *Sicilian Cookery*. Florence: Casa Editrice Bonechi, 1996.

Root, Waverly. *The Food of Italy*. New York: Atheneum, 1971.

Simeti, Mary Taylor. *Pomp and Sustenance*. New York: Knopf, 1989.

Tornabene, Wanda and Giovanna. *La cucina Siciliana di Gangivecchio*. New York: Alfred A. Knopf, 1996.

Vada, Simonetta Lupi. *La pasta e'in tavola*. Milan: Fabbri, 1990.

Verge, Roger. *Roger Verge's Vegetables in the French Style*. New York: Artisan, 1994.

Valentini, Beatrice. *La cucina della mamma*. Rome: Edizioni Polaris, 1995.

Waters, Alice. *Chez Panisse Vegetables*. New York: HarperCollins, 1996.

———. *Chez Panisse Pasta, Pizza, and Calzone*. New York: Random House, 1984.

Wolfert, Paula. *Paula Wolfert's World of Food*. New York: Harper & Row, 1988.

Acknowledgments

This, my first book, was an exhilarating and sometimes nerve-racking experience that veered in several directions before taking form. I am grateful to the many friends who helped me along the way. I'd first like to thank Elise Goodman, who discussed the project with me in its infant stage and gave me many good organizational ideas. Thanks to Tina Ujlaki at *Food & Wine* magazine, who was the first to publish my articles on Italian cooking and continues to support me and publish my work. Thank you to Enzo Carollo for introducing me to Sicilian sea salt. I give a giant thank-you to all the farmers who sell their beautiful vegetables, meats, and fish at the Union Square Green Market in Manhattan; they've made my dream of seasonal cooking a glorious reality. I am grateful to my good friend Jay Milite for his endless encouragement and for his love of Italian food. I thank my two friends since childhood, Barbara Calamari, who suggested the title and talked me through the rough times, and Tobi Seftel, who photographed me for the jacket. Thank you to Van Dyke Parks for providing me a lifelong outlet for my creativity. I am also grateful to Scott Berkson for sharing his artistic soul with me for so many years. A special thank-you to my agent, Susan Lescher, for believing in this project from the start. And a very huge thank-you to my wonderful editor, Maria Guarnaschelli, for her amazing energy and dedication to making this book the best it could possibly be. A huge thank-you to Barbara Bachman, my designer; to M. C. Hald, my production editor; to Laura Maestro, my illustrator; and to Matthew Thornton, whose help throughout this project was invaluable. And finally, thank you to my family: my sister, Liti De Mane, for always being there for me; my brother, Richie De Mane, for his love and culinary expertise; my very special husband, Fred Allen, for giving me self-confidence and for sampling every pasta dish in this book and loving every one; and my parents, to whom this book is dedicated.

Index

a

Abruzzo, 14, 84, 344
acini, 29
    chicken sausage and parsnip soup with, 260–61
    grated zucchini soup with saffron and, 66–67
aglio e olio (garlic and oil sauce), 10, 45–51, 54–57, 68, 81, 187, 349
    crab in, 201
    as no-cheese sauce, 84
    sautéed, 54
    sautéed, spaghetti with black olives, anchovies, orange zest, bread crumbs and, 54–55
    uncooked, 56
    uncooked, tubetti with parsley, celery leaves and, 57
aioli, 213
    late-summer minestrone with tomato, fennel, and broken spaghetti—served with, 106–7
allspice, 67
almond(s), 55, 73, 346
    arugula pesto, 141
    arugula pesto, soft-shell crab over linguine with, 202–3
    -basil pesto and béchamel, lasagne with, 140–41
    bucatini with fresh sardines, dill, capers and, 168–69
    and caper pesto, clams with, 189
    and caper pesto, spaghetti with poached skate and, 182–83
    in cauliflower, saffron, basil, and preserved garlic sauce for ziti, 76–77
    in gemelli with haricots verts, potatoes, and preserved garlic, 48
    ground, *zuppa di pesce* with spaghetti and, 218–19
    tomato tagliatelle with basil butter and, 105
    in trout cannelloni with pancetta and sage sauce, 242–43
    ziti with peperonata, green olives and, 82–83
amatriciana sauce, 14, 84

anchovy(ies):
    about, 163
    in basil lasagne with scallops and zucchini, 250–51
    butter, 105, 339
    canned or preserved in salt, 338
    in cauliflower, saffron, basil, and preserved garlic sauce for ziti, 76–77
    cream, green penne with baby artichokes, fava beans and, 94–95
    crespelle with zucchini, mozzarella and, 156–57
    and fennel seed sauce for spaghetti, 164–65
    in fish stew with couscous, black olives, and bay leaves, 216–17
    in fresh cod, yellow peppers, and thyme with ziti, 225
    fusilli lunghi with mushrooms, black olives and, 124–25
    garganelli with roasted radicchio, black olives and, 118–19
    in grilled paprika shrimp on spaghetti with summer tomato sauce, 186–87
    in large shells filled with *baccalà mantecato* and baked with red pepper and garlic purée, 246–47
    in lasagne with fresh tuna, caciocavallo, and marjoram, 252
    in lasagne with sautéed greens, mascarpone, and olives, 142–43
    marinated, penne salad with grilled red onions, dandelions, black olives and, 166–67
    in orecchiette with mako and cranberry beans, 178–79
    as recipe alternative, 43, 77, 78, 104, 116, 307, 319
    spaghetti with cherry tomatoes, capers, marjoram, lemon zest, and (a puttanesca sauce), 27
    spaghetti with sautéed *aglio e olio* (garlic and oil), black olives, orange zest, bread crumbs and, 54–55

anchovy(ies) (*cont.*)
    in squid stuffed with pistachios and greens, served over bucatini, 210–12
    ziti with lamb, tarragon and, 308–9
anellini, with beef, currants, and pine nuts, baked, 312–13
arrabbiata sauce, 84
artichoke (hearts), 45
    baby, green penne with fava beans, anchovy cream and, 94–95
    baby, notes on, 94, 235
    baked veal ragù with saffron and, 316–17
    braised baby, penne salad with mussels and, 234–35
    and duck ravioli with savory butter and Parmigiano, 335
    fusilli lunghi with prosciutto, lemon and, 270–71
    as recipe alternative, 230, 309
arugula, 135, 167, 279
    almond pesto, 141
    almond pesto, soft-shell crab over linguine with, 202–3
    cavatelli with Montasio cheese, morels and, 90–91
    -chicken meatballs, baked cavatappi with, 304–5
    -chicken meatballs, lasagne with mozzarella, tomato and, 323
    in fusilli with veal, capers, and lemon, 282–83
    lumachine tossed with uncooked tomato sauce with avocado, croutons and, 37
Asiago, 358
    cannelloni with escarole, tomato-basil cream and, 154–55
asparagus, 51, 73, 230
    gemelli with potatoes, preserved garlic and, 49
    in pasta primavera in shades of green, 96–97
    roasted, in lasagne with fontina, 138–39
    saffron tagliatelle with orange zest, ramps and, 86–87

asparagus (*cont.*)
    spaghetti with zucchini blossoms, egg and, 88–89
avocado, lumachine tossed with uncooked tomato sauce with arugula, croutons and, 37

B

baccalà with ditali, sweet onion, chickpeas, and rosemary, 180–81
bacon:
    in gemelli with haricot verts, potatoes, and preserved garlic, 48–49
    orecchiette with chicory, walnuts, capers and, 130
    in peperonata sauce, 79
    as recipe alternative, 109, 129, 189
balsamic vinegar, 353–54
basil, 38, 43, 65
    -almond pesto and béchamel, lasagne with, 140–41
    black pepper tagliatelle with seared scallops, lemon and, 194–95
    butter, tomato tagliatelle with almonds and, 105
    cauliflower, saffron, and preserved garlic sauce with ziti, 76–77
    dried, 61
    lasagne with scallops and zucchini, 250–51
    in monkfish and escarole soup with toasted orzo and mint pesto, 222–23
    as recipe alternative, 65, 89, 100, 107, 109, 187, 197, 243
    in spaghetti nest with Genoese pesto and goat cheese–stuffed tomatoes, 102–4
    summer couscous with chanterelles, yellow squash and, 98–99
    -tomato cream, cannelloni with escarole, Asiago and, 154–55
bay leaf (leaves):
    fish stew with couscous, black olives and, 216–17
    as recipe alternative, 149
    -tomato sauce, scallion and ricotta ravioli with, 148–49
beans:
    ceci, *see* chickpeas
    cranberry, orecchiette with mako and, 178–79
    dried and canned, 339–40
    fava, *see* fava beans
    fresh, cooking of, 179
    kidney, cavatappi with cabbage and, 132–33
    white, *see* cannellini

béchamel, lasagne with basil-almond pesto and, 140–41
beef:
    baked anellini with currants, pine nuts and, 312–13
    bresaola, *see* bresaola
    cannelloni with rosemary, mushrooms and, 336
    tagliatelle with, 319
beet pasta, 369
Bel Paese, 358
black pepper pasta, 26
  recipe for, 368
    tagliatelle with seared scallops, lemon, and basil, 194–95
    three-egg, in roasted asparagus lasagne with fontina, 138–39
bluefish, 173
Bolognese ragù, 306
boscaiola, 23
bottarga, 207
boudin blanc, penne with escarole, capers and, 264–65
bouillabaisse, 223
Boulud, Daniel, 122
bread crumbs, 84
    chervil, tagliatelle with mussels and, 190–91
    as garnish, 111
    homemade, 340–41
    in recipes, 74–75, 77, 104, 118–19, 126, 142–43, 164–65, 168–69, 184–85, 200–201, 210–12, 225, 246–52, 302–5, 312–13
    spaghetti with sautéed *aglio e olio* (garlic and oil), black olives, anchovies, orange zest and, 54–55
bresaola:
    about, 269
    cavatelli with mozzarella, roasted fennel and, 272–73
    goat cheese, and radicchio in cannelloni with tomato and rosemary sauce, 332–33
broccoli, 58, 273
    about, 69
    baked penne with feta, black olives, thyme and, 74–75
    green tagliatelle with purée of roasted garlic and, 51
    Romanesco, 183
broccoli rabe, 69–73, 273
    cavatelli with mortadella, pistachios, tomatoes and, 70–71
    gemelli with potatoes, preserved garlic and, 49
    and Italian pork sausage sauce, 71
    tagliatelle with mascarpone and, 72–73

broth, 341–42, 373–77
    mushroom, 377
    shrimp, 376
    shrimp and tomato, paprika ravioli with shrimp in a, 244–45
    see also chicken broth; fish broth, light; mixed-meat broth; veal broth, light; vegetable broth
bucatini:
    with crab, parsley, and lemon verbena, 200–201
    with fresh sardines, dill, capers, and almonds, 168–69
    with peperonata and bacon, 79
    with red clam sauce, 38
    with shellfish and a soffritto, 219
    with Sicilian pasta sauce, 77
    squid stuffed with pistachios and greens, served over, 210–12
Bugialli, Giuliano, 206
butter, 283, 342–43
    anchovy, 105, 339
    basil, tomato tagliatelle with almonds and, 105
    brown, tagliatelle with poached skate and, 183
    plum tomatoes, and shallots sauce, 21
    plum tomatoes, and shallots sauce, in recipes, 22–23, 25
    savory, duck and artichoke ravioli with Parmigiano and, 335
butternut squash, ziti with roasted garlic and, 120–21

C

cabbage, Savoy:
    cavatappi with kidney beans and, 132–33
    and potato ravioli with poppy seeds, 150–51
    seasoning of, 133
cabbage and *boudin blanc* with pasta, 265
cacciatorini sausage, 71
    in big shells with radicchio filling and fontina, 152–53
caciocavallo cheese, 84–85, 358
    in baked anellini with beef, currants, and pine nuts, 312–13
    in farfalle with ricotta, mint, and sweet pepper purée, 83
    lasagne with fresh tuna, marjoram and, 252
    in lasagne with tiny chicken meatballs, mozzarella, and tomato, 323
    in tagliatelle with *saucisson à l'ail,* green olives, and savory, 268–69

chicken (cont.)
-based ravioli, 245
cacciatore, 281, 287
cannelloni filled with capers,
ricotta and, 335
cavatelli with saffron, green olives
and, 286–87
meatballs, tiny, lasagne with mozzarella, tomato and, 323
chicken broth:
canned, doctoring up, 375
duck trimmings in, 291
in pasta recipes, 48–49, 76–77,
86–87, 90–91, 98–99, 114–15,
118–21, 130, 194–95, 204–5,
210–12, 225, 228–30, 238–41,
244–45, 266–71, 276–93,
308–13, 316–17, 320–22,
330–31
recipe for, 374–75
in soup recipes, 66, 67, 106–7,
128–29, 222–23, 260–61
in stew recipe, 216–17
chicken livers:
cooking of, 281
gemelli with leeks, tomato, sage
and, 280–81
lasagne with wild mushrooms,
Marsala and, 320–21
chicken sausage and parsnip soup
with acini, 260–61
chicken stock, in simmered tomato
sauce, 29
chickpeas (ceci beans), 311
baccalà with ditali, sweet onion,
rosemary and, 180–81
fresh Neapolitan pasta with celery,
carrots and, 134–35
pappardelle with eel, white wine,
saffron and, 198–99
ziti with oven-roasted tomato
sauce, prosciutto, black olives,
chile pepper and, 39
chicory:
in lasagne with sautéed greens,
mascarpone, and olives, 142–43
orecchiette with bacon, walnuts,
capers and, 130
as recipe alternative, 119, 167
seasoning of, 130
chile pepper:
dried, 344
in uncooked tomato sauce with
arugula, avocado, and croutons
tossed with lumachine, 37
ziti with oven-roasted tomato
sauce, prosciutto, black olives
and, 39
chive blossoms, 57
chocolate, pappardelle with rabbit,
Chianti and, 292–93
chorizo, 189

cinnamon:
orecchiette with roasted eggplant,
walnuts, ricotta and, 60–61
penne with squid simmered in
white wine and, 208–9
clams:
about, 188
linguine with pancetta, marjoram
and, 188–89
in zuppa di pesce with ground
almonds and spaghetti, 218–19
clam sauce, red, 189
oven-roasted tomato sauce as base
for, 38
clam sauce, white, 189
Classic Techniques of Italian Cooking
(Bugialli), 206
cloves, 67
cocoa powder, in eggplant dishes, 61
cod, fresh, 173, 181
baked with white wine and shallots, fazzoletti over, 254–55
as recipe alternative, 199
yellow peppers, and thyme with
ziti, 225
cod, salt:
with ditali, sweet onion, chickpeas, and rosemary, 180–81
in large shells filled with baccalà
mantecato and baked with red
pepper and garlic purée, 246–47
note on cooking of, 181
cognac, 45
pappardelle with duxelles, walnuts
and, 122–23
saffron tagliatelle with lobster,
tomato and, 204–5
conchiglie with veal sausage, radicchio, and cream, 259
coq au vin, 287
corn:
cavatappi salad with grilled
swordfish, mint, tomato and,
174–75
recipe alternatives for, 109
roasted, orecchiette with red peppers and ricotta salata and,
108–9
cotechino sausage, 133
couscous:
with chanterelles, yellow squash,
and basil, summer, 98–99
fish stew with black olives, bay
leaves and, 216–17
crab(meat):
about, 200
bucatini with parsley, lemon verbena and, 200–201
soft-shell, over linguine with
arugula almond pesto, 202–3
tomato and orange sauce with
farfalle and, 25

cranberry beans, orecchiette with
mako and, 178–79
cream, 23, 29, 65
anchovy, green penne with baby
artichokes, fava beans and,
94–95
anchovy, tagliatelle with, 95, 165
in baked saffron tagliarini with
shrimp and fennel soffritto,
184–85
in baked spinach tagliatelle with
endive, leeks, and prosciutto
cotto, 114–15
in basil lasagne with scallops and
zucchini, 250–51
in cannelloni with Spanish ham
and spiced leeks, 330–31
conchiglie with veal sausage,
radicchio and, 259
in farfalle with Gruyère, eggs, and
broiled pancetta, 274
fontina, big shells with radicchio
filling and, 152–53
fusilli with grappa, tomato, concassé and, 44–45
in garganelli with simmered
tomato-fig sauce, 30–31
in green lasagne with capocollo,
roasted peppers, and tarragon,
324–25
in lasagne with chicken livers, wild
mushrooms, and Marsala, 320–22
in lasagne with sautéed greens,
mascarpone, and olives, 142–43
Parmigiano, 95, 321–22
in peperonata sauce, 79
as recipe alternative, 155
in roasted asparagus lasagne with
fontina, 138–39
in saffron tagliatelle with asparagus, orange zest, and ramps,
86–87
in tagliatelle with sweetbreads,
green peppercorns, and watercress, 278–79
tomato and olive, sausage ravioli
with, 328–29
veal and eggplant meatballs with
cavatelli in a sauce of tomato,
caper and, 302–3
crème fraîche:
in cannelloni with escarole, Asiago,
and tomato-basil cream, 154–55
in lasagnette with braised duck
and black olives, 290–91
as substitute in recipes, 23
in trout cannelloni with pancetta
and sage sauce, 242–43
cremini:
in fusilli lunghi with mushrooms,
black olives, and anchovies,
124–25

flounder, 173
flour, 345
fontina, 359
   big shells with radicchio filling
     and, 152–53
   roasted asparagus lasagne with,
     138–39
food processor, use of, 366–67
frisée, 119, 167
frittella, 97
fusilli:
   with cream, grappa, and tomato
     concassé, 44–45
   with drained canned tomatoes
     flavored with soppressata and
     pine nuts, 33
   with haricots verts, potatoes, and
     preserved garlic, 48–49
   with pureed roasted garlic and
     butternut squash, 121
   with roasted radicchio, anchovies,
     and black olives, 118–19
   with rock shrimp, pureed onions,
     and peas, 230–31
   with veal, capers, and lemon,
     282–83
fusilli lunghi:
   with mushrooms, black olives, and
     anchovies, 124–25
   with prosciutto, lemon, and arti-
     chokes, 270–71
   with tuna ragù, 220–21

G

garganelli:
   with baked veal ragù with saffron
     and artichokes, 316–17
   with roasted radicchio, anchovies,
     and black olives, 118–19
   with scallops, chanterelles, and
     fava beans, 228–29
   with simmered tomato-fig sauce,
     30–31
garídes mikrolímano, 75
garlic, 283
   blanching of, 47
   cherry tomato sauce with olive oil
     and, 26
   large shells filled with baccalà man-
     tecato and baked with purée of
     red pepper and, 246–47
   and oil sauce, see aglio e olio
   pasta, 369
   sausage, tagliatelle with green
     olives, savory and, 268–69
   young vs. old, 46
garlic, preserved, 46–47
   cauliflower, saffron, and basil
     sauce with ziti, 76–77
   gemelli with haricots verts, pota-
     toes and, 48–49

garlic, roasted, 49
   and potato ravioli, 151
   purée, green tagliatelle with red
     pepper and, 50–51
   ziti with butternut squash and,
     120–21
garnishes, for pasta, 110–11
gemelli:
   with chicken livers, leeks, tomato,
     and sage, 280–81
   with haricots verts, potatoes, and
     preserved garlic, 48–49
Genoese pesto, spaghetti nest with
     goat-cheese-stuffed tomatoes
     and, 102–4
ginger, as recipe alternative, 209
goat cheese (caprino), 83, 107, 359
   bresaola, and radicchio in cannel-
     loni with tomato and rosemary
     sauce, 332–33
   in green tagliatelle with red
     pepper and roasted garlic-
     purée, 51
   lasagne with greens and, 143
   pasta with chanterelles and, 99
   rigatoni with ratatouille and, 97
   -stuffed tomatoes, spaghetti nests
     with Genoese pesto and, 102–4
   watercress, and prosciutto ravioli
     with pine nut pesto, 147
   ziti with merguez sausages,
     tomato, parsley and, 262–63
gorgonzola, 123, 360
Grana Padano cheese, 91, 360
   in baked spinach tagliatelle with
     endive, leeks, and prosciutto
     cotto, 114–15
   in orecchiette with turkey and
     wild mushroom cacciatore,
     288–89
   in roasted asparagus lasagne with
     fontina, 138–39
   in scallion and ricotta ravioli with
     tomato-bay leaf sauce, 148–49
   in spaghetti nest with Genoese
     pesto and goat cheese-stuffed
     tomatoes, 102–4
   in tagliatelle with broccoli rabe
     and mascarpone, 72–73
   in ziti with roasted garlic and but-
     ternut squash, 120–21
   in ziti with tripe, prosciutto, and
     rosemary, 296–97
grapeseed oil, 68
grappa, fusilli with cream, tomato
     concassé and, 44–45
gravy, leftover meat, to flavor pasta
     sauces, 297
green pasta:
   recipe for, 367
   in recipes, 50–51, 114–15,
     324–25

greens, 335
   lasagne with goat cheese and,
     143
   and pistachios stuffed squid,
     served over bucatini, 210–12
   prevention of bruising of, 22n
   sautéed lasagne with mascarpone,
     olives and, 142–43
   see also arugula; chicory; dande-
     lion greens; escarole; kale
gremolata, 171, 297
Gruyère:
   farfalle with eggs, broiled pancetta
     and, 274
   in penne with boudin blanc, esca-
     role, and capers, 264–65
   roasted zucchini, and fennel
     tossed with penne, 65

H

halibut, 173
ham, Spanish:
   cannelloni with spiced leeks and,
     330–31
   rigatoni with potatoes, celery and,
     276–77
hands, as kitchen utensils, 40
hare, 85
haricots verts, gemelli with
     potatoes, preserved garlic
     and, 48–49
Hazan, Marcella, 12
hazelnuts, 346
herb pasta, 45, 50
   basil, lasagne with scallops and
     zucchini, 250–51
   recipe for, 368
   sage, 121
   sage, in lasagne with chicken
     livers, wild mushrooms, and
     Marsala, 320–22
   three-egg, in basil lasagne with
     scallops and zucchini, 250–51
herbs:
   chopping of, 35
   dried, 61
   as garnish, 110
   mild, spaghetti with snails sim-
     mered in tomatoes, Marsala
     and, 214–15
   mild fresh, ravioli with veal and,
     326–27
   overkill with, 101
   in peperonata sauce, 79
   prevention of bruising of, 22n
   sautéed summer, spaghetti with,
     100
   see also specific herbs
hot pepper, 78, 84
   and herb oils, 110
   see also chile pepper

olive(s), green, 348
    cavatelli with chicken, saffron and, 286–87
    in fresh cod, yellow peppers, and thyme with ziti, 225
    tagliatelle with *saucisson à l'ail*, savory and, 268–69
    ziti with peperonata, almonds and, 82–83
onion(s), 349
    and Marsala sauce for baked ziti, 126–27
    outside grilling of, 167
    pureed, fusilli with rock shrimp, peas and, 230–31
    sautéing of, 24
onions, red:
    cherry tomato sauce with olive oil and, 26
    grilled, penne salad with marinated anchovies, dandelions, black olives and, 166–67
    ziti with grilled squid, black olives, mint and, 196–97
onion(s), sweet:
    baccalà with ditali, chickpeas, rosemary and, 180–81
    white, 73
orange (juice), 169, 349–50
    cannelloni with lamb and, 334
    in grilled squid and mushroom skewers over rosemary tagliarini, 236–37
    lasagne with tomato and orange sauce and fennel-flavored ricotta, 144–45
orange zest, 181, 283
    and fennel seed marinade for shrimp, 187
    pasta, 368
    saffron tagliatelle with asparagus, ramps and, 86–87
    spaghetti with sautéed *aglio e olio* (garlic and oil), black olives, anchovies, bread crumbs and, 54–55
orecchiette:
    with chicory, bacon, walnuts, and capers, 130
    with drained canned tomatoes flavored with soppressata and pine nuts, 33
    with mako and cranberry beans, 178–79
    with roasted corn and red peppers and ricotta salata, 108–9
    with roasted eggplant, walnuts, ricotta, and cinnamon, 60–61
    with turkey and wild mushroom cacciatore, 288–89

oregano, 38, 69, 75, 79
    dried, 32, 61
    fresh, about, 32
orzo, 29
    as recipe alternative, 217
    toasted, monkfish and escarole soup with mint pesto and, 222–23
oven-dried tomatoes, *see* tomatoes, oven-dried
oven-roasted tomato sauce, *see* tomato sauce, oven-roasted
oxtail:
    and Chianti ragù, rigatoni with, 318–19
    cooked, removing of meat from, 319
    ravioli, 334

P

pancetta, 350
    about, 269
    in baked cavatappi with chicken-arugula meatballs, 304–5
    in baked saffron tagliarini with shrimp and fennel soffritto, 184–85
    broiled, farfalle with Gruyère, eggs and, 274
    in cannelloni with escarole, Asiago, and tomato-basil cream, 154–55
    in cavatappi with cabbage and kidney beans, 132–33
    in cavatelli with chicken, saffron, and green olives, 286–87
    in conchiglie with veal sausage, radicchio, and cream, 259
    in gemelli with haricots verts, potatoes, and preserved garlic, 48
    in grated zucchini soup with saffron and acini, 66–67
    in lasagne with chicken livers, wild mushrooms, and Marsala, 320–22
    leeks, sage, and scallops with pasta, 195
    linguine with clams, marjoram and, 188–89
    in malloreddus with lamb, pork, and roasted red peppers, 310–11
    note on cooking of, 133
    in orecchiette with roasted corn and red peppers, and ricotta salata, 108–9
    in orecchiette with turkey and wild mushroom cacciatore, 288–89
    in pappardelle with eel, chickpeas, white wine, and saffron, 198–99
    as recipe alternative, 73, 79, 125, 135, 217, 307

pancetta (*cont.*)
    in rigatoni with oxtail and Chianti ragù, 318–19
    and sage sauce, trout cannelloni with, 242–43
    in spaghetti with asparagus, zucchini blossoms, and eggs, 88–89
    in veal and eggplant meatballs with cavatelli in a tomato, caper, and cream sauce, 302–3
pans, 24
Pantelleria, capers of, 343
pappardelle, 311
    cutting of, 369
    with duxelles, cognac, and walnuts, 122–23
    with eel, chickpeas, white wine, and saffron, 198–99
    lobster with small diced fall vegetables and, 238–39
    with rabbit, Chianti, and chocolate, 292–93
paprika:
    grilled shrimp on spaghetti with summer tomato sauce, 186–87
    note about, 187
    pasta, 368
    ravioli with shrimp in a shrimp and tomato broth, 244–45
    Spanish (*pimentón*), 186–87, 213
    Spanish, in *zuppa di pesce* with ground almonds and spaghetti, 218–19
Parmigiano-Reggiano, 84, 360, 361
    baked tagliatelle with veal juices and, 298–99
    cream, 95, 321–22
    in lasagne with basil-almond pesto and béchamel, 140–41
    in lasagne with chicken livers, wild mushrooms, and Marsala, 320–22
    -lemon sauce, crespelle with spinach and, 158–59
    in onion and Marsala sauce for baked ziti, 126–27
    in pappardelle with duxelles, cognac, and walnut, 122–23
    in roasted asparagus lasagne with fontina, 138–39
    and savory butter, duck and artichoke ravioli with, 335–36
    in tagliatelle with sweetbreads, green peppercorns, and watercress, 278–79
parsley, 43, 69
    bucatini with crab, lemon verbena and, 200–201
    leaves and fried sage, as garnish, 110

parsley (*cont.*)
  as recipe alternative, 23, 35, 83,
    89, 109, 201, 203, 309
  in spaghetti with poached skate and
    caper and almond pesto, 182–83
  tubetti with uncooked *aglio e olio*
    (garlic and oil), celery leaves
    and, 57
  ziti with merguez sausage, goat
    cheese, tomato and, 262–63
parsnips:
  and chicken sausage soup with
    acini, 260–61
  farfalle with a soffritto of fennel
    and, 113
  in lobster with small diced fall
    vegetables and pappardelle,
    238–39
  recipe alternatives for, 113
pasta:
  cooking of, 15, 17
  as first vs. second course, 145
  garnishes for, 110–11
  matching sauce with, 15, 117
  sauce ideas for, 371–72
  traditional, Italians tampering
    with, 115
pasta:
  alla gricia, 269
  alla norma, 58
  con le sarde (pasta with sardines),
    164, 168
pasta, dried, 350
  cooked with its sauce, 81
  cooking time for, 17
  how to buy, 127
pasta, fresh:
  cooking time for, 17
  cutting of, 369–71
  making of, 363–71
  see also egg pasta, plain; three-
    egg pasta; *specific recipes*
pasta primavera:
  green penne with baby artichokes,
    fava beans, and anchovy cream
    as, 94–95
  in shades of green, 96–97
  variations of, 95
pasta salads, 57
  about, 56
  cavatappi with grilled swordfish,
    corn, mint, and tomato, 174–75
  grilled squid in, 197
  penne, mussels, and braised arti-
    chokes, 234–35
  penne with marinated anchovies,
    grilled red onions, dandelions,
    and black olives, 166–67
  penne with oven-roasted tomato
    sauce, prosciutto, black olives,
    and chile peppers, 39

pasta salads (*cont.*)
  salt in, 273
  shrimp for, 184
  tubetti with oven-dried tomatoes,
    white beans, sage, and celery,
    42–43
peas:
  fusilli with rock shrimp, pureed
    onions and, 230–31
  in pasta primavera in shades of
    green, 96–97
  as recipe alternative, 45, 127, 209
Pecorino cheese, 91, 361
  in green lasagne with capocollo,
    roasted peppers, and tarragon,
    324–25
  in spaghetti nest with Genoese
    pesto and goat cheese–stuffed
    tomatoes, 102–4
Pecorino Romano, 84, 360
Pecorino Toscano, 360
  in baked cavatappi with chicken-
    arugula meatballs, 304–5
  in baked veal ragù with saffron
    and artichokes, 316–17
  in conchiglie with veal sausage,
    radicchio, and cream, 259
  in fresh Neapolitan pasta with
    chickpeas, celery, and carrots,
    134–35
  in gemelli, with chicken livers,
    leeks, tomato, and sage, 280–81
  in orange lasagne with tomato and
    orange sauce and fennel-fla-
    vored ricotta, 144–45
  in soft-shell crab over linguine with
    arugula almond pesto, 202–3
  in spaghetti with asparagus, zuc-
    chini blossoms, and eggs, 88–89
  in watercress, prosciutto, and goat
    cheese ravioli with pine nut
    pesto, 147
penne, 135
  with *boudin blanc,* escarole, and
    capers, 264–65
  with drained canned tomatoes fla-
    vored with soppressata and pine
    nuts, 33
  with feta, black olives, broccoli,
    and thyme, baked, 74–75
  green, with baby artichokes, fava
    beans, and anchovy cream,
    94–95
  and grilled eggplant slices with oil
    and herbs, 63
  with grilled squid and basil pesto,
    197
  with haricots verts, potatoes, and
    preserved garlic, 48–49
  with roasted radicchio, anchovies,
    and black olives, 118–19

penne (*cont.*)
  roasted zucchini, fennel, and
    Gruyère tossed with, 65
  salad with marinated anchovies,
    grilled red onions, dandelions,
    and black olives, 166–67
  salad with mussels and braised
    artichokes, 234–35
  salad with oven-dried tomatoes,
    white beans, sage, and celery,
    42–43
  salad with oven-roasted tomato
    sauce, prosciutto, black olives,
    and chile peppers, 39
  with squid simmered in white wine
    and cinnamon, 208–9
  with uncooked *aglio e olio* (garlic
    and oil), 56
  uncooked tomato sauce with
    arugula, avocado, and croutons
    tossed with, 37
penne alla vodka, 45, 84
pepato, 63
peperonata:
  about, 77
  farfalle with ricotta, mint and,
    83
  sauce, 78–79
  ziti with almonds, green olives
    and, 82–83
pepper, chile, *see* chile pepper
peppercorns, green, tagliatelle with
    sweetbreads, watercress and,
    278–79
pepperoni, orecchiette with drained
    canned tomatoes flavored with
    pine nuts and, 33
peppers, bell:
  color of, 77
  diced roasted, as garnish, 111
  in peperonata sauce, 78–79
  seasoning of, 77
peppers, green bell, 77
  pasta, 369
peppers, Italian frying, rigatoni with
    eggplant, shaved provolone
    and, 62–63
peppers, jalapeño sauce, tubetti with
    celery, potatoes and, 116
peppers, orange bell, 77
pepper(s), red bell, 33, 58, 73, 77
  cavatappi with octopus, red wine,
    star anise and, 212–13
  green tagliatelle with roasted
    garlic purée and, 50–51
  large shells filled with *baccalà
    mantecato* and baked with
    garlic purée and, 246–47
  orecchiette with roasted corn and
    ricotta salata and, 108–9
  pasta, 369